Frommer's®

Great Outdoor Guide to Northern California

Also Available:

Frommer's Great Outdoor Guide to Southern California & Baja
Frommer's Great Outdoor Guide to Washington & Oregon

Frommer's®

Great Outdoor Guide to
Northern California

by Andrew Rice, with Marc Herman

IDG Books Worldwide, Inc.
An International Data Group Company
Foster City, CA • Chicago, IL • Indianapolis, IN • New York, NY

IDG Books Worldwide, Inc.

An International Data Group Company
919 E. Hillsdale Blvd.
Suite 400
Foster City, CA 94404

Find us online at **www.frommers.com**

ISBN: 0-02863693-7
ISSN: 1522-8134

Editor: Jeff Soloway
Production Editor: Tammy Ahrens
Photo Editor: Richard Fox
Design by Madhouse Studios
Staff Cartographers: John Decamillis, Elizabeth Puhl, and Roberta Stockwell
Page Creation by Angel Perez and Kendra Span

Special Sales

For general information on IDG Books Worldwide's books in the U.S., please call our Consumer Customer Service department at 1-800-762-2974. For reseller information, including discounts, bulk sales, customized editions, and premium sales, please call our Reseller Customer Service department at 1-800-434-3422.

Manufactured in the United States of America

5 4 3 2 1

Contents

Getting Underway   4

*Ballooning 4, Bird Watching 4, Boardsailing 5, Canoeing 6,
Cross-Country Skiing 7, Downhill Skiing & Snowboarding 8,
Fishing 9, Hang Gliding 10, Hikes, Bushwhacks & Backpack Trips 10,
Horseback Riding 11, Kayaking 12, Mountain Biking 13,
Road Biking 15, Rock Climbing 15, Sailing 17, Scuba Diving 17,
Surfing 18, Swimming 18, Walks & Rambles 20, Whale Watching 20,
White-Water Rafting 20*

Outfitters   21

Schools   24

Maps   24

Books   24

Spas   25

Camping Reservations   25

Cycling the California Coast   27

FEATURES

*Backcountry Equipment Checklist   6
Backpacking for Beginners   12
The Hiker-Biker Program   16
Sail for Free   19
A Note on Equipment   26*

FEATURES

FEATURES

FEATURES

7 The Gold Country 239

List of Maps

Map Legend

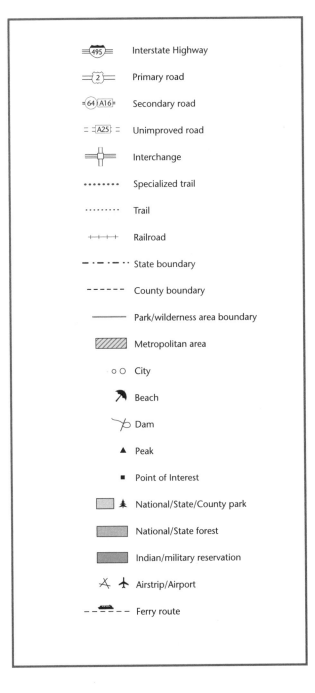

495	Interstate Highway
2	Primary road
64 A16	Secondary road
A25	Unimproved road
	Interchange
········	Specialized trail
·········	Trail
++++	Railroad
– · – · – ··	State boundary
– – – – –	County boundary
——	Park/wilderness area boundary
	Metropolitan area
·○ ○	City
	Beach
	Dam
▲	Peak
■	Point of Interest
♠	National/State/County park
	National/State forest
	Indian/military reservation
⊀ ✈	Airstrip/Airport
– – – – –	Ferry route

Acknowledgments

Marc Herman would like to thank KC Swanson for suffering through 4 months of arduous beachcombing and wine tasting, Misty Henry for still speaking to me after I crashed her sailboat, and the High Sierra Trail group for its fine company and good cheer: Seth, Dan, Kathe, Mary, Jake, and particularly Lark, who got stung by a bee.

Invitation to the Reader

In researching this book, I crisscrossed the state in search of the very best places to get outside. I'm sure you have your own favorite spots, or at least will find new ones as you explore. Please share your secrets with me, so I can pass them on in upcoming editions. If you were disappointed with a recommendation, I'd love to know that, too. Please write to:

Frommer's Great Outdoor Guide to Northern California, 2nd Edition
Frommer's Travel Guides
1633 Broadway
New York, NY 10019

An Additional Note

Please be advised that travel information is subject to change at any time. Every effort has been made to ensure the accuracy of the information provided in this book, but we suggest that you write or call ahead for confirmation when making your travel plans. The authors, editors, and publisher cannot be held responsible for the experiences of readers while traveling. Outdoor sports are, by their very nature, potentially hazardous activities. In doing any of the activities described herein, readers assume all risk of injury or loss that may accompany such activities. The Publisher disavows all responsibility for injury, death, loss, or property damage which may arise from a reader's participation in any of the activities described herein, and the Publisher makes no warranties regarding the competence, safety, and reliability of outfitters, tour companies, or training centers described in this book.

Find Frommer's Online

www.frommers.com offers up-to-the-minute listings on almost 200 cities around the globe—including the latest bargains and candid, personal articles updated daily by Arthur Frommer himself. No other Web site offers such comprehensive and timely coverage of the world of travel.

Introduction to the Second Edition

This second edition expands on Andrew Rice's first edition, and tries to build on his already vast catalogue of things to see and do in Northern California. It wasn't easy—every time I thought I'd found an undiscovered trail, his footprints were already in the snow. Therefore, many of the listings in this edition remain more or less unchanged from the last, though all were checked and fully updated.

Nonetheless, the book has grown a lot since the first edition. I've greatly expanded the introductory chapter "The Basics," which contains new information on sports ranging from boardsailing to hang gliding. It's designed to give you a sense of the local interest in each sport, a few points of reference, and a more detailed introduction to the area's possibilities. I've also added to the sections that cover activities on the state's enormous bays.

And throughout the book, I've added new beaches, hikes, bike rides, and parks. Many are within half an hour of downtown San Francisco or Sacramento, while others are in the remote backcountry. For those who'd like to tackle something more ambitious, there is now a primer on how to bike California's famous Highway 1, either in sections ranging from a day to a week, or as a 2-week odyssey that would test your will but also change your view of the state for good, and likely for the better.

In this second edition, I've tried to give you the region in its many dimensions: the look and feel of the coast and the mountains, the forests as well as the cities. I realize that activities like hiking, surfing, wine tasting, and downhill skiing all represent different Californias. I've tried to show you pathways to all of them, or at least alert you to their presence. Something, no doubt, still got missed. Even after expanding the guide, I know there are still more places out there. But you've got a good road map to begin exploring, and signposts to some hidden spots. Fortunately, it's hard to take a wrong turn in Northern California—this is not a place that easily disappoints. You've chosen a remarkable destination. Good luck. Have fun.

—*Marc Herman*

1

The Basics

No way could anyone write the definitive guide to every outdoor activity between Big Sur, Mount Whitney, and the Oregon border even if they had 10 years, much less just one. But I've given it a good whack. The Great Outdoor Guide to Northern California isn't the end of my journey; it should be a starting point for your own personal adventure, like a trail sign pointing you down an inviting path. It's arranged in eight regions, following the natural boundaries between different areas of Northern California. Some particularly hefty chapters are broken down even further into smaller regions. The core of each chapter is the "What to Do & Where to Do It" section (or sections, if there are several regions), an A to Z list of sports or activities from bird watching to white-water rafting, with a whole lot of hiking, fishing, kayaking, and more in between. If you're in, say, Mount Shasta and want to go mountain biking, look under "Mountain Biking" in the Northern Mountains chapter. There you'll find an assortment of good rides around Mount Shasta, plus tips on where to find local wisdom. But maybe your thing is whale watching and you're in Half Moon Bay. Or you want to snowboard and you're headed to Mammoth Lakes. Well, I've covered that too, plus rock climbing in Yosemite, diving in Monterey, boardsailing in the San Francisco Bay, and a whole lot more.

Under each sports heading, you'll find specific trails, routes, waterways, and activities chosen because they are the best in Northern California. These featured activities are described in detail. Distance, time, level of difficulty, terrain, location, and availability of maps have all been included when appropriate. Of course, time and level of difficulty are relative terms, but if you're in decent condition you should do just fine following these recommendations. Level of difficulty also varies from sport to sport. For example, all Walks & Rambles are easy, but a hike designated as easy is more strenuous, since hikes, by nature, involve a climb uphill or more rugged terrain. A difficult cross-country ski trail or white-water kayak run is something that you should never attempt unless you're sure of your technical ability,

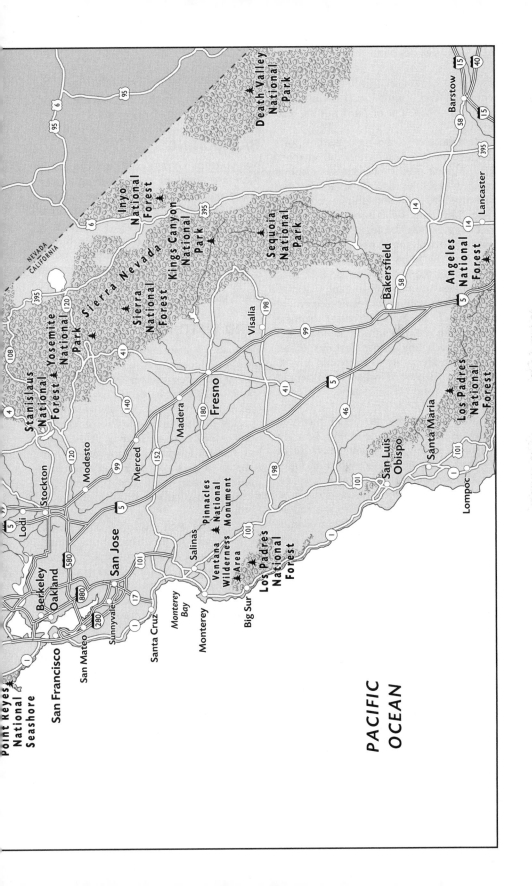

whereas a difficult road-biking trip mainly involves lots of hard huffing and puffing.

Introductory essays precede the sports and activities in each regional chapter. Since I don't think these kinds of sports and activities take place in a vacuum, I've also tried to say something about the geography and the natural character of each region—its biology and geology, and how people have interacted with the land over the years. This section is called "The Lay of the Land."

Because it's also important that you know where you are in relation to where the action is, each chapter also contains a section that discusses the most important towns, roads, and other features of an area—if you're trying to figure out how to cross the Sierra, or what town would make a good base camp, look at "Orientation."

And because it's important that you know exactly *where* the action is, each chapter contains a long annotated list of "Parks & Other Hot Spots," which includes the state forests, wilderness areas, beaches, rivers, lakes, and mountains that you'll be in, or on, as you paddle, hike, ski, and so on. And to ensure that you sleep well after all this action, each chapter concludes with a list of recommended campgrounds and a list of special inns and lodges for those who prefer to sleep in a bed but want to wake up with someplace wild right outside the door.

Getting Underway

By far the largest chunk of this book is broken down by sport, telling you just what you can do and where you can do it. Where is the best mountain bike ride in Marin County? How do you go about getting a California fishing license? Who's the best whale-watching tour operator?

Below is a list of most of the sports covered in this book, with information on organizations, outfitters, schools, and some of the best places to go.

BALLOONING

No, you can't rent a balloon. Fortunately there are plenty of people willing to give you a ride in theirs. Most of the ballooning in Northern California is found in the Napa and Sonoma wine country (see chapter 5), and that means two things: excellent food and drink before going aloft, and views right out of a French postcard during the ride. There's also some ballooning in the eastern Sierra.

BIRD WATCHING

Because it has so many different types of habitat, California is either home or a temporary stopover for literally thousands of species of birds. In each chapter, you'll find a list of some of the distinctive species in that area, plus recommendations of places to go birding. If there are any special activities, like ranger-led bird tours or a seasonal migration through a particular area, you'll find that included too, plus particularly good local guidebooks.

Any state with this many birds would be expected to also have birding clubs. The **National Audubon Society** is still, 100 years after Mr. Audubon started it, one of the best resources for birding information in the state. Local chapters can provide up-to-date information on the movements of specific species of birds and the people who follow them, and in some cases offer schedules of guided bird-watching trips. For a complete listing of chapters, contact the state office at ☎ 916/481-5332.

For a catalogue of species in the state, a 1944 book, *The Distribution of the Birds of California,* by Joseph Grinnell and Alden H. Miller, remains an authoritative text. Reproductions of the original edition are available for $20 hardback, $12 paperback from the Audubon Society.

There are so many special places to view birds in Northern California that it's almost impossible to list them all. Due to the nature of the sport, on any given day, one spot could be far better than the next. However, you can hardly go wrong with these six locales:

- **Point Reyes** If the weather allows, you can see more different species here than any other place in North America. It's often foggy, and Point Reyes is huge, so plan on spending a few days to really explore all the different environments of the park. This is a great place for sighting pelagic seabirds blown off course. See chapter 2.

- **Mono Lake** Strange as it may seem, most of the gulls in California are hatched here on the east side of the Sierra Nevada, not on the Pacific Coast. The birds nest on two small islands, visible with powerful spotting scopes or accessible by canoe, though you must stay at least 200 yards away to avoid stirring up the nesting birds. See chapter 6.

- **Pinnacles National Monument** Raptor heaven. The towering volcanic spires of this little-known coastal-range park are a stunning backdrop and, more importantly, offer nesting sites for many birds of prey. The surrounding mountains are completely undeveloped, a wonderful hunting ground. You can see golden eagles, peregrine falcons, Cooper's hawks, black-shouldered kites, and numerous other species here. See chapter 4.

- **Tule Lake National Wildlife Refuge** Tule Lake is synonymous with huge numbers of waterfowl. Canada geese, snow geese, canvasbacks, and sandhill cranes wing over this huge wetland complex. To top things off, this is also a major bald-eagle nesting habitat. A self-guided canoe tour and a self-guided auto tour make seeing this 40,000-acre refuge easier than you'd think. See chapter 8.

- **Klamath Basin** Located just east of Tule Lake, Lower Klamath National Wildlife Refuge adds another 46,000 acres of freshwater marshes and grasslands to the area's bird-watching opportunities. The refuge offers a 10-mile auto tour route, as well as a number of photo blinds. Waterfowl, including several species of heron, predominate, with peak migrations in late February through April and throughout November. Species include bald eagles, hawks of various kinds, ducks, swans, sandhill cranes, white pelicans, and sandpipers. Lower Klamath, established in 1908, was the nation's first waterfowl refuge. See chapter 8.

- **Elkhorn Slough** This huge tidal estuary feeding into Monterey Bay is one of the most spectacular birding spots around. You can either hike the surrounding hills, or better yet, take to the slough in a canoe or kayak. The record for the most species spotted in one place in one day was set here. Besides the marsh birds and waterfowl you'd expect, you'll also see numerous hawks and songbirds. See chapter 3.

BOARDSAILING

Boardsailing is a sport with a steep learning curve and complex, expensive equipment, and by its very nature it depends on two fickle variables—wind and water. With that in mind, this book assumes that you're either a beginner looking to get some introductory lessons, or an experienced sailor who just needs to be pointed to a local spot.

As with most ocean sports in Northern California, the best boardsailing is found around San Francisco and Monterey bays, plus the 50 miles of coastline in between. Beginners will find **Cowell's Beach** in Santa Cruz, the **Berkeley Marina** on San Francisco Bay, and **Richardson Bay** in Marin County to be the most forgiving spots. More experienced boardsailors will want to head towards **Coyote Point,** near the San Francisco airport, or **Waddell Beach,** about 15 miles north of Santa Cruz. See chapter 2 for spots near San Francisco and Marin County, and chapter 3 for those near Santa Cruz.

There are several phone numbers in the area to call for **wind, weather, and surf conditions.** Two of the most popular public reports are from San Francisco Airport (Coyote Point) at ☎ **650/ 877-3585,** and Sherman Island, in the Bay Delta, at ☎ **916/777-7007.** The recorded reports are updated several times daily.

The best places for sailboarding instruction are Santa Cruz and Berkeley. Try **Club Ed Surf and Windsurf School** (☎ **831/459-9283**) in Santa Cruz at Cowell's beach, or the **Cal Sailing Club** in the marina in Berkeley (no phone; see www.cal-sailing.org for info).

CANOEING

There was a time when canoes were the premier craft for exploring wild waterways, but in recent years the sea kayak seems to have taken over, even in freshwater. Nonetheless, there are still places where canoes are still king.

For information on canoeing, contact **California Canoe and Kayak,** a chain of canoe outfitters, with locations in Oakland, Sacramento, and Half Moon Bay. They offer rentals and lessons and also often supply advice that's free, thoughtful, and comprehensive. Call ☎ **510/893-7833** (Oakland), 916/353-1880 (Sacramento), or 650/728-1803 (Half Moon Bay). The

BACKCOUNTRY EQUIPMENT CHECKLIST

Below is a list of things you'll need for a backcountry trip. This is mainly a backpackers' list, for a 4- to 7-day summer or fall trip on a Northern California long-distance trail. But the list will also do for canoeing, backcountry skiing, whatever—there will be a few extra items of equipment you'll want for different kinds of trips, but this is a good checklist from which to start packing.

KITCHEN
- [ ] lightweight water-filter pump (Pür, First Need, Sweetwater Guardian)
- [ ] two to three Nalgene quart-size water bottles
- [ ] 5-gallon camp water bag
- [ ] stainless-steel cook set
- [ ] wooden spoon
- [ ] backpacking stove (like MSR Whisperlite or Coleman PEAK 1)
- [ ] 1.5 to 2 quarts stove fuel
- [ ] kitchen matches
- [ ] biodegradable soap
- [ ] scouring pad
- [ ] washcloth/pot holder/towel

PANTRY
- [ ] coffee singles or tea bags
- [ ] breakfast foods, like instant oatmeal
- [ ] lunch items, like peanut butter and jelly, crackers, cheese, hard sausage
- [ ] trail snacks, like gorp, beef jerky, dried fruit
- [ ] dinners—macaroni and cheese, freeze-dried dinners, couscous and Knorr gravy, other one-pot meals, in resealable (Ziploc) bags
- [ ] spices/seasonings
- [ ] big chocolate bar
- [ ] separate sacks for lunch/snacks and breakfast/dinner foods

CLOTHES CLOSET
- [ ] boots
- [ ] two pairs heavy socks
- [ ] polypropylene socks
- [ ] polypropylene long johns
- [ ] shorts or swimsuit
- [ ] baseball cap, or other sun hat
- [ ] knit wool cap
- [ ] bandanna
- [ ] water/wind-resistant, breathable shell (Gore-Tex or equivalent)
- [ ] rain pants
- [ ] cotton/synthetic T-shirt
- [ ] fleece jacket
- [ ] fleece pants
- [ ] sport sandals
- [ ] clothes stuff sack

California Floaters' Society is a network of canoeists and rafters who organize trips on Northern California rivers. For a recorded listing of upcoming trips, call ☎ **415/435-7936.** A membership may be required for some trips.

In addition, **The Flow Phone** (☎ **916/368-8682**), is a recorded listing of flows and dam releases for most of Northern California's major rivers. Updated every few days, the recording is worth checking before heading out on any canoe trip, particularly if you're not sure whether that Class II river is acting like a Class V that week. The only hitch is that, with several rivers to report on, the Flow Phone reporter always speaks *really fast,* and often seems to list the rivers in no particular order. Keep your pen and paper ready.

Some of the best places to canoe are the **American River** (see chapter 7), **Lake Alpine** (see chapter 6), the **Russian River** (see chapter 9), and **Elkhorn Slough** (see chapter 3).

CROSS-COUNTRY SKIING

Cross-country skiers seem to be evenly split between those who love nothing more than gliding down a freshly set mechanical track at a Nordic ski area and those who much prefer to bust their own trail along snow-covered logging roads, meadows, and trails. Accordingly, in the cross-country skiing section you'll find some of both: listings and descriptions of commercial resorts in that area, plus a selection of backcountry trail listings.

BEDROOM

- [ ] waterproof groundcloth
- [ ] tent
- [ ] sleeping bag rated to 20°F
- [ ] sleeping pad (Therm-A-Rests are great)

ALL-PURPOSE ESSENTIALS

- [ ] maps/compass
- [ ] bug repellent
- [ ] lighter
- [ ] whistle (for bear country, or rescue)
- [ ] sunglasses
- [ ] watch
- [ ] toothbrush, razor, other toilet gear
- [ ] Mini-Mag flashlight, or headlamp
- [ ] extra batteries
- [ ] battery-powered or candle lantern
- [ ] Swiss army knife

- [ ] 75–100-foot rope (parachute cord), for hanging food, etc.
- [ ] toilet paper
- [ ] toilet trowel
- [ ] extra quart sealable bags
- [ ] extra gallon sealable bags
- [ ] extra stuff sack
- [ ] notebook/pen
- [ ] a good book

FIRST-AID KIT

- [ ] 2-inch by 3-inch moleskin
- [ ] pair small shears
- [ ] thermometer
- [ ] safety pins
- [ ] acetaminophen/ibuprofen/aspirin
- [ ] diarrhea pills
- [ ] antacid tablets
- [ ] sunscreen
- [ ] sting-relief pads

- [ ] iodine solution
- [ ] iodine ointment
- [ ] triple antibiotic ointment
- [ ] antiseptic towelettes
- [ ] single-edge razor blade or scalpel
- [ ] 1-inch by 3-inch fabric bandages
- [ ] fabric knuckle bandages
- [ ] sterile wound-closure strips (butterflies)
- [ ] 4-inch by 4-inch sterile gauze pads
- [ ] adhesive tape
- [ ] elastic (ace) bandage
- [ ] 5-inch by 9-inch combine dressings
- [ ] irrigation syringe
- [ ] wire mesh splint

LUXURIES

- [ ] camera gear
- [ ] binoculars
- [ ] fishing gear

Cross-country skiing can be totally relaxing—an easy shuffle around a mountain meadow—or extremely demanding. Some of the more difficult trails involve steep climbs and speedy descents.

If you haven't cross-country skied in a while, you're in for a big surprise. There are now a variety of skis to tackle the variety of terrain. First, there's the old touring ski, good for diagonal striding on groomed trails. Skating skis or racing skis are shorter and more narrow than the traditional track skis and are used with a speed-skating technique for quickness. Backcountry skis are wider than touring skis to give extra maneuverability on ungroomed trails. Telemark skis are similar to backcountry skis with the addition of metal edges. Telemarking is a gracefully lunging turning technique that gives free-wheelers something close to the kind of control on steep slopes that alpine skiers have. Finally, there are *randonee* skis with lock-down heel bindings enabling you to climb a slope like a cross-country skier and descend using downhill parallel technique, bridging the gap between cross-country and downhill skiing.

The most obvious and popular destination for cross-country skiers is the Sierra Nevada, particularly the **Lake Tahoe** region and **Yosemite** (see chapter 6), and those places are rightfully deserving of the attention they get. Often overlooked is the great cross-country skiing in the northern mountains. **Mount Lassen** and **Mount Shasta** (see chapter 8) are especially beautiful destinations and receive tons of snow. You can often ski Mount Shasta well into June and even July.

DOWNHILL SKIING & SNOWBOARDING

There's both too much and not enough to say about downhill skiing in California. Obviously it's an important sport or there wouldn't be so many resorts. You could write an entire book describing every single California ski resort in endless detail

and people would probably line up to buy it, but this isn't it. I've tried to give you a feel for the personalities of some of the various resorts in each area, but I don't presume to be writing a comprehensive encyclopedia. If you want that, *California City-Sports* magazine publishes an annual ski preview issue every November with the latest prices, rules, snowmaking equipment, number of lifts, trails, new programs, vertical drop, and phone numbers, plus special tips on each mountain. You can contact the magazine at 214 South Cedros, Solana Beach, CA 92075 (☎ 619/793-2711) or find it in any California ski shop.

Here's a list of my favorite skiing/snowboarding hills, all covered more fully in chapter 6:

- **Squaw Valley** It's a little big and glitzy for my taste, but Squaw has unarguably the most radical terrain in the Tahoe area. Tons of steeps and moguls. Also miles and miles of easy cruising runs.

- **Northstar-at-Tahoe** This north-shore resort is one of the best-managed in California. Tons of high-speed lifts whisk you up the mountain. Coming down is generally a well-groomed intermediate run. Good family mountain.

- **Kirkwood Ski Resort** Kirkwood is just far enough outside of the Tahoe area to avoid the crowds. Much of the mountain is above the tree line. A clear day here is striking; a stormy one is awful.

- **Bear Valley Ski Area** I grew up skiing Bear Valley and went from stem christies to gonzo cornice drops here. The view into the Mokelumne River Canyon is one of the best anywhere. The back side is intermediate heaven. Below the lodge are two little-known and incredibly steep bowls served by the Kodiak and Grizzly lifts. A very diverse mountain.

FISHING

If it has fins, you can probably find it swimming somewhere in California. Fishing, both inland and saltwater, is big-time fun in this state, where people catch everything from trophy-sized largemouth bass and salmon to the small and extremely rare golden trout, the state fish. In each area, you'll find a description of the chief fishery there, as well as some recommendations about guides or shops, but remember that there are literally thousands of tackle shops, boat rentals, and fishing guides, and fishing schools are just waiting for you to give them a call or drop by.

To help make sense of the huge numbers, get your hands on a copy of the *Cal/North Boating–Fishing–Diving Directory,* a wonderful phone-book–style directory of all kinds of different services relating to, you guessed it, boating, fishing, and diving. The price is right—free.

Contact **Cal/North Marine Publishing Company,** P.O. Box 410483, San Francisco, CA 94141 (☎ **415/243-0426**). Inland anglers might want to pick up another great publication, with an exhaustive listing of fishing streams, lakes, and rivers: *California Fishing,* by Tom Stienstra, an award-winning outdoors writer for the *San Francisco Examiner.*

If you're over 16, you need a **license** to fish anywhere in California waters and you must display it at all times. The only exception is fishing from recreational piers in the Pacific, but only from piers. Cast from the beach or a boat and you need a license. California has an extremely complicated license program, where you buy a base license for a certain price and then have to buy different stamps for different types of fishing and different areas. To make things even easier, they change these stamps and areas just about

---

It Costs *How* Much?

A day fishing in Monterey or San Francisco Bays, the most popular ocean fishing spots in northern California, can cost very little or quite a bit. It all depends on whether you bring your own rod and reel, buy live bait, need to buy a 1-day fishing license, or specify a particular kind of fish you're trying to catch.

Boats out of Half Moon Bay's Pillar Point harbor, for example, tend to charge between $30 and $45 per person for a day sail, though it's a long day, beginning at sun-up and returning late. You'll have to tack on another $10 to $15 if you're leaving from San Francisco or Monterey's better-known waterfronts, or chasing a specific kind of fish requiring the captain to take the boat farther out. Half-day trips are sometimes available for half price. That's often a good option—spend 12 hours straight on the water, and you begin to understand why old fishermen look the way they do.

If you don't have a fishing license, you'll need to purchase one, with costs varying according to a complicated regularity system. Renting a rod and reel will run about $10. Most bait is fairly inexpensive, a few dollars, but live bait, preferred for catching some kinds of fish, will cost between $10 and $25.

As you can see, fishing costs add up. Plan to spend about $100 per person for the day, with some discounts for children.

every year. For nonresidents they keep it a little more simple: you can buy a fishing license for a single day, 10 days, or a year. For up-to-date license information, contact the **California Department of Fish and Game License Section,** 3211 S St., Sacramento, CA 95816 (☎ **916/227-2244**).

HANG GLIDING

With rock climbing, bungee jumping, downhill mountain biking, and helicopter skiing all garnering great enthusiasm over the past decade, it's no surprise that hang gliding has gained in popularity too. After all, long before anyone had heard of those other "extreme" sports, there were hang gliders.

Several options for hang gliding and learning to hang-glide present themselves in Northern California, though I strongly recommend you read the legend of Icarus first, and don't say I didn't warn you. **Mission Soaring Center,** located at 1116 Wrigley Way in the San Jose suburb of Milpitas, has been around since 1973. Equipment sales, lessons, and nearly 3 decades of institutional wisdom on gliding are available here. Lessons are taught in Hollister, about an hour south. Call ☎ **408/ 262-1055** for details and schedules.

Popular hang-gliding spots include **Hat Creek Rim,** 20 miles north of Lassen National Park and roughly 75 miles east of Redding (see chapter 8), and **Mount St. Helena,** 7 miles north of Calistoga in the wine country (see chapter 5). Wind and weather information for various areas around Mount St. Helena can be found at a Web site, www.sonomawings. com. Similar information is available for San Jose and points south from Northern California's largest hang-gliding club, **Wings of Rogallo** (www.wingsofrogallo.org).

HIKES, BUSHWHACKS & BACKPACK TRIPS

This is consistently the biggest part of each chapter: the list of hikes and possible overnight backpacking trips for the

area. Each recommended hike listing will give you the approximate mileage, difficulty, recommended map, and trailhead access, plus a description of each hike, including terrain, wildlife you might see, points of interest, and things to look out for. For overnights I've also included a lot of possible side activities, and where you should go to get current trail conditions and wilderness permits.

Bear in mind that these listings are not an exact description of every fork in the trail or every rock where you should turn right, cross a stream, and crawl over three logs before climbing 300 feet and turning southwest. If you don't know how to follow a trail or use a map, this book isn't going to save you. It's intended to give you the information you need to decide which hikes you want to do, not to take the place of backcountry skills and a good map. Once you leave the trailhead, you're on your own. For easier walks that usually don't require a map, check out the "Walks & Rambles" sections.

The great thing about hiking in California is that you can do it year-round and you can do it everywhere. Options include hiking to isolated wilderness beaches on the north coast, finding a backcountry hot spring in Big Sur, or trekking to a granite-shrouded lake in the High Sierra. It's the best way to really see the state: slow enough to catch the details, but with a view that changes with every hill and valley.

Favorite Day Hikes

- **High Peaks Trail, Pinnacles National Monument** A wonderful day hike in the coast range mountains of the Pinnacles. The trail winds through a wild formation of hoodoos and wind-carved rocks. The remnant volcanic spires here are more reminiscent of New Mexico than California. See chapter 4.

- **Mount Tam to Stinson Beach Loop, Mount Tamalpais State Park** This trail offers a bit of everything, including a wonderful series of cascades and second-growth redwoods. See chapter 2.

• **Tuolumne Meadows to Glen Aulin High Sierra Camp, Yosemite National Park** Beginning with a hike across one of the largest alpine meadows in the state and ending at a spectacular waterfall, this hike is a good introduction to one of the most important watersheds in the Sierra Nevada. Lots of wildlife along the route. See chapter 6.

• **Giant Forest, Sequoia & Kings Canyon National Parks** Numerous short loops will let you see the giant sequoia trees here, but if you want to really see the forest, take one of the longer hikes into the far corners of this spectacular grove. There you can be alone with the towering sequoias, the largest living things on earth. See chapter 6.

• **Berry Creek Falls, Big Basin State Park** An all-day walk to the falls and back is one of the best ways to get a taste of a remote redwood forest. Big Basin State Park is within half an hour of downtown San Jose and an hour and a half from San Francisco. The trails to and from the falls are generally forgiving, though with enough up-and-down to let you know you've worked. The falls themselves, the last in a series of cascades encountered along the trails through Big Basin, are magnificent. The park's extensive trail system makes it possible to hike the falls as a loop, including ocean vistas and sunny patches, or as an out-and-back, staying in the misty, cool redwood environment. See "Skyline to the Sea/Sunset Trail Loop" under "Hikes, Bushwhacks & Backpack Trips" in chapter 3, for the most popular approach to the falls. See chapter 3.

Favorite Overnights

As nice as day hiking is, nothing compares to the experience of spending a few days or even weeks away from the rat race. Literally thousands of good weekend backpacking trips can be done year-round in California.

If you have more than a weekend, several long-distance trails cross Northern California:

• **John Muir Trail** This 200-plus-mile trek through the heart of the Sierra Nevada is the most famous backpacking trail in Northern California. It begins in the Yosemite Valley and ends at the summit of Mount Whitney. In between is the finest high-country hiking in California. Plan on at least 3 weeks to cover the whole route.

• **Pacific Crest Trail** Running the length of California from near Mount Shasta, through Lassen National Park, and down the spine of the Sierra, the PCT links Canada, the United States, and Mexico. Most people hike it in small segments, but a few thru-hikers trek the whole length.

• **The Lost Coast** This 25-mile-long stretch of roadless wilderness coastline in Humboldt County is the finest coastal backpacking in the Lower 48. It's a longer 25 miles than you might think; 5 to 6 miles a day is a reasonable goal. Steep and densely wooded mountains soar out of the stormy Pacific. You'll spend lots of time clambering over rocks, slogging through soft sand, and waiting for the tides to let you pass.

HORSEBACK RIDING

More than 100 different dude ranches, pack-horse guide services, and livery stables are dispersed around the northern half of the state, with options ranging from 1-hour trail rides to weeklong

BACKPACKING FOR BEGINNERS

No other activity requires more preplanning than backpacking. You have to eat and sleep for days or weeks without the luxury of a refrigerator, oven, and bed. Obviously, the first items you need are good hiking boots, a good sleeping bag and sleeping pad, and a **backpack.** As far as packs go, the debate over the merits of the old-fashioned external-frame pack and the more new-fangled internal-frame pack has raged on for years. External-frame packs are generally a little cheaper; they're well suited to carrying heavy loads on fairly straight-ahead trail. But internal-frame packs have clearly outdistanced their rivals in most ways. They're more stable over rough going—rock-hopping and steep-and-twisty switchbacks—because they distribute the weight more evenly across your hips and shoulders and cinch more snugly to your back. They let you carry greater loads with more comfort, a combination that I find hard to beat. Whichever you choose, get one that really fits you—don't try to fit yourself to a pack. A good pack will have plenty of padding and support; a wide, firm hip belt; and a lumbar support pad. Most of all, it will simply feel good.

Now comes the hard part—trying to pare down your load so you don't feel like a beast of burden on your hike. All the essentials are listed in the "Backcountry Equipment Checklist" feature, above. I'm a terrible gear hound and a pack rat and always want to take everything. I indulge myself the luxury of pulling out every bit of gear I think I need and trying to fit it in my backpack; then I put 80% of it away. I used to haul a lot of stuff around I never used. These days, I'm a big proponent of going very light—leave the extra pants, three fishing reels, 10 pounds of chocolate, and encyclopedia set at home.

My meals on the trail are a mixture of dried foods (rice, beans, lentils, pastas, dried meats, dried fruits); Swiss-type crackers; plastic jars of peanut butter and jelly; cereal; a trail mix of nuts, carob, and raisins; granola bars; cookies; and premade meals, from Lipton's Cup-a-Soups to freeze-dried backpacker dinners. Water, of course, depends on where you're going. Most places in the Sierra Nevada or Northern Mountains have plentiful water. In the backcountry around Big Sur, water can be scarce in summer. Take lots of containers and inquire at the ranger station before heading out. No matter where you are in California, treat your water to remove *Giardia.*

wilderness adventures. While virtually anyone is capable of short day rides, some riding experience is useful before setting out on a multiday packstock trip. Contrary to the movie *City Slickers,* horseback riding is not a sport where you ride for 4 days straight unless you have some idea of what it's like to sit in a saddle. Otherwise, your visions of *High Noon* might turn into great doom and you could be walking bowlegged for the next month.

Excellent pack trips are available in **Sequoia National Park** and **Yosemite.** Contact the park offices for details (see chapter 6). Most pack trips take three or more days, about the same amount of time it would take to hike the trail yourself. Of course, this way you don't have to hike it. **Point Reyes** makes a popular day trip on horseback (see chapter 2).

For a complete list of the commercial outfitters and stables operating in California, write to the California Trade and Commerce Agency, 801 K St., Suite 1700, Sacramento, CA 95814. Include a self-addressed stamped envelope.

KAYAKING

The beauty of the kayak is its ruggedness, portability, and maneuverability, and California can put all these characteristics to the test. A good kayaker is the epitome of grace under pressure, and a bad kayaker is, well, swimming.

The advent of the **sit-on-top kayak** has opened the sport to casual dabbling, mostly in the ocean and lakes, and to a much smaller degree in white-water rivers. Instead of sitting *in* the kayak, where beginners tend to feel claustrophobic and the consequences of tipping are much more serious, you sit *on* the kayak, in a molded cockpit or well. That way if you tip over (and you just might) there's no panicked fear session of hanging upside down while trying to Eskimo roll. You just take a nice dip and climb back on top of your boat. Of course, you give up a lot of handling and performance when you use a sit-on-top; I'd never recommend them for serious adventuring, but they're a great way to get a taste of the sport.

California Canoe and Kayak is one of the better sources of information along the coast. It has three locations: Oakland (☎ 510/893-7833), Sacramento (☎ 916/353-1880), and Half Moon Bay (☎ 650/728-1803), south of San Francisco.

White-Water Kayaking

A white-water kayak is to a sea kayak what a Ferrari is to a school bus. The level of performance here is much higher, as is the steepness of the learning curve. You can become a competent kayaker in Class III (screw up and you won't die) rapids with a week's worth of classes, but you may never be able or have any desire to run Class IV (screw up and you *might* die) and Class V (screw up and it is *likely* that you'll die) white water. The problem is that there's a lot of hard Class IV and V white water out there mixed in with all that forgiving Class III water, making it imperative that you know what lies below before you venture down any stretch of river.

With that in mind, each white-water kayaking entry in this book describes the general nature of an area's rivers, along with overall descriptions of the popular runs, but stops short of giving you mile-by-mile or rapid-by-rapid descriptions. This is not a river guidebook. *Read this very carefully:* We by no means intend

this book to be used as the primary source of information for any white-water run. That is why we list local experts and local guidebooks that do give extremely detailed descriptions of each run tailored to your individual level of skill.

I don't mean to imply that kayaking is terribly dangerous or scary. It's not, and done right it's one of the purest thrills I've ever felt. But if you've never kayaked in white water before, take it from me—go get at least a few basic lessons. The fundamental building blocks of the sport are incredibly subtle and counterintuitive. Let someone show them to you.

There are three main kayaking schools in California. The most deluxe and widely acclaimed is **Otter Bar Lodge** on the Salmon River (see chapter 8), a wilderness resort and intensive kayaking program that operates week-long sessions. The others are **Sierra South** in Kernville (see chapter 6) and **California Canoe and Kayak** (see chapter 2). The latter two are both highly recommended schools with no lodging or resort features where you can take classes as short as a single day or as long as you like.

Sea Kayaking

The most popular sea-kayaking area in Northern California is the waterfront of **Monterey** (see chapter 3), followed closely by the bay shore of **Marin County** (sea chapter 2), but you can have a blast on a sea kayak just about anywhere (including lakes—don't take the name that seriously). Since a kayak trip depends so much on weather, surf conditions, tides, and how energetic you're feeling that day, what you'll find here is a description of local conditions and a list of good places to put in with general trip suggestions.

MOUNTAIN BIKING

It's no wonder that the mountain bike was invented in California. We've got good weather and lots of backcountry fire roads and trails, and distances in this state are huge. There are a lot of places you can reach in an easy 25-mile mountain bike ride over the course of an afternoon that would take days to reach on foot. Unfortunately, the sport is in a major flux right now. Many trails are being closed to bikers because of conflicts with hikers and horses. Please do what you can to ease the tension: ride within your ability to stop quickly if you see a hiker or horse; dismount and let horses pass you instead of whizzing past them; don't shortcut or otherwise thrash trails; smile, say hi, and generally kill everyone on the trail with kindness.

Single tracks, double tracks, and dirt roads dominate the mountain biker's terrain. Dirt roads can range from hard-packed gravel logging roads to sandy fire roads. Double tracks vary in width from former railroad beds to old carriage paths. These are ideal trails for the beginner to intermediate biker. Single track—narrow trails created by hikers or horseback riders—whisk you in and out of the forest, within arm's length of trees and bushes on both sides. Unfortunately for us mountain bikers, the number of available single tracks has declined drastically since many of the national and state parks began banning mountain bikes from most of their trails. So-called "technical" single-track trails are the most challenging. They wind up and down hills, over rocks, roots, and soft mud that often feels like quicksand. On these trails, it's not uncommon (or embarrassing) to have to get off your bike and walk around or over an obstacle.

In my opinion, the best mountain biking in the state is in the coast range, much of which has unfortunately been declared off-limits. Still, great places like **Wilder Ranch State Park** near Santa Cruz and **Forest of Nisene Marks State Park** near Aptos continue to allow largely unfettered mountain-bike access to their fantastic networks of trails and roads (see chapter 3).

All across the state, national forestlands are crisscrossed with an elaborate network of logging roads and fire roads that doubles as the world's hugest mountain-bike park.

Here's a list of my favorite rides:

- **Deadman Creek to June Lake**   This backcountry route between Mammoth Lakes and June Lakes epitomizes mountain biking in the eastern Sierra—changing terrain, spectacular views, and challenging conditions. You'll probably get lost, but so what—wherever you end up will be really nice. See chapter 6.

- **Flume Trail, Lake Tahoe**   Once the route of an old logging flume, this trail today is the gem of all Tahoe area mountain biking. Riding it is a strenuous, all-day event but the sight of the lake below while you whiz down the perfect single track is enough to make the most jaded biker smile. See chapter 6.

- **Wilder Ranch State Park, Santa Cruz**   My favorite coastal biking within a day's drive of the Bay Area. Wilder is an explorer's dream. Lots of fire road and single track through redwood groves, creeks, and open grasslands—and endless ocean views too. See chapter 3.

- **Mount Shasta**   So many trails surround Mount Shasta that you could ride for weeks. What sets this area apart from others is the looming presence of the mountain. Wherever you go, Shasta is there and always changing. One of the most difficult rides in the state is a single-day circumnavigation of the mountain using a combination of fire roads, paved road, and railroad grade. See chapter 8.

- **The Lost Coast**   In an era when mountain bikers seem to be losing their right to ride from all sides, the Lost Coast in Humboldt County is one of the last places you have to worry about access battles. What you do have to worry about is the incredible steepness and difficulty of the hundreds of miles of old logging roads through this redwood-filled wilderness. See chapter 9.

ROAD BIKING

Cycling devotees in Northern California have created a calendar of events and favorite routes to match anything in the world. On the somewhat absurd end, the annual Davis Double (200 miles around Sacramento), Markleeville Death Ride (a ride over five Sierra passes in 1 day), and Mr. Bill's Nightmare (150 nearly vertical miles over the Santa Cruz mountains) supply proof of a vibrant lunatic fringe. On the other, healthier end of the spectrum, a system of bike paths and lanes is growing in many locations, with city planners in Palo Alto, Davis, and Santa Cruz turning out some widely imitated thinking on how to integrate bikes and cars on the city streets safely. It doesn't hurt that the area's coastal scenery lends itself to bike paths in many places, and that, inland, back roads wind through redwood groves and alpine towns.

It's no coincidence that some of the country's greatest racing cyclists have lived and trained in Northern California, using the reliable climate and variety of terrain to get themselves ready for international competition. Champion Greg Lemond, as a kid in Carson City, Nevada, used to ride across the state line to climb in the Sierra, or so the legend goes.

Of course, you don't have to be training for the Tour de France to explore the back roads. **Napa and Sonoma counties** are laced with an extensive network of flat, forgiving routes through the grape fields (see chapter 5). Monterey's coastal bike path spills directly onto the well-known 17-Mile Drive, a toll road cyclists can ride for free (see chapter 3). The far northern counties, such as Humboldt, are virtually free of traffic and offer hundreds of miles of canopied riding in the forests.

Northern California is also a long-distance touring destination to rival any other. The coast, the wine country, and the mountains all host hundreds or thousands of multiday trips every year, some organized, many solo or undertaken by small groups of friends. For details on one of the best long-distance rides anywhere, see "Cycling the California Coast," below.

If you're looking to go with an organized tour, the largest outfitter for California road biking is **Backroads** (☎ **800/245-3874**), a Berkeley-based outfit running tours all over the state. Other operators offering guided tours of the wine country and other regions are listed in the appropriate chapters.

If you're cycling on your own, several route guides exist. Along Highway 1, the guide used by hundreds of cycle tourists year after year is *Bicycling the Pacific Coast,* by Tom Kirkendall and Vicky Spring (The Mountaineers, 1998). For elsewhere in the state, try *Adventure Cycling in Northern California,* by the Adventure Cycling Association (The Mountaineers, 1997).

Another great source of information is the local bike shop. Beyond being able to do basic repairs for you, Northern California's many bike shops are often informal two-wheeler community centers, where local routes are discussed, traffic warnings posted, and advice given. In much of the state's midsize cities, there seems to be a bike shop every few blocks, which is greatly to your benefit. Your best resources here are usually the mechanics, many of whom are fonts of local cycling information beyond anything you could find on a map.

ROCK CLIMBING

From sandstone outcroppings overlooking the Pacific Ocean to the huge granite walls of the Yosemite Valley, California is

THE HIKER-BIKER PROGRAM

For those of you who think there's no justice in the world, we humbly submit California's hiker-biker program for your cynical evaluation. The program allows campers who arrive at state camping grounds "under their own power," usually on foot or bike, to camp for the ridiculously affordable price of $2. That's right, two dollars. The catch is, you have to be traveling under muscle power exclusively. No driving to the edge of the park and walking in (or if you do, don't let them catch you).

In popular locations, principally **Big Sur,** hiker-biker sites are located in separate (usually quieter) areas of the park, away from the car camping areas. Each hiker-biker camp is a little smaller than a regular site, but has the same amenities: fire rings, picnic tables, nearby bathroom facilities, and a water source.

There are usually between 5 and 10 such sites in participating parks, each big enough for two tents. Camping is on a first-come, first-served basis, but people will usually make room for each other if it's an unusually busy night. Fortunately, it's very rare for the hiker-biker area to get crowded. Frequently, you'll be the only person there.

In parks without a designated hiker-biker area, you may be assigned a regular space among the car-campers, but charged only the hiker-biker fee. Policies on the program vary from park to park and with the season. Before planning your trip, call ahead to the parks on your itinerary to ask whether they have hiker-biker sites, or at least discounts. Also, keep in mind that this is a state program, so it won't help you in federally-administered national forest, national parks (such as Yosemite), or other public lands outside the California state park system. It will, however, help you in many parts of the Sierra, most of the coast, and the northern wine country, where there are numerous state parks.

Though some hardy souls do walk to state parks, the most common beneficiaries of the hiker-biker program are mountain bikers and touring cyclists, who plan multiday rides in park-to-park segments to take advantage of the cheap sleeps. In the high summer and fall season, hiker-biker areas serve as a crossroads for many types of people, who each night compare road stories, swap weather and topography reports, loan each other inner tubes, and share campfires. For some, the friendships that result become the highlight of the trip.

At its most fundamental, two bucks for a clean campsite with hot water—not to mention a view of the Pacific or the Sierra—may be the best camping deal in the country. After a long day's walk or ride, it also feels like a nice reward for leaving the car at home.

—Marc Herman

studded with great climbing spots. Not surprisingly, people here are just crazy about climbing. Listing all the different routes and rocks would be impossible, so the rock-climbing coverage in this book is designed to give you an idea of what each climbing area is like and point you in the direction of what you hope to find.

As with white-water kayaking, I cannot emphasize enough how important it is to know what you're doing when rock climbing. Screw up and you *will* get hurt. There's no other way around it. Wile E. Coyote can fall off a cliff and walk away because he is made of ink—you are not. There are numerous excellent schools and guides throughout Northern California that will teach you everything from the definition of *belay* to how to place protection in a finger-wide crack. They are also great sources of information on local climbing options. Here are some of the best:

- **Alpine Skills International,** located in Tahoe's Donner Pass area, offers classes not only in basic climbing, but in leading, anchoring, and self-rescue. It even has women-only classes. For information, call ☎ **530/426-9108.**

• **Mountain Adventures,** located halfway between Tahoe and Yosemite in Bear Valley, offers a similar range of climbing courses, as well as special trips to Pinnacles and Southern California's Joshua Tree. Most instruction takes place at the organization's base, located on the Sierra's west slope off Highway 4. Call ☎ **800/36-CLIMB.**

• Made famous by its "Go Climb a Rock" T-shirts, the souvenir every visitor to Yosemite seemed to buy during the 1970s, **Yosemite Mountaineering School** has the advantage of location. You might not scale Half Dome by the end of your first lesson, but it'll be there, over your shoulder, waiting. Instructors are seasoned Yosemite climbers. The basic battery of classes is divided into "Rock I," "Rock II," and "Rock III"—multiday packages including all three are available. Advanced classes tackle some of the park's famous walls. The school will also, for a hefty price (a few thousand dollars), provide a guide for ascents of the legendary El Capitan.

SAILING

The two great sailing spots of Northern California are **Monterey Bay** (see chapter 3) and the **San Francisco Bay** (see chapter 2). Monterey Bay is less sheltered from the open sea, with higher winds and bigger waves. San Francisco Bay is a sailor's dream, even though it does have heavy recreational and commercial traffic. If you're looking to learn how to sail, there are several schools in both areas that will teach you. If you're already an experienced skipper looking to rent a bareboat by the day or week, you'll find listings to help you locate the best one. Boatless

sailors, experienced or not, should note that many day-sailing captains will take you out in the California bays for free, provided you do your job as a faithful member of the ship's crew in return (see "Sail for Free," below).

Certification requirements for renting, or "bareboating," vary from outfit to outfit, but some sort of proof that you can sail is almost always required before anyone lets you leave the dock with their $50,000 boat. Be prepared to present a sailor's resume—basically a list of what kinds of boats you've sailed, where you sailed them, and for how long. If you have a certification from a good sailing school, bring that too.

Finally, if you learned to sail by stealing your uncle's leaky skiff on some unnamed lake in Wisconsin 20 years ago, be prepared to be asked to take a **sailing test** on the water—and to pay for the privilege. A 1- to 2-hour checkout ride is standard for anyone just showing up for a bareboat, and can cost as much as $100. You might want to think of that as the price of lasting certification. In the future, other marinas where you might want to rent will be able to call the place you checked out with and get their opinion of you. Often a nearby marina will let you go without a test if your previous checkout vouches that you're not going to sink the boat.

SCUBA DIVING

People have been known to scuba dive just about everywhere on the Northern California coast, but there's a huge difference between where you *can* dive and where you'd really *want* to dive. **Monterey** and its surrounding area offer some of the finest cold-water diving in the world; see chapter 3 for a description of some of the most popular dives and informational listings for the best dive shops and boats. The other good Northern California diving is in **Sonoma** and **Mendocino** counties, but access is restricted to just a few state parks (see chapter 9).

Though scuba diving isn't particularly difficult or dangerous, it does require some safety techniques that aren't naturally intuitive. As a result, instruction is not only strongly advised, it's mandatory. You must be certified by the National Association of Underwater Instructors (NAUI) or Professional Association of Dive Instructors (PADI) to rent scuba equipment, get tanks filled, or go on dive boats. This only goes for scuba diving, though. To snorkel or free-dive, you just need to be a confident swimmer.

SURFING

When people think of surfing and California, they think of Malibu, Huntington Beach, San Onofre, Blacks Beach, and other famous Southern California surf spots, but they rarely think of Northern California. "It's cold up there," they say. "There are sharks." Well, they're right on both counts. It is cold up here—full wet suits are the prescription year-round, and in winter you'll probably want a hood, gloves, and booties. And yes, there are sharks. On the average, one surfer gets bitten by a great white shark each year in Northern California. Considering how many people go in the water, though, your odds of getting bitten by a shark are a lot less than getting killed crossing the street on the way to the beach.

Santa Cruz is surf city, the center of all Northern California surf culture, and also has some excellent surfing schools (see chapter 3). Other popular spots are **Pacifica,** just south of San Francisco, and **Ocean Beach,** located in the San Francisco city limits (see chapter 2). North of Marin County on the real north coast there are hundreds of secret little breaks hidden at the bottom of a cliff or down a winding trail, some of which you even have to backpack to (see chapter 9). By the way, if you're considering learning to surf, try renting the film **Big Wednesday,** with Gary Busey and Jan Michael Vincent. It'll get you started, anyway.

SWIMMING

Swimming off Northern California's beaches can be great, but it's a lot colder up here than in Southern California, and the riptides can get serious. **Ocean Beach,** in San Francisco (see chapter 2), has had a rash of tragic drownings lately, owing in part to the deceivingly placid appearance of its riptide-torn water. And unlike Southern California, very few Northern California beaches have lifeguards on duty. Take care swimming at any beach, especially with children.

There are, of course, a number of tried and true beaches that are safe and a lot of fun. **Cowell's Beach,** in Santa Cruz (see chapter 3), is crowded with swimmers every summer, as is the nearby beach in front of the Santa Cruz boardwalk. **Stinson Beach,** on the shore below Mount Tam in Marin County (see chapter 2), is also a good swimming beach, though it gets a little sharky now and again. The beach just north of **Crissy Field,** in San Francisco (see chapter 2), is popular. Most placid of all is **Alameda Beach,** on the east side of San Francisco Bay; it's so shallow that you may not be able to get wet past your ankles without walking halfway to the Bay Bridge. Which means it's perfect for kids, and at high tide, a good place to swim without dealing with Pacific waves.

All of these waters are only swimmable without a wet suit in winter, notwithstanding the few hearty souls of the Dolphin Club in San Francisco who go in year-round dressed only in their Speedos. They are, of course, insane, but you're welcome to join them in their insanity if you're so inclined. The Dolphin Club takes to the water at **Aquatic Park** in San Francisco, just east of Fort Mason, early on weekend mornings but on no particular schedule.

Northern California also offers a lot of freshwater swimming options. **Pinecrest**

SAIL FOR FREE

One of the better-kept secrets in Northern California's outdoors is the availability of free sailboat rides on San Francisco and Monterey bays. That sounds suspiciously like a joke—but in fact, it makes perfect sense.

Sailing a boat is a lot of work. But owning a boat often takes only one or two people. That means a lot of boat owners, either because their friends can't make it every time, or because they simply don't know anyone else who likes to sail, could use some help. It's a great exchange: They get a less hectic sail (and maybe enjoy feeling like the captain of the ship), while you get an afternoon on the bay, and if you keep your eyes open, free sailing lessons. Add to that the natural enthusiasm many sailors have for both their sport and their boat, and you begin to feel silly for not taking up the hundreds of free rides that are there for the asking.

Many of the day sailors on the bays actually prefer crews of novice or intermediate sailors. The logic is pretty sound: Boat owners have made enormous investments in their vessels, so even the calmest, most laid-back skipper wants things done his or her way out on the water, where a mistake can mean damaging the boat or worse. Novices don't second-guess the captain, and they take orders pretty well. If they can understand what's going on as it's explained, and learn quickly, they make the perfect crew members.

So lack of experience shouldn't deter you from checking out a crew list and, if the boats interest you, trying to get on one.

If you have access to the World Wide Web, a good place to start is a Web site called **SF Sailing** (www.sfsailing.com), which despite its name covers Monterey Bay as well as San Francisco. Click on "crew list," at the top of the screen, for lists divided into racing, offshore cruising, and day sailing. Each ad will contain a description of the boat, its location, the skipper's name, some details about when the boat sails and where, and contact information.

Another good resource is a free magazine, a virtual Bible among local sailors, called *Latitude 38.* It's available at most marinas, plus other seemingly random locations (I get mine every month at an ice cream shop; I suppose sailors like ice cream, or perhaps this ice cream vendor likes to sail). Crew lists are located in the back, with the classifieds.

Usually, you get on a crew the same way you get a job: Call up the number in the ad and chat with the skipper, and see if it's a good fit. It's an informal process, but you do want to get a feel for each other. You'll be spending the afternoon in a small space with this person, and probably several others. Is this a lazy, sail-in-the-sun captain, or a heeled-over, go-for-broke, bury-the-rail sort of captain? A few ads, it must be said, will also have romantic overtones ("Skipper seeks first mate for day sailing and companionship"). Most don't, and if that's the case it is usually made clear up front. The assumption with crew lists is that you are there to sail, and the captain needs a crew, and nothing more. Still, at first contact you might want to ask how many people are going out that day, and stick to boats with more than two onboard.

As with any such system, crew lists require a certain amount of honesty and good faith among all involved. It's a little like a blind date. So be honest about your skills—understating your nautical experience is much better than overselling it, and the truth will come out on the water anyway. And keep in mind that you're a guest on someone else's boat. Bringing enough water and food to share with the rest of the crew, and wearing nonstaining shoes with white soles, are both good ways to make sure your first ride goes well and you're invited back. Then sample a lot of boats and meet a lot of new people, and have a few great afternoons on the water.

—*Marc Herman*

Lake, near Sonora Pass in the Sierras (see chapter 6), is popular for swimming, as are the concrete pools at Grover Hot Springs State Park, south of Tahoe on Route 89. **Lake Tahoe** itself can also be swum in late summer, though even then it's not terribly warm (see chapter 6). The lower **Russian River** has several stretches good for what might be called swimming, but really are better for splashing and rope swinging (see chapter 9). Ditto the **Eel River** and **Benbow Lake** at Richardson Grove State Park, near Benbow. Both have access year-round, but are best after July.

But perhaps the best swimming in Northern California is in the **Sierra** backcountry, where lakes too numerous to name dot hundreds of trails. See the hiking section in chapter 6.

WALKS & RAMBLES

The difference between "Walks & Rambles" and "Hikes, Bushwhacks & Backpack Trips" is the degree of physical exertion. Whereas hikes involve sweating, sore feet, and the like, walks and rambles are generally short (between 0.5 and 2 miles) and relatively flat. Most involve some sort of destination: a landmark, historic building, or vista. Others are interpretive trails, with signs along the way explaining a particular natural feature or ecosystem. The listings contain distance and trailhead directions, but no listing of difficulty—by definition they are all easy. You could take your grandmother or your toddler on most of these, and probably should.

Short walks and afternoon rambles are especially appropriate for a trip to Northern California's cities. For example, the **East Bay Regional Park System,** located in the hills above Oakland, offers a wide variety of trails and short nature walks within a few minutes of downtown Oakland or Berkeley, and not more than 15 miles from San Francisco (though the traffic might make that a slog). Visitors in San Francisco can walk to the **Cliff House** and **Fort Point** or head to nearby **Muir Woods.** See chapter 2 for more information.

WHALE WATCHING

Every spring and fall more than 17,000 California gray whales swim through state waters on their annual migrations between the Gulf of Alaska, where they feed in summer, and secluded lagoons in Baja California, where they breed and give birth in the winter. The best season for whale watching is the fall migration, when mothers and their calves travel up the coast in pods of five or six, sticking close to shore to avoid predators like the orcas that sometimes will attack the young calves. During the height of the migration, it's not uncommon for whale-watching boats out of Monterey, Santa Cruz, Half Moon Bay, and San Francisco to spot 20 or 30 whales in 1 day.

You don't need to go to sea to see these huge creatures, however. All you need to do is pick a spot with a good view of the ocean, almost anywhere along the coast (look for someplace with a high cliff or hill to give you some height and perspective) and watch the whales go by. The difference, of course, is that they're a lot farther away—pack your binoculars. Favorite places include **Garrapata State Park** in Big Sur (see chapter 4), **Lighthouse Point** in Santa Cruz (see chapter 3), and **Point Reyes** in Marin County (see chapter 2). In each regional chapter along the migration route we list commercial whale-watching tours as well as good places to spot the whales from shore.

WHITE-WATER RAFTING

Last time I counted there were more than 40 different outfitters offering trips in California, on about 20 different major runs. It's a big business here, and getting bigger. The reason is that over the last 5 to 10 years, innovations in raft design and improvements in technique have made it

---

Thar She Blows!

In an afternoon spent whale watching, you might catch the whales performing a few classic moves, if you're lucky. You'll certainly see their **spouts**, formed by the condensed moisture of their exhalation, which can rise 10 to 15 feet in the air and be seen from 10 miles away. You may also see their powerful **flukes** rising out of the water in preparation for a dive. Occasionally you may see their heads popping out above the surface for a look around—this is called **spy-hopping**—or, most amazingly of all, their whole bodies lurching right out of the water in what's called a **breach**. Why the whales perform the last two is a mystery. Some speculate that when they spy-hop they're actually checking coastal landmarks. As for breaching, who knows? Perhaps it's sheer jubilation.

---

possible to run virtually anything in self-bailing paddle rafts, which are a hell of a lot of fun. The difference between a paddle raft and an oar raft is that in a paddle raft you, the client, are part of the paddling team coached by a guide who sits in the stern barking directions and trying to steer. Riding in an oar raft is more leisurely; the guide rows the boat from the middle and you just sit there looking pretty without having to lift a finger—a little like watching the Discovery Channel in a cold shower. Most people prefer to go in paddle rafts for the sense of camaraderie and group achievement.

With minor exceptions, most of the good white-water runs in the state are in the Gold Country, the southern Sierra Nevada, and the northern mountains. The single most popular river in the state is the **American River,** east of Sacramento (see chapter 7). The most exciting? Well, these days they're running just about everything: Burnt Ranch Gorge on the Trinity, the Salmon, Cherry Creek, the Forks of Kern Run. Any of these will jack your adrenaline levels through the roof.

It'd be easy to get confused with so many rivers and outfitters to choose from. Luckily, the state's white-water guides are a fairly organized bunch. **California Outdoors,** P.O. Box 401, Coloma, CA 95613 (☎ 800/552-3625) is the statewide professional organization of white-water guides and outfitters. Don't hesitate to call with questions about a particular river or outfitter. **River Travel Center,** Box 226, Point Arena, CA 95468 (☎ 800/882-RAFT) is a free, centralized booking service for every outfitter on every river in California.

Outfitters

"Yeah, yeah. All these sports, I love them, but the problem is I don't have time. I don't have time to buy a bike. I don't even have time to pedal. Listen, I get 2 weeks off a year and then it's back to the floor of the stock exchange. For those 2 weeks, I'd like to breathe in some fresh air while I'm outside. A nice bike trip in Sonoma, hiking in the Sierra, you know what I mean. And I don't want to take care of a damn thing—no flat tires, no rentals, no accommodations, no food, nothin'. Ya got it?"

So you want to participate in some sort of outdoor activity in the day and be pampered at night? You want someone to guide you on your sporting excursion, and you don't want to be bothered with equipment problems, finding a trailhead, renting a canoe, or setting up a tent and cooking over a fire? You want someone to deal with all your arrangements, but you still want to take the best trips as outlined in this book? Then you'll need to find an outfitter.

The irony is that even finding a good outfitter and trip takes time. Hopefully, I'll save you hours of research by listing my favorite outfitters under each sport heading in the regional chapters. However, certain questions should always be asked. Most are commonsensical. Some are related to specific sports:

1. *What level of fitness is required?*

   By far, the most important question. Get a feeling for the tour. Is this an obstacle course better suited for Marines, a walk in the park for couch potatoes, or something in between? Do I have to bike 20, 40, or 60 miles a day? Do I have options for each day? Can I go shopping or sightseeing 1 day while my wife bikes to her legs' delight?

2. *What's the cost and what's included in the price?*

   First and foremost, discuss the type of accommodation and whether all meals are included. Some companies skip lunch or an occasional dinner. Is liquor included? Then ask about shuttles to and from airports, cost of rentals, bikes, skis, etc.

3. *How long have you been in business?*

   Good outfitters stay in business; bad ones don't. If they've been around a long time you can expect that they're doing things right.

4. *What's the experience level of the guides?*

   Many outfitters are desperate enough to hire guides who, until very recently, had no experience in that sport or are from an entirely different part of the country. The American River is notorious for having white-water "guides"

with only marginally more experience than most of the clients. Depending on the intensity level of the activity, this can be a real problem.

5. *How many people are in the group?*

   What is the guide-to-client ratio? Do I have to compete with 30 or 5 other people for the guide's attention?

6. *Is it mostly singles or couples?*

   Guided tours are a great place to befriend other singles or couples. Make sure you get on the trip that's right for you.

7. *What equipment is required? What type of equipment can I rent?*

   Some outfitters, particularly fly-fishing companies, request that you bring your own equipment. Others will rent you gear. Find out what they offer, especially bikes. Do they rent 10-speed Raleighs or 21-speed Cannondales and Treks?

8. *What happens if it rains?*

   Do you have alternative plans or do you expect me to bike around the Napa Valley in a downpour?

9. *How much free time do we have?*

   Is every minute of the day accounted for or should I bring a good book?

10. *How far in advance do I need to book?*

    Don't miss out on a limited amount of spaces by waiting until the last minute. Some of these tours are booked a year in advance.

11. *Can I bring young children?*

    Most outfitters will usually answer affirmative to this. A buck is a buck, no matter who hikes or sits on the bike. However, you should take yourself and the other guests into account. Do you really want to bring the kids along? Do the other guests really want you to bring your kids along? Is this trip appropriate for children? Will they have a good time?

The main pro to hiring a guide is the complete and utter lack of responsibility on your part. Most outfitters will find a way to relieve all your vacation worries, from accommodations to food to equipment. You also have a chance to make new friends. The con is the additional cost. Most of these trips can be done on your own for much less money. The other con is the lack of privacy. There's no place better than a mountaintop, lonely backcountry road, or tranquil river to collect your thoughts and gain a sense of serenity. On vacation, you've earned a certain amount of peace and quiet. This fragile state can easily be shattered by the woman with the shrill voice and the constantly running video camera, or the man in the next tent who snores all night. Or maybe you just won't *like* the people fate throws your way. The best way to eliminate this problem is to simply book the whole trip with a group of your friends.

Below is a list of seven of the largest outfitters in the country—it's just the tip of the outfitter iceberg, but it gives you a place to start:

- **American Wilderness Experience,** P.O. Box 1486, Boulder, CO 80306 (☎ **800/444-0099**). Offers backpacking, dude ranches, mountain biking, and river running (canoes, kayaks, and rafts). Trips are fully supported, and last from 5 to 22 days.

- **American Youth Hostels,** 733 15th St. NW, Suite 840, Washington, DC 20005 (☎ **202/783-6161**). Bike tours, hiking trips, and, of course, the largest selection of hostels in the state. Hostels and programs are open to all ages, despite the name.

- **Backroads Bicycle Touring,** 801 Cedar St., Berkeley, CA 94710 (☎ **800/245-3874** or 510/527-1555). The biggest and best-organized bicycle touring operation in the world.

Backroads leads weekend and weeklong tours specifically geared to a special set of interests; for example, singles weekends, family outings, wine tastings, wilderness trips. Sag wagons accompany all trips, so if you find yourself waning, you'll have a ride back to your accommodations, usually an inn or B&B.

- **ECHO: The Wilderness Company,** 6529 Telegraph Ave., Oakland, CA 94609 (☎ **800/652-ECHO** or 510/ 652-1600). Specializes in rafting trips all over the world, and also runs fishing seminars and river trips in inflatable kayaks.

- **Outward Bound USA,** 384 Field Point Rd., Greenwich, CT 06830 (☎ **800/243-8520**). Outward Bound strives to foster personal growth by pushing people to the edge of their personal physical and emotional limits through challenging outdoor experiences. Unlike most outfitters, whose job it is to make sure that your trip is a seamless montage of perfect moments, Outward Bound teaches you to fend for yourself, then puts you in tough situations where you'll need that training. Some people love it. Some hate it. Just don't go into it with false expectations.

- **Sierra Club Outings,** 730 Polk St., San Francisco, CA 94109 (☎ **415/ 977-5630**). Since its creation in 1892, the Sierra Club has been dedicated to protecting and enjoying the outdoors. Each year the club offers hundreds of trips and expeditions around the world: bike tours, raft trips, ski touring, canoeing, canyoneering, backpacking, you name it. Two basic kinds of programs are offered: the Travel Program and the Service Program. Both involve travel in the wilderness, but the Travel Program is more geared toward recreational enjoyment. Service trips combine volunteer work like trail maintenance, archaeological surveys, and wildlife counts with outdoor enjoyment.

• **The Nature Conservancy,** 4245 N. Fairfax Dr., Arlington, VA 22203 (☎ **703/841-5300**). Primarily dedicated to purchasing and preserving large tracts of endangered land, the Nature Conservancy also offers trips and work-study options for people wishing to explore its extensive holdings.

Schools

Instruction is an important aspect of outdoor recreation. For sports like sailing, scuba diving, sea kayaking, white-water kayaking, and rock climbing, schooling is imperative. Lessons in cross-country or downhill skiing, mountain biking, horseback riding, fishing, and canoeing can only improve your skills and make the sport more enjoyable.

The same questions you should ask to outfitters (see above) apply to schools. Group size is extremely important. You want to be in a small group where you get personal attention. Be blunt with your initial questioning. If you want to be able to bareboat charter a sailboat in Monterey Bay or kayak down a Class III river, ask whether you'll be able to achieve those goals by the end of the course. Also ask how much time is spent in the classroom compared to time spent actually participating in the activity. Lectures are one thing, but nothing compares to the lessons of hands-on experience. I've found that the best schools and instructors impart their knowledge through guided activities rather than abstract theories. As a starting point, try the outfitters listed in the section above; most outfitters run instructional programs, just as most schools also rent equipment. Throughout the regional

chapters, you'll find more schools that pertain to each activity.

Maps

As anyone who has ever gone backcountry hiking knows, a good map can be your best friend. Many hikes simply have maps at the trailhead or park visitor center. In other cases, I have mentioned the appropriate United States Geological Survey (USGS) maps—topographical maps designed by the U.S. government. Many of these maps can be found at local bookstores or sporting-goods stores. If you can't locate the map for a particular section, go to the source: **U.S. Geological Survey,** Federal Center, Building 810, P.O. Box 25286, Denver, CO 80225 (☎ **800/USA-MAPS**).

Books

For many activities covered in this book, such as white-water kayaking or hiking the John Muir Trail, a specialized guidebook is absolutely indispensable. In many of the sports listings, I refer to specific books. Below is a list of more general books about Northern California:

• *California Coastal Resource Guide,* California Coastal Commission (University of California Press, 1987). An unbelievably detailed inventory of the coastal resources in the state, arranged north to south. This guide will tell you everything, from what that weird salamander is to where to go surfing. The Coastal Commission has also published a *Coastal Access Guide.* The only problem with both these books is their unwieldy size. They don't really fit into a travel pack.

• *California Hiking,* Tom Stienstra and Ann Marie Brown (Foghorn Outdoors, 1999). Regularly referred to as "The Bible," this massive book lists virtually every major hiking trail in the state. It also rates each trail for scenic beauty and difficulty. Several overnights and the Pacific Crest Trail are also included. An unparalleled catalog.

• *California State Parks: A Complete Recreation Guide,* by Rhonda and George Ostertag (The Mountaineers, 1995). An excellent guide to California state parks, including information on hikes, camping, history, wildlife, and practical travel matters.

• *Great Hot Springs of the West,* by Bill and Ruth Kaysing (Capra Press, 1993). It's unfortunate that this book is bound in a large-page format because it's such a handy travel resource. Hot springs throughout the West are included, with good maps and accurate descriptions. Not very comprehensive but it will get you to the major springs.

• *Roadside Geology of Northern California,* by David Alt and Donald Hyndman (Mountain Press, 1994). What's neat about this book is that it doesn't speak in generalizations; instead, it points to specific features along Northern California roadways and explains what they mean and where each particular region of the state fits into the big geological picture.

• *The High Sierra: Peaks, Passes and Trails,* by R. J. Secor (The Mountaineers, 1992). Ostensibly a book of climbing routes and backcountry trails, this volume is one of the best researched and most authoritative books about the history, geology, and practicalities of traveling in the High Sierra.

Spas

There's a hard way and an easy way to do everything. If you like the easy way, Northern California's spa scene is the thing for you. Usually centered around natural hot springs or in out-there resort areas, most California spas offer massage, hot pools, mud baths, and comfortable lodging and great food. Most are in the Napa and Sonoma valleys, but there are also several spas, or at least hotels with spa services, in Big Sur and the Sierra Nevada.

What's great about combining, say, a bike trip to the Napa Valley with a stay at some of the spas in Calistoga is that you'll experience the satisfaction that can only come from working your muscles until they're sore, then turning your body over to expert hands to feel better again.

One of the best resources for finding spas is *California Spas and Urban Retreats* by Laurel Cook (Foghorn Press, 1993). Though Cook doesn't really get into outdoor sports at all, her information about the spas themselves can be really useful.

Camping Reservations

It's an unfortunate fact of life that in a state with 30 million residents and millions more visitors, it's sometimes tough to find the perfect campsite. There are two main approaches to the problem. One is to get your reservations far in advance. The state parks (☎ 800/444-PARK), national parks (☎ 800/365-CAMP), and large national forest campgrounds (☎ 800/280-CAMP) all have centralized reservation numbers. Unfortunately they are all managed by a reservation service called MISTIX, based

A NOTE ON EQUIPMENT

In the 263 pages of John Muir's *Wilderness Essays,* there is not a single mention of camping gear. Muir, one of the fathers of the modern park system, spent months at a time hiking California's spine in the Sierra, blazing his own trails. But in his writings, there's scant mention of his backpack, his sleeping bag, his ropes, or his hat.

What, then, would Muir have thought upon walking into one of today's camping stores, with their pastel climbing walls and piles of plastic gadgets? Probably the same thing a lot of us think: *What the hell is all this stuff for?*

It's for sale, is what. In the past 20 years or so, walking on a simple forest trail has become part of the exploding recreation industry. What some call a love of the outdoors, others call a lifestyle, one with rules and, of course, products. In many ways that's great—more people than ever are heading to the outdoors, and the equipment they use is better than it used to be— more comfortable, more useful, and often a lot of fun to employ and wear.

But encounters with the recreation industry can also be confounding, particularly for the casual outdoors enthusiast. With such an astonishing variety of products now geared toward active recreation, it's sometimes hard to distinguish between what you absolutely need and what you don't. Meanwhile, even familiar items like tents, bikes, and backpacks have become major investments, likely to cost as much as a month's rent. Outfitting just one person for the backcountry could easily pass $500; outfitting a family for a camping trip could get into four figures. To top it off, there's the inevitable sales clerk warning of blisters, cold nights, and injury if you make the wrong equipment choices.

Unavoidably, many of the activities in this book *do* require some specialized equipment. But there are ways to minimize costs considerably. If you're new to camping, skiing, kayaking, mountain biking, or any other outdoor sport, try getting your equipment from a general sporting-goods store or a department store first, and avoid the boutique prices at outdoors-specific stores. The equipment won't be as fancy and might not last as long; if you're camping every weekend, it definitely won't. But not too many of us are so lucky as to get out 20 times a year, and most of us aren't climbing Mount Shasta. So pretty good stuff is probably good enough. A $50 tent from Big 5 won't stand up as well as a $300 model in a gale force wind, but it will probably do just fine for a 4-day trip in moderate weather, or years of car camping.

Better still, if you only use your gear once or twice a year, it may be worth renting what you need from outfitters instead of buying. Since outfitters need their own equipment to last, they tend to buy good stuff—meaning you get to use the comfy $300 backpack after all, only for $40. This is also a good way to shop for equipment, since the backpack that felt great in the shop might feel totally different after a week on the trail. If, after your first few tastes of a sport with rented gear, you decide you're going to be doing it often, you can make investments with the hindsight of experience, and buy whatever you think is appropriate for your interests.

However you ultimately decide to approach your equipment needs, I'd encourage you to dwell on them as little as possible while reading through the following chapters. It's easy to feel that buying gear is an essential part of the outdoor experience, as if a swipe of the credit card were the first step down the trail. Thankfully, that's not so for many of California's best outdoor experiences. To enjoy many of the most memorable places in this book, the most you'll ever need is what John Muir had, a sensitive eye and a good pair of shoes. Enjoy your trip.

—Marc Herman

out of Florida or somewhere, that appears to be run entirely by computers. Not hardworking, trustworthy computers, mind you, but computers that only work during normal business hours and follow a bizarre system of logic. For the pleasure of dealing with seemingly endless multiple-choice computerized voice loops to reserve your campsite, you get to pay MISTIX the cost of your site, plus a $6 to $8 reservation fee. Know the exact name of the park you are visiting, the exact campground, and hopefully, the exact campsite you're seeking, and have your credit card ready, or dealing with MISTIX is pretty much a lost cause.

The second method, which is the one I usually subscribe to, is flexibility. Instead of camping at the famous national park on a busy weekend, I find some tiny national forest campground nearby that doesn't take reservations, or I camp in the most far-flung corners of Yosemite or Kings Canyon. Show up around noon, when people are leaving. Think back roads and out-of-the-way places, many of which are actually more beautiful and more relaxing than the overrun "famous" spots. I've won some and lost some this way, but at least I didn't spend 45 minutes on the phone with a computer only to end up camped next door to the annual Hell's Angels road rally.

Cycling the California Coast

Most cyclists keep a mental list of the roads they've ridden, and another of those they hope someday to ride. Montana's Going to the Sun highway, Mississippi's Natchez Trace, and Vermont's Highway 7 make a lot of people's lists. California's Highway 1 seems to make almost everyone's.

It isn't just the ocean views. Stretching over 1,000 miles from Oregon to Mexico, Highway 1 encompasses an astonishing cross-section of terrain and natural environments. The road passes through redwood forests, farmland, chaparral-covered hills, fishing villages, vineyards, cosmopolitan cities, and remote mountain ranges.

To ride the section of coast encompassed by this book, from the Oregon border to Big Sur, would take a fit cyclist between 10 days and 2 weeks. Within that distance, however, are several shorter stretches that make excellent overnight or weekend trips, giving you the best of the coastal touring experience without forcing you to tackle the whole winding monster.

None of those rides are beyond the capability of an average rider, though the coast can be hilly and shouldn't be taken lightly. Dozens of campgrounds and motels are available along the Northern California coast, conveniently spaced about a day's bike ride apart. To enjoy a multiday trip, you should probably be able to ride at least 25 miles in a day comfortably. Most cycle tourists riding the coast average between 40 and 60 miles a day. Here are my favorite stretches of the road:

- **Mendocino to San Francisco:** This classic Northern California tour has it all: the area's most striking stretch of coastline, light traffic during weekdays, and a dramatic finish at the Golden Gate Bridge. A 3- to 4-day, 150-mile ride.

- **Half Moon Bay to Monterey:** This 90-mile trip starts with some impressive climbs, then levels out into a long stretch of state parks and farms. Pacific views on one side, fresh-produce stands on the other, and Highway 1's widest shoulder for much of the way.

- **Avenue of the Giants to Russian Gulch State Park:** It seems strange to spend most of your time inland on a road called the Coast Highway. But for much of this stretch between

---

Go South, Young Man

Prevailing winds blow from north to south along the coast. You don't want to bike north on Highway 1 if you can avoid it. The wind blows hard along the water. Better to have it at your back.

Humboldt Bay and Mendocino, that's what you'll do. Just south of Eureka, Highway 1 turns away from the water and joins Highway 101 in the redwoods, before crossing the King Range on a fantastic, though narrow, ride back to the water.

- **Bodega Bay to San Francisco:** A shorter version of the Mendocino–San Francisco trip, this 90-mile overnight takes you through a ragged coastline, past Point Reyes, and inland via Marin's redwoods, ending with a good stretch of bike path through Sausalito.

CREDIT CARDS & SADDLE BAGS

Every approach to biking the coast has advantages and disadvantages. For **loaded tours,** where you carry everything you need on the bike, stay in a tent, and cook over a camp stove or fire, state parks provide the best accommodations. You can also take advantage of low-cost "hiker-biker" campsites (see "The Hiker-Biker Program," above). This type of self-reliant touring allows the greatest amount of freedom for planning your route and deciding how far you'll ride each day. Plus you can sleep more or less anywhere in a pinch. The downside is that you have to lug 40 pounds of gear up the coastal hills. You'll need proper pannier-style bags to hang on your bike.

Other cyclists prefer to go the **credit card** route, staying in motels, eating at restaurants, and carrying only a credit card and a camera. Having a completely unencumbered bike means you can cover more ground more comfortably. Plus you

get hot showers and a warm bed each night.

Group tours are the luxury cruises of the coastal touring experience. Most are "sagged" tours, which means that you'll still camp and cook your meals outside but that a sag wagon (read: a van) carries your gear for you. In other cases, you get bed-and-breakfast stays, meals cooked for you, and bikes provided. Some tours include stops at wineries, gourmet meals, mechanics who'll fix the inevitable flats, and as much other pampering as you can hope for while still riding a bike 30 to 50 miles a day. The downside of organized tours, of course, is the cost, which runs from $400 for a short trip to $1,200 dollars and up for a longer one. A good group tour company is **Backroads** (☎ 800/245-3874).

Lastly, a unique option is the annual **AIDS Ride** from San Francisco to Los Angeles, a group ride that raises money for AIDS research. Starting on the bay shore in San Francisco, the AIDS ride covers a section of northern Highway 1 as far as Big Sur, then continues another 250 miles to Los Angeles. The ride is a sagged, fully supported trip, and in recent years has become an annual media event along the coast. It's probably the best way to make an extended trip down Highway 1 in a large, safe group of riders. The catch is that participants are responsible for raising $2,500 in pledges to the AIDS Foundation. But it's for a good cause. For information call the AIDS Ride information line at ☎ 800/825-1000.

SAFE CYCLING

Many sections of Highway 1 are narrow and have blind curves. While that's part of the route's beauty, it also makes the ride undeniably treacherous in spots. A few basic practices can make a trip down Highway 1 much safer and more pleasant.

- **Wear a helmet.** You can be injured by even a small mishap.

- **Stay within your level of fitness.** When you get tired, you're less safe on your bike. Fatigue makes you weave going uphill, and tempts you to cheat across intersections without stopping. If you've never ridden 40 or 50 miles in a day, plan for 30 or 35, and maybe go farther a few days later when you're used to it.

- **Get off the road at dusk.** Drivers don't all have their lights on yet, and twilight can play tricks on their eyes. Highway 1 has no street lamps, so it's dark. Be in camp by sunset.

- **Get a rear-view mirror.** For $10 or $15, a cycling mirror mounted on your helmet or handlebars provides enormous peace of mind. In areas like Big Sur and Bodega Bay, the wind and terrain mask the sounds of a car engine; you'll need to see to know if somebody wants to pass you.

- **Ride during the week.** If your schedule allows you to ride on off-days, do so. Monday through Wednesday are generally low-traffic times.

- **Schedule your trip sensibly.** Riding through Big Sur on Memorial Day weekend, for example, is foolish. This may mean juggling your vacation schedule around traffic patterns hundreds of miles away. Absurd as that sounds, you'll be thankful for the space on the road when you arrive.

September and October are the best months to ride the coast. Northern California is characteristically cold in the summer, which comes as a rude surprise to many visitors ("The coldest winter I ever spent was a summer in San Francisco," goes the famous quip attributed to Mark Twain). But by early fall, temperatures rise and the fog gives way to blue skies from Humboldt all the way to Monterey. The days are still on the long side, and with Labor Day past, the traffic also slows.

- **Respect trucks.** Humboldt and Mendocino county have large logging industries, and Highway 1 is used to ship the lumber from the forest to the mill. The heavy trucks don't come too frequently, but when they do, you'll know it. If you hear a truck coming, stop and wait on the side of the road until it passes. It's safer for you and the truckers both.

THE WHOLE ENCHILADA

Riding the entirety of the Northern California coast, from the Oregon border to Big Sur, is a serious undertaking and a grand adventure. You'll cover 600 miles. That may sound impossible, but it isn't. Every year people who have never toured before ride this route or significant portions of it. Many go a great deal farther, starting as far north as Alaska and heading as far south as Patagonia.

Here's a summary of the trip. For a more detailed account, indexed to the tenth of a mile, get a copy of *Bicycling the Pacific Coast* by Tom Kirkendall and Vicky Spring (The Mountaineers, 1998).

California State Line to Mendocino

The northernmost portion of the trip passes through **Redwood National Park** south to **Eureka** and beyond to the coast, with few climbs longer than a mile. Traffic is minimal, but shoulders thin toward the southern part of Humboldt County. A few excellent side trips offer alternatives to the main road without adding much distance.

The weather is reliably cool this far north, in the 50s and 60s most days, ranging into the 80s late in the summer and early fall—perfect cycling weather. State parks in the Patrick's Point area, the Humboldt Redwoods, the banks of the Eel River, and the King Range come at ideal 40-to-60-mile intervals, and the campsites are usually uncrowded and clean.

At the small town of **Leggett,** Highway 1 heads up the first major climb, 6 miles up to the unnamed pass over the King range, then down through the trees and a dramatic descent to the ocean at Westport. Thirty miles later you're on the beach in Mendocino.

Mendocino to San Francisco

Highway 1 curves, dips, and falls through a seemingly unceasing series of picturesque coves for the next 150 miles. This is for many the most striking stretch of road on the north coast, with towering rock formations offshore, sea lions on the beach, and virtually no towns larger than a few hundred people to spoil the view. There's a serious climb north of **Jenner,** at the Russian River's mouth, and another getting out of the river valley. Be careful not to get your wheels caught in the cattle grates on the way down, or hit the cattle themselves, which sometimes wander onto the road.

Highway 1 continues to wind along the ragged coastline to **Bodega Bay,** rising steeply for a few hundred yards, then falling mercifully the same distance, all within earshot of the water hitting the cliffs below. Finally it turns inland to the **Sonoma** dairy lands and the east side of **Point Reyes.** Turning east from Point Reyes, away from the coast and across Marin, spares you a beautiful, but dangerously narrow section of Highway 1 south of Stinson Beach. In its place you get a ride through the Sam Taylor Park redwoods and the undeveloped, lazy hills of west Marin. If you don't have a place to stay in San Francisco, you might want to stay out here. If pressing on, you'll follow Sir Francis Drake Boulevard to San Francisco Bay and the city streets to

Marin's bike path, which leads to **Sausalito** and your dramatic arrival at the **Golden Gate Bridge.**

San Francisco to Big Sur

After crossing San Francisco, Highway 1 picks up the coast again at the beach town of **Pacifica** and climbs over a somewhat harrowing set of cliffs appropriately called the **Devil's Slide.** Again, exploring an inland route might be advisable here, though a Monday or Tuesday afternoon might not be so bad for this challenging but short (5-mile) section of coastline. From there it's on to **Half Moon Bay** and 50 miles of good shoulders into **Santa Cruz.** South of Santa Cruz you'll ride through some suburbs and then into the Monterey Bay's farmlands, before hitting the boutiques around Carmel and beginning the final ride into **Big Sur.**

Big Sur has a reputation for both the best and the worst of California north coast cycling. On one hand, after riding all the way from Oregon, it's a fitting finish line, the dramatic last gasp of the rocky northern coast. On the other hand, Highway 1 has virtually no shoulder most of the way through Big Sur, and you ride atop cliffs hundreds of feet high. On weekends, the tourist traffic is heavy, with RV's crowding you toward oblivion. The famous **Bixby Bridge** is wonderful to ride across, but it leads to **Hurricane Point,** which feels like riding on an airplane wing.

The trick to enjoying the ride to Big Sur is to time your departure right. **Carmel,** the last civilization before the road gets hairy, is 26 miles from the town of Big Sur, your destination. If you depart Carmel on a Monday or Tuesday between 2:30 and 3pm, you should be able to miss most of the traffic. Riding 10 miles an hour in summer or early fall, you should also get to Big Sur's camping areas and hotels just before dusk. Day-trippers will all be heading north on their way home by then, and evening traffic south will be fairly light. Relatively few people head to

Big Sur for the evening so early in the week.

If you want, you can continue south from Big Sur the next day, covering another 45 miles of the headlands. Traffic eases considerably south of Big Sur proper, since many cars turn around there and head back to Monterey Bay. You'll get some memorable views before leaving the area, and a last long hill to scale before descending to **San Simeon.** The beaches here are long strands, flat and straight, a welcome rest after the climbs of the past 2 days.

Farther south the terrain continues to ease, leaving the northern environs. Beyond are the broad, flat deserts of Southern California.

2

The San Francisco Bay Area

Perhaps no other major metropolitan region in the United States is as blessed with outdoor recreation as the Bay Area. From its defining feature—the bay itself—to Golden Gate Park, the mountains of Marin County, wild Pacific beaches, and the inland parks and hills of the East Bay, the Bay Area attracts people from all over seeking outdoor adventure, something you just don't find in a lot of cities.

A study conducted by People for Open Space, a San Francisco–based environmental group, counted more than 700,000 acres of open space within San Francisco, Marin, San Mateo, Santa Clara, Alameda, and Contra Costa counties. Those acres include several national parks, monuments, and seashores, a dozen state parks, watershed preserves, and many excellent county and city parks. The survey didn't include the bay itself as open space, which adds another 400 square miles of potential sailing, fishing, boardsailing, kayaking, and swimming.

A number of factors played an important role in preserving so much open land. When the area first began growing rapidly around a century ago, city planners realized that if they wanted to develop the bay waterfront, which lacks any sort of good groundwater, they would have to preserve the high watersheds of the surrounding hills to provide water. As a result, thousands of acres were preserved for the sake of catching rainwater runoff. Today, these lands offer some of the best mountain biking and hiking in the region.

Other large tracts of land were set aside by private landowners and early environmentalists who foresaw the need to preserve large areas of pristine land long before most realized it would someday be such a scarce commodity. Muir Woods is one such example; a wealthy philanthropist outbid a lumber company to purchase this dramatic grove, narrowly saving it from becoming redwood siding in some San Francisco Victorian.

Weather and dramatic geology also conspired to keep parts of the Bay Area protected. Not many people live on the Pacific side of the peninsula

---

Fear Not the Dreaded Fog

San Francisco Bay went undiscovered by Europeans until 1769, because the omnipresent marine fog shrouding the Golden Gate kept early Spanish explorers from seeing the great harbor entrance. But you shouldn't let the famous San Francisco fog keep you away, too. Fog is only one of the Bay Area's many faces. While on any given day it can be foggy and cold somewhere in the Bay Area, this is a region of dramatic microclimates. It might be freezing at Golden Gate Park but sunny and beautiful on Angel Island. An open mind and a flexible schedule are the key. If it's too hot to go mountain biking on Mount Diablo, head to Point Reyes for a hike. If the surf is too big at Ocean Beach, go kayaking in Richardson Bay instead.

---

simply because it's remote, windy, and foggy much of the year. Marin County, now a swanky bedroom community to San Francisco, was separated from the city by the current-swept channel of the bay mouth until the Golden Gate Bridge was completed in 1937. Most people in the Bay Area are clustered in a relatively narrow strip of land around the tip of the peninsula and along the inside edge of the bay. Some sprawl spills over the eastern hills, and the South Bay suburbs around San Jose seem to go on forever, but for most Bay Area residents a large undeveloped tract of land is only a short distance away.

Finally, in a great irony, the closure of several military bases has opened up arguably the best open space to use as parkland. Swords into plowshares and all. A few years ago, Marin's Fort Cronkite (formerly a nuclear missile site) became the Headlands Center for the Arts, open to the perfect black sand of Rodeo Beach. The Presidio, on the south end of the Golden Gate Bridge, has become a cycling area. Crissy Field, previously part of the Presidio, is being relandscaped with trees and pathways on the shore beside the Golden Gate Bridge. The Alameda Naval Air Station has been in part converted to a bird sanctuary. And Treasure Island is now accessible, with a sailing marina and a set of bay views you previously had to enlist in the Navy to enjoy.

The two big urban park districts in the Bay Area, the **Golden Gate National Recreation Area** and the **East Bay Regional Parks District,** have done an admirable job of connecting the region's urban areas with the necklace of wild parklands that surrounds them. As a result, it is possible to bike from the city's crowded Marina District across the bridge to the wild and scenic Marin Headlands in about 15 minutes. Pedaling another 15 to 20 minutes will take you to the old-growth redwoods of Muir Woods. Try that in New York City, Los Angeles, or Chicago.

Though San Francisco owes its status as a city to the gold rush of 1849—one of the worst disasters man has ever inflicted on California's natural surroundings—since then it has historically been a city with a green conscience and a hankering for environmental action. The Sierra Club, formed here by John Muir and a number of his San Francisco friends to protect their favorite hiking and climbing areas, went on to become one of the world's most influential environmental groups. Greenpeace, Forest Action Network, and the Earth Island Institute are all based in the Bay Area. Like any big metropolitan area, the Bay Area has its environmental horror stories (such as the City of San Francisco drowning Yosemite's Hetch Hetchy Valley under a reservoir, or the continual air pollution of the East Bay),

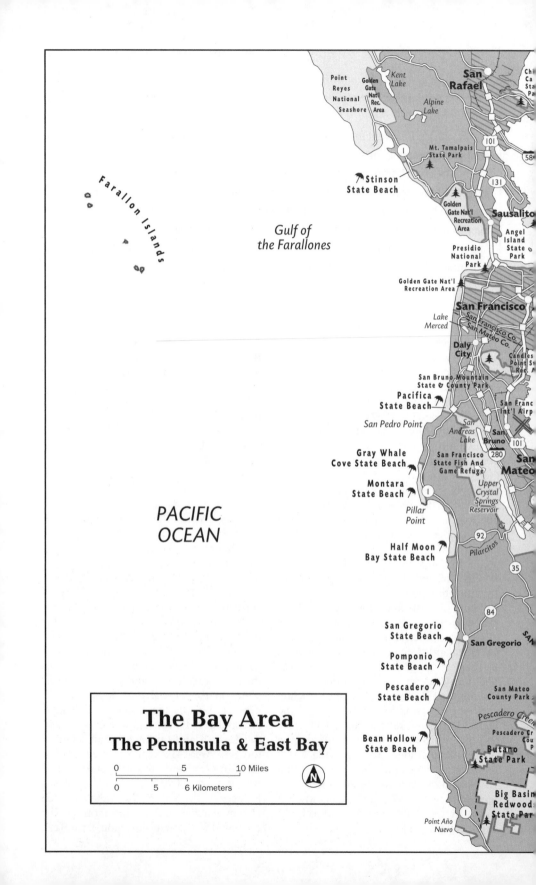

Point
Reyes
National
Seashore

Golden
Gate
Nat'l
Rec.
Area

*Kent
Lake*

**San
Rafael**

Ch
Ca
Sta
Pa

*Alpine
Lake*

101

58

1   Mt. Tamalpais
State Park

131

🌴Stinson
State Beach

Golden
Gate Nat'l
Recreation
Area

Sausalito

Angel
Island
State
Park

Presidio
National
Park

Golden Gate Nat'l
Recreation Area

*Gulf of
the Farallones*

F a r a l l o n   I s l a n d s

*Lake
Merced*

San Francisco

San Francisco Co.
San Mateo Co.

**Daly
City**

Candles
Point S
Rec. A

San Bruno Mountain
State & County Park

**Pacifica
State Beach**🌴

San Franc
Int'l Airp

San Pedro Point

*San
Andreas
Lake*

**San
Bruno**

101

**Gray Whale
Cove State Beach**🌴

San Francisco
State Fish And
Game Refuge

280

**San
Mateo**

**Montara
State Beach**🌴

1

*Upper
Crystal
Springs
Reservoir*

*Pillar
Point*

**PACIFIC
OCEAN**

92

35

Pilarcitos

**Half Moon
Bay State Beach**🌴

84

**San Gregorio
State Beach**🌴

San Gregorio

SA

**Pomponio
State Beach**🌴

**Pescadero
State Beach**🌴

San Mateo
County Park

Pescadero Creek

Pescadero Cr
Cou
P

**Bean Hollow
State Beach**🌴

**Butano
State Park**

The Bay Area
The Peninsula & East Bay

| 0 | | 5 | | 10 Miles |

| 0 | | 5 | 6 Kilometers | |

(N)

**Big Basin
Redwood
State Par**

1

*Point Año
Nuevo*

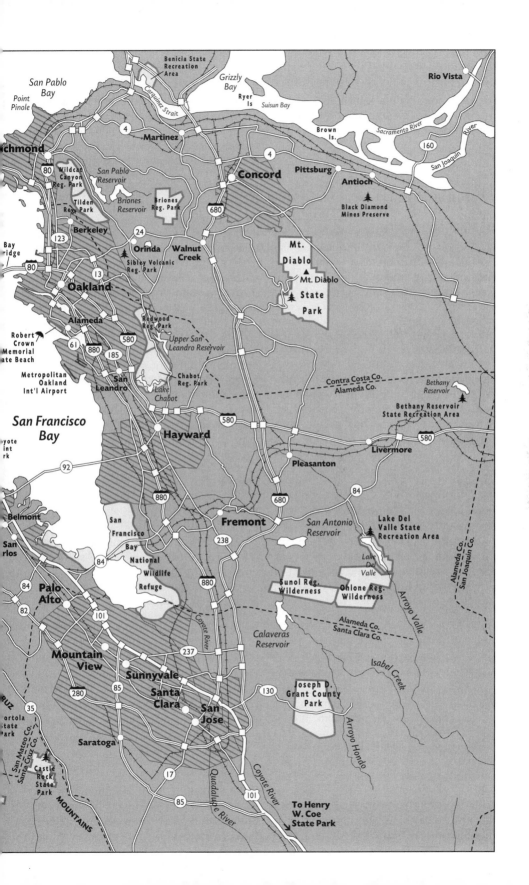

but it has also been a leader on the progressive edge of urban planning and environmental preservation.

The Lay of the Land

The very bay that defines the Bay Area also serves to separate and distinguish between the surrounding communities and diverse geographic features. The **coastal mountains** of Marin County and the peninsula are a lush mix of oak woodland, rolling grassland, and dramatic redwood and Douglas fir forest. In the **canyon bottoms,** an understory of poison oak and blackberry vines grow alongside ferns, dogwoods, and bay laurel under a covering of first-growth, or more likely second-growth, redwoods, or Douglas fir. Along the **bay shore,** wetlands were once predominant, but most of the bay's marshy habitat (300 square miles, worth) has been filled in to build airports, housing tracts, and shopping malls, and only a few undeveloped miles of shoreline remain, mostly in the East Bay and Marin.

Because they lie in the rain shadow of the coastal mountains and are farther from the temperature-moderating effect of the Pacific, the hills of the **East Bay** are relatively hot and dry. The highest point in the Bay Area is the East Bay's 3,849-foot Mount Diablo, visible for hundreds of miles on a clear day and a great lookout. When conditions are right, you can see as far as Mount Lassen in the Cascades or make out the distinctive shape of Half Dome in the Yosemite Valley. Diablo, like the rest of the East Bay mountains, is covered by rolling grass, oak savannah, and brushy chaparral, and a few more heavily vegetated areas occur where stream canyons concentrate the runoff. One species, the eucalyptus tree, tends to dominate as it's particularly well adapted to the East Bay's climate. Imported from Australia in the 19th century, the exotic

blue gum eucalyptus took off, eventually crowding out native species. Recently, the eucalyptus has fallen into disfavor after several wildfires fueled by the volatile wood devastated homes and parkland in the East Bay. An ongoing debate between those who want to remove the trees because they don't belong in the area and those who think they're a historically and ecologically important part of the California landscape flares up every time one of the park districts cuts down a eucalyptus grove. Eucalyptus or not, many excellent hiking and biking areas are hidden in the folds of the East Bay's rolling hills.

The **Pacific coast** of Marin, San Francisco, and San Mateo counties is a completely different world from the more urbanized parts of the Bay Area. Other than a short stretch of developed coast inside the San Francisco City limits and into Pacifica, you'd never know that millions of people live within a 20-mile radius. **Point Reyes National Seashore** anchors one end of this beautiful coast with 65,000 acres of protected land, 32,000 of it designated wilderness. From here south to the Golden Gate, the Marin coast is a wild mix of long sandy beaches popular with surfers and sunbathers, and sheer, rocky ocean cliffs that ward off even the most daredevil adventurers.

Across the Golden Gate, **San Francisco** has some incredible coastline within city limits. Baker Beach in the Presidio is a favorite summertime hangout. Ocean Beach, a 4-mile sandy beach between the Cliff House and Fort Funston, is a world-renowned surfing spot made even more famous by a two-part *New Yorker* piece a few years ago profiling San Francisco surfer Mark "Doc" Renneker.

South of San Francisco the coast quickly becomes wild again, passing through the precipitous Devil's Slide just south of Pacifica. The main town between San Francisco and Santa Cruz is **Half Moon Bay,** a small port backed by steeply rising forested hills. Once a hardscrabble fishing town, Half Moon Bay has become something of a tourist destination. Whale-watching tours and salmon fishing out of Pillar Point Harbor are big business here now, and bed-and-breakfasts are springing up all over town. Maverick's, the once-secret big-wave riding spot, is located just outside the north harbor jetty—it became the center of a worldwide media feeding frenzy when professional surfer Mark Foo died there after wiping out on a 20-foot wave on Christmas Eve, 1994.

Other beaches near Half Moon Bay are popular for camping and swimming, though the water is chilly. From Half Moon Bay along the shore, a number of **state beaches,** such as San Gregorio, Pompanio, and Bean Hollow, line the west side of the Highway 1 strip and draw flocks of visitors on busy summer weekends. Other times of the year they can be nearly deserted. On the inland side of Highway 1, many of these state parks reach into the coastal hills and forests for great hiking, biking, and camping that is often overlooked by visitors intent on spending the day at the beach.

Then there's **the bay** itself. The mile-wide Golden Gate is the largest break in the California coast range, yet the looming headlands on either side are so dramatic they nearly obscure the bay entrance. Four times a day the tides pour in or out through this narrow channel, surging past the pillars of the Golden Gate Bridge at what can be a terrifying clip if you've misjudged your kayaking ability or broken some vital piece of equipment on your sailboard just as the tide begins going out. Which doesn't discourage anyone; hundreds of boardsailors

put in at Crissy Field to sail the bay every time the wind blows, and people swim across the Golden Gate every year. Just be extremely cautious: know the limits of your ability and time your voyage to coincide with slack or incoming tides so you don't end up halfway to the Farallon Islands. Look out for busy ship traffic, too, if you venture into the open bay.

Other parts of the bay are more forgiving and better suited to casual exploration. **Aquatic Park** in the Marina District is a favorite with swimmers, many of whom swim here every day without wet suits even though the water is a chilly 52° to 58°F. A small sand beach makes getting in easier than staying in. **Richardson Bay** is the catchall name for the protected waters of the Marin Coast between Sausalito, Tiburon, and Angel Island. Ideally suited to sea kayaking and sailing, this is a great area for all ability levels to get on the bay. **Angel Island,** the largest and most pristine of the bay islands, is accessible by ferry or private boat. A military garrison between the Civil War and World War II, Angel Island is now a state park. You can set up a tent at the island's environmental campsites, and hike or bike the old military roads to the top of Mount Livermore, the highest point on the island.

Though pollution and cutbacks in the amount of freshwater pouring into the bay have left some species reeling, fishing is still a popular pastime when large game fish like striped bass, salmon, and steelhead come through the bay on the way to their spawning or feeding grounds in the rivers of Northern California's central valley and delta. A

San Francisco's Average Temperatures and Precipitation											
	Jan	Feb	Mar	Apr	May	June	July	Aug	Sept	Oct	Nov	Dec
High (°F)	56	60	61	63	64	66	66	66	70	69	64	57
Low (°F)	46	48	49	50	51	53	54	54	56	55	51	47
Precipitation (in.)	4.1	3.5	2.9	1.5	0.5	0.2	trace	trace	0.2	1.1	2.6	3.9

number of long piers provide fishing access in Berkeley, San Francisco, and the South Bay.

Orientation

THE PENINSULA

San Francisco

San Francisco lies at the northern end of a 50-mile-long peninsula dividing the bay from the Pacific. The city has a reputation for fog and fierce weather drawn in off the ocean by the Golden Gate's break in the coast range. While it's true that San Francisco gets more than its fair share of bad weather, it also gets more than its fair share of wonderful ocean breezes, amazing scenery, and plentiful outdoor activities. In the last decade, the city has become the center of a high-tech youth culture, full of computer and information workers who labor behind computers all day and play hard all weekend. The list of activities that go on all the time within the city limits ranges from base jumping (skydiving from a stationary object) off Financial District skyscrapers, to surfing at Ocean Beach, to trout fishing in Lake Merced.

Within the city are numerous large parks, including the Presidio, Land's End, Golden Gate Park, Ocean Beach, Lake Merced, the Marina Green, Aquatic Park, Baker Beach, and Fort Funston, where you can fish, hang-glide, boardsail, surf, sail, hike, or have a picnic. The largest park authority in the area is the **Golden Gate National Recreation Area** (☎ 415/556-0560), headquartered in Fort Mason on Marina Boulevard, which manages the bay islands and the entire coast from the Golden Gate to Fort Funston. A fantastic book put out by the Golden Gate National Parks Association is the *GGNRA*

Recreation Area Park Guide. This 100-page, hip-pocket-size book is a valuable reference for the historical, the practical, and the trivial; in short, just about anything you could want to know about outdoor recreation in the city. The thousand acres of **Golden Gate Park** (hiking, picnicking, playing fields, fly-casting ponds, museums, and more) are managed separately by the City of San Francisco. Park Headquarters (☎ 415/556-0560) are located in McLaren Lodge at Fell and Stanyon, where you can get maps and activity schedules.

Fort Mason

Located at water's edge in San Francisco, between Fisherman's Wharf and Crissy Field.

Fort Mason is the best spot in San Francisco to see sailboats, boardsailors, and the occasional kayak up close. The sailboat races out of the St. Francis yacht club frequently pass by here; don't miss the brilliant scene of snapping white canvas spread against the blue bay, Marin's green headlands, and the Golden Gate Bridge.

The Golden Gate

Between Fort Point to the south and the Marin cliffs to the north.

A trip "outside the gate" is a right of passage for day cruises, fishing boats, and sailboats. This is where the Pacific enters San Francisco Bay. The famous fog enters this way also, spilling over the bridge seductively, but dropping visibility to a few feet.

Pacifica

Once south of the city and county limits of San Francisco, the coastal zone of San Mateo County passes through Pacifica, a ticky-tacky little town of trailer parks and 1950s tract homes, and then quickly becomes less populated. Sharp Park Beach and Pier is a popular fishing and surfing spot right in Pacifica. The pier stretches a quarter mile out and is open 24 hours a day for fishing. Rockaway and San Pedro beaches are also popular, and the Sweeney Ridge segment of the Golden Gate National Recreation Area rises above Rockaway, where you can find miles of hiking trails into the coastal mountains. The main Sweeney Ridge Trailhead starts near the nursery at 2000 Cabrillo Hwy. (Hwy. 1).

Devil's Slide

Exactly 1 mile south of San Pedro Point, Highway 1 passes through the Devil's Slide, an aptly named stretch of road on the shoulder of one incredibly unstable area of coastal cliff. The road here, hundreds of feet above the ocean, is in a state of perpetual repair as it slides downhill after nearly every heavy rain. There is talk of replacing it with a tunnel through Sweeney Ridge.

MARIN COUNTY

Sausalito

Just inside the Golden Gate, this town on the bay side of Marin County is famous for its nautical history and views of the water. It's a bit of a tourist trap now, but remains a convenient place to experience the bay. Several marinas are here, near "Hurricane Gulch," a pocket of reliably high wind just off the town's waterfront. Sea kayaking is popular at the town's north end. A ferry runs to San Francisco and Angel Island several times a day; the fishing fleet here offers charters daily; and several sailing schools and sailboat-rental operations reside in town.

Bolinas

Bolinas is located north of Bolinas Lagoon on Olema-Bolinas Road and back about 30 years in time. Less than 1,000 people live in this wonderful, 1968-style tiny town surrounded by Bolinas Lagoon, Point Reyes, and the Pacific Ocean. Dogs and children run wild and loose in the

town's four streets. The people here have everything they need: a bar, a good cafe, an organic grocery, sandy beaches, and virtually no traffic. To keep it this way, they tear down the street signs from Highway 1 as soon as Caltrans put them up. Now if only they could change the name of the Bolinas Lagoon they could really hide out. Several good trailheads into the southern reaches of Point Reyes leave from Mesa Road.

Panoramic Highway

From Mill Valley to Stinson Beach, this windy two-lane road goes over the crest of Mount Tam instead of sticking to the coast like Highway 1. Many great hikes and vistas are reached from here, including the summit of Mount Tam.

Angel Island

Angel Island, located in the bay across the "Raccoon Straights" from Marin, is accessible only by ferry or private boat. Its well-sheltered harbor is a popular overnight sailing destination that feels remote despite sitting in the center of San Francisco Bay; it also has easy access to the island's hikes and few stores. Angel Island is also one of the more important topographical influences on San Francisco Bay's environment, with kayakers rarely braving the fast water squeezed between the island and the mainland, and sailers hiding in the huge rock's protected east side when the winds get too hairy. Behind the island lies a blustery, unprotected stretch called "the Slot."

Bodega Bay

Ninety miles north of San Francisco, this fishing bay is home to a significant sport fleet and some pleasure craft. The rocky shores north of town host a nearly unbroken strand of state beaches ending at the Russian River, and the seafood is as good as you might expect in a historic fishing village.

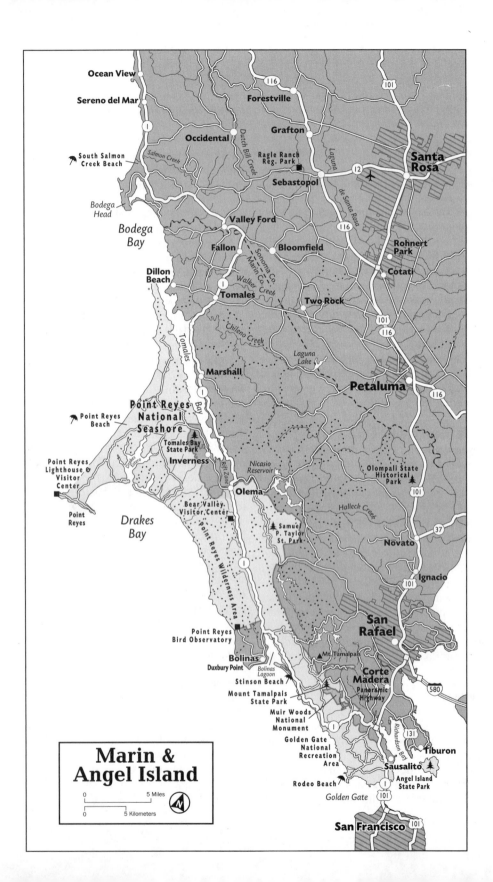

Marin &
Angel Island

0   5 Miles

0   5 Kilometers

Parks & Other Hot Spots

THE PENINSULA

The Presidio
Southern base of the Golden Gate Bridge. For information call the Presidio Army Museum (☎ **415/561-4323**) or the GGNRA Headquarters (☎ 415/556-0560). Hiking and biking trails, beaches, golf course, historic buildings, rest rooms, outdoor showers, picnic areas. Fishing, golfing, swimming, surfing, boardsailing.

For more than 2 centuries the Presidio was a huge military base guarding the Golden Gate. Though it has long been open to the public, it is now in the process of being converted into a National Park. Baker Beach, Fort Point, and Crissy Field are popular for sunning, surfing, and boardsailing. Wooded paths and dramatic views of the bay and the Golden Gate make hiking and walking in the Presidio very rewarding—one of the best urban nature experiences in the United States. See the feature on the Presidio a little later in this chapter.

Golden Gate Park
From the Bay Bridge, take Hwy. 101 north toward the Golden Gate Bridge. Take the 9th St. exit, and follow the signs to Fell St., which you follow east to the park. ☎ **415/666-7035**. Picnics, hiking, soccer fields, basketball, bicycling, row and paddle boats.

Stretching from Stanyan Street to the Pacific Ocean, Golden Gate Park provides miles of walking and cycling trails, a rowboating area, a botanical garden, athletic fields, Pacific beach access, and a modicum of piece of mind amid the city streets. It also has a small herd of buffalo.

The park proper is a rectangle about 2 miles long beginning at the west end of Fell Street. The bike and walking path begins another mile east, however, and follows a narrower strip of green called the Panhandle into the park.

Though an urban park, it's possible to hike all day between the Panhandle and the ocean, passing an excellent botanical garden, the Japanese Tea Garden, two lakes and several athletic fields that have pickup soccer and football most weekends. Make sure to dress appropriately for the shore. The microclimates are different from one end of the park to the other, so a hot walk across the polo fields can turn into a very cold visit to the fog in 10 minutes.

The Farallon Islands
25 miles offshore from the Golden Gate. Sailing, wildlife.

The Farallones are a rocky collection of small islands that provide homes to a variety of species, including seabirds, sea lions, and a large population of great white sharks. Protected by their own marine sanctuary, the waters around the islands are popular for cruising and sailing. On a clear day, the Farallones are visible from the Golden Gate, as a jagged, mysterious outline on the horizon.

San Bruno Mountain State and County Park
Access from Guadalupe Canyon Pkwy. from Bayshore Blvd. or I-280. ☎ **415/355-8289**. Hiking and biking trails, rest rooms, picnic area.

What's remarkable about this park is that it is here at all. At one time the mountain was targeted to be torn down, dumped in the bay, and used as fill for an airport (mind you, we're talking about a mountain, not just a hill). Other plans would have covered the mountain with condos. Two endangered butterflies, the Mission Blue and San Bruno elfin, are responsible for the preservation of these 2,700 acres of the last large coastal scrub habitat on the peninsula.

Coyote Point Recreation Area and Museum
Take U.S. 101 southbound exit at Poplar Ave. and follow signs to park, which is on Coyote Point Dr. ☎ **650/**

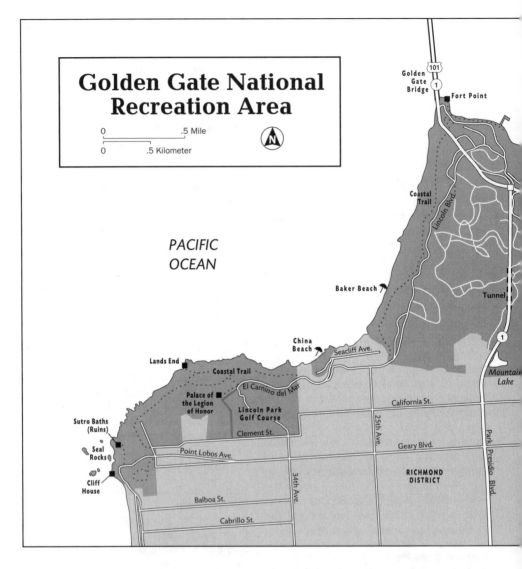

Golden Gate National Recreation Area

0   .5 Mile
0   .5 Kilometer

PACIFIC OCEAN

Golden Gate Bridge · 101 · 1 · Fort Point

Coastal Trail · Lincoln Blvd.

Baker Beach

Tunnel

China Beach · Seacliff Ave.

Mountain Lake

Lands End · Coastal Trail

El Camino del Mar

Palace of the Legion of Honor · Lincoln Park Golf Course

California St.

Sutro Baths (Ruins)

Clement St.

25th Ave.

Geary Blvd.

Seal Rocks

Point Lobos Ave.

Cliff House

34th Ave.

RICHMOND DISTRICT

Park Presidio Blvd.

Balboa St.

Cabrillo St.

573-2592. Natural history museum, beach, showers, rest rooms, restaurant, bike path, marina, rifle range. Swimming, boating, boardsailing.

This is one of the few actual waterfront beach accesses on the bay, but the main reason for coming here is the incredible **Museum for Environmental Education** (☎ 650/342-7755). The museum is designed to allow visitors to explore fully the six biotic communities in San Mateo County: broadleaf forest, coniferous forest, chaparral, grassland, badlands, and seacoast. Computer games, working bee-hives and ant colonies, food-chain diora-mas, and a continually changing list of exhibits are displayed in a high-tech, environmentally friendly building.

Montara Area Beaches and Parks

Both sides of Hwy. 1 between Devil's Slide and Half Moon Bay. ☎ 650/573-2592. Beaches, parking, rest rooms, outdoor showers. Hiking, biking, swimming, whale watching.

South of the Devil's Slide the coast turns inland, but a number of state beaches provide ocean access. Most of them have parking and rest rooms. Some, but not all, charge day-use or parking fees. None have camping. **Gray Whale Cove State Beach** (☎ 650/728-5336) is the first, a

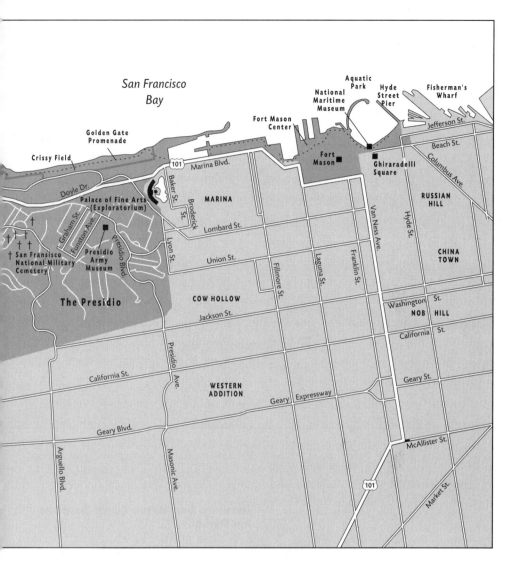

beautiful sandy cove beach reached by a stairway. Montara State Beach comes soon after, a particularly popular mile-long stretch of sand that is matched on the other side of Highway 1 by 2,000-acre McNee Ranch State Park, the site of some great mountain biking and hiking. The **Montara Lighthouse** (☎ 650/728-7177) just south of Montara is a popular youth hostel. South of here about a mile is the **James V. Fitzgerald Marine Reserve** (☎ 415/728-3584), a wonderful zone of rocky intertidal reefs and tide pools where, since its declaration as a reserve in 1969, scientists have found 25 new species. Interpretive programs and tide-pool walks

are led by park docents on a regular basis; call for current schedules.

Pillar Point Harbor

West of Hwy. 1 and Capistrano Rd. ☎ 650/728-3377 for harbor activity information. No lifeguard or facilities available. Parking along the side of Hwy. 1. Surfing, swimming, bird watching.

You can't miss Pillar Point; it's the huge headland with a huge radio telescope and satellite tracking station just west of Highway 1. The harbor here in the lee of the point is an important fishing and boat-building port; plus it's the only safe harbor between San Francisco and Monterey

Bay. Charter fishing boats and whale-watching cruises leave from the port town of Princeton daily. A nice wetland and beach are found in the northernmost corner of the harbor—perfect for children.

Half Moon Bay State Beaches
West of Hwy. 1 in Half Moon Bay. ☎ 650/726-8820. Picnic tables, rest rooms, motor-home and hike/bike campsites, beach, outdoor showers. Swimming, kayaking, sailing, fishing, hiking.

Half Moon Bay stretches from Pillar Point to Miramontes Point about 5 miles south. In between, this 3-mile-long stretch of several adjacent beach parks allows public access to the longest uninterrupted sand beach on the San Mateo Coast. El Granada Beach is a popular beginning-surfers' hangout as well as a motor-home campsite. Farther south you come to Roosevelt, Dunes, Venice, and Francis beaches, all of them broad sandy beaches linked by the bluff-top Coastside Trail.

Half Moon Bay is also growing as a sea-kayaking and sailing destination, and is home to a small sportfishing industry.

Southern San Mateo Coast Beaches and Parks
Both sides of Hwy. 1 between Half Moon Bay and Año Nuevo. ☎ 650/879-0227. Wild beaches and parks with nonflush rest rooms, picnic areas, lighthouse, hostel, campground. Wildlife viewing, hiking, swimming, biking.

From Half Moon Bay to the San Mateo County line, Highway 1 passes through one of the best concentrations of state parks anywhere. The state beaches, Bean Hollow, Pomponio, Pescadero, and San Gregorio, provide fantastic ocean access in this otherwise rugged coast. On the mountain side of the road, Pescadero Marsh, San Gregorio estuary, Bean Hollow State Park, and Butano State Park offer great hiking, bird watching, and camping. The wetlands and redwoods of

Golden Gate Park

this area are a good example of what much of the peninsula looked like prior to development.

San Mateo Memorial County Park and Pescadero Creek County Park

8 miles inland of Pescadero on Pescadero Rd. ☎ **415/879-0173.** Hiking, creek swimming, camping, nature museum, bird watching.

More than 6,000 acres of virgin redwoods and the upper watershed of Pescadero Creek. Trails connect the two parks and Portola State Park.

Portola State Park

From State Rte. 35 (Skyline Blvd.) go west on Alpine Rd. 3.5 miles to State Park Rd. ☎ **415/948-9098.** Camping, rest rooms, showers, visitor center, hiking, mountain biking, wildlife viewing.

This hidden jewel is located in the upper headwaters of Pescadero Creek. The second-growth redwood forest, creek, and campground get much less use than other Santa Cruz mountain redwood parks.

Castle Rock State Park

From State Rte. 9, take State Rte. 35 south 2.5 miles. ☎ **408/867-2952.** Backcountry camping, picnic tables, hiking and horse trails, rock climbing, nonflush toilets, water.

Known mostly as the closest rock climbing to the South Bay (on Castle and Goat Rocks, 100-ft.-high sandstone outcroppings), Castle Rock is also the starting point of the 37-mile Skyline to the Sea Trail that traverses the Santa Cruz mountains and is a popular spot for picnics and short walks.

MARIN COUNTY

Point Reyes National Seashore

Access from Hwy. 1 or Sir Francis Drake Blvd. ☎ **415/663-1092.** Flush toilets, running water, restaurant, museums, 100 miles of hiking trails, 44-bed hostel,

Native American history exhibits, horse farm. Bird and whale watching, biking, swimming.

Point Reyes, set aside as a national seashore in 1962 by President John F. Kennedy, is paradise found for birders, whale-watchers, beachgoers, and hikers. The best backcountry camping in the Bay Area is here in the wooded southern part of the seashore (36,000 acres of which are designated wilderness). Other areas are set aside as agricultural preserves, continuing an old tradition of coastal dairy farming on the ocean bluffs, and some areas are used for commercial oyster farming. For more information see the feature on Point Reyes later in this chapter.

Tomales Bay State Park

Access from several points on Bear Valley Rd. or Hwy. 1. ☎ **415/669-1140.** Beaches, rest rooms, parking, picnic tables. Hiking, bike-in and walk-in camping, bird watching, fishing, biking, kayaking, swimming.

This shallow rift bay is on the San Andreas Fault. It's more than 13 miles long yet only a mile wide and often less than 10 feet deep. At low tide large mud-flats are exposed. Relatively undeveloped, the bay is an important wildlife breeding and feeding area as well as a popular fishing, clamming, and kayaking spot. Birders have identified more than 100 different water birds in the bay. The state park encompasses several different properties on the waterfront and ridges around the bay.

Samuel P. Taylor State Park

5 miles east of Olema on Sir Francis Drake Blvd. ☎ **415/488-9897.** Camping, hiking trails, showers, flush toilets, running water, creek, picnic grounds.

The closest good car camping to Point Reyes, Samuel Taylor is also a great destination on its own with redwood groves and hiking into the headwaters of Lagunitas Creek.

Point Reyes Bird Observatory

Mesa Rd. ☎ **415/868-1221.** Ornithological research station open to the public. Call for hrs. Small donation requested. Bird watching.

Visitors can observe and participate in some of the fieldwork going on at this cutting-edge ornithological research station. The visitor center explains the birds' habitat and behavior.

Audubon Canyon Ranch

Access from Hwy. 1 between Stinson and Olema. ☎ **415/868-9244.** Open to public on weekends and holidays. Small fee. Bird watching.

This 1,500-acre ranch owned by the Audubon Society is best known for its egret and great-blue-heron nesting trees, visible from the Henderson Overlook at the end of a half-mile trail.

Stinson Beach

Access from Hwy. 1 north of intersection with Panoramic Hwy. ☎ **415/868-0942** (Ranger Station). Open daily 9am–10pm. Picnic grounds, rest rooms, showers. Swimming, surfing.

This long sandy beach is the most popular weekend getaway for Marin residents and many visitors from the city. In addition to the state beach, there is the small town of Stinson, which has a few B&Bs, a surf shop, grocery store, and private homes.

Mount Tamalpais State Park

Access from Panoramic Hwy. between Mill Valley and Stinson Beach. ☎ **415/388-2070.** Fees charged. Camping, hiking, biking, picnic grounds, scenic drive, group camp.

The buffer between developed east Marin and wild and scenic west Marin is this 6,200-acre state park. Encompassing most of Mount Tamalpais (known simply as Mount Tam), the park is most famous for the network of trails that lace its high ridges and wooded flanks, connecting the summit to the sea. Camping is severely limited and fills up fast.

Muir Woods National Monument

Muir Woods Rd., 3 miles north of Hwy. 1. ☎ 415/388-2595. No fee. Interpretive trail, visitor center, rest rooms, wheelchair accessible. Biking, hiking.

Completely enclosed by Mount Tamalpais State Park, Muir Woods was the first part of Marin set aside to protect the old-growth redwoods, in 1908. Short trails loop through the park; other longer ones extend into the state parklands.

Rodeo Beach

At the end of Bunker Rd., across from the former Fort Cronkite buildings, now called the Headlands Center for the Arts. Parking available near the bridge to the beach. No lifeguard or facilities. Surfing, swimming.

Rodeo Beach is the official name of a stretch of black sand half an hour from downtown San Francisco, just north of the Marin headlands. It's one of the best beaches that close to the city, though the fog closes in some days and can turn a good day cold in 10 minutes. That aside, there are few places that allow you faster access from the city to Pacific surf (there's a popular break on the beach's north end); the cliffs on either side of the sand also make the beach memorable. Rodeo is a neighborhood spot. Marin residents take their dogs here to run, which is always good for a show, and cyclists riding up from Sausalito often make the beach a turnaround point. Swimming is good, but watch the riptides and be prepared for very cold water. Rodeo Lagoon, behind the beach, connects to the open ocean part of the year and is good for bird watching, especially for pelicans.

There are no lifeguards or services at Rodeo Beach, so bring lunch and be careful in the water.

Golden Gate National Recreation Area: Marin Headlands

From San Francisco, take the Alexander Ave. exit off of U.S. 101 just over the Golden Gate Bridge. Southbound traffic should take the second Sausalito exit after the Waldo tunnel. ☎ 415/331-1540. Hiking trails, backcountry campsites, swimming, marine-mammal rescue center, youth hostel.

The GGNRA, a branch of the National Parks Service, manages a number of facilities on the Marin Headlands, the striking northern half of the Golden Gate. You'll even find some old military installments tucked away in these steep and wild headlands.

Richardson Bay and Angel Island

Take the ferry from Tiburon or San Francisco. ☎ 415/435-1915. Hiking, biking, camping, kayaking, sailing, boardsailing.

Inland from the harsh conditions of the Golden Gate, Richardson Bay stretches back into a long harbor and tidal basin that has the best sea kayaking in the entire bay. Raccoon Strait separates 740-acre Angel Island from Richardson Bay and the Marin mainland. The island has served various roles, from the West Coast version of Ellis Island to prison produce gardens for Alcatraz, but today it is maintained by the GGNRA and left virtually wild to be enjoyed by hikers and bikers. Several environmental campsites dot the island. Slips and mooring buoys are available for private boaters, and a ferry runs to the island several times daily from San Francisco or nearby Tiburon.

THE EAST BAY

East Bay Regional Park District Headquarters

2950 Peralta Oaks Court, Oakland. ☎ 510/562-7275. 60,000 acres of parks, trails, preserves, shorelines, bike and horse paths, wildlife corridors, camping areas, and lakes. Fees vary from none to $3 per vehicle.

The East Bay Regional Parks District controls most of the large open space in the East Bay and is a wonderful resource for hikers, bikers, and equestrians. The major trails, important parks, and wild places managed by the EBRPD are listed individually below, but for general information, reservations, or advice call or visit the headquarters.

Skyline and Ohlone Trails

For access and other info, contact the EBRPD. ☎ 510/562-7275. Hiking, biking, horseback riding.

These two trails, managed by the EBRPD (see above), connect the six biggest wilderness parks together. The Skyline Trail is open to bicycles, hikers, and horses and follows the crest of the Berkeley/Oakland hills for 31 miles. The wilder Ohlone Trail runs for 29 miles through remote areas and over 3,817-foot Rose Peak. It's not open to bicyclists and is used mostly by backpackers en route to the several backcountry camps.

Point Pinole Regional Shoreline

From I-80, exit Hilltop Dr. west to San Pablo Ave.; go right on Atlas Rd., then left on Giant Hwy., which will take you to the park. ☎ 510/562-PARK for the East Bay Regional Park District. Fishing pier, bird watching, hiking, swimming, water, rest rooms, picnic areas.

The square mile of Point Pinole was left relatively unsullied while the rest of Pinole and Richmond became an industrial hell, for the simple reason that an explosives factory sat here from the 1880s until 1960. The plant occupied only a portion of the point and the rest was left open as a safety buffer. Now it is the site of the best fishing pier in the whole bay, a 1,225-foot-long mother that puts you right over the migration routes of salmon, striped bass, and sturgeon. It also puts bird-watchers right under the flightway of waterfowl migrating into the Delta from the bay.

Wildcat Canyon Regional Park

From Berkeley, take Arlington Blvd. to Park Ave. Also several more remote entries. ☎ 510/562-PARK for the East Bay Regional Park District. Water, picnic areas, rest rooms, views, creek. Hiking, biking, wildlife watching, horseback riding.

Wildcat Canyon is one of the least developed East Bay Regional Parks. At 2,000 acres, it is plenty big enough for you to wander off into wooded canyons and across the grassy hillside and pretend you're not, in fact, on the edge of a huge metropolis. The Skyline Trail begins here. The one road through the park is a popular cycling route, connecting San Pablo Dam Road to Tilden Regional Park. It's a hill, of course. Both ways.

Tilden Regional Park

Surrounds Berkeley. Use a Berkeley street map to find any number of entrance points. ☎ 510/562-PARK for the East Bay Regional Park District. Camping, hiking, biking, picnicking, archery range, botanic garden, golf course, beach and lake with swimming, rest rooms, environmental education center.

Tilden Park is the most developed and well-used park in the whole EBRPD, with everything from merry-go-rounds to a golf course. Fortunately, it also holds miles of nice hiking and numerous quiet picnic grounds. The Environmental Education Center is the headquarters for the EBRPD's naturalist program and home to numerous educational displays, maps, and brochures. A small farm with pigs, rabbits, goats, horses, and chickens gives kids a look at the rural life.

Robert Sibley Volcanic Regional Preserve

1.5 miles north of Skyline Blvd. Shepherd Canyon junction. ☎ 510/562-PARK for the East Bay Regional Park District. Water, rest rooms, picnic tables, hiking.

The hill in the center of this park used to be a volcano. Years of quarrying by a sand-and-gravel company revealed many old volcanic features that are now explained with a great self-guided walking tour, maps, and brochures provided in the park.

Huckleberry Botanic Regional Preserve

Adjacent to Oakland at 7090 Skyline Blvd. ☎ 510/562-PARK for the East Bay Regional Park District. No water, 1 toilet, nature trail.

This small preserve was set aside to protect rare plants that grow on the hillside above urban Oakland. In addition to the namesake huckleberry, here would-be botanists can check out a rare blend of chaparral community plants including three distinct species of manzanita and the endangered western leatherwood.

Redwood Regional Park

Several entrances. The most commonly used one is on Redwood Rd.: Take the 35th Ave. exit off I-580 southbound. E. 35th becomes Redwood Rd. ☎ 510/562-PARK for the East Bay Regional Park District. Picnic ground, rest rooms, swimming pool, hiking, biking.

It's hard to believe now, but once the East Bay was covered with redwoods, the two tallest of which were located here, so tall that sailors entering the bay reputedly used them as a landmark to steer by. The demand for redwood lumber after the gold rush quickly caused the forests to be razed, but more than 100 years later, the second-growth forest here is pretty nice too. This is also the spot where the rainbow trout was first identified as a separate species in Redwood Creek. Tons of good hikes roam the hills and canyons. Big trout swim in Redwood Creek but fishing is prohibited.

Anthony Chabot Regional Park

Several entrances off Redwood Rd. and Skyline Rd. ☎ 510/562-PARK for the East Bay Regional Park District. Campground, picnic area, livery stable, lake, marina, rest rooms, showers. Fishing, boating, hiking, swimming.

Lake Chabot, a popular fishing and boating lake (no private boats, rent them at the marina), is the main draw of this large

park. At 315 acres it's large enough for a nice afternoon of canoeing. Hikers can follow the trail around the lake and others within this 5,000-acre park.

Black Diamond Mines Regional Preserve

End of Somersville Rd. in Antioch. ☎ 925/757-2620. Water, rest rooms, picnic tables, underground mining museum, nature walks, 30-plus miles of hiking trails. Bird watching.

Once a working coal mine, the Black Diamond Preserve is an interesting example of land turning back to nature. Once there was a town, mill, and huge mine here. Now there are 30 miles of trails, incredible bird watching, and a fascinating tour of the old mine tunnels (by reservation only; phone the park before coming).

Briones Regional Park

Bear Creek entrance is accessible from Orinda exit off State Rte. 24. ☎ 925/370-3020. Water, rest rooms, picnic tables. Hiking.

This 5,000-acre park is mostly open ranch land, where cattle still graze to keep the grass and subsequent fire hazard down. Many hikes in the 2- to 8-mile range are here. The view from Briones Peak is spectacular.

Mount Diablo State Park

From I-680 in Danville take Diablo Rd. 3 miles to the park's south entrance. ☎ 925/837-2525. Campsites, horse camp, picnic ground, rest rooms, hiking trails, equestrian trails, mountain bike trails, observation tower on summit of Mt. Diablo.

Miwok Indian myth held 3,849-foot Mount Diablo to be the home of Eagle and Coyote, two of their most sacred spirits. The Spaniards put a negative spin on this spirituality and named the mountain after the devil. Today, this 29,000-acre park has not just a little for everyone but a lot. Fifty miles of backcountry hiking

MUIR WOODS NATIONAL MONUMENT

Leave San Francisco, cross the Golden Gate Bridge, and within 20 minutes you can be in Muir Woods, where the old-growth coastal redwoods of Northern California stand much as they did prior to the influx of European settlers in the 19th century. While the rest of Marin County's red-wood forests were being devoured to feed the San Francisco building spree around the turn of the century, Muir Woods's trees, which are located in a remote ravine on the flanks of Mount Tamalpais, escaped destruction in favor of easier pickings. By 1905, however, lumber compa-nies had designs on the 200-foot-tall, 800-year-old giants. They were thwarted when farsighted congressman, philanthropist, and conservationist William Kent purchased the grove for $45,000. But only 2 years later the trees faced a different threat: The local water agency sought to condemn the land and build a dam on Redwood Creek, which would have inundated the for-est. Kent appealed to President Theodore Roosevelt and in 1908 secured the National Monument status that the woods still enjoy today. It was on Kent's request that the park was named after John Muir.

Muir Woods is a small park, only 553 acres tucked in a V-shaped canyon, but it's com-pletely encircled by enormous Mount Tamalpais State Park, lending the national monument a wildness beyond its size. Most visitors know the park for the easy **paved loop trail** that leaves from the visitor center and circles along the banks of Redwood Creek into the heart of the mon-ument's Bohemian and Cathedral groves. Hikers seeking more solitude should consider the longer trails such as **Fern Creek Loop,** 4 miles of spectacular canyon and redwood views, or the more strenuous **Dipsea Trail,** an 8-mile mix of shady creek-side, high ridges, and ocean views.

The monument is 17 miles north of San Francisco, with well-marked signs leading from U.S. 101. From 101 you can enter the park from either Highway 1 or the Panoramic Highway. The National Monument Visitors Center and the state park both sell good hiking maps for a small fee. Muir Woods is open every day from 8am to sunset. Admission is free. For more infor-mation contact **Muir Woods National Monument,** Mill Valley, CA 94941 (☎ **415/388-2595**). There is no picnicking, camping, or accommodations in Muir Woods. The nearest campground is a first-come, first-served, 13-site walk-in camp at Pantoll Station or the heavily wooded Alice Eastwood Group Camp (reservations required; ☎ **800/444-7275**), in **Mount Tamalpais State Park.**

trails, miles of unpaved fire roads for mountain biking, three year-round camp-grounds, winter-only backcountry camps (closed in summer due to fire hazard), and some of the most stunning spring wildflowers you'll ever see. The summit can be reached by car, and after a rain you can see as far as Mount Lassen in the north.

Henry W. Coe State Park

From U.S. 101 in Morgan Hill, exit at East Dunne Ave. Go east 13 miles. Road is extremely narrow and winding. ☎ **408/ 779-2728.** Car, horse, and backpacking camps; visitor center/ranch museum; rest rooms and water at the visitor center. Fishing, hiking, swimming, horse-back riding, biking.

This park, once a private ranch home-steaded by the Coe family, is the second largest in the state. Its 79,500 acres are lit-tle visited, and the harsh elements of the Diablo range make it unlikely that it will be overrun anytime soon. The park has become popular with mountain bikers in recent years, and given the considerable distances involved, a bicycle is the ideal way to cover ground, but the terrain is not for beginners. Steep rough trails, long dis-tances, and scarce potable water make this a spot for the experienced backcoun-try rider.

Point Reyes National Seashore

The national seashore system was created to protect rural and undeveloped stretches of the coast from the pressures brought on by soaring real-estate values and increasing population, in an effort to preserve both the natural features and unique culture of the coast. Nowhere is the success of the system more evident than at Point Reyes. Seventy road miles north of San Francisco via U.S. 1, Point Reyes is a 100-square-mile peninsula of dark forests, wind-sculpted dunes, endless beaches, and plunging sea cliffs. It offers a window to California's coastal history, with lighthouses, turn-of-the-century dairies and ranches, and the site of Sir Francis Drake's 1579 landing, plus a complete replica of a coastal Miwok Indian village.

Layers of human history coexist peacefully here with one of the world's most dramatic natural settings. Residents of the surrounding towns, **Inverness, Point Reyes Station,** and **Olema,** have steadfastly resisted runaway development. You'll find no strip malls and fast food here, but rather a laid-back culture of cafes, country inns, and gentle living. The park itself is loaded with wildlife, including Tule elk, birds, and bobcats; just offshore are gray whales, sea lions, and white sharks. During Audubon's annual Christmas bird count, Point Reyes regularly scores the largest concentrations of bird species in the continental United States—as many as 350.

For information, contact **Point Reyes National Seashore,** Point Reyes Station, CA 94956-9799 (☎ **415/663-1092;** www.nps.gov/pore).

GETTING THERE

Point Reyes is only 30 miles northwest of San Francisco, but it takes at least 90 minutes to reach by car (it's all the small towns, not the topography, that slows you down). The easiest route is via Sir Francis Drake Boulevard from U.S. 101 south of San Rafael; it takes its bloody time getting to Point Reyes, but does so without any detours. For a much longer but more scenic route, take the Stinson Beach/Highway 1 exit off U.S. 101 just south of Sausalito and follow Highway 1 north.

SEASONS & WEATHER

Weather at Point Reyes is very fickle. The point itself is the foggiest place on the West Coast. Inland, however, it can be warm and balmy while the coast is socked in. Generally the seasons here reverse normal expectations, with summer cold and foggy, and winter clear and, if not exactly warm, often at least tolerable. But there's no hard-and-fast rule about the weather. Winter storms can rage for weeks and sometimes the summer fog stays away. The best bet is to be flexible with your itinerary.

VISITOR CENTERS

As soon as you arrive at Point Reyes, stop at the **Bear Valley Visitor Center** (☎ **415/663-1092**) on Bear Valley Road (look for the small sign posted just north of Olema on Hwy. 1), and pick up a free trail map, talk with the rangers about your plans, and check out the natural history and cultural displays. It's open daily year-round.

The **Ken Patrick Visitor Center,** located at Drakes Beach, houses a 250-gallon saltwater aquarium and a 16-foot minke whale skeleton, among other exhibits. Open weekends and holidays only (except Christmas) from 10am to 5pm. The **Lighthouse Visitor Center,** located at the most westerly point of the Point Reyes Peninsula, offers information on the lighthouse and lifesaving services performed over the 125 years of its use, as well as natural-history exhibits on whales, seals, and wildflowers. Hours are from 10am to 5pm. It is closed Tuesday, Wednesday, and Christmas.

SEEING THE HIGHLIGHTS IN A DAY

First, stop at the **Bear Valley Visitor Center** and pick up the free Point Reyes map, which lists all the trails and roads open to cars, bikes, horses, and hikers. While you're here, spend some time at the nearby **Kule Loklo,** an authentic reconstruction of a village of the indigenous Coast Miwok Indian tribe, and **Morgan Horse Ranch,** a good place to see park patrol horses. Afterward, take a short stroll along the **Earthquake Trail,** an informative 0.6-mile walk along the infamous San Andreas Fault.

By far the most popular, and crowded, attraction at Point Reyes National Seashore is the venerable **Point Reyes Lighthouse,** located at the westernmost tip of Point Reyes. The drive alone on the **Sir Francis Drake Highway** is worth the trip, a 45-minute, 20-mile scenic excursion through rolling, windswept meadows and working dairy ranches (watch out for cows on the road). When the fog burns off, the lighthouse and the headlands provide a fantastic lookout point for spying common murres, basking sea lions, and gray whales as they make their migration along the coast from December through March. A free shuttle operates from the lighthouse area to Drakes Beach

If there's still some time left, the **Point Reyes Bird Observatory**—an ornithological research organization located at the southeast end the park—is a must for bird-watchers.

BEACHES

Beachgoers have lots of options here. The **Great Beach** is one of California's longest sand strands and also one of the windiest. You can't swim here, due to the large and dangerous waves, but the beachcombing is some of the best in the world. Tide-poolers should go to **McClures Beach** at the end of Pierce Point Road at low tide or hike out to **Chimney Rock.** Swimmers will want to stick to **Limantour Beach** or **Drakes Beach** in the protected lee of Point Reyes. Drakes Beach is home to the **Kenneth C. Patrick Visitors Center,** which has exhibits about the area's whale fossil beds and **Drakes Beach Café,** the only food concession in the park (famous for great oysters). Sir Francis Drake reputedly slid the Pelican (later rechristened the Golden Hind) onto the sandy shore of Drake's Bay in June 1579 for repairs and replenishing of supplies before sailing home to England.

HIKING & BIKING

There's a little of everything for hikers here: 32,000 acres of the park, containing 70 miles of trails, are set aside as wilderness where no motor vehicles or bicycles are allowed. One great sight that's worth the hike required to see it is **Alamere Falls.** The falls, which lie near Wildcat Camp on the **Coast Trail** (see "Day Hikes" under "Marin County: What to Do & Where to Do It," below), plummet 40 feet down to the beach and into the Pacific Ocean from an ocean bluff. They can also be reached via the Palo Marin Trail or Five Brooks Trail in the south of the park. Bicycles are permitted in the park but not on the wilderness area trails, making for complicated navigating. Check with the visitor center for specific information.

SPECIAL PROGRAMS

Rangers lead special programs year-round, with everything from wildlife hikes and history lessons to habitat restoration. All are free and open to the public. Call the Bear Valley Visitors Center for up-to-date schedules. Other groups, such as the Marin chapter of the **Sierra Club** (☎ **510/526-8969**), **Golden Gate Audubon Society** (☎ **510/843-2222**),

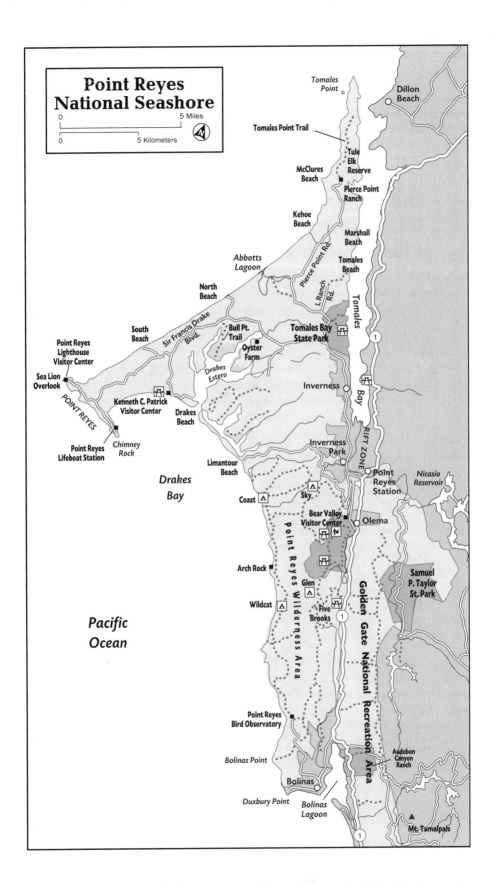

and **Oceanic Society Expeditions** (☎ 415/474-3385), run special excursions and outings to the park.

The Peninsula: What to Do & Where to Do It

There's a lot to be said for keeping the city in the city and the country in the country without a lot of in-between, and San Francisco says it well. Though the city is extremely densely populated, within a 15-minute drive or even a short walk you can be in—if not exactly wilderness—places that can safely be called nature, such as the Presidio, Fort Funston, Lake Merced, Land's End, and Ocean Beach. As you progress down the peninsula, the same holds true: cities like Palo Alto, Atherton, and Sunnyvale line the inside of the bay shore, but once over the mountain crest the land is still wild evergreen forests, flower farms, and wild, wild beaches. The ridgeline that divides the peninsula is a steep and powerful barrier to suburban spillover; development is largely contained on the east side of U.S. 280.

As a result of this division, much of the sporting scene on the peninsula relates directly to the sea: hikes along coastal marshes, beachfront bike paths, surfing the beautiful waves of Ocean Beach, or boardsailing at Crissy Field. Even when you're high in the hills of the southern peninsula, the occasional glimpse of blue, or sometimes a smothering cloud of gray ocean fog, will remind you that you're playing on the edge of the continent.

BIRD WATCHING

The variety of ecosystems on the peninsula is reflected in the variety of birding—the bay provides important shorebird habitats, the high ridges and forests offer feeding and nesting areas for raptors, and the wild Pacific coast is home to many pelagic and nearshore species.

Sweeney Ridge Preserve is a great raptor watching spot. During a 95-hour survey by the Golden Gate Raptor Observatory in 1988, volunteers saw 143 turkey vultures, 4 osprey, 2 bald eagles, 31 northern harriers, 58 sharp-shinned hawks, 49 Cooper's hawks, 2 red-shouldered hawks, 1 golden eagle, 24 American kestrel, 1 prairie falcon, and 47 other unidentified raptors. All this within line-of-sight of downtown San Francisco.

The wetland marshes around the southern San Mateo County beaches are known for their incredible variety of migratory species. At **Pescadero Marsh,** just inland of Pescadero State Beach, 230 separate species have been counted and 66 species are known to nest in the marsh and surrounding woodlands (see "Walks & Rambles," below). Commonly seen are rare varieties of sandpipers, great blue herons, Virginia rail, willet, marsh wrens, and downy woodpeckers. The state park maintains a checklist.

BOARDSAILING

Coyote Point is an endangered sailing spot on San Francisco Bay, near the San Francisco airport. A proposal to expand the airport's runways would require filling in part of the bay—the part with the good boardsailing—and has raised hackles from both wind enthusiasts and environmentalists. Until that happens, however, Coyote Point is the primary boardsailing site on San Francisco Bay. The conditions can be deceiving close to shore, with calm winds and little apparent wave action. But get a little bit out and suddenly the bay wakes up. Not a first-time spot, but a good site for the slightly more advanced.

Crissy Field is the end of the rainbow. If you can handle the demands of this remarkable spot, you get to sail in a blustery 30 knots with the Golden Gate

THE PRESIDIO

In 1989, the Department of Defense announced what once had been inconceivable: The army, which had held the Presidio as a military base since before the Civil War, was pulling out and leaving the most prized piece of real estate in San Francisco to the National Parks Service as an example of post–Cold War retrofitting. At press time, the last soldiers were leaving and a new Presidio era was beginning.

Frankly, it's too early to tell what will become of the conversion, but some signs are promising: The Clinton administration mandated that the Presidio should become a global center for the study of environmental policy, technology, and sustainability.

Unlike many military complexes, with their machine-gun–toting guards and high fences, much of the Presidio has always been open to the public; city residents have long escaped San Francisco's teeming streets into the base's forests and beaches. Now those uses will be encouraged even more. The base golf has gone public (yes, they had their own golf course), former military buildings are being leased out, and the base theater is opening as a private repertory theater. In addition, many bicyclists like to use the Presidio roads as a warm-up before venturing across the Golden Gate Bridge and into the Marin hills.

Walkers and joggers can also enjoy the forests of the Presidio. Once a bleak field of wind-blasted rock, sand, and grass, the area is now a thriving woodland habitat. In a strangely humanitarian gesture that perhaps foreshadowed San Francisco's future, 60,000 trees were planted in the 1880s to make the place more livable for the troops. Today, on the 2-mile **Ecology Loop Trail,** walkers can see more than 30 different species of those trees including redwood, spruce, cypress, and acacias. Other good walks are the 2.5-mile **Coast Trail,** which follows the bluff top from Baker Beach to the southern base of the Golden Gate Bridge, and **Lover's Lane,** a short and romantic walk from ritzy Pacific Heights straight downhill to the former officers' housing.

Anyone interested in the military history of the Presidio should stop at the **Presidio Army Museum,** which is loaded with military arcana from 200 years of base history. Another interesting chunk of military history is **Fort Point,** a National Historic Site that lies directly under the Golden Gate Bridge. During the Civil War, the fort held 140 men and 90 pieces of artillery to prevent a Confederate takeover of California. Rangers in Civil War regalia lead regular tours and sometimes fire the old cannons. Call ☎ **415/556-1693** for schedules and information.

Two of the most popular beaches in San Francisco lie in the Presidio. **Baker Beach,** a small and beautiful strand just outside the Golden Gate, is packed on sunny days with sunbathers and fishermen. Because of the cold water and the roaring currents that pour out of the bay twice a day, swimming is not advised here for any but the most confident. On very low tides it's possible to walk all the way from here to the Golden Gate. On the other side of Fort Point is **Crissy Field,** a former airfield that in recent years has become known as one of the see-and-be-seen proving grounds of California's boardsailing culture. Between March and October, hundreds come to try their hand. The Crissy beach provides easy water access and plenty of room to rig up. This is also a popular place for joggers en route from the Marina District to Fort Point and back. At the west end of Crissy Field is a pier that can be used for fishing and crabbing.

For schedules, maps, and general information about ongoing developments at the Presidio, the best source is the **Golden Gate National Recreation Area Headquarters** at Fort Mason, Building 201, San Francisco, CA 94123 (☎ **415/556-0560**).

bridge over one shoulder and San Francisco's skyline over the other. On the other hand, you need to know what you're doing or you will almost certainly get in trouble here. Tides are not to be ignored this close to the Gate, and when the fog comes in, so should you, lest a container ship on its way in from Singapore swat you like a gnat. The coast guard earns its pay pulling people out of the 50° water here. Don't overestimate yourself. But if you can handle the location, on San Francisco's breezy northern tip just downhill from the Golden Gate Bridge, this site could offer the ride of your life.

FISHING

Pier and shore fishing for halibut, surf perch, and the occasional striped bass is a popular pastime all over the bay, but the big **saltwater fishing** news around here is chasing **salmon.** When they run, numerous charter boats will take you outside the Golden Gate to fish the rich waters between Point Reyes and Half Moon Bay, or to wherever the fish are running in the bay.

In San Francisco, it's difficult to miss the local fleet, based amid the wax museums and general tourist mayhem at Fisherman's Wharf. Among the boats making open and charter trips, there are the **Wacky Jacky** (☎ 415/586-9800).

Half Moon Bay's fishing fleet tends to stay close to Pillar Point, where it originates. June and July are said to be your best bets for the widest range of fish, but each species has its traditional high months. As with the entire central coast, winter is a little slower, but the fleet goes out year-round. **Huck Finn Sport Fishing** runs five boats out of Pillar Point, located 4 miles north of Half Moon Bay on Highway 1. Call ☎ 800/572-2943 for reservations and the latest fishing reports.

Freshwater fishing is surprisingly popular and good in the many small lakes

in several of the **East Bay Regional Parks,** several of the **Mount Tamalpais water district lakes,** and at **Lake Merced** in San Francisco. Lake Merced regularly delivers up trophy-worthy (5- to 10-lb.) trout and bass. Access to the lake is difficult on most of the shoreline because of steep banks and reedy shoreline. At Harding Park, at the south end of the Great Highway, **Lake Merced Boating and Fishing Co. (☎ 415/753-1101)** rents boats and canoes, and there is bank fishing as well.

HIKES, BUSHWHACKS & BACKPACK TRIPS

Day Hikes

Sweeney Ridge

4.8 miles round-trip. Moderate. 2–3 hr. Access: Take Fairway Dr. from Hwy. 1 in Pacifica to the dead-end near a nursery. Map: GGNRA hiking map.

Sailors had missed the Golden Gate for over 200 years before the bay was discovered by Captain Gaspar de Portola on November 4, 1769, and he discovered it by hiking. Portola was looking for Monterey Bay when he climbed Sweeney Ridge that day, but quickly realized the potential of this huge natural harbor. The rest, as they say, is history. The Sweeney Ridge Trail climbs about 600 or 700 feet to a scrub and grassland ridgeline from which you can see the entire Bay Area: Mount Diablo, Mount Tam, the Golden Gate and Bay bridges, and the Farallon Islands 25 miles out to sea. You can stand here and imagine Portola's surprise when he crested the ridge.

Under the Bridge and Out to the Sea

San Francisco–area saltwater fishing takes place almost entirely outside the bay, which means you get a trip beneath the bridge and through the Golden Gate in addition to a good day on the open water. Most trips originate from San Francisco, Sausalito, Emeryville, and Berkeley.

Jackson Flats Trail, Butano State Park

3.5 miles round-trip. Easy. 2 hr. Access: Near Butano State Park Headquarters on Cloverdale Rd. Map: Butano State Park map.

Butano State Park protects a series of lush forests mixed with vernal pool wetlands, small seasonal ponds caused by geologic slumping that are important breeding habitat for many amphibians. The Jackson Flats Trail passes through a small redwood forest and then follows the side of a ridge for about a mile. At about 1.5 miles from the trailhead you can see a few small ponds and a large marsh on a flat plain of forest. A few hundred yards more brings you to an awesome stand of virgin redwoods. The trail continues further, but this is where I like to turn around and head back.

Overnights

Butano Trail Camp, Butano State Park

13 miles round-trip. Moderate. Access: Butano State Park Headquarters, Olmo Fire Trail. Map: Butano State Park map.

It's hard to find a place where you can hike almost 7 miles through first- and second-growth redwoods and over running creeks, and then camp in a primitive trail camp this close to a big city—but this hike is it. The flora, fauna, and geography here are otherworldly, from the earthquake fault to the periodic ocean views. The camp itself has a single pit toilet, no water, and no fires allowed.

MOUNTAIN BIKING

It's unfortunate that the place that invented mountain bikes should become the epicenter of the backlash against them, but that's exactly what has happened. Ten years ago, just about every trail in the Bay Area was open to bicycles; now they are prohibited from most trails and strictly regulated on fire roads. On Mount Tamalpais in Marin, rangers actually use radar guns to enforce the 15 mph speed limit. Ever tried descending a huge mountain at 15 mph? It sucks. Ever been ticketed or had your bike taken away for riding on single track? Me neither, but I bet it sucks too. The truly committed have taken to poaching trails at night under full moons or using halogen lamps. Others just drive to Santa Cruz or into Sonoma and Mendocino. It's out there, but it's not nearly as convenient as it once was. A couple of places in the area rent bikes. **American Bike Rental,** 2715 Hyde, (☎ 415/931-0234) rents tandems as well as mountain bikes.

Old Haul Road, Portola State Park

13 miles. Moderate. Access: Portola State Park Headquarters.

From the parking area at the state park headquarters pedal down the road, over a bridge, and through the service road gate. In about three-fourths of a mile you'll pass employee housing and come to another gate—this one is the boundary with Pescadero Creek County Park. Turn right here onto Old Haul Road. It's about 6 miles from here to Memorial County Park through rolling evergreen woodlands, and the total elevation gain is only 400 feet, though you do it twice since it comes in the middle. At the Memorial Park Trailhead turn around and pedal up and over that hill again. From there it's a coast back to your car.

Butano State Park Ranger-Led Rides

11 miles round-trip. Easy to moderate. Fire roads and wide trails. Access: Ride begins at the Butano State Park Visitors Center. Map: Butano State Park map.

This is a beautiful ride, but, sadly, the only way to do it is with a ranger. Park staff have made arrangements with private landowners inside and surrounding the park to open access to a 5.5-mile-long logging road that leads through dense, tall stands of redwoods and Douglas fir. At several points the trail passes onto open ridges with views of the surrounding coast range and the ocean below. Along the way you'll stop several times to rest and to hear your ranger guide talk about natural history. The rides are only offered on summer weekends and fill up quickly. Make reservations in advance at the Butano State Park ranger station (**☎ 650/ 879-2040**).

ROAD BIKING

Despite its hills, San Francisco is actually a really bike-friendly city, and the open country in southern San Mateo County is even better. The best resource for anyone interested in doing a lot of road rides here is *Touring the San Francisco Bay Area by Bicycle* by Peter Powers (Terragraphics, 1990). Small enough to stick in a jersey pocket yet incredibly detailed, this book shows hundreds of potential routes in the city and all over the Bay Area. *Bay Area Bike Rides* by Ray Hosler (Chronicle Books, 1994) is also very good for outlying areas, but not nearly as detailed in the city.

San Francisco Ocean Front and Golden Gate Bridge

20–30 miles depending on turnaround point. Moderate. Access: Park in lot at Sloat and Great Hwy. on Ocean Beach. Follow bike path north. Map: San Francisco city map or GGNRA trail and road map.

One of my favorite rides here follows the oceanfront path between Fort Funston and Golden Gate Park along Ocean Beach, weaves through the woods of Land's End, drops down through the Presidio, and then crosses the Golden Gate Bridge to Sausalito. It's easy to get confused getting on the bridge because the bike path from Lincoln Boulevard heads toward the west (ocean) side of the bridge but a seemingly hidden tunnel then ducks under the toll plaza to the east (bay) side. Be patient and you'll find it. On weekends the bay side is closed to cyclists, but I like to do this ride early in the morning on a weekday so I can ride

with the view of the city. Usually the fog is lifting when I hit the bridge. You can see the ships entering and leaving the bay below and the sun rising behind the city skyline. Pedestrians aren't really a problem this early, but as you round the bridge pillars, watch for bicycles coming the other way. Once on the Marin side I ride into Sausalito, fuel up on scones and coffee, then ride home.

ROCK CLIMBING

Rock climbing is one thing there just isn't a lot of around here. Most serious climbers either trek over to Yosemite or down to the Pinnacles. **Castle Rock State Park** (**☎ 408/867-2952**) is the closest decent-size rock to the peninsula and it's nothing to write home about. To stay in shape for those Yosemite treks, a lot of San Francisco climbers go to **Mission Cliffs,** 2295 Harrison (**☎ 415/550-0515**), in the Mission District. This newly constructed climbing gym in a converted garment factory has numerous difficult routes and seems to be in a growth phase. It also offers introductory and beginning lessons, good for getting the basics down or refreshing after a few years away from climbing.

SAILING

The bay is one of the finest sailing grounds on the West Coast—the Golden Gate allows Pacific winds through but stops much of the open ocean's rollicking swell. Richmond's **Tradewinds Sailing School and Club,** Brickyard Marina, Port Richmond (**☎ 510/232-7999**), rents boats from 20 feet to 40 feet, and runs a respected sailing school. Rental rates decrease with membership in the Tradewinds sailing club, but a membership is not required. Proof of seamanship skills is, however. Sailing lessons range from novice to "bareboat chartering," the highest level. Among rental and sailing schools on San Francisco Bay, Tradewinds has some of the most forgiving air, owing to its location on the bay's east side, in the

---

Join the Crew

For information on hitching a ride for the day on someone else's sailboat, see "Sail for Free" in chapter 1.

---

lee of Angel Island and Tiburon. By the time the lack of heavy wind frustrates you, it's probably time to graduate to a harder class and a bigger boat.

Cass' Marina (☎ **415/332-6789**), in Sausalito, rents sailboats for the half day, full day, and weekend. It's the outfit located closest to the Golden Gate Bridge, Angel Island, Alcatraz, and the SF waterfront, so renting here minimizes the time spent chugging out of the marina or through the shipping lanes. Particularly when you're paying by the hour, the proximity is no small advantage, and means more time under sail and less spent getting to and from the dock.

One of the area's largest sailing operations, **Club Nautique** has locations in Sausalito, San Mateo, and Alameda. The club offers a broad menu of instruction and an extensive bareboat fleet, ranging from 24-foot to 41-foot boats. It's best known for its sailing courses, which aren't cheap—most are $300 to $1,000—but are comprehensive and guaranteed to give you enough skills to sail safely under most conditions. A certification from Club Nautique should allow you to pass requirements for rentals elsewhere.

To go through the complete series of Nautique's classes, from novice to "basic cruising" level, takes between 1 and 2 weeks. One-day or evening classes are also available, on topics such as celestial navigation, sailing catamarans, and using charts. Call ☎ **800/559-2582** for information on the **Sausalito** location, at Kappas Marina, 100 Gate Six Rd. The **San Mateo** location is at Coyote Point, also a popular boardsailing destination; call ☎ **888/693-7245**. The Alameda is located at Ballena Bay harbor west of Oakland, and occasionally offers a Wednesday-night dinner and bay cruise; call ☎ **800/343-7245**.

Spinnaker Sailing offers rental and instruction at Mountain View and Redwood City's marina, on the peninsula about 30 miles south of San Francisco and the same distance north of San Jose. An advantage of sailing in the South Bay is the considerably smaller amount of traffic on the water, both from other recreational sailors and commercial vessels. It's just a much wider body of water south of the Bay Bridge. Of course, the view and the wind, while not bad, just aren't the same as what you will get north of the Bay Bridge. For the **Mountain View** school, call ☎ **650/965-7474**. In **Redwood,** slightly farther north but not too different in sailing terms, Spinnaker can be reached at ☎ **650/363-1390**.

SCUBA DIVING

Given that the area between Point Reyes, Point Año Nuevo, and the Farallon Islands is commonly known as the "Blood Triangle" because of all the great white sharks that live here (see "Shark Watch" feature, below) plus the fact that the water is generally murky and rough, not many people go diving here. The exception is the large number of people who go **abalone diving** on the ocean side of **Tomales Point** in Point Reyes. You can't really call it diving, though, since most of them just poke around in large tide pools looking for these mollusks. I don't blame them at all. Biologists have seen more white sharks at Tomales Point than any other mainland spot.

Some of the best dive shops in the San Francisco Bay area teach diving off the Sonoma Coast to the north (see chapter 9). **Marin Skin Diving** in San Raphael (☎ **415/479-4332**) and **Cal School of Diving** in Berkeley (☎ **510/524-3248**)

THE BAY BITES BACK

As if you needed proof that San Francisco Bay is a real sailing ground, consider the following sad sea tale.

My friend Misty and I had finally made her 26-foot sailboat seaworthy, and taken a few light tours around the harbor near Oakland to test it out. Finally, it was time to head out of the channel's mouth and into the bay. It was a day for which we'd been waiting a whole year.

We had new sails up, and the boat was moving better than it ever had. We started hitting the real wind for the first time in the narrow channel between Alameda and Oakland, and were making a good course to open water with some help from an outboard motor. After motoring for nearly an hour, we reached the channel's mouth and killed the engine, tacked out to the south edge of the harbor, and got ready to sail into the bay.

Then everything went severely wrong. First, a tanker the size of an office building made us tack off our course. Then the traffic from other sailboats pushed us too close to the channel's rocky edge. Then a fishing skiff decided to stop right in the center of the channel's mouth, forcing another tack. Then we hit the current, which I hadn't seen, and started drifting toward the rocks.

Misty leapt to the outboard. The motor, normally reliable, wouldn't start. The boat's bow turned away from the wind and the sails started flapping. I leaned on the tiller; nothing happened. By then we were within feet of the channel's edge, and I began to accept the terrible fact that I'd steered us aground.

Ten seconds later we were smashing onto the rocks, vainly trying to hold the boat's hull off them, until a more level-headed sailor on a passing boat called to us to take the sails down and ease away. Taking his advice, we frantically untied the lines and dropped the sails, and the boat sloughed down into the water.

Fortunately, the boat didn't sink and no one got hurt. The only injury was to our pride, most acutely when the coast guard towed us back into the channel's center and sent us limping home with our sails splayed all over the deck. We never did make it out into the bay, and felt very lucky to have just gotten home in one piece.

Back at the marina, while Misty dove under the boat to check for leaks, the lesson of that stressful afternoon was clear. California's coastal bays may feel like home, but they act like the open ocean. That day we failed to respect the bay, and despite never making the high seas, we still got in over our heads.

—Marc Herman

are among the area's best-known dive schools.

SURFING

San Francisco was an underground surfing scene, a deeply held secret until the late 1980s. The water here is really cold year-round, which scared off all but the most diehard surfers. Then, a vast explosion in the sport's popularity, coupled with improvements in wet-suit materials, made this cold-water kingdom more accessible. It's still not a cakewalk: The main break on the peninsula is **Ocean Beach,** a hollow, unforgiving beach break known for breaking boards and basically kicking ass. **Fort Point, China Beach,** and **Baker Beach** are all semi-point breaks inside the Golden Gate with smaller but still unforgiving conditions. Only when you get down to **Pacifica** and **Rockaway Beach** will you find anything approaching beginner- or intermediate-level surf breaks. And there's always **Maverick's,** the Half Moon Bay reef break where professional big-wave rider

Mark Foo died in 1994. On a good day, 20- to 25-foot sets roar through Maverick's with a sound approaching that of a jet on takeoff. The lineup is pretty far out in the ocean, but nearby cliffs offer a good viewpoint. Just follow the trail around Pillar Point from the parking area below the radar station. If Maverick's is breaking, you can't miss it.

The main surf shop in San Francisco is **Wise Surfboards,** 800 Great Hwy. (☎ **415/750-9473**), which also runs the San Francisco surf hot line (☎ 415/273-1618). The staff is taciturn almost to the point of unfriendliness, but the place stays in business despite itself simply because it stocks the best selection of boards on the North Coast.

WALKS & RAMBLES

Cliff House to Land's End

Distance varies. Access: Park at the Cliff House at the junction of Geary Blvd. and the Great Hwy.

Perched on a rocky outcrop at the northern headland of Ocean Beach, the Cliff House is a historic restaurant and museum overlooking the sea. Park here and follow the sidewalk a short distance until you come to the ruins of the Sutro Baths on the shore below. Pass through the Merrie Way parking area and pick up the Coastal Trail. Actually a series of interweaving trails, the Coastal Trail curves through the cypress forest and along the cliff top until the Golden Gate Bridge comes into sight. Across the channel you can see the Marin Headlands and Point Bonita Lighthouse. Several ships have run aground on the rocks below Land's End and are sometimes visible during low tides. At several points, benches and coin-operated telescopes are placed along the trail.

Pescadero Marsh Trails

Distance varies. Access: Pescadero State Beach.

Two trails with numerous observation decks allow nature lovers and birders to get a good look at the wealth of wetlands here. Bring binoculars and park at either of the main Pescadero Beach parking lots. The marsh is across Highway 1 and stretches up this striking coastal valley for what seems like miles. You, however, only need to go a few hundred yards before you'll start seeing the hundreds of species of birds that use the marsh as their breeding ground and shelter.

Fort Point

2 miles. Access: Park at Marina Green.

Beginning in the swanky Marina District of San Francisco, this walk follows the best of the bay front from near the Saint Francis Yacht Club through Crissy Field and the Presidio to end up at Fort Point. This Civil War–era emplacement was designed to keep Confederate ships from taking over California. It must have worked. Construction of the Golden Gate Bridge, which passes directly over the fort, was headquartered here. Originally the fort was slated for demolition to make way for the bridge but was spared when project engineer Joseph Strauss decided it should stay. The walk to the fort is level but often windy. The view back to the city from here is one of the best.

WHALE WATCHING

Whale watching isn't quite the big deal on the peninsula that it is in Monterey Bay to the south or Point Reyes to the north. The whales tend to be farther offshore here and the weather and coastline aren't as hospitable to cliff-top viewing. Several San Francisco and Half Moon Bay area charter companies run trips to see the whales as they pass offshore. Many tours originate at Fisherman's Wharf in San Francisco. Check at the Red and White Fleet office at Pier 39. (You can't miss it; look for a giant red and white boat that says RED AND WHITE on it.) Inquire dockside for schedules.

SHARK WATCH

In a skiff bobbing off the Farallon Islands, some 30 miles west of San Francisco, Scot Anderson watches a 16-foot great white shark approach a battered surfboard floating nearby. The surfboard is a decoy, modified to hold an underwater video camera. The shark is familiar, one Anderson calls Stumpy because of its chopped-off tail fin. Stumpy seizes the decoy like a dog fetching a stick. Then, no longer interested, the shark is suddenly gone.

Great white sharks come to the Farallons specifically to feed, mostly on elephant seals, which find these rocky, windswept, deserted islands an ideally located refuge. On land the seals are safe, but in the surrounding waters it's another story. As a result, the seals and their predators form a natural marine laboratory for students of the great whites: In a single 3-month span last year, the scientists from the Farallon Islands Shark Project witnessed almost 80 attacks by great whites.

One of the things the Farallon researchers have learned is that the sharks arrive at the same place every year on a predictable schedule. They noticed that one shark, called Half-Fin because it's missing the top of its dorsal fin, came to the same rocky point between October 7 and October 10 for 3 out of 4 years. After feeding, it disappeared. Other sharks in the Farallons follow similar patterns of arrival and departure.

The surfboard decoy is one of the project's most useful research tools. Seen from below—the shark's view—the decoy resembles the silhouette of a young elephant seal. White sharks regularly approach Anderson's unbaited contraption, bumping, biting, or just eyeing it. Their curiosity satisfied, they vanish back into the depths.

September to November is the project's observations season. "What really goes on most of the time," Anderson says, "is that we go up to the lighthouse and look around the island all day long. You look at the nearshore waters for gulls or blood or whatever catches your eye."

A shark attack triggers a rapid sequence of actions. First the observer takes a location fix from the lighthouse, then turns on a telephoto-equipped video camera calibrated to register the size of the shark. Word of the sighting is relayed to others on the island. If ocean conditions allow, researchers race out in a small boat to get a better view of the feeding shark. The scientists try to gather as many details as possible: type of prey, weather, tide, time of day, and—using visible scars and marks—the identification of the shark.

In coming years, the scientists hope to attach sonic tracking devices to individual sharks. This will help them learn much more about what sharks are doing, because, as marine animal behaviorist Peter Klimley explains, "Right now we only know where they are when they feed or hit the decoy."

My favorite is the trip offered by the **Oceanic Society** (☎ 415/474-3385), a nonprofit research organization based in Fort Mason. These multifaceted cruises on an 85-foot boat leave the San Francisco Yacht Club and last 8 or 9 hours, sometimes traveling as far as Point Reyes or the Farallon Islands. Trained naturalists explain many different aspects of the marine environment on each trip, so even if you don't see whales, you'll come back satisfied. Departure time is 9am on Saturday and Sunday.

Marin County: What to Do & Where to Do It

Marin County's most famous inventions are the mountain bike and the hot tub—it's hard not to like a place with that kind of initiative. From the top of Mount Tamalpais (known simply as Mount Tam) to the seaward tip of Point Reyes, Marin is the most fabulous natural playground near any major U.S. city. Grassy ridges and forested ravines dominate the high country while steep sea cliffs alternate with occasional long sand beaches on the coast. The people who live here do so because they value their surroundings and hold fierce opinions as to how those surroundings should be used. Mostly this is a good thing; just look around—it's hard to argue with success. But other times it leads to factionalism and infighting such as the ongoing war between hikers and mountain bikers that has closed so much of Marin to off-road bicycling and resulted in actual fisticuffs and arrests. Because it's so close to San Francisco, the backcountry of Marin can sometimes be overrun on summer weekends or big holidays. The off-season—fall, winter, and spring—is often the best time to visit. Between winter storms are long stretches of warm weather when there is nothing better than a long hike on Mount Tam or a trip to Stinson Beach.

BIRD WATCHING

No two ways about it, Marin County is the single best place in California for birders to buff out their life list while seeing numerous species in a still-wild setting. Practically anyplace in the North Bay you stand a good chance of seeing something interesting, but **Point Reyes** is the Chartres Cathedral of birding. The park's 100 square miles contain plentiful and varied habitats, which, as the result of a geological quirk, have been thrust miles out into the Pacific Ocean. Because of this, the point is both a magnet for migrating birds coming down the Pacific Coast in search of land and the stop-off point for a lot of vagrants that were separated from their flock and blown wildly off course. Many East Coast and Siberian species are spotted here on a regular basis. An amazing total of 430 recorded species, ranging from the Cooper's hawk to the Cape May warbler, are listed on the park's bird list, available at the **Bear Valley Visitors Center** (☎ 415/663-1092).

Located just south of the park on Mesa Road near Bolinas, the **Point Reyes Bird Observatory** (☎ 415/868-0655) is a good place to get up close and personal with many land birds. The staff here offer tours and special programs. They also run year-round netting and banding operations and welcome public participation. The observatory is a privately supported, nonprofit ornithological research organization and welcomes any donations.

Bolinas Lagoon is a coastal wetlands at the south end of Tomales Bay, north of Point Reyes. It's open to the public from mid-March to mid-June. In addition to hundreds of coastal species, Bolinas is the best place on the coast to see the great blue heron and the massive-winged great egret, which looks like a pile of powdery snow come to life. Not to be missed. The **Audubon Canyon Ranch,** located in a forested canyon across Highway 1 from the Bolinas Lagoon (☎ 415/868-9244), is also an important nesting area for egrets and the great blue heron. The birds congregate by the hundreds in high tree branches on the south side of the canyon while a vista point on the other side offers a perfect place to set up a spotting scope.

BOARDSAILING

The Marin side of the bay is less windy and less accessible than most other corners of the bay. **Larkspur Landing,** in Marin County, is the opposite of Crissy Field, with a more modest view (of San Quentin prison and a ferry dock). Still, it's a popular intermediate spot, with low waves and moderate winds that build over the course of the day. The entire U-shaped area is sheltered by the surrounding hills, though afternoon gusts can get interesting. And like anywhere in the bay, Larkspur can go from placid to a stiff blow at any time, so be prepared. Regular traffic from the Larkspur–San Francisco ferry means you have to keep your eyes and ears open, but it's easy to stay well clear.

FISHING

There are a wide variety of saltwater and freshwater fishing options available all over the Bay Area; see the other "What to Do & Where to Do It" sections in this chapter for more information. In Sausalito, **Caruso's Sportfishing Center** (☎ **415/332-1015**) coordinates several Marin operators.

HIKES, BUSHWHACKS & BACKPACK TRIPS

Day Hikes

Mount Tam to Stinson Beach Loop

7 miles. Moderate. 4–5 hr. Access: Pantoll Ranger Station on Panoramic Hwy., Mt. Tamalpais State Park. Map: Mt. Tam trail map available at trailhead.

This 7-mile hike dishes out a little of everything Marin has to offer: It begins just below the summit of Mount Tam but quickly plunges downhill in the thickly wooded Steep Ravine Trail (one portion of this trail is a ladder). The trail follows Web Creek and crosses five or six wooden bridges under the cover of redwoods and California laurel. When you come to the junction with the Dipsea Trail, bear right. Steep Ravine continues to the ocean and a nice campground, but for the sake of making a loop you want to go right. The Dipsea will take you through hillsides of open chaparral with stunning views of Stinson Beach, San Francisco, and even the Farallon Islands on a clear day. You'll hit paved roads at the junction of the Panoramic Highway and Highway 1 just above Stinson. Once in town you can stop for an ocean swim or lunch at a cafe, or else start the long climb home.

The Matt Davis Trail begins just above Highway 1 at the other end of Stinson Beach. From this trailhead it is almost 4 miles home. After the first mile or so of hiking through the heavy forest above Stinson, you'll break out onto an open ridge with more amazing vistas of the beach below and the city to your south. After several steep switchback sections the trail descends and crosses the Panoramic Highway back at Pantoll.

Muir Woods Lose-the-Crowd Loop

4-plus miles. Moderate. 2–3 hr. Access: Trail begins near Muir Woods Visitors Center. Map: Muir Woods map. Mt. Tamalpais State Park hiking map.

More than a million people every year come to Muir Woods, but 98% of them walk the 1-mile Redwood Creek Loop. To get away from the crowd while still enjoying the redwoods, take the trail that bears uphill from the Gifford Pinchot Tree. Depending on which map you use, it may be called either the Ocean View Trail or the Panoramic Highway Trail. Either way, this trail will take you through Muir Woods and past a nice waterfall. Before reaching the Panoramic Highway (and the ocean view) you'll come to a junction with the Lost Trail. Go left and follow it downhill to Fern Creek. The Fern Creek Trail follows its namesake until you reach the Bootjack Trail, which will shortly deposit you back at the visitor center.

Hassle Free Loop, Muir Woods

5 miles. Moderate. Access: Trailhead is off the Panoramic Hwy. in Mt. Tamalpais State Park. Map: Muir Woods map. Mt. Tamalpais State Park hiking map.

On busy weekends and summer vacation when Muir Woods's 200-space visitor-center parking area can be a real headache, consider avoiding the traffic jam with the Hassle Free Loop. It begins on the Panoramic Highway in Mount Tamalpais State Park and descends into the redwood grove and fern canyon via the Panoramic Trail, Ocean View Trail, and Fern Canyon Trail, a total of about 5 miles. It is also a short but steep hike from this parking area to the top of Mount Tamalpais, one of the best views in the Bay Area.

Tennessee Valley to the Beach

4.25 miles round-trip. Moderate. Access: Tennessee Valley Rd., Mill Valley, off the Stinson Beach exit of Hwy. 101. Tennessee Valley Rd. ends at the trailhead. Parking is available. Map: USGS Point Bonita.

Tennessee Valley is not a remote trail by a long shot, but what it lacks in solitude it makes up for in scenery. Popular with mountain bikers, the trail is actually a gravel road for about a mile, then continues on dirt through an unshaded glen. After just over 2 miles, the trail arrives at the ocean amid a grouping of massive cliffs. If you want to keep going, there is a trail up the cliffs that gives excellent views of the beach below, adding a stiff climb to the generally flat walk between the beach and the trailhead. This is one of the most popular hikes in the Bay Area, so expect company. Allow 3 hours to ensure some beach time.

Bass Lake

5.8 miles round-trip. Moderate. Allow 4–5 hr. to give yourself swimming time. Access: Palomarin Trailhead at end of Mesa Rd. north of Bolinas. Map: Point Reyes map or USGS Double Point topo.

This relatively flat hike takes you through rolling oak forest and grasslands where deer are common, past striking ocean overlooks, and into a cool and wooded freshwater swimming lake. From the trailhead the route is obvious. The trail skirts several steep cliffs and then heads over a steep ridge and inland. At about 2 miles you are faced with an unsigned fork. Go left. Soon you will pass a few small ponds and meadows. If it is a hot day you'll probably sense Bass Lake before you see it; it always seems to exude a cool, wet smell. The trail passes Bass Lake and a short spur trail will take you left to a grassy area and several steep trails to the water. Though there isn't any real beach, there is a rope swing, and the water is perfect for swimming. When you've had enough, return the way you came.

Bear Valley Trail, Point Reyes

8 miles round-trip. Easy. Compressed rock Park Service road. Allow 4 hr. Access: Bear Valley Visitors Center. Map: Park map or USGS Inverness topo.

The Bear Valley Trail leads through wooded hillsides and past Divid Meadow until it hits Arch Rock, where Coast Creek splashes into the sea through a "sea tunnel." While the compressed rock path takes away a bit from the nature experience, it does make the trail wheelchair accessible.

Coast Trail, Point Reyes

7 miles round-trip. Easy to moderate. Access: Palomarin Trailhead, just off Mesa Rd. at the southern tip of the park. Map: Park map.

Recommended by locals, this trek is one of Point Reyes's prettiest. This section of the trail skirts a cliff offering stunning views and then passes several small lakes and meadows before it reaches **Alamere Falls,** a freshwater stream that cascades down a 40-foot bluff onto Wildcat Beach. Easily the longest trail at the national seashore, the Coast Trail continues on for a 15-mile one-way hike along the coast that is usually done in 2 days, camping a third of the way through at Wildcat Beach. (There's another campground at Santa Maria Beach.) The trail ends at the American Youth Hostel. You'll need a second car, however, to shuttle you back to the trailhead where you began.

Estero Trail, Point Reyes

Various trails ranging from 4–8 miles round-trip. Easy to moderate. Access: Estero Trailhead in Point Reyes. Map: Park map or USGS Drake's Bay topo.

This relaxing group of trails is a favorite with birders. The trails meander along the edge of Limantour's Estero and Drake's Estero. "Estero" is the Spanish word for estuary, and the brackish waters of these two draw flocks of waterfowl and shorebirds as well as many raptors and smaller species.

Tomales Point Trail, Point Reyes

11 miles round-trip. Easy to moderate. Access: Trailhead is at the Pierce Ranch parking area in Point Reyes. Map: Park map or USGS Tomales topo.

The Tomales Point Trail is one of the best hikes in the state to see wildlife. In addition to the views of rugged shoreline, the watering hole 3 miles into this hike is home to the park's herd of tule elk. Elk trails lead off the main trail, offering many side-trip possibilities. Keep an eye out for poison oak's waxy three-leaf clusters. Also be sure to check for ticks as the Lyme disease–carrying black-legged tick is common here.

Stewart Trail, Point Reyes

9 miles round-trip. Moderate. Access: Five Brooks Parking Area. Map: Park map.

This trail to Wildcat beach is one of the few unpaved trails in the park open to mountain bikes and is also quite popular with horseback riders. It's quite steep and not nearly as scenic as most other trails.

Abbotts Lagoon Trail

3 miles round-trip. Easy. Access: Abbotts Lagoon Trailhead Parking Area on Pierce Point Rd. Map: Park map.

If you're looking for a short, easy trail located well away from the masses, this is the one. After climbing a small ridge, you're led down to Abbotts Lagoon, a popular watering hole for migratory birds.

Mount Wittenberg Trail

2 miles one-way. Moderate to difficult. Access: Bear Valley Trailhead. Map: Park map.

This huffer-puffer weeds out the weenies due to its steep elevation, peaking at 1,407 feet rather abruptly. Start at the Bear Valley Trailhead, south of the parking area, and turn right on to the Mount Wittenberg Trail after 0.2 miles. The trail up the ridge is steep but rewards hikers with great views back east across the Olema Valley. Instead of turning around directly, if you still have the energy, you

can loop back along Baldy Trail and take an alternative path such as the Meadow Trail back to Bear Valley Trail, the main route home.

Phoenix Lake

2.75 miles. 1.5 hr. Easy to moderate. Access: Trailhead is at the end of the small parking lot 1 mile west on Lagunitas Rd., at the road's end. Map: USGS San Raphael.

It is one of the small tragedies of Bay Area life that swimming is prohibited in Phoenix Lake. This small body of water, only 25 acres in total area, would be a swimming hole straight out of Mark Twain, were it not off-limits as part of the local drinking supply. Fortunately, the trail around the lake is a beautiful, quick hike through the cattails and along the sandy hills beside the water. After a short climb to the lake's edge, head left and follow the shoreline trail toward the cove at the lake's south end. Past the turnoff toward Mount Tam's summit, the trail climbs to a small overlook that's popular for fishing (bass mostly). Continue another 10 minutes to a glade with welcome shade and a small bridge to the opposite bank, where you pick up the trail along the west shore. For about a mile, you'll follow a rolling path beside a creek, then emerge onto a wide dirt road for the walk back to your car. There's a drinking fountain about a hundred yards east of that intersection. There's also a porta-potty at the trailhead.

Overnights

Wildcat Camp and Beach, Point Reyes National Seashore

11.4 miles. Moderate to difficult. Allow 2 or 3 days. Access: Palomarin Trailhead at end of Mesa Rd. north of Bolinas. Map: Point Reyes trail map or USGS Double Point topo.

This continuation of the Bass Lake day hike passes three more freshwater lakes, the largest of which, Pelican Lake, is enhanced by having its own ocean view, but is almost impossible to reach because of thick brush. The coastal trail here winds through the eucalyptus and past thick berry vines. In the spring and summer the whole trail is lined with sticky monkey flowers and lupine. After almost 6 miles of hiking from the trailhead, you'll reach Wildcat Camp, a large meadow with running water. Several picnic tables mark the campsites, and sandy Wildcat Beach is a short walk away. Reservations to camp here are required and are available from the park headquarters at Bear Valley (☎ 415/663-1092).

HORSEBACK RIDING

A popular day trip on horseback is to ramble around **Point Reyes.** Horses are available at **Five Brooks Stables,** in the small town of **Olema** near the park office (☎ 415/663-1570). Horse trails head up the back of the Point Reyes ridge, which is shaded in the afternoon, to an overlook offering views of the coast below and the oak-covered hills to the east.

KAYAKING

Marin is a sea kayaker's dream come true. In addition to the bay itself, Tomales Bay, Drakes Bay, Bolinas Lagoon, and Richardson Bay are all classic sea-kayaking adventures. **Sea Trek Ocean Kayaking Center** in Sausalito (☎ 415/488-1000) teaches sea kayaking and has a rental fleet of sit-on-top and closed-cockpit boats right on the edge of Richardson Bay. The center also offers guided night-kayaking tours in Richardson Bay nearly every full moon. **Pacific Currents** (☎ 800/465-2925) also leads trips, particularly at north-county spots like Tomales Bay and Drakes Bay.

One of the better sources of kayaking information in the area is **California Canoe and Kayak,** which rents and sells sea kayaks at two locations. The Half Moon Bay branch (☎ 650/728-1803) rents kayaks and runs tours, which generally head along the bay coast, where

there's a good chance of seeing sea lions and, if you're lucky, even whales.

Tomales Bay
Access: Pt. Reyes National Seashore, 1 mile north of the town of Inverness.

This long, narrow finger of Pacific water separates the northern half of Point Reyes from the Marin mainland, offering a vast tidal marsh to explore. The bay is placid enough on its southern end to invite excursions out of the tree-lined coves and onto the open water. Rentals and instruction are available at **Blue Waters Kayaking** in Inverness (☎ 415/669-2600). Blue Waters also runs overnight kayak trips on Tomales Bay.

MOUNTAIN BIKING

The mountain bike was officially invented here in 1977, and well into the 1980s Mount Tam was the hub of the off-road biking world. When mountain biking really took off, the pressure became too much for Marin to bear, and the forces of hiking and horseback riding united to ban bikes from all Mount Tamalpais single-track trails. Luckily, numerous fire roads web the mountain, and these remain open, though a 15-mile-per-hour speed limit is enforced. For maps of bikeable areas in **Mount Tamalpais State Park,** contact the visitor center (☎ 415/388-2070). The Marin Municipal Water District also owns much of Mount Tam, though they also enforce the single-track ban and speed limit. Point Reyes also allows mountain bikes on the Abbotts Lagoon Trail, the Stewart Trail, the Estero Trail, the Olema Valley Trail, and part of the Bear Valley Trail. For maps of other trails in the area contact the **Bicycle Trails Council of Marin,** P.O. Box 13842, San Rafael, CA 94913 (☎ 415/456-7512). For bike rentals, try **Start to Finish** (☎ 800/600-BIKE), which has several locations around the Bay Area, or **Mike's Bike Center** (☎ 415/454-3747) at 1601 4th St. in San Rafael.

Old Railroad Grade to Mount Tam Summit

13 miles round-trip. Strenuous. Steep with tons of switchbacks. Access: West Blithdale Ave., Mill Valley. Map: Mount Tam State Park.

This ride is the most popular route to the summit (other than the paved road). Following the bed of an old narrow-gauge railway that served a mountaintop hotel, it switchbacks over 100 times on the way to the summit. Pick up the Old Railway Grade about a mile out of Mill Valley on West Blithdale Avenue at the Blithdale Summit Gate. From here you just put it in a low gear, crank, and try to enjoy the scenery. After about 5 miles, you reach the Panoramic Highway and the West Point Inn. Cross the highway and pick up the grade again on the other side. From here it gets *steep* and switch-backy. Don't worry—it's only about 1.5 miles more, most of it straight up. You'll get there eventually and after a long rest it's all downhill. If riding down at 15 miles per hour sounds just too boring for you, there's always the paved road, but watch out for traffic there.

Bolinas Ridge Trail

28 miles. Moderate. Access: Hwy. 1 near Audubon Canyon Ranch and Bolinas Lagoon. Map: None needed.

Mountain biking is pretty much forbidden in Point Reyes, since most of the good trails are in the wilderness sections, but this trail just on the other side of Highway 1 gives you the same sort of terrain and no headaches. From the intersection of Bolinas Road and Highway 1, follow the Fairfax-Bolinas Road to the 1,300-foot summit overlooking the lagoon, Stinson Beach, the San Andreas Fault, and Point Reyes. Here you turn left on the Bolinas Ridge Trail, a wide path. For almost 10 miles you ride through redwoods, keeping pretty much to the ridgeline. The road begins to descend and breaks out into grazing land. Watch for cattle and shut all gates behind you. About 4 miles after leaving the redwoods you'll reach Sir Francis Drake Drive, giving you two return options. One is to simply go back the way you came. The other is to turn left on Sir Francis Drake into Olema and then take Highway 1 south to your car. The road is pleasant, but traffic sometimes whizzes through the windy curves here.

ROAD BIKING

Over the Hill and Around Muir Woods

30 miles. Strenuous. Steep climbs, fast descents. Access: Park at Vista Point on north side of Golden Gate Bridge. Map: Marin County road map or GGNRA trail and road map.

From Vista Point, a bike path descends down Sausalito Lateral and then weaves through Sausalito along the waterfront, where it is simply a bike lane, not a separate path. Soon a separate path branches off. Follow it until it forks left under U.S. 101. From here just follow the signs to Panoramic Highway, Stinson Beach, or Mount Tamalpais. After passing through Mill Valley, the Panoramic Highway catapults up the side of Mount Tam, alternating hideous climbs with outrageous views of the surrounding countryside and of the Pacific. Once you pass Pan Toll Station, it's a solid downhill blast to the intersection of Panoramic Highway and Highway 1. This stretch of road is winding, steep, and narrow. If you're up for the speed, I'd try to ride a little faster than the prevailing car traffic down the hill to avoid getting run off the road. Once you reach Highway 1 above Stinson Beach, you'll follow it south along one of the most stunning coastal roads in the world. Muir Beach is the last oceanfront on this ride and a good resting point. Then Muir Woods Road will take you back to the Panoramic Highway just outside Mill Valley. Turn right and return through Sausalito the way you came.

SAILING

The bay is one of the finest sailing spots on the West Coast—the Golden Gate allows Pacific winds through but stops much of the open ocean's rollicking swell. For a list of charter fleets and sailing schools in the Bay Area, see "Sailing" under "The Peninsula: What to Do & Where to Do It."

SURFING

Marin's surf conditions are tame compared to San Francisco's fierceness. **Stinson Beach** and **Bolinas** are the main spots. They are generally small and mushy, since both lie in the shelter of Duxbury Reef. **Livewater Surf Shop** on Highway 1 in the heart of Stinson Beach (☎ **415/868-0333**) rents wet suits, surfboards, and boogie boards. For wave info, call the **Marin Surf Report** (☎ **415/868-1922**).

WALKS & RAMBLES

Redwood Creek Trail, Muir Woods National Monument

1 mile. Access: Muir Woods headquarters.

Muir Woods is the striking remnant of the virgin redwoods that once covered Mount Tamalpais. The Redwood Creek Trail is a great way to get acquainted with these 400- to 800-year-old giants. The tallest tree in the park is 253 feet tall. Many others top 200 feet. Perhaps the most charming feature of this short trail is its proximity to Redwood Creek. The gurgling of the creek and the wind in the trees is a wonderful white noise filter to cover up the sounds of others on this popular (over a million visitors a year) trail.

Slide Ranch Tidepools

Short but steep. Access: Driveway on ocean side of Hwy. 1, 2 miles north of Muir Beach.

Slide Ranch is possibly the best tidepooling spot in Marin. Several large pools here contain nudibranchs, starfish, urchins, anemones, crabs, and tiny fish. Don't be intimidated by the steep driveway—you'll make it. Also on site is a small organic farm and environmental education center. Closed from November through February. Call ☎ **415/381-6155** for information.

Earthquake Trail, Point Reyes National Seashore

0.6 miles. Access: Bear Valley Visitors Center, Point Reyes.

The earth is alive here, as the Earthquake Trail will show you. The trail takes you through a brief but fact-filled informational tour of the San Andreas Fault as it slices through Point Reyes. You'll see sink ponds left when the earth collapses, slumping hillsides, broken fences, and a barn knocked off its foundation—all caused by the gradual but relentless movement of the fault.

WHALE WATCHING

Point Reyes juts nearly 10 miles out to sea from the surrounding coastline, creating an incredible bottleneck for coast-hugging whales on their migration. As a result, you can see more whales in a day here than any other place in the state. Of course that presumes that the fog cooperates. On a good day hundreds of visitors gather at the **Point Reyes Lighthouse** for the chance to spot 50 to 60 whales in an afternoon. Bring binoculars, as the point is several hundred feet tall and you'll be looking a long way down. During peak season, from December through March, the Park Service runs a shuttle from Drake's Beach to the lighthouse. Two other spots in Point Reyes, **Chimney Rock** and **Tomales Point,** offer just as many whales without the crowds. Other favorite lookouts are the **Muir Beach Overlook** and the **Pacific bluff tops** between Muir Beach and Stinson Beach on Highway 1.

During whale season **Oceanic Society Expeditions** (☎ **415/474-3385**) takes naturalist-led whale-watching boats from the San Francisco Marina to Point Reyes every weekend that the weather permits. The all-day trip costs $48 for adults and $46 for kids and senior citizens. No children under 10 are allowed.

The East Bay: What to Do & Where to Do It

The East Bay differs dramatically from the peninsula and Marin County. The terrain here is more rolling and the climate much drier. The cities also tend to be more sprawling, long fingers of development fragmenting the wildlands. Still, the parklands of the East Bay Regional Parks District (EBRPD) and the State Parks System hold many square miles of wonderful hiking and biking opportunities. The bay shore is another outlet; boardsailing, fishing, and sailing are extremely popular here.

BIRD WATCHING

The **East Bay Wilderness System,** operated by the East Bay Regional Parks District, is an important nesting and feeding zone for numerous species, especially the larger raptors. Though this part of the bay is often developed right to the water's edge, a few preserves like **Point Pinole Regional Shoreline** have sheltered the last remaining salt marshes. Migratory species heading into the Delta are often seen passing through here too. The EBRPD maintains a bird list and offers bird-watching interpretive programs at several regional parks. Call the main office (☎ **510/635-0135**) for more information.

BOARDSAILING

With predictable high winds that funnel in through the Golden Gate, but little surf to speak of, the East Bay Area is a popular hangout for boardsailors looking for a speed fix or beginners working on their oceangoing skills. Access to the bay, however, can be tough. **Berkeley's** waterfront, location of the city's marina and the Cal Sailing Club, is free of power boats and too shallow for anything much bigger than a dingy. That makes it a perfect spot for beginners. It's also sheltered by a breakwater and the nearby Ashby Shoal, which cuts your swells up for you into bite-sized chunks. The basin can get crowded on good days, and the local crowd includes boardsailing students and neophyte sailors. You'll see a lot of entertainingly frantic capsizes and "agony of defeat" wipeouts. Don't laugh. You might be next.

For the beginner, there are two primary areas on the San Francisco Bay offering respites from the demanding winds found elsewhere, plus reasonable equipment rentals and patient boardsailing instruction. **Cort Larned Windsurfing** (☎ **415/925-0543**), at Crown Beach, west of Oakland, offers boardsailing lessons and rentals by the hour, half day, or full day. You won't confuse Crown Beach with a postcard—it's a small strip of mostly landfill sand; the water is barely deep enough to swim in at high tide; and the shore turns to muck at low tide. But it's a perfect place to learn.

The second option, better for those who live in the area or will be staying a while, is Berkeley's **Cal Sailing Club,** located at Berkeley's marina (www. cal-sailing.org; no phone). It's among the better sailing bargains on the coast, but be advised that the club's sailboards tend to need some fixing before you head out. Members are expected to volunteer at the club for 4 hours over the course of a 3-month membership, plus pay a $48 membership fee. But lessons are free, and after you pass a sailing proficiency test, you can take the boards out whenever you want and sail the basin between Berkeley and Emeryville, a stretch of good air just less than a mile long.

FISHING

The town of **Emeryville,** located on the bay shore south of Berkeley, boasts a small but uncrowded sportfishing center at its marina; call ☎ **800/575-9944.** Berkeley's marina is a few miles north, at the west end of University Avenue, and runs one of the bay's newest fleets of boats, including a few up to a comfortable 60 feet. Live bait is available. For reservations call the marina at ☎ **510 849-2727.**

The best inland fishing spot in the area is **Lake Chabot,** located at the center of Lake Chabot Regional Park (☎ **510/ 892-2177**), which is part of the East Bay Regional Parks system. Like most of the East Bay parks, Lake Chabot seems more remote than it is. Located in the otherwise featureless suburb of Castro Valley, the lake is tucked into a narrow glen that obscures the surroundings and blocks out most of the surrounding sound. Chabot is regularly stocked with trout, largemouth bass, catfish, crappie, and sturgeon, and is a favorite spot among local freshwater anglers. The record bass to come out of the lake was a good 17 pounds, 10 years ago.

Private kayaks, canoes, waders, and sculling boats shorter than 20 feet may be brought to the lake and launched for a $2 fee. Other boats must be rented, or you can drop your line from the pier at the lake's west end, or head out on a boat. The boat launch is located at the west park entrance, which is the terminus of Lake Chabot Road.

At 315-acres, the lake is a little big to fish from a rowboat, but if you're looking for a workout, or just want to paddle around, you can rent one for $12 an hour or $32 a day. The same boat with a slow but quiet electric outboard costs a little more, but gets you fishing faster; it's $14 an hour, $33 for 3 to 5 hours, or $48 for the whole day. The required fishing license, which can be purchased at the boathouse, costs $10 for 2 days or $27.50 for the year, good anywhere in the state.

A small tackle shop sells hooks, lines, and sinkers at the boathouse, and several kinds of live and packaged bait. There is also a cafeteria at the boathouse. (You won't need the cafeteria, of course, since you'll be cooking trout on the park's picnic grills that afternoon.) Parking is $3.50 at the park.

GONDOLAS

Gondola Servizio

Access: At the Lake Merritt Boathouse, 568 Bellevue, downtown Oakland. Look for the Venetian gondolas. They're pretty obvious. ☎ **510/663-6603.**

Former Venetian gondolier Jeff Fischer decided in 1999 that what downtown Oakland really needed was two genuine Italian gondolas poling around Lake Merritt. He brought two with him when he moved back from Venice, and he now offers rides on the lake, with antipasto included. You won't confuse the experience with exercise. Then again, you won't confuse exercise with romantic nights on a lake ringed with lights. It's $55 for the hour sunset ride, $65 if you include food. In addition, for $225 a couple you get the *promessi sposi* special, for which the gondoliers wear 17th century costumes—you're supposed to be asking for someone's, y' know, hand. It's not a cheap fling, but it's a lot cheaper than a ticket to Italy, and you don't have to do any of the rowing yourself. All that's missing is the Ponte di Rialto.

HIKES, BUSHWHACKS & BACKPACK TRIPS

Day Hikes

Around Mount Diablo

7-mile loop. Strenuous. 6 hr. Access: Juniper Camp Trailhead, 2.5 miles up the summit road from south entrance. Map: Mt. Diablo State Park map.

Most visitors flock to the summit of Mount Diablo for the incredible view, but if you'd like to get a good look at the different ecosystems and geological zones on the mountain, this hike is better. Mount Diablo can get scorching in the summer and has little to no water, so get an early start on the day and bring more water than you think you'll need. The trail begins in a forest of giant live oaks, passes through chaparral, into a digger pine forest, over grassland, through more chaparral, more oaks, and of course, tons of poison oak. As you crest each ridge, you'll get a sample of what the view is like from the summit before plunging back into the next canyon. Eventually you'll have done a complete circle and will be back at Juniper Camp.

Little Yosemite

3.5 miles round-trip. Easy. 2 hr. Access: Canyon View Trailhead at Sunol Regional Park Headquarters. Map: Sunol trail map available in park.

This short trail crosses several creeks and wanders through an oak and wildflower wonderland on a hillside overlooking Alameda Creek. After a junction with an old ranch road you'll descend to Little Yosemite, a boulder-strewn, rock-walled canyon that seems more Sierra Nevada than Alameda County.

Redwood Loop

4 miles. Moderate. 1 or 2 hr. Access: Skyline Gate entrance to Redwood Regional Park, off Skyline Dr. in the Oakland hills. Trailhead is located behind the water fountain. Maps: Available free at the trailhead, in the wooden bin beside the parking lot.

This loop passes several interesting natural features, including redwoods, brushy hillsides, a stream, and a few non-native but sweet-smelling Eucalyptus groves. It involves three short but stiff hills, but is flat most of the way.

From the trailhead, follow the Stream Trail downhill until you reach a gate, where there is a picnic area. Walk around the gate, and then follow the stream for a few minutes through an open, brushy area. You may see a few snakes here, but they are likely harmless king snakes.

In less than a mile you'll descend from the grassland into the shade of a cool redwood grove. Go right off the Stream Trail at the end of the descent, cross the creek, and follow the path a few yards to where it forks. Take the left fork, called French Trail, up the steep hill 0.6 of a mile to Mill Trail, which winds further through the redwoods along a ridge and then descends. At the bottom of the hill you'll hook back up with the Stream Trail for the walk back. There is another picnic area at the intersection, as well as potable water and bathroom facilities. The site used to be an old logging mill, which may explain how quickly the redwoods thin as you head back and the forest becomes a eucalyptus grove. Follow the Stream Trail back the way you came. It's a little over a mile back to the trailhead.

Around Lake Chabot

9.1 miles. Moderate. Allow all day. Access: East Shore trailhead, Lake Chabot Regional Park. Maps: East Bay Regional Park District, Lake Chabot Map.

The circuit hike around V-shaped Lake Chabot follows four connected trails and includes a climb to an oak-covered ridge with a good view of the water, excellent bird watching, and several opportunities to drop a fishing line. It's a good hike for early in the morning. The trail is flat for the first half, and then meanders through the hills before dropping back to the water's edge. Starting at the Lake Chabot Marina, near the park office, follow East Shore Trail 1.7 miles along the shore until you come to a footbridge. East Shore trail leads through an open grassland next to the water, then connects to Honker Trail—perhaps named for the local ducks living along the lake's north shore marsh. Twenty minutes past the bridge, at 2.6 miles, you pass a pier that's said to be the best fishing spot on the lake.

At the pier Honker Trail turns uphill for 0.5 of a mile and connects with the Columbine Trail, which you should follow west, winding past the campsites at

Lost Ridge and back to the waters edge. After descending from the bluffs, you'll pass two other camping areas, Lookout Ridge and Hawk Ridge, both of which have views of the lake's narrow northern estuary, Bass Cove. The Columbine Trail then crosses the end of Bass Cove and hooks up with the Bass Cove Trail, which heads south nice and flat along the water. Somewhere in there you'll cross the Oakland city limits, but you wouldn't know it from the open hillsides. Traffic gets busier here, and you may see some mountain bikes. In 1.3 miles you reach the West Shore Trail, which you'll follow the last 1.8 miles along the lakeshore, passing a few more piers and paralleling Lake Chabot Road before ending back at the marina.

Most of the circuit is out in the open, and the Columbine Trail in particular gets hot. Bring sun screen, food, and enough water for an all-day walk. You might be able to drink out of the lake, but it's probably easier to drink from a bottle. Unfortunately, swimming in Lake Chabot is limited to a few designated areas, most near the marina.

Overnights

Oristimba Wilderness, Henry W. Coe State Park

22-plus miles round-trip. Strenuous. Allow 3 or 4 days. Access: Henry Coe State Park Headquarters, Pacheco Rte. Trailhead. Map: Henry Coe State Park map.

This state park is the largest wild tract of public land in the East Bay, and this hike will take you to the most remote corner. Because the park was formerly a ranch, many of the trails are old ranch roads. That's actually a good thing, because the area is steep, and poison oak lines the trail in many areas so the extra width is a nice buffer. You'll go through an interesting dry woodland of Digger pines, laurel, buckeye, and several different kinds of oak. The main destinations, though, are the three biggest lakes in the park: Coit, Kelly, and Mississippi reservoirs. With

plentiful water, good swimming, and sometimes spectacular bass fishing, these lakes are a good place to spend a couple days in the spring or fall.

KAYAKING

One of the better sources of kayaking information in the area is **California Canoe and Kayak,** which has a branch in Oakland on the water at Jack London Square (☎ **510/893-7833**), providing access to the Oakland estuary. A least tern refuge is located nearby.

Newark Slough

Access: Off Hwy. 880 in Newark. Drive to the east end of the Dumbarton Bridge, taking the frontage road half a mile north to the San Francisco Bay National Wildlife Refuge visitor center. Put-ins are available past the visitor center at the marsh's edge.

Often overshadowed by the East Bay and Marin, the wetlands on lower San Francisco Bay's east shore are little-known and not often visited. They're also far enough from the Golden Gate to make for placid, easy kayaking. Much of these wetlands were lost to development in recent decades, so the refuge is off a lot of people's radar; you may have it to yourself. This is a good place for spotting waterfowl—ducks of several kinds, grebes, and cormorants, among others— or just getting out on the bay in an unusually uncrowded corner. The Dumbarton Bridge, connecting Newark on the east shore to Palo Alto, is an unfortunate drawback, with occasionally heavy traffic and unremarkable architecture.

MOUNTAIN BIKING

The backcountry of the East Bay is laced with an elaborate network of fire roads and water district maintenance grades that link the major East Bay parks. Due to heavy use, however, there is virtually no single track open to bikes. Still, it's great to be able to do a nice fire road ride within an easy pedal of Berkeley and Oakland. For info on renting a bike try **Start to Finish** (☎ 800/600-BIKE), which has several locations throughout the Bay Area, or **Missing Link Bicycles** (☎ 510/843-7471) at 1988 Shattuck Ave. in Berkeley.

Tilden and Wildcat Canyon Regional Parks
16 miles. Moderate. Access: Wildcat Canyon Dr. in Tilden Park. Map: Tilden and Wildcat Canyon maps.

From the Lone Oak Picnic Area, take the Meadow Canyon Trail to the Curran Trail. Soon you'll reach Wildcat Gorge Trail, which veers right. Both these trails run in a beautiful and narrow canyon lined with springs and lush riparian growth. They are often closed in the rainy season, in which case you should simply detour on the Meadow Canyon Trail. Either way, you end up on the Wildcat Creek Trail edging along the boundary of Tilden Nature Area, an ecological study area, and Jewel Lake. Bikes aren't allowed in the nature area. After almost 5 miles along Wildcat Creek, the Belgum Trail veers right and uphill almost to the top of "No Way Hill." At this point you're on the San Bruno Ridge Trail, which soon hooks up with Nimitz Way and a smooth coast down to your starting point.

Henry W. Coe State Park
Distance varies. Strenuous. Access: Park Headquarters 20 miles southeast of San Jose. Map: Henry W. Coe State Park map.

Some of the roughest, toughest mountain biking in California is here in the ranch country of this huge coast range park. More than 200 miles of old ranch roads and single track climb and plunge over, down, and around the neck-straining topography of the park. Almost all of it is open to bikes, with the exception of the Orestimba Wilderness in the east end of the park. This is not the place for a first-time ride or a new-bike shakedown cruise. The terrain is extremely unforgiving, the climate can be positively brutal,

and if you blow it and break something it's going to be a long walk home or a long wait for rescue. That said, this is heaven for solid riders. There is little hiker traffic, and the distances between points of interest are perfect for the pace of mountain biking. In spring the weather is best, the creeks are flowing (lots of swimming holes in Coyote Creek), and the wildflowers are amazing.

Mount Diablo State Park
Distance varies. Moderate to strenuous. Access: South Park entrance near Danville. Map: Mount Diablo State Park map.

Until 1990, bikes were banned on Diablo, a terrible waste of some of the best fire roads in the Bay Area. Thanks to the constant lobbying of the Bicycle Trails Council of the East Bay and other mountain-biking advocates, the park officials relented and threw open most fire roads and a few short sections of single track. Park elevations range from the 3,849-foot summit to down around 500 feet, and fire roads range all over the mountain. If you're looking to pound some vertical, you can bike up the summit road on asphalt and then drop down the Summit Trail or North Peak Trail. Not looking for that much of a thrill? Well, then the Wall Point Road near Sentinal Rock and Barbecue Terrace Road makes a nice 7-mile loop. Bring lots of water bottles as it gets really hot here.

ROAD BIKING
Mount Diablo Summit Ride
29 miles (14.5 up, 14.5 down). Access: Downtown Danville. Map: Diablo State Park map.

Begin in downtown Danville, a pleasant little town with plenty of cafes and water fountains to fuel up for the grind ahead. Take Diablo Road to the south entrance of the state park, marked by two stone pillars and a sign. From here, South Gate Road begins climbing at a steady but not oppressive 6% grade. Eventually you turn right on Summit Road and the climb continues. From the Summit Road turnoff, it is 5 miles and 1,500 feet to the summit parking lot and observation building, all but the last 300 yards a gentle climb. (The last 300 yd. is a killer, but it's only 300 yd.) On a clear day you can soak up the view while resting. I'm not sure if I believe them, but according to people who tally these kinds of things, Mount Diablo is second in the world to Mount Kilimanjaro for the number of square miles of land you can see from its summit, something like 400,000 square miles. When you're good and ready, check those brakes and whoosh home.

Grizzly Peak

12–30 miles. Moderate/Strenuous. Access: Old Tunnel Rd., Hwy. 24 just before the Caldicott Tunnel. Map: East Bay road map, Compass Maps.

The Oakland and Berkeley hills, marking the eastern borders of those adjacent cities, are among the Bay Area's most popular road-riding areas, and Grizzly Peak is one of the most popular rides. Starting at Old Tunnel Road, you'll climb past homes rebuilt after the devastating fire of 1991. In the first mile you should pass one shaped like a saxophone, or you're not on the right road. You'll know when you see it.

Continue winding uphill on the narrow road—watch out for bikes descending—until it flattens out, right before the intersection of Grizzly Peak and Skyline Drive. You can turn around here and head back, or turn left onto Grizzly peak. After a few yards of more shallow climbing, the road will drop and then begin gently rolling, offering excellent views off your left shoulder of the bay, San Francisco, Mount Tam, and the Golden Gate Bridge. You'll then descend to Fish Creek Road. A left brings you screaming downhill into Berkeley. Turn left again at the Claremont Hotel to return to Old Tunnel Road and your car.

If you go straight at Fish Creek Road instead, you'll climb considerably and

steeply again for a little over a mile, then continue along the ridge of the Berkeley Hills. At the signs for Tilden Park, a left will again bring you plummeting down into Berkeley, while a right will put you into Tilden Park, where you can tour the quiet roads before circling, climbing out of the park, and heading back the way you came.

SAILING

Lake Merritt, located in the center of downtown Oakland, offers the safest, calmest water on the coast for dinghy sailing. It's a small, shallow (only 8 ft. deep at its deepest point), attractive body of water with a view of town and a good bend in the center, so you feel like you've gotten somewhere. It also drains to the Oakland estuary, so is responsive to tides and gets low twice a day, limiting the sailable area slightly. Granted, this is not the open ocean, but it's a perfect place for novice sailors to practice their tacks and gibes, and find some inexpensive, placid sailing within walking distance of the subway. Access to the water is on the west shore of the lake, at 568 Bellevue Ave. in downtown Oakland (☎ 510/444-3807). Boat rental and sailing lessons are very affordable, and make a good activity after a hike in the nearby Oakland hills. El Toros are $6 an hour; a faster Sunfish is $8. You must also leave a $10 deposit. Despite the urban environment, the lake also has excellent bird watching. Snowy egrets and pelicans live here, and there's an aviary just north of the boathouse.

WALKS & RAMBLES
Mount Diablo Fire Interpretive Trail
0.7 miles. Access: Summit Observation Tower, Mt. Diablo State Park.

This short hike, best done in spring, circles just below the summit of Mount Diablo through an area swept by wildfire in 1977. A brochure that you can purchase at the summit visitor center will explain the fire recovery process, now nearly completed. From February through

---

Seafaring from Oakland

Oakland's waterfront at Jack London Square is an excellent place to kayak, with rentals available. Dinghy's are also available for sailing in the Oakland estuary, and boats for the bay can be rented just across the estuary (via a tunnel), at Ballena Bay in Alameda. Just be advised that the Port of Oakland is notable as the source of all those enormous container ships bearing down on you. There's supposed to be some sort of regulation allowing small vessels to have the right of way over powered vessels. If there is, it's irrelevant. Those behemoth intercontinental ships move faster then you might think, and take 2 miles to slow down, so it's important to glance over every once and a while and make sure the *Titanic* isn't heading your way. They're the windshield, you're the bug.

May, wildflowers bloom on the slope that the fire once charred.

Monument Trail, Henry W. Coe State Park

1.6 miles. Access: Headquarters, Henry W. Coe State Park.

After exploring the 19th-century ranch headquarters at the visitor center, you can take this brief but interesting trail up to a good view knoll that overlooks much of this huge park. Again, spring is the best time to take this hike. The wildflowers and clear days make for spectacular views of the Sierra Nevada to the east and the Santa Cruz Mountains to the west.

Campgrounds & Other Accommodations

CAMPING

The Peninsula

As you might imagine, camping on the San Francisco Peninsula is less than plentiful and in high demand. There is no official camping in San Francisco, so if you must stay in the city, see "Inns & Lodges" later in this section. It's still possible to find a nice place to camp on the peninsula outside of San Francisco, however, if you're willing to make reservations through the dreaded PARKNET service or to travel in the off-season, which really isn't as bad as it might be, since the weather is better here in winter than summer anyway. As tempting as it might be to pull your van to the side of the road along Highway 1 and crash in the back, don't do it unless you're prepared to deal with rude cops with bright spotlights. San Mateo County, which controls most of the wild area in this chapter, has draconian laws against sleeping in your car. You're much better off paying for a site in Butano or Half Moon Bay State Park, if you can get one, or guerrilla camping in a residential neighborhood or remote mountain road. Better yet, plan your visit to leave time to get to either Marin or Santa Cruz before nightfall.

Half Moon Bay State Beach

7 miles south of Pillar Point Harbor on Hwy. 1; turn west on Kelly Ave. to park. ☎ 650/726-8820. 51 tent or motorhome sites. Flush toilets, water, fire pits, pets accepted. Fishing, hiking, swimming, biking, surfing, whale watching. No reservations. $16 per night.

The beach is a short walk from this level and unfortunately wide-open campground. On weekends it's a little too crowded for my taste. Still, the beaches of San Mateo County stretch in both directions; Pillar Point Harbor is a few miles north; and the mountains rise in the background.

Butano State Park
Just west of Pescadero Beach and south of the tiny town of Pescadero on Cloverdale Rd. ☎ **415/879-2040.** 40 sites. Flush toilets, running water, fire pits, pets accepted. Bird watching, hiking, swimming, biking. Reserve through PARKNET (☎ 800/444-PARK). $16 per night.

The best real camping on the peninsula. You can hike for miles from here or take the short drive down to Pescadero State Beach for a day by the sea. Also really interesting is the Pescadero Marsh nature preserve—miles of undisturbed freshwater creek and estuary at the mouth of Pescadero Creek.

Marin County
Angel Island
Reached by ferry from San Francisco Fisherman's Wharf or Tiburon Landing. ☎ **415/435-1915.** 9 environmental walk-in campsites. Tables, water, pit toilets, no fires. Hiking, biking, boating. Arrange ferry transport through Blue & Gold Fleet (☎ 415/705-5555). $7–$9 per night plus ferry (ferry runs weekends only).

The most unique camping option in the whole Bay Area is the Angel Island walk-in sites. It requires planning far in advance to get reservations, but where else can you be practically alone on a several-square-mile wild island with the Golden Gate Bridge, Bay Bridge, and San Francisco skyline all practically within reach? The closest sites are a mile from the ferry landing, so bring your gear in a backpack and go light.

Olema Ranch Campground
Junction of Hwy. 1 and Sir Francis Drake Blvd. in Olema. ☎ **415/663-8001.** 200 sites. Running water, flush toilets, showers, laundry, pets accepted. Hiking, horseback riding. Reservations accepted. $18–$25 per night.

Since Point Reyes doesn't have any car camping within park boundaries, this private campground picks up most of the business. Nearby is Olema, a quaint little town, and Tomales Bay to the north.

Samuel P. Taylor State Park
Sir Francis Drake Blvd., 6 miles east of Hwy. 1. ☎ **415/488-9897.** 60 sites. Rest rooms, running water, fire pits, food lockers. Pets accepted in campground but not on trails. Hiking. Reserve through PARKNET (☎ 800/444-PARK). $12–$16 per night.

Samuel P. Taylor is the closest public campground to Point Reyes but is also a great destination in its own right. The sites are right in a forested creek canyon. It can get cold here in winter, as the sites get little sun through the trees.

Pan Toll Campground, Mount Tamalpais State Park
Panoramic Hwy., Mt. Tamalpais State Park. ☎ **415/388-2070.** 16 walk-in sites. Flush toilets, running water, fireplaces, tables, wood for sale. Biking, hiking. No reservations. $12–$16 per night.

The little-known secret of camping on Mount Tam is that the best campground doesn't take reservations or fill up early. If you're willing to hoof it up a small hill, you can camp at the beginning of the Steep Ravine Trail and within a short hike of the mountain summit. I've camped here on busy weekends and had no problem getting a site as long as I arrived before dark.

Point Reyes Campgrounds
Point Reyes National Seashore. ☎ **415/663-1092.** 50 walk-in sites total. Water, pit toilets, fire pits, food lockers. No pets.

Biking, bird and whale watching, hiking, swimming, horseback riding. Reservations accepted. Free.

Camping within the park is limited to four hike-in camps. Two, **Wildcat Camp** (6.5-mile hike) and **Coast Camp** (1.8-mile hike), sit just above the beach. They are often foggy and damp, so bring a good tent and sleeping bag. **Sky Camp** (1.7-mile hike) and **Glen Camp** (4.6-mile hike), set in the woods away from the sea, are more protected from the coastal elements. Individual sites hold up to eight people. Camping is free, but permits are required and stays are limited to 4 days. Sites can be reserved up to 2 months in advance, Monday through Friday, from 9am to noon only.

The East Bay
Mount Diablo State Park
South Gate Rd. outside Danville. ☎ 925/673-2890. 60 sites in 3 separate campgrounds. Running water, flush or pit toilets, showers. Biking, hiking, horseback riding. Reserve through PARKNET (☎ 800/444-PARK). $12–$15 per night.

Hot and dry in summer, this is a great getaway in the winter or spring, when the view from Diablo's summit is clearer and the temperatures more bearable.

Anthony Chabot Regional Park
Redwood Rd. in Castro Valley. ☎ 510/562-2267. 10 walk-in and 35 regular sites. Running water, showers, flush toilets. Pets accepted. Boating, fishing, hiking, swimming. For reservations call East Bay Regional Park District (☎ 510/635-0135).

With 5,000 acres and a large fishing lake, Chabot is a popular local camping getaway. Fishing is great in the winter and spring, as is the hiking.

Henry W. Coe State Park
Exit Dunne Ave. from U.S. 101 in Morgan Hill. Go east 13 miles to end of road. ☎ 408/779-2728. 7 walk-in and 13

regular sites. Pit toilets, water available at the visitor center. Fishing, hiking, swimming, horseback riding, biking. $8–$12 per night.

Few people bother to drive all the way out to this huge state park, leaving more of it for the rest of us. The mountain biking is amazing here, as is the spring and winter hiking. Also of interest are the early California ranch buildings and equipment.

INNS & LODGES
The Peninsula
If you want to stay in San Francisco, the best place to look for hotel or other accommodation information is the **San Francisco Convention and Visitors Bureau,** P.O. Box 429097, San Francisco, CA 94142 (☎ 415/391-2000). You can also stop by the bureau's **Visitors Information Center** at 900 Market St. downtown.

Montara Lighthouse Hostel
Located just off Hwy. 1 on 16th St. in Montara. P.O. Box 737, Montara 94037. ☎ 650/728-7177. Reservations by mail only. Rates $9 and up.

The Montara Lighthouse Hostel is a beautiful conversion of the old coast-guard buildings into simple lodgings. Everything is deliberately simple but functional. It's always hard to beat a lighthouse for a view, and this is no exception.

Marin County
Steep Ravine Cabins
Rocky Point, south of Stinson Beach on Hwy. 1. Reserve 8 weeks in advance through PARKNET (☎ 800/444-PARK). $30 per night.

Once the getaway of wealthy and powerful San Franciscans, these 10 simple redwood cabins on Rocky Point south of Stinson are now available to the general public. Overlooking the raw surf as it strikes the rugged Marin shoreline, these simple two-room cabins are a deal you just can't beat—$30 per cabin per night, and they sleep four or five. With their woodstoves, outhouses, and no electricity, you'll be transported back to a different century.

Point Reyes Hostel

Limantour Rd., Point Reyes National Seashore, P.O. Box 247, Point Reyes Station 94956. Reservations by mail only. $9 per night.

With a well-equipped shared kitchen, this old ranch compound is a great way to be self-sufficient while staying in the park. If you do feel like eating out, nearby Point Reyes Station and Olema have a number of great restaurants. Within walking distance of the hostel is Limantour Beach and Drakes Estero, plus miles of great hiking. The hostel fills up early, so reservations are recommended. Maximum stay is 3 nights.

The East Bay

Claremont Resort and Tennis Club

Ashby and Domingo Aves., Oakland, CA 94623-0363. ☎ **800/551-7266** or 510/843-3000. Fax 510/848-6208. 269 units. $235–$395 double; from $300 suite. Packages available, including a 1-night package from $281. AE, DC, MC, V.

This 22-acre resort overlooking San Francisco and the bay straddles the municipal line between Oakland and Berkeley. The main draw is the spa, which offers five different types of massage and a variety of body care treatments—loofah scrub, mud and herbal wraps, aromabath, and Turkish scrub. Many fitness facilities are available, including an exercise room for aerobics and yoga classes, a weight room, two lap pools, and 10 tennis courts. The beauty salon offers a complete range of skin and beauty treatments. The cuisine—which is fairly standard—consists of nutritionally balanced menus of seafood, salad, and pasta.

3

The Monterey Bay Area

To write about Santa Cruz and Monterey in the same chapter at first seems ironic. Santa Cruz is bohemian and loose at the seams, a throwback to a more experimental time in American culture. Monterey and Carmel, on the other hand, seem to inhabit a loftier—some would say snootier—frame of mind.

In Santa Cruz, manners and mores are such that people will take off their clothes or otherwise get out of hand simply to make a point. In Monterey and Carmel, by contrast, everything is neat and orderly. I'm convinced no one has done anything overtly impolite here in decades. At least not since the wild and woolly days John Steinbeck documented in *Cannery Row* and *Tortilla Flats*—the sardine boom of the 1940s was perhaps the most famous (some would say notorious) period of Monterey Bay history. All those little fish made Monterey a rich town, but by 1951 the boom was over—the sardine population had been decimated by overfishing in the bay. They're only now beginning to recover, but squid, anchovy, salmon, and ling cod are all still commercially fished in the bay.

It's **Monterey Bay** that brings these cities and the surrounding landscape together. Besides its fringe of beaches, tide pools, sand dunes, surf breaks, and scuba-diving spots, the bay is something much more. This is one of the most alive patches of ocean you'll ever find.

Comparable in size to the Grand Canyon, the **Monterey Submarine Canyon** begins just offshore of Moss Landing in the middle of the bay's crescent, and extends more than 90 miles out to sea. Within a half-mile of its head, the canyon is already 300 feet deep. It quickly deepens even more, and well offshore reaches a depth of more than 10,000 feet. Scientists speculate that the canyon began more than 30 million years ago as an onshore canyon (rather than a submarine trench) just west of present-day Santa Barbara.

All that cold, deep water creates a nutrient-filled soup for hundreds of species each year during the spring and summer upwelling season, when currents and wind push the warmer surface water out to sea and bring highly oxygenated water up from the canyon. That in turn creates a feeding and breeding frenzy on the lowest end of the food chain. Phytoplankton bloom in a huge bounty that doesn't stop until it reaches the highest level on the food chain: the whales, sharks, birds, and people who are the final recipients of the bay's riches.

Monterey Bay came by its name during the 1602 voyage of Sebastian Vizcaino, who christened it after his Mexican viceroy, the count of Monte Rey. Though it was one of the first major harbors discovered by early explorers and was an important stopover for many voyages, it wasn't settled until much later. Gaspar de Portola and Padre Junípero Serra made things permanent for the Spanish in 1770 when they built a *presidio* in present-day Monterey and a mission, the Mission Basilica San Carlos Borromeo del Rio Carmelo, in present-day Carmel.

The settlement of Monterey sounded the death knell for the culture of the Costanoan Indians who had inhabited this area for at least 10,000 years. To save their poor pagan souls (and provide a cheap and easy source of labor to construct the new city), the Spaniards rounded up the Indians in *rancherias,* small settlements where the missionaries converted them to Christianity. Syphilis, smallpox, and general despair ripped through the Costanoans and decimated their population.

The city was built and became the capital of Spanish California. From then until the gold rush, it was the busiest port on the coast and the political and cultural center of Alta California. However, the stormy half-circle embayment was never quite sheltered enough to use as a major commercial port in later years. And it was here, of course, that the Constitutional Convention met to set up the state's first government in 1849 prior to California becoming an official U.S. state in 1850.

With the onset of the gold rush, statehood, and increasing traffic to California, Monterey Bay was eclipsed by San Francisco Bay, leaving it and its surroundings to the fishermen, loggers, smugglers, and scientists.

The Lay of the Land

Officially Monterey Bay extends from Point Piños in Pacific Grove to Lighthouse Point in Santa Cruz. Unofficially, it exerts a much larger influence on the surrounding land and ocean. This chapter covers the coastal area from Point Lobos just south of Carmel to Año Nuevo Island just north of the Santa Cruz/San Mateo County Line, and inland to the Santa Cruz Mountains, which wrap down as far as Watsonville, and the Carmel Valley and surrounding hills.

On the northern edge of the bay, the redwood-covered **Santa Cruz Mountains** border a rugged coast of cove beaches and steep, fast-eroding sea cliffs. Though the mountains have been logged for over 100 years, numerous groves of beautiful *Sequoia sempervirens,* the coast redwood, were saved with the creation of Big Basin State Park in 1902 and the later creation of Henry Cowell, Wilder Ranch, and Forest of Nisene Marks state parks.

Año Nuevo Island and State Preserve just north of Santa Cruz are, together with the Farallon Islands off San Francisco, the most important breeding habitat of the northern elephant seal and an important feeding ground for the great white shark, which preys on the juvenile and adolescent seals.

Santa Cruz, a city of nearly 40,000, is known throughout California as the capital

of Northern California surfing. Famous breaks like Steamer Lane and Pleasure Point, plus numerous lesser-known spots, keep one of the world's most intensely competitive surfing scenes alive. The city gets great waves on almost any swell direction year-round and there are more surf shops per capita here than anywhere on earth. Mountain biking is another booming sport in Santa Cruz, with the fire roads and skid trails through the mountains behind town seemingly designed for long steep rides through the forest.

The redwood- and pine-covered **Santa Cruz Mountains** stretch all the way from Santa Cruz to the sprawling cities of the south bay. In the northern part of Santa Cruz county, a series of marine terraces demonstrates the continuing uplift caused when the Pacific Plate and North American Plate collide. (The Forest of Nisene Marks, a state park just outside Aptos, was the epicenter of 1990's disastrous Loma Prieta earthquake that did so much damage in the Monterey and San Francisco Bay areas.) Because of this uplift, the geology of the mountains is an interesting mix of metamorphic rock blended in alternating layers with sedimentary rock formed when this land was the ocean floor.

To the south, the mountains give way to the fertile **Salinas River Plain.** This is some of the richest land in the state. Also here is **Moss Landing,** an important commercial port, and **Elkhorn Slough,** a huge and relatively undisturbed freshwater estuary. Between Moss Landing and Monterey is a long stretch of coastal dunes caused by the omnipresent wind.

Monterey itself sits in the crook of a large and wooded peninsula with hills at its back and a rocky shoreline. The Pacific side of the peninsula is more windswept. Sandy beaches are here at **Asilomar** and **Carmel,** but also there is mile after mile of rocky, wave-swept coves and sheer drops into the sea. Sadly, in my opinion, this beautiful stretch has been overly commodified by the famous **17-Mile Drive.** The segment of Highway 1 just south of Carmel is equally beautiful and free of the toll booth, the busloads of tourists, and the ostentatious wealth. **Carmel** itself is a cute little town. Quaint almost to a fault, it is one of those former artists' colonies where the artists can no longer afford to live, but the beach here is wonderful for surfing, walking, kite flying, and just about anything else.

Outside Carmel you'll come to **Monastery Beach,** a famous diving spot (and also a rock-climbing area), then you'll reach the entrance gate of **Point Lobos State Reserve,** an unbelievable piece of coastal wildland. Inland from Monastery Beach, the **Carmel Valley** is beautiful ranch land quick becoming mini-ranchettes, and the secret access way to much of the Ventana Wilderness.

Orientation

Highway 1 is the main road of interest, running more or less within striking distance of the coast the entire way from Point Lobos to Año Nuevo. Between Santa Cruz and Año Nuevo the road runs right alongside the ocean with virtually no development save for the occasional Brussels sprout field or farmhouse. Several times the road climbs up to follow the top of precarious sea cliffs, and then plunges down to creek crossings and beautiful beaches like Scott Creek Beach or Waddell Beach. As Highway 1 heads south around the crescent bay, affluent tourist towns like Aptos and Capitola give way to busy agricultural centers like Watsonville and Castroville, home to much of the world's artichoke-growing industry.

Within the Santa Cruz Mountains, the two chief thoroughfares are **State Route 9,** a beautiful and winding two-lane road that leads to Big Basin and Castle Rock state parks, and **State Route 17,** connecting

Santa Cruz to San Jose with a four-lane freeway.

Pigeon Point Lighthouse
6 miles north of Año Nuevo on Hwy. 1.

The second tallest lighthouse on the West Coast at 115 feet, the Pigeon Point Lighthouse is still an important navigational marker for boat traffic between San Francisco Bay and Monterey Bay. It's accessible from 9am to 4:30pm. There is also an **AYH Youth Hostel (☎ 650/879-0633)** at the lighthouse's base.

Santa Cruz Surfing Museum
West Cliff Lane. ☎ 831/429-3429.

You can buy a T-shirt saying "real surfers don't have real jobs," or check out the very first wet suits (invented by Santa Cruz's Jack O'Neill) in this old lighthouse building. With its collection of historic and modern boards and a great exhibit of photographs and videos, the tiny museum is perfectly located on West Cliff Lane at Lighthouse Point—about 50 feet from Steamer Lane, Northern California's most famous surf spot. Hours vary and donations are appreciated.

Santa Cruz County Conference and Visitors Council
701 Front St. ☎ 831/425-1234.

The best source of practical information like hotel reservations, restaurants, and businesses is the Visitors Council office, located downtown. The staff isn't great for outdoor recreation queries but can probably point you to a local person who can answer your questions.

Capitola Town and Wharf
Unlike Santa Cruz, Capitola is probably a little too quaint for its own good. Its Victorian cottages and 1920s bungalows are beautiful, but Capitola seems to be succumbing to the kind of civic narcissism that allows a town to base its economy and self-image on T-shirts and coffee cups with the city name emblazoned on them because it's just so damn cute. The municipal pier is good for fishing and there is a nice sandy beach. If you visit after a storm, look for the fossilized shells that erode out of the cliff at the Capitola bluffs.

Moss Landing
For a look at what Monterey was really like during the *Cannery Row* era, go to Moss Landing. Named after Charles Moss, a New England sea captain who sailed these waters in the 19th century and turned Moss Landing into a whaling port, the little town is home to one of the largest commercial fishing fleets in California. Fishing boats are built here in large numbers and every day the fleet sets out to fish the rich waters of the Monterey Submarine Canyon, which begins about 200 feet beyond the harbor mouth. This is a town that instinctively faces the sea. It smells like fish, looks like fish, and is full of fish, most of which are immediately whisked to markets around the state. The California State University Marine Biology Laboratories have a laboratory complex on Sandholdt Road. On a clear day, the huge 500-foot twin smokestacks of the Moss Landing Power Plant make it easy to spot the harbor from anywhere in the bay.

Fisherman's Wharf
A major fishing pier during the sardine boom, Monterey's Fisherman's Wharf is now where they set the hook on huge

Monterey's Average Temperatures and Precipitation												
	Jan	Feb	Mar	Apr	May	June	July	Aug	Sept	Oct	Nov	Dec
High (°F)	60	62	62	63	64	67	68	69	72	70	66	61
Low (°F)	43	44	45	45	48	50	52	53	53	51	47	43
Precipitation (in.)	3.8	2.7	3.1	1.6	0.4	0.2	0.1	0.1	0.3	0.8	2.5	2.9

schools of tourists. Seafood restaurants, art galleries, barking sea lions, deep-sea fishing trips, and a constantly changing array of nautical-theme kitsch are the bait. It's located at the foot of Oliver Street and Del Monte.

Cannery Row

This street in Monterey was actually named after John Steinbeck's novel *Cannery Row,* rather than the other way around. Once the home to more than 20 separate canneries, the area is now a tourist trap anchored on one end by the Coast Guard Breakwater and by the Monterey Bay Aquarium on the other. Several small beaches and stairways provide water access to some of the best shore-launched scuba diving anywhere, but parking is tough.

Monterey Bay Aquarium

886 Cannery Row, Monterey. ☎ 831/648-4888 for information, 831/648-4937 for advance tickets. Open daily 10am–6pm.

The best way to understand the workings of Monterey Bay and its surroundings is to spend an afternoon in this amazingly designed aquarium. From a three-story-tall kelp forest exhibit to the first successful jellyfish display, the staff of the Monterey Bay Aquarium keeps on the cutting edge of aquarium design. Particularly notable is the way the museum displays ecosystems rather than individual species. Indoors and outdoors interact beautifully in the sparsely constructed building. The kelp forest, tide-pool tank, and shorebird aviary lead to outside decks where you can watch whales go by and sea otters play. The museum is extremely popular on weekends and holidays, so make reservations if you can.

Pacific Grove Museum of Natural History

165 Forest Ave. in Pacific Grove. ☎ 831/648-3116.

Often overshadowed by the Monterey Aquarium is this great natural-history museum. With its large collection of area birds, fish, and mammals, you can learn a lot about terrestrial flora and fauna and the Monterey Bay area. There's also a selection of Native American artifacts. The museum is open Tuesday to Sunday from 10am to 5pm.

Point Piños Lighthouse

Asilomar Ave. and Lighthouse Ave. in Pacific Grove. ☎ 831/648-3116.

The Point Piños Lighthouse, which marks the southern boundary of Monterey Bay, has been operating longer than any other lighthouse on the West Coast—since 1855. The point is a great tide-pool area and also home to some small dunes. Whales are often sighted from here. The lighthouse and museum are open for tours Saturday and Sunday from 1 to 4pm.

17-Mile Drive

Travel writers love to gush about the beautiful, scenic, glamorous, quaint, dramatic, extravagant, natural, otherworldly 17-Mile Drive through the Del Monte Forest between Pacific Grove and Carmel. Well, in my humble opinion, it is way overrated. Basically, a bunch of filthy rich people have successfully monopolized a beautiful—but by no means the most beautiful—stretch of coastline and are charging you money at five separate toll booths to drive through their neighborhood and look at their ostentatious wealth under the guise of checking out a bunch of natural wonders. I'm not denying that there are nice beaches, vistas, etc., here, but I think that these people should be hung by their gilded thumbs for trying to cut you and me off from beaches and oceanfront that by law we own. To do that they've promoted a road as a tourist attraction. Come on, it's just a road. We already own the beaches and ocean. Just let us drive to them.

Carmel-by-the-Sea

I'm waiting for the hyphenators in City Hall to change the name to Ye-Olde-

Scenic-Carmel-by-the-Sea-Great-Paradise-of-All-Arty-and-Quaint-Plus-Lots-of-T-Shirt-Shops-Scenic-Area-and-Historical-Zone-Aren't-We-Cute? But then again, that would be too hard to fit on a coffee mug. Nonetheless, Carmel is actually a nice place to go to the beach. The city beach at the foot of Ocean Avenue is backed by great dunes and is a really fun place to fly a kite, run down the dunes, roll in the sand, and splash in the waves. During the winter, surf can get really good here.

And if you look past entrepreneurs' attempts to capitalize on the town's inherent quaintness, some of the charm that made Carmel an artists' colony in the first place still remains. Walk some of the narrow residential streets of small beach cottages. Street numbers aren't allowed in Carmel, so many of the houses have distinctive names to match their look. Call ☎ 831/624-2522 for information.

Monterey Bay Submarine Canyon

This unseen feature of Monterey Bay's floor provides a unique laboratory for marine biologists and other oceano-graphic research. Research vessels from around the world come to the area to study the bay floor's features and envi-ronment. The canyon itself is immense and mysterious, teeming with species normally found only in the deepest parts of the ocean. Picture the Grand Canyon, only hundreds of feet beneath the water's surface.

Though you can't visit it without a few million dollars in scientific grants, a bathosphere, and a damn good reason, the canyon affects much of what goes on in the bay's waters, and thus many of the experiences you'll have along the coast. Intertidal life, including rich tide pools and a large population of sea lions, are only the most visible parts of one of the world's most complex marine environ-ments, a picture of which is still just emerging.

Parks & Other Hot Spots

Año Nuevo State Preserve

21 miles north of Santa Cruz on Hwy. 1. ☎ **650/879-0227.** Open 8am to sunset. Fee and reservations generally required for guided elephant-seal–colony tours (☎ 800/444-PARK), but some spaces may be available first-come, first-served. Other park areas and beaches open at no fee. Bathrooms, visitor center, picnic tables, water. Bird watching, hiking, swimming, surfing.

This former dairy farm is most popular now as the site of California's largest breeding colony of elephant seals. From late fall to early spring, throngs of tourists come to see one of the most amazing close-up views of these gigantic seals as they breed and give birth (see "Hikes, Bushwhacks & Backpack Trips," below). The park is also great for hiking, bird watching, picnicking, and (if you aren't afraid of the great white sharks who cruise the area looking for tender seal pups) surfing. The old ranch buildings and visitor center let you look back to a more slow-paced time on the California coast.

Waddell Beach and Creek

2 miles south of Año Nuevo on Hwy. 1. Parking on road only. Bird watching, hik-ing, swimming, surfing, boardsailing.

Actually part of Big Basin State Park (see below), this beautiful beach is popular with surfers and boardsailors who come to ride the waves and bird-watchers or nature lovers who come to explore the beautiful wetland habitat of Waddell Creek.

Big Basin State Park

9 miles west of Boulder Creek on State Rte. 236. ☎ **831/338-8860.** Open daily year-round. Entrance and camping fees.

THE MONARCH BUTTERFLY

The gray whale may be the Monterey Bay's most famous visitor, but there's another migration that's equally impressive. And if you can figure out how it works, they might well give you a Nobel Prize.

Each winter, the monarch, a brilliantly-marked orange and black butterfly about 3 inches long, travels thousands of miles from Northern California to the warm southern air of Mexico. Leaving in fall and returning in spring, the species travels as much as 3,000 miles in total, taking several generations to complete one round-trip.

How these tiny animals can travel so far, through air streams that routinely toss about large shorebirds and knock over sailboats, is only the first mystery. The really odd part—and the part you can witness—comes when the butterflies stop to rest.

Miraculously (and somewhat disconcertingly), each new group of monarchs stops to rest in the same groves of trees, and often *the exact same trees,* as the previous generation. Keeping in mind that each butterfly lives less than a year, flying only part of one circuit and then dying, how does the next year's group know where to go? "Somehow they know their way, even though the butterflies returning to Mexico or California each fall are the great-great-grandchildren of the butterflies that left the previous spring," notes an organization called Monarchwatch, which tracks the peculiar circuit. "No one knows exactly how the system works."

Two of the best butterfly-viewing stops are located along Monterey Bay, one at the northern tip in Santa Cruz, the other on the southern tip in the town of Pacific Grove. (Pacific Grove takes its butterfly responsibilities particularly seriously, calling itself "Butterfly City," and levying a $500 fine on anyone caught "molesting a monarch.") The northern stop in the Monterey Bay area is **Natural Bridges State Beach,** 2531 W. Cliff Dr. in Santa Cruz. A wheelchair-accessible wooden path leads directly to the trees where the monarchs roost (See "Walks & Rambles," below).

Forty miles away as the monarch flies, the southern stop in the bay area is a grove of eucalyptus at the intersection of Lighthouse Avenue and Ridge Road in Pacific Grove, called the **Monarch Grove Sanctuary.** Look for the sign at the intersection reading CAUTION BUTTERFLY ZONE, beside the Butterfly Grove Inn.

Though solitary fliers, monarchs cluster together for warmth in the trees, where they can be found hanging by the thousands in bulbous clumps. These can be hard to spot at first, with the undersides of the butterflies' wings camouflaged a nut-brown color, making their little confabs look a lot like leaves or boughs in the tree. But look closely and eventually you'll spot individuals coming and going from the clumps, betrayed by the brilliant orange top-side of the wings. Occasionally, if you're lucky, a group will break apart, erupting in a burst of bright color.

For more information call **Friends of the Monarch,** in Pacific Grove, at ☎ 831/375-0982, between 9am and 5pm PST.

Camping, grocery store, picnic grounds, natural science museum. Wildlife, bird watching, hiking, swimming, surfing, camping, boardsailing.

Created in 1902, Big Basin was the first California state park. With more than 14,000 acres, beaches, waterfalls, virgin redwoods, and 40 miles of hiking trails, it is also one of the nicest. Rising from the ocean to high redwood forests, the park encompasses the entire Waddell Creek drainage and is home to all sorts of wildlife.

Wilder Ranch State Park
2 miles north of Santa Cruz on Hwy. 1. ☎ 831/423-9703. Parking fee inside park. Plenty of free parking on Hwy. 1. Toilet, no water. Mountain biking, hiking, bird watching.

One of the newest state parks, Wilder Ranch is paradise for mountain bikers. Where other state parks ban bikes from all but a few roads, Wilder encourages them to ride on almost all the trails, including miles of single track through redwood forests and open meadows. The beach here is closed to protect the snowy-plover nesting habitat, but the bike and walking trail along the coastal bluff is magnificent. The old ranch headquarters are operated as a historical site several days a week.

Henry Cowell Redwoods State Park
Main park 3 miles north of Santa Cruz on State Rte. 9. Fall Creek unit 2 miles farther. ☎ 831/335-4598. Fee for day use and camping. Toilet. Hiking, mountain biking, swimming, fishing.

Covering more than 6,000 acres of forest land, the two units of this park have numerous short trails through the redwoods and along the headwaters of the San Lorenzo River. There are 15 miles of hiking trails and swimming and fishing holes on the river.

Natural Bridges State Beach
2531 W. Cliff Dr., Santa Cruz. ☎ 831/423-4609. Fee. Changing rooms and toilet. Swimming, surfing, bird watching, butterfly viewing in season.

This park was named for a pair of natural rock bridges that once adorned the eastern end of this pocket beach. Only one bridge remains, however, and with the current rate of erosion, its days are numbered. But the cove beach and eucalyptus grove in the center of the park aren't going anywhere. Visitors are split between those who come to use the biggest sandy beach on the west side of Santa Cruz and those who come here to see the monarchs that nest in the butterfly grove every winter. The park is also home to good tide pools and the Secret Lagoon, a small freshwater wetland where you can find ducks and geese.

Steamer Lane
West Cliff Dr. at Lighthouse Point. Surfing.

Steamer Lane is one of the best surf spots in Northern California—a long point break set off by dramatic water-carved cliffs. Because it is sheltered from most prevailing winds yet exposed to virtually all swells, the Lane is great in everything from 2 feet to 15 feet. When the surf gets big, the waves crashing on the cliffs make entry and exit a bit dicey—plus it gets crowded. But if you can manage those factors, the waves more than make up for it.

Santa Cruz Yacht Harbor
E. Cliff Dr., 5 miles south of downtown Santa Cruz. ☎ 831/475-6161. Fishing, bird watching, kayaking, sailing.

Several outfitters, charter services, sailing schools, and fishing operations call Santa Cruz's harbor home. The U.S. Coast Guard, among others, is involved in boating instruction, with courses on how to handle a boat and navigate taught year-round. UC Santa Cruz also offers summer sailing classes here that are open to the public. Numerous excursion boats also originate here, for whale watching, fishing, and wildlife trips. Kayak rentals are available at several spots in Santa Cruz and points south. Be advised that winter storms shoal up the harbor mouth for weeks at a time, and the entrance can be really hairy on a big swell.

Inland Arana Gulch, the wetland from which the harbor was dredged in the 1950s, continues back and is a great spot for birding.

Schwan Lake
E. Cliff and 9th St. Boating, bird watching, swimming.

Once a brackish estuary, Schwan Lake is now a freshwater lagoon adjacent to a beautiful beach. A number of important wetland habitats are here and a corresponding number of birds come to take advantage of the biological bounty. Canoes and kayaks are allowed on the lake.

Pleasure Point
E. Cliff Dr. between 32nd and 41st aves. Fishing, swimming, surfing.

When the macho chest beating at Steamer Lane is too much to bear, Pleasure Point usually lives up to its name. Santa Cruz is famous for mean locals and hassles in the water, but I've never felt anything but good vibrations at Pleasure Point. The waves are good too. During big winter swells, the entrance and exit can be spooky because there is no beach; you leap off rocks and clamber back up when you want to leave.

New Brighton State Beach
1500 Park Ave., off Hwy. 1. ☎ 831/464-6330. Camping and beach activities, rest rooms. Fee. Reservations accepted for camping. Swimming.

From New Brighton to Monterey, the bay is practically one long sandy beach. The state beach here is really two separate parks. The beach is a popular swimming and play beach. On top of the bluff is the campground, wooded with Monterey pines; it's quiet, shady, well laid out—arguably the best in the immediate Santa Cruz area.

Forest of Nisene Marks State Park
Aptos Creek Dr. off Soquel Dr. in the town of Aptos. ☎ 831/763-7063. Hike-in camping, hiking, biking.

This primitive 10,000-acre state park is a favorite with mountain bikers and hikers looking for a bit of solitude. The formerly logged forest is now mature second-growth redwood. Though stripped bare by 1923, 70-plus years later the forest is starting to diversify back to a more complex redwood forest with layers of dogwood, bay laurel, Douglas fir, and tanbark oak. The Loma Prieta earthquake that demolished much of downtown Santa Cruz as well as huge portions of the bay area was focused here, and you can hike to the epicenter—fissures and fallen trees marked the spot for a few years, but these signs seem to have faded after heavy rains and erosion.

Seacliff and Rio Del Mar Beaches
State Park Dr., Rio Del Mar. 5 miles south of Santa Cruz. ☎ 831/685-6442. Trailer camping, fishing pier, picnic grounds, interpretive center, swimming.

These two wide and sandy beaches stretch 2 miles from the 500-foot pier made out of a former World War I supply ship to the mouth of Aptos Creek. They're popular summertime hangouts for people from the inland valleys and nearby neighborhoods of Aptos and Rio Del Mar.

Manresa Beach State Park
Sand Dollar Dr. off San Andreas Rd. exit from Hwy. 1, Watsonville. ☎ 831/724-3750. Fee for day use and camping. Camping, swimming, surf fishing, surfing, 64 tent camping sites.

Extremely popular with both locals and visitors from out of town, Manresa is a stunning park set on a bluff overlooking the bay. The bluff is covered by a mature grove of Monterey pines, where you find picnic grounds and campsites.

Sunset Beach State Park
201 Sunset Beach Rd., Watsonville. ☎ 831/763-7063. Fee for day use and camping. Toilet. No water. Swimming, surfing, bird and whale watching.

Sunset Beach is located on the northern edge of the huge dune fields that line the back of Monterey Bay. It has the best-preserved coastal dune habitat in Santa Cruz County. Important dune and beach plants like the mock heather, sea rocket, and the endangered Monterey paintbrush live here in healthy quantities. It's rare to find such a well-preserved dune habitat with all its strata intact from the water line to upland bluff. The beach is often windy, as it lies right in the crux of Monterey Bay, and fog is not uncommon. Birds, dolphins, whales, and sea otters can frequently be seen offshore.

Pajaro Valley Wetlands
Between Watsonville and the sea. Bird watching.

This 21-square-mile expanse of five sloughs is one of the most important wetland habitats in the Monterey Bay area, after Elkhorn Slough near Moss Landing. The five sloughs here—Gallighan, Hanson, Harkins, Struve, and Watsonville—however, are freshwater rather than brackish and support a different type of ecosystem.

Moss Landing State Beach

End of Jetty Rd. on north side of Moss Landing Harbor. Parking fee within the park; plenty of free parking a short walk away. ☎ 831/649-2836. Water, toilet available. Surfing, fishing, board sailing, bird watching, kayaking.

This relatively small beach park offers an inordinate number of things to do in the park or the waters surrounding it. Located on a sandy isthmus between Moss Landing Harbor, Elkhorn Slough, and the bay, the park is popular with surfers, surf casters who fish off the rock jetty, board-sailors, and kayakers and canoers who use the east side of the park as a convenient launch point to explore Elkhorn Slough. This is also one of the most popular spots to view huge numbers of shorebirds in the exposed low-tide mudflats.

Elkhorn Slough

East of Hwy. 1 at Moss Landing, reaching inland 7 miles to Watsonville. Kayaking, wildlife, bird watching, hiking, swimming.

The largest relatively undisturbed wetland in California, Elkhorn is a complex tidal embayment covering 2,500 acres of tideland, and several more thousand acres of grasslands and rolling oak woodland habitat. Archaeological evidence suggests this was an important center for the Ohlone Indians, who subsisted on the incredible population of tule elk and waterfowl that congregated here. The elk are gone but the waterfowl still come in huge numbers. More than 250 bird species congregate here during the winter and spring migrations, often crowding the back bays. Exposed tidal mudflats are an incredible source of food for both indigenous and migratory shorebirds on their way elsewhere. The **Monterey Bay Area Rare Bird Alert** (☎ 831/375-2577) posts a recorded message of interesting bird sightings in the slough and bay area each week. Many saltwater fishes use the slough as a breeding ground, including leopard sharks, halibut, starry flounder, bat rays, and smaller species like the northern anchovy.

Thirteen hundred acres of the slough are owned by the state as part of the **Elkhorn Slough National Estuarine Research Reserve and State Ecological Reserve** (☎ 831/728-2822). There is a visitor center at 1700 Elkhorn Slough Rd., hiking trails, guided walking tours, kayak tours, fishing access, and displays about the slough and Monterey Bay Marine Sanctuary. The visitor center is located in the middle of nowhere. To get there, follow the signs from Moss Landing and don't give up; it's a long way out here, but it is the best place to see and understand the slough in a single visit. **Kirby Park** (☎ 831/633-2461) on Kirby Road is the best place to get your own kayak or canoe to the water.

Salinas River Wildlife Area

1 mile west of Del Monte Ave. exit from Hwy. 1. ☎ 831/649-2870. No facilities. Bird watching, hiking.

The Salinas River flows 170 miles, mostly underground, to surface and enter the ocean here. A large and important nesting and feeding area for shorebirds that occupy a number of small islands in the river, the river mouth is also an important resting and congregating area for brown pelicans, gulls, and terns. Several endangered species of plants and animals are found here, including the Smith's blue butterfly and the snowy plover, which nests on the beach. South of here are miles of private sand dunes accessible only by hiking down the beach.

Marina State Beach
Dead end of Reservation Rd., Marina. ☎ 831/384-7695. Toilet. Water. Hang gliding, hiking, swimming.

Hang gliders have turned a Marina curse—constant onshore winds—into a blessing here. When the onshore breezes encounter the huge dunes, they create a powerful updraft. A hang-glider launch area and concession with equipment rentals and lessons is located here (☎ 831/384-2622). Even if you aren't here to fly, it's fun to watch and explore the dunes.

Jacks Peak Regional Park
End of Olmstead County Rd. off Hwy. 168, Monterey. ☎ 831/647-7799. $2–$3 per vehicle. Horse and hiking trails.

Monterey Jack cheese is named after David Jacks, an early dairy farmer after whom this park is also named. Equestrian and hiking trails lead through Monterey pines to views of the bay and Pacific.

Coast Guard Breakwater
Southern end of Cannery Row, Monterey. Parking, diving, rest rooms, boat ramp. Fee for parking.

The Coast Guard Breakwater marks the southern end of Cannery Row. Sea lions haul out on the jetty, and little San Carlos beach is a popular entry spot for scuba divers. Parking is up the hill with only a few spots for unloading gear at the beach.

Lover's Point
Ocean Blvd. at 17th St. Hiking, swimming, diving.

A dramatic headland with granite boulders and wandering trails, Lover's Point is a fantastic dive spot on calm days and a stunning place to watch the waves crash on other days. From the grassy hilltop, park trails lead down to Pacific Grove Beach, Lover's Point Beach, and Otter Cove. All three are used by divers to access the **Pacific Grove Marine Gardens Fish Refuge,** an underwater reserve reaching from the mean high-tide line down to 60 feet, all the way from the aquarium to Asilomar Beach. No collecting is allowed other than taking fin fish with a valid license. Shoreline Park runs the same distance between Ocean View Boulevard and the bay. One of the few **hyperbaric chambers (☎ 831/ 372-6660** in case of emergency), a recompression device used to treat diving accidents, on the West Coast is just to the east of Lover's Point.

Asilomar State Beach
Sunset Dr. and Asilomar Ave. in Pacific Grove. ☎ 831/372-4076. Toilet, water available. Diving, swimming. *Warning:* tides are unpredictable.

Sandy beaches are few and far between south of Point Piños, but Asilomar Beach is one of the most exceptional beaches anywhere. The fine-grained sand interspersed with granite rocks and tide pools has a brilliance unrivaled by any other nearby beach. Sandbars and offshore rock reefs form the best surfing waves on the Monterey coast. Diving can be good on calm days. In the 1970s a diver was killed by a great white shark here and his body was never recovered. The attack, chronicled in a *Rolling Stone* magazine story, began an era of shark-attack hysteria that has only faded in recent years.

Monastery Beach
South of Carmel on Hwy. 1. ☎ 831/ 624-4909. Toilet, water available. Swimming, diving, whale watching, surf fishing.

Part of Carmel River State Beach, Monastery Beach is one of the most fantastic dive spots in the world. The Carmel Submarine Canyon starts literally a few yards from shore, and dives on the canyon wall can be really spectacular. Surf conditions can be really scary here while you're diving. Swells come up out of the deep water with virtually no warning and whomp in a crashing shore break. To avoid this, enter on the northern end of Monastery Cove, not in the middle. This is an ecological reserve, so all marine invertebrates and plants are protected. Fin fish may be taken with a license. Rock climbers often climb on the 15- to 20-foot-tall granite boulders on the beach below Ribera Road, some of which are bolted.

Point Lobos State Reserve
4 miles south of Carmel off Hwy. 1. ☎ **831/624-4909.** Open 9am–5pm. Fee. Hiking, diving.

Point Lobos is everything the 17-Mile Drive is supposed to be but isn't. Wild and pristine, the landscape here is so beautiful that everywhere you turn you'll feel like crying. Entrance into the park is limited to only 450 people to preserve the solitude of the place, and a line often forms as people wait for one group of visitors to leave so rangers will let another enter. The 1,300-acre site includes several rocky headlands, coves, a creek, rocky beaches, offshore rocks, and Monterey pine forests. Though short, the hiking trails here are truly magical. Divers can enter the water in Whaler's Cove by reservation or by lining up for entry early in the morning. It's worth the hassle. Underwater, the granite rocks and spires are covered with extravagant numbers of sea anemones, nudibranchs, and gorgonians. Schools of bluefish, ling cod, and red snapper are seen in the kelp forests along with seals and sea otters. Proof of certification is required before entering the water.

What to Do & Where to Do It

BIRD WATCHING
Raptors such as the golden eagle, osprey, and peregrine falcon regularly hunt the grasslands surrounding all of Monterey Bay's wetland areas. Thousands of waterfowl use these same grasslands as an important layover on the Pacific Flyway, and all along the bay shore you'll find sandpipers, curlew, snowy plovers, brown pelicans, gulls, shearwaters, grebes, stilts, and avocets, to name just a few.

The world record for most bird species seen in a single day from one spot was set on the **Five Fingers Loop Trail** at **Elkhorn Slough,** with 116 separate species sighted in one day in 1982. The combination of the rich marine and wetland environments with the nearby mountains and forests makes this a particularly rich area for spotting diverse species.

The **Interpretive Center** at Elkhorn Slough, 1700 Elkhorn Rd. (☎ **831/728-2822**), keeps a master list of species sighted there, and also leads canoeing and kayaking trips into the heart of the slough. To find out the latest sightings in the area, call the **Monterey Bay Area Rare Bird Alert** (☎ **831/375-2577**), a recorded message of recent spottings and their location. **Moss Landing Beach** and the **Salinas Rivermouth** are particularly good for **shorebirds.**

BOARDSAILING
With fairly reliable wind and good waves, the beaches northwest of Santa Cruz are the best bet for wave jumping and surfing. **Cowell's Beach** is a traditional beginner's area, offering forgiving, predictable water sheltered by the northern lip of Monterey Bay. Equipment rentals and lessons are available from sail shops along Beach Street. It's also within walking distance of the Giant Dipper roller coaster at the nearby boardwalk, an excellent post-sail activity if the waves haven't tossed you around sufficiently. The only downside to Cowell's is the crowds. The beach sits right in the heart of Santa Cruz's summer tourism strip. You might find yourself dodging swimmers.

The location of **It's Beach,** opposite Steamer Lane's legendary surf break, means it's technically on the Pacific

Ocean and not Monterey Bay. That makes it a whole different kettle of fish, if you will, from Cowell's Beach, despite being only a mile north. Waves are higher and less predictable, and the wind blows harder, though still calmer than beaches farther north. There's a good sandy area below the cliffs to launch from, and the area has parking at the lighthouse. Casual observers may note a fair amount of nude sunbathing going on at It's, despite the beach's location in the heart of the West Cliff residential area. Welcome to Santa Cruz.

Davenport Beach, 10 miles north of Santa Cruz, is for neither the inexperienced nor the faint of heart. But those with expert-level confidence will find a good place to push their limits. Waves get as high as small buildings, and there's nothing blocking the wind for several miles up the coast. And there are sharks around. A surfer was munched here in the early nineties (he lived).

Waddell Beach, located 20 miles north of Santa Cruz in Waddell Creek State Park, is one of the best-known boardsailing areas in the state. The setting is spectacular, below a set of red cliffs at the mouth of a long, pretty canyon. This is definitely an expert sailor's spot, with consistently high winds. Though more broadly distributed, the waves get as big here as they do at Davenport, and the riptides can get you in trouble if you don't pay attention. The sharks spend some time around here too—an elephant-seal breeding ground is nearby. Don't dangle the feet.

FISHING

Inland fishing is pretty limited. The creeks and rivers of the northern half of the bay are either closed to fishing because of endangered runs of steelhead trout, or simply don't have any fish. The **San Lorenzo River,** which runs through Santa Cruz, is an exception, with decent but not extraordinary fly-fishing all along its reach.

Ocean and surf fishing is another story. Monterey Bay is one of the richest fisheries in the world and with a little conviction you can catch just about anything here. The fall catch of ling cod is a great deep-sea fishing adventure, with party boats pulling up fat 30-pounders every day. Salmon also run in the bay on an unpredictable schedule. Surf casters will find plenty of rocky points from which to cast their lines, but beware, fishermen die almost every year in Santa Cruz and Monterey when they're swept from the rocks by rogue waves. Stay well above danger's reach.

Greyhound Rock County Park between Waddell Beach and Scott Creek is a popular surf-fishing area with free parking and a trail down the bluffs. The **Santa Cruz, Capitola,** and **Monterey piers** are all popular with crabbers and bait fishermen after halibut and other game species. And an added benefit of fishing from these piers is that no license is required.

On the Monterey Bay, **Stagnaro's** (☎ 831/427-2334) is a local institution in Santa Cruz, with a venerable seafood restaurant on the city wharf to prove it. In addition to the restaurant, the company runs fishing trips that leave early and rarely leave anyone skunked. Call for reservations. Bait and tackle are available for purchase and rental.

A few miles away at the Santa Cruz yacht harbor, **Pleasure Point Charters** (☎ 831/464-3045) runs the 40-foot *Margaret Mary* for bay fishing daily. Near the *Margaret Mary* is the *Makaira,* a 50-foot bay boat owned by **Santa Cruz Sport Fishing** (☎ 831/426-4690). Chartering is available here, along with bait and tackle. Also in the main harbor is **Scurfield's Landing,** 2210 E. Cliff Dr. (☎ 813/476-2648), which sails daily. Scurfield's also has a good bait-and-tackle shop and can offer recommendations for what's biting and where.

On Monterey Bay's south end, most of the sportfishing fleet is conveniently located at the far end of **Fisherman's Wharf,** a 10-minute walk east of Cannery Row. Many of the boats in Monterey do double duty as whale-watching vessels, and are labeled as such. Indeed, if you go whale watching, you'll probably notice a few fishing poles stowed around the boat.

Two of the more popular sportfishing operators on the wharf are **Randy's Fishing Trips,** 66 Fisherman's Wharf, (☎ 831/372-7440; head to the right beyond the saltwater taffy shops); and **Sam's Fishing Fleet** (☎ 831/372-0577). If it's whale-watching season, you might try the less touristed harbor in Moss Landing, a small town half an hour north, easily found beneath the two towers of the local power plant; **Tom's Sportfishing** (☎ 831/633-2564) is a good choice here.

On Monterey Bay, many of the fishing operations also run whale-watching trips and bay tours. Late December to early February is peak time for whale watching. During those months, Randy's, Sam's, Santa Cruz Sport Fishing, Stagnaro's, and Scurfield's run whale-watching trips first, and the fishing has to wait.

HANG GLIDING

Marina, a town about 15 minutes north of Monterey on Highway 1, is popular with novices for its forgiving sand landings. **Western Hang Gliders**, located at the intersection of Highway 1 and Reservation Road in Marina (☎ 831/384-2622), offers lessons 7 days a week. There's also a pro shop there for experienced pilots. Launches are from the ridges over Marina State Beach, most of which top out at a few hundred feet. It's less grand than flying off Mount Tam, or Mount St. Helena in Sonoma, but the views of the Monterey peninsula and the surrounding bay aren't bad.

HIKES, BUSHWHACKS & BACKPACK TRIPS

Day Hikes

Point Año Nuevo Elephant Seal Colony

2.5 miles. Easy. Mostly flat. Allow approximately 4 hr. Access: Año Nuevo Main entrance off Hwy. 1. Map: Park map. Hike is docent-led Dec–Apr. By permit other times.

The elephant-seal breeding colony at Año Nuevo is truly amazing. Beginning in November, the 16-foot, 6,000-pound elephant-seal bulls begin staking out their turf on the beach and dunes of Año Nuevo Point. By January, the females, comparatively small at only 1,500 to 2,000 pounds, arrive to give birth and to mate. Yes, that's right—they give birth and then are almost immediately impregnated again. An elephant-seal cow spends most of her adult life pregnant.

The mating ritual is the most dramatic wildlife display I've ever witnessed. The huge alpha male bulls stake out a harem of anywhere from 2 to 20 cows and proceed to mate with as many as possible. All that sex makes them tired and vulnerable to attack from younger bulls waiting to sneak in and steal their harem. The vocal and physical conflicts between these 3-ton monsters literally shake the ground. Meanwhile, the cows and pups are just trying to stay out of the way. By the peak of the elephant-seal season as many as 1,000 seals line the dunes of the point.

Docents lead hikers within what seems like a few feet of the seals and share a wealth of biological information. The hike itself is easy, a flat couple miles round-trip along a beautiful coastal bluff and over a few dunes. Reservations (☎ 800/444-7275) are required for the hikes from December through April. A number of slots are kept open every day for people who show up early in the morning, but they go quickly. Call the state park (☎ 650/879-0227) for more information.

During the rest of the year, some elephant seals are in residence but not in the same numbers. Still, this beautiful dune landscape is one of the wildest oceanfront hikes in the area. You can enter the wildlife protection area with a permit from the state park visitor center.

Skyline to the Sea/Sunset Trail Loop, Big Basin State Park

10.5 miles round-trip. Strenuous. Allow 6 to 8 hr. Access: Big Basin Park Headquarters. Map: Big Basin trail map.

By combining a portion of the famous Skyline to the Sea Trail with a return on Big Basin's Sunset Trail via the Berry Creek Falls cutoff, you can see the best of Big Basin's backcountry in a single hike. The trail runs through lushly vegetated redwood forests and through a canyon adorned with several beautiful falls. The forest is very primordial after a winter rain, and 65-foot Berry Creek Falls is a roaring torrent. This is old-growth rather than second-growth redwood forest; some of the trees here reach 240 feet tall and are as large as 17 feet in diameter. There is an understory of dogwood and azalea and, like everywhere in the Santa Cruz Mountains, poison oak is common.

From the Park Headquarters, take the Redwood Trail (itself a great short hike) to the Skyline to the Sea Trail, which follows Kelley and Waddell creeks to the Berry Falls Trail. Continue up Berry Creek to Sunset Trail and return to the headquarters.

Ridge Trail, Henry Cowell State Park

3 miles round-trip. Moderate. Allow 2 hr. Access: Main entrance to park, off State Rte. 9 just south of Felton. Map: Henry Cowell State Park map.

Though the redwood forests along the creek bottoms in Henry Cowell State Park are the most popular attraction, the Ridge Trail is an interesting hike that passes through the redwoods and then climbs to a high ridge and former fire tower with observation deck. Along the way you pass through several different plant communities: the redwood forest, chaparral, and finally oak and pine forest. From the observation deck you can see for miles down into Santa Cruz and surrounding mountain canyons. There are so many crisscrossing trails in this park that it's difficult to stay on the right one. Just keep

bearing uphill and you'll eventually get to the ridge top.

Loma Prieta Grade–Bridge Creek Loop, Forest of Nisene Marks State Park

7.5 miles. Moderate to difficult. Access: Porter Family Picnic Area. Main entrance of Forest of Nisene Marks State Park. Map: Park map.

This hike takes you up a dramatic creek canyon through second-growth redwoods, then up a steep ridge and back down to the trailhead through the hillside that is the namesake of the October 17, 1989, Loma Prieta earthquake, which was centered near here. Begin by hiking up the Bridge Creek Trail from the picnic area. The trail follows Aptos Creek a short distance until heading up the lush canyon of Bridge Creek. After about a mile, you are forced to choose between a clockwise or counterclockwise loop. Counterclockwise gives you a better perspective as you go up the creek canyon. After about 3 miles you come to an old homestead site, now mostly gone after floods carried away the ruins. Here the Loma Prieta Trail veers left. It's possible to hike up the creek another half mile to delicate Maple Falls by rock hopping and bushwhacking along a faint trail. After switchbacking up a steep ridge, the Loma Prieta Grade will carry you back down to the trailhead.

Wilder Ranch Old Landing Cove Trail

3.6 miles. Easy. Access: Wilder Ranch parking lot. Map: Park brochure trail map.

This flat and wide trail allows some of the best lateral access along the bluff tops north of Santa Cruz. You'll walk out along a farm road through flower and brussels-sprout fields until you come to Wilder Beach. This beautiful beach is off-limits to protect nesting habitat for the endangered snowy plover. The trail veers north along the coastal cliffs and in about a mile a trail leads down to the old landing cove. A fern grotto below a cliff-top spring is a unique site here, only 25 feet above the Pacific. The very next cove north contains Seal Rock, a flat offshore rock popular with harbor seals and the occasional sea lion. Several trails descend to Sand Plant Beach. Most hikers turn around here and return to the park headquarters; however, the trail continues upcoast for another 3 miles to the 4-mile beach at Wilder Ranch's northern boundary. From there you can walk back along Highway 1 to your car.

Point Lobos Perimeter Trail
6.5 miles. Moderate. Access: Whaler's Cove, Point Lobos. Map: Point Lobos Park map.

Actually several shorter loop trails strung together to allow a hiker to traverse the entire waterfront of Point Lobos in a day, the perimeter trail is an ambitious hike. Not that it is so difficult; there is just so much to see. You'll want to go slow and stop for lots of lookouts. The perimeter trail is accessible from seven different spots along the park road, so don't feel obligated to do the whole thing. My favorite portion of the trail is the segment near Sea Lion Cove and Point Lobos. A spur trail leads out to the dramatic headland of Point Lobos where churning surf meets the harsh granite coast. Sea lions and seals play in the water and haul out on the rocks in Sea Lion Cove. Whale-watchers flock to this point in winter to see gray whales that sometimes come within 100 feet of the point. South of here along China Cove the water is more tranquil in the lee of the point and the beach is sandier. Pelicans, gulls, and cormorants are visible in large numbers in the air and on offshore Bird Island.

Skyline Nature Trail, Jacks Peak Regional Park
2 miles. Moderate. Access: Olmstead County Rd. off Hwy. 168 south of Monterey. Map: None needed.

Though only a 515-acre park, Jacks Peak is the highest point on the Monterey Peninsula, at 1,068 feet. The Skyline Nature Trail leads you up through oak forests and poison oak to a forest of Monterey pines and the summit where you can see all of Monterey Bay and the Carmel Valley on a clear day.

Overnights
Skyline to the Sea (Big Basin Headquarters to Waddell Beach)
11.5 miles. Difficult. 2 or 3 days. Access: Big Basin Headquarters. Park second car or arrange pickup at Waddell Beach on Hwy. 1, 18 miles north of Santa Cruz. Map: Big Basin trail map.

Big Basin is a remarkable park because it encompasses nearly the entire watershed of Waddell Creek from mountain crest to the sea. This trail takes you from the lush old-growth redwood forests near the park headquarters to stunning and wild Waddell Beach, following the creek most of the way. Several overnight camps make this a great 2- or 3-day hike; Camp Herbert is closest to midway at 7.5 miles. The other camps are within 2 miles of Highway 1 but are great for camping one last night before an early-morning shuttle. In summer, you must make reservations to use any of the three backcountry camps along this route by calling the park (☎ 831/338-8860) at least 2 weeks in advance. Fires are prohibited and there is a charge for camping. Though you can hike this trail either way, do it from headquarters down to the sea and save yourself a lot of climbing.

Sand Point Overlook, Forest of Nisene Marks State Park
12 miles round-trip. Difficult. 2 days. Access: Aptos Creek Trailhead in Forest of Nisene Marks State Park. Map: Nisene Marks trail map.

This 6-mile-each-way hike up the west ridge of the Aptos Creek drainage has many things to recommend it. Besides the hike up through mature second-growth redwoods and Douglas firs, you end up at Sand Point Overlook, one of the most dramatic vistas in the Santa Cruz Mountains. The view from here stretches all the way across Monterey Bay and down into the Bridge Creek and Aptos Creek drainages. The trail camp is a short distance north on the West Ridge Trail.

From Sand Point it is also possible to return down the Aptos Creek fire road and China Creek. Though this extends the hike to nearly 20 miles, it does allow you a different return route through some interesting terrain. Mountain bikers use this road a lot, so keep your ears open for descending cyclists.

HORSEBACK RIDING

Redwood Riding Adventures rents horses for forest rides in the Santa Cruz Mountains. The stables are located in Felton, 6 miles east of Santa Cruz on State Highway 9. Call ☎ **408/335-1334** for information.

KAYAKING

With much less recreational traffic and virtually no large ships to bother you, Monterey Bay is even better than San Francisco Bay when it comes to kayaking. The coves on the Pacific side of the Monterey Peninsula, as well as the beachfront area near the town of Pacific Grove and Monterey proper, are prime areas for kayak views of sea lions, whales, dolphins, and tide pools. **Monterey Bay Kayaks,** 693 Del Monte, Monterey (☎ **831/373-KELP**), is one of the biggest dealers of ocean kayaks in the world. It has a complete line of rental boats and leads tours and classes on a regular basis. Reservations are recommended.

On the other end of Monterey Bay, Santa Cruz has more surf and swimming traffic to contend with, and the coast is generally more developed, but excellent open water opportunities remain. In Santa Cruz, **Venture Quest,** 125 Beach St. (☎ **831/427-2267**), is both a shop and a rental and teaching facility. The **Kayak Connection** (☎ **831/479-1121**) in the

yacht harbor, rents and sells equipment, plus offers guided bird watching, sunset, and moonlight bay tours. Some companies run trips to explore the wetlands of **Elkhorn Slough,** and the state park system (☎ **831/728-2822**) also periodically offers kayak tours of the slough.

Getting your kayak to the water without too much of a hike can be a challenge in parts of the bay. **Davenport Landing Beach,** about 8 miles north of town, is one popular launching point. In Santa Cruz, **Twin Lakes, Seabright,** and **Capitola beaches** are commonly used. To access the Elkhorn Slough wetlands you can either launch at **Moss Landing State Beach** and paddle up the slough through a large tidal basin or put in at **Kirby Park,** at the end of Kirby Road off Elkhorn Road (☎ **831/633-2461**), in the heart of the slough. Monterey kayakers deal with huge parking hassles along the bay front to unload their boats. The **Coast Guard Breakwater** at the south end of Cannery Row is the closest you can get your car to the water and has loading zones. Parking is up the hill in the city lot. **Lover's Point** is another possibility, though you'll have to carry your boats a little farther.

The only **white-water kayak** run in the Monterey Bay area is the **San Lorenzo River** between Henry Cowell State Park and town. An extremely reactionary river, it flows very dramatically with even a small rain. The best time to run it is a few days after a good rain when the river calms down again. The rapids on this run are all Class II and III, but the potential for logjams and strainers makes the run potentially dangerous for inexperienced boaters. Be careful.

MOUNTAIN BIKING

Santa Cruz is to Northern California mountain biking what Marin County once was. One positive aftereffect of the unfortunate logging history of the area is a vast network of old and new logging roads deep into the Santa Cruz Mountains. With the crackdown and closure of most good Mount Tamalpais trails, many of California's top-level mountain bikers have moved here for the plentiful back-country roads and trails that remain large-ly unrestricted. Two state parks, **Wilder Ranch** and **Nisene Marks Forest,** are extremely friendly to mountain bikers. Wilder, in fact, seems to cater to bikers more than hikers. Many rides outside the two parks are semi-secret and trespass on private lands. Because of the active com-petitive and casual biking scenes around the area, several good bike shops do a booming business, including **The Bicycle Trip,** 1127 Soquel Ave. (☎ **831/ 427-2580**).

Wilder Ranch

30 miles of trails. Easy to difficult. Access: 1 mile north of Santa Cruz on Hwy. 1. Map: Wilder Ranch has a special bike trail map.

Wilder Ranch is one of my favorite places in the world to mountain bike. The first time I rode here I was stunned. I'd passed the park on Highway 1 for years and dis-missed it as another state beach. What I didn't realize was that the park stretches for 3,900 acres up into the forest high-lands of the Santa Cruz Mountains. The 30 or so miles of trails and fire roads loop and intersect their way up the hills, pass-ing meadows, redwood forests, old barns, a eucalyptus grove, and creeks—all with a striking view of the bay. That first day I covered at least half the trails and saw everything from a bobcat to banana slugs. This place is amazing. From gently mean-dering fire roads to hairy switchbacked single track, Wilder has it all. My favorite trail is any trail that takes you to the very top of the ranch where the Charcoal Trail and Sequoia Trail loop around a eucalyp-tus grove, marking the park boundary with Gray Whale Ranch. (Also a popular but illegal riding area. Won't talk about that here.)

From the top of the park any number of loops and forks will eventually lead you back down to your car or the road to town. I'm particularly fond of the Peasley Gulch Trail, a steep single track through a creek bottom. Don't, however, get hung up on following any one "ride" because eventually you'll get where you're going anyway. Enjoy.

Forest of Nisene Marks State Park

Distances and difficulty vary. Access: Aptos Creek Trailhead. Map: Park map.

Almost as popular as Wilder Ranch is the Forest of Nisene Marks State Park (or Nisene Marks for short). Though the reg-ulations say bikes are only allowed on the Aptos Creek fire road, I've seen bikes all over the park and nobody seems to be complaining, perhaps because horses are not allowed here. The best ride in the park, however, is on the Aptos Creek fire road anyway. From the trailhead the fire road ascends China Ridge, a steep work-out. The epicenter of the 7.1-on-the-Richter-scale Loma Prieta quake of 1989 was right here.

As you climb China Ridge, you'll alter-nate between shade and stretches of sun. Bring plenty of water because there's none available in the park. After what seems like endless miles uphill through redwood and tan oak forest, you'll pass a small meadow and soon come to the Sand Point Overlook. Drink in the huge view and then bomb the road home. An option is to overnight at the trail camp about a mile farther along the fire road and ride down the next day.

Soquel Demonstration Forest

Distances and difficulty vary. Access: take Old San Jose Rd. up from Soquel, turn right on Stetson and then right again on Comstock Mill Rd. in another 1.5 miles. From State Rte. 17, turn east on Summit Rd., south 2.4 miles on Old San Jose Rd., then left on Stetson. Map: Forest map.

Attached to Nisene Marks is a 3,000-acre forest owned by the State Department of Forestry as an experimental timber forest.

Though not technically a park, all the forest trails are open to hikers and bikers. A number of trails loop through the forest and some connect down to Nisene Marks. The Sulfur Springs and Tractor Trail connects to the Ridge Trail. It in turn can connect you to the Sand Point overlook and eventually all the way down to Aptos. For information about the forest, call ☎ 831/475-8643.

ROAD BIKING

Road biking in the Monterey Bay area has its ups and downs, so to speak. On one hand, there's a lifetime's worth of back roads to explore, traversing redwood forests, topping spectacular ridges above the coast, and offering excellent opportunities for from-the-saddle whale watching. On the other hand, the climbs can be brutally steep and long (particularly on the Santa Cruz end of the bay), the coastal winds unyielding, and the roads narrow. They used to call the old dash up notorious Alta Road, in the Santa Cruz Mountains, the hardest race in the state (the event has since been canceled). Another ride through the hills carries the gaudy but all-too-accurate title "Mr. Bill's Nightmare." Olympians train here. Enough said.

That shouldn't keep the less fanatical among us from bringing a bike to the Monterey Bay, however. In addition to its more serious offerings, the area has coastal bike paths perfect for a balloon-tired beach cruiser, and some hidden shorter routes with great views, flat roads, and no traffic. Both Santa Cruz and Monterey are unusually bike-friendly towns, and the ocean breezes are just right for a morning spin.

Natural Bridges Beach to Lighthouse Point
1.5–3 miles. Easy. Access: Natural Bridges State Beach, W. Cliff entrance, 2531 W. Cliff Dr. Free parking available on the street or in the lot above the beach. The path begins next to the lot, where W. Cliff Dr. meets the park entrance.

At sunset, the thin concrete bike path between West Cliff Drive and the Pacific is one of Santa Cruz's most popular low-impact exercise spots. This a good, lazy ride. The path is flat and meandering, while the scenery is spectacular—crashing waves, shorebirds, surfers, sailboats. From the Natural Bridges Beach entrance, pick up the path on the ocean side of West Cliff, then ride it 1.5 miles to Lighthouse Point, the recommended endpoint. The path continues as a regular sidewalk another half-mile toward Cowell's Beach, but becomes increasingly congested and disappears just before the hill down to the boardwalk, where streets become busier still.

Lighthouse point is a good place to observe Steamer Lane's indigenous species, the sea lion (look at the rock just off the point), and the surfer (look to the right of the lighthouse). It's also a good way to see a cliff-side environment without venturing out onto the cliffs themselves, onto busy Highway 1, or further south to windy Big Sur.

Monterey Shore
18 miles. Easy to moderate. Access: Various points along the shoreline between Seaside and Lover's Point.

From the small town of Marina south to 17-Mile Drive, an excellent paved bike path traces the Monterey coastline with only a handful of breaks or intersections. Pick up the trail on Del Monte Boulevard in Marina. The path will parallel Del Monte for a few miles. There are a few small hills to climb straight away, none of which are long but all of which are maddening, with Del Monte running nice and flat 10 feet away, while you scramble up and down the ungraded bluffs the bike path follows. After 4 miles the path crosses under the freeway and rides through the former Fort Ord army base, now a university campus, before passing through the suburban-style town of

Seaside and temporarily breaking onto the city streets. Follow the green bike-route signs and the lane painted prominently on the pavement.

The break lasts less than a mile and then the concrete bike path begins again. You'll follow a long downhill through some dunes, popular for hang gliding, and then down into Monterey, where the path becomes temporarily crowded. It continues through downtown Monterey, past Cannery Row and the famous aquarium, breaking onto the city streets once at Ocean View Boulevard, but picking up again half a mile later. From there it stays hard on the shore, and has a brilliant coastline view (watch for whales in winter). The path continues south through Pebble Beach and the path's terminus at 17-Mile Drive. You can continue there for free, or turn back along the path.

Santa Cruz to Davenport

20 miles. Moderate to strenuous. Access: Begin at the intersection of Hwy. 1 and Western Dr. Head north on Hwy. 1 to Davenport, the turnaround point.

Hate the wind and love the wind, all in 2 hours. For such a heavily-traveled road, Highway 1 has some good shoulders, making the 10-mile stretch of undeveloped coastline between Santa Cruz and the tiny whale-watching town of Davenport, a pleasant, popular ride. The prevailing winds blow from the north along the coast, and blow hard, so you'll be fighting all the way there. But going back, with the Pacific to your right and the wind behind you, is effortless.

Empire Grade

30 miles. Strenuous. Access: Intersection of High and Bay sts., at the main entrance to University of California, Santa Cruz. Street parking. Empire Grade is the road High St. becomes west of the intersection. Take the road northwest as it heads around the perimeter of the university. A large barn at the university entrance should be on your right as you begin.

It's not called Empire Street, or Empire Avenue, but Empire Grade. That should tell you something. But this ride, which follows one of many mountain roads hidden in the Santa Cruz Mountains, is worth the work. Passing from chaparral-covered hills dotted with immense oak trees, the climb away from the coast into the hills follows a twisting two-lane path with a few blessed level sections. Along the way, you'll pass redwood groves, old farms, a llama ranch, several excellent meadow views, a tree farm, and very few cars or people. You'll also be able to say you really rode Santa Cruz: this is not an easy ride; it's uphill most of the way out, steeply in sections.

Fortunately this is an out-and-back trip, so the ride home is almost free, owing to the price paid getting up there. Loop routes are available by heading left down Ice Cream Grade to the coast, or right down nearly vertical Alba Road or Jameson Creek Road to Highway 9, which heads back into Santa Cruz. If you do decide to deviate to the side roads, don't plan on returning back the way you came—you want to ride down and not up them. This is a fantastic road ride for the fit and ambitious, the stubborn and foolish, or Lance Armstrong.

ROCK CLIMBING

Most rock climbers from here travel to the Pinnacles (see chapter 4) to do any serious climbing, but there are a few small outcroppings in the Monterey Bay area to practice on. **Castle Rock State Park,** State Route 35 between State Route 17 and State Route 9 (☎ 831/867-2952), offers large sandstone outcroppings with numerous top-roped routes. **Monastery Beach** in Monterey is another great practice area, with a formation of granite outcropping rising right out of the sand at the northern end of the beach. The beach is best reached by driving to the end of Ribera Road and walking down a short access trail. **Bugaboo Mountain Sports** (☎ 831/429-6300) in Santa Cruz is by far

> ### Join the Crew
>
> For information on hitching a ride for the day on someone else's sailboat, see "Sail for Free" in chapter 1.

the best source of local climbing information and has a great selection of gear.

SAILING

Monterey Bay is often incredibly windy, perfect for learning to sail in open ocean conditions. Santa Cruz yacht harbor is the center for all your sailing needs. **O'Neill Yachts and Charters,** Santa Cruz yacht harbor, 2222 East Cliff Dr. (☎ **831/476-5200**), was founded by yes, *that* O'Neill, the guy who invented the wet suit so he could surf all day without getting hypothermia. He subsequently became a local tycoon, though apparently in a very Santa Cruz sort of way (tycoon-hood being just one of many excuses for hanging out at the beach all day). His sailing center offers lessons for all levels, as well as boat rentals and charters with professional crews.

Pacific Yachting and Sailing, also located at the Santa Cruz yacht harbor (☎ **831/423-7245**), has a fleet of 18 bareboats, ranging from 27 feet to 43 feet. Like O'Neill's, Pacific offers sailing instruction for all levels of experience, plus skippered charters by reservation.

If you are going to learn how to sail safely, who better to ask than the people who rescue you when you wreck? Perhaps believing that an ounce of prevention is indeed worth a pound of cure, the brave men and women of the **United States Coast Guard** offer courses in sailing, navigation, and powerboat driving at their office in Santa Cruz. Boat rentals are not available; classes use vessels from the coast guard auxiliary flotilla. As you can imagine, they're kept up handsomely. Courses last 13 weeks and are offered year-round. Call ☎ **831/423-7119** for more information.

During the summer months, the office of Recreation and Sports at the **University of California, Santa Cruz,** offers sailing classes to the public. Boat rental is available with a membership in the UCSC Sailing Club, available to the public year-round. The club is located below the bridge on the harbor's north side. Call the UCSC Boating Center at ☎ **831/425-1164.**

Chardonnay Sailing Charters (☎ **408/423-1213**) offers a great chance to see how the other half-percent lives. Its million-dollar racing yacht, *Chardonnay,* is one of the fastest and sexiest boats on the water today, and you can rent it, fully crewed, for a basic rate of $500 per hour (2-hr. minimum from Santa Cruz, 3-hr. minimum from Monterey). With tons of deck space, a bar, stereo, cellular phone, and all the other amenities a boat can have, the *Chardonnay* is a great way to throw a party while touring the bay in style.

SCUBA DIVING

Monterey and Carmel are without a doubt the best and most well-known diving sites in Northern California. The incredible concentration of marine life here in combination with relatively good visibility (averaging 20 to 60 ft.) makes putting up with chilly bay waters seem like a treat, not a burden.

Most of the best underwater scenery and wildlife in the Monterey Bay area centers on the **kelp forests** around its edges. These forests form an incredibly beautiful underwater environment, but they take some getting used to. It's important to have a good sense of where your body and equipment are at all times to avoid getting tangled. Also, be more conservative with your air supply. Instead of waiting until you are nearly out of air and then looking for the boat or your path to shore, make sure you have enough air to swim under any kelp beds between you and your destination. One time crawling across the surface of a huge kelp bed wearing full scuba gear will teach you why this is important.

One of the best things about Monterey is how easy it is to dive from the shore. You can find great diving just a few hundred feet off **Cannery Row, Monastery Beach,** or (best of all) **Point Lobos,** which is near Carmel, just south of Point Piños, and offers reef dives near Whaler's and Bluefish coves, Granite Point, Cannery Point, and Coal Chute Cove. For information on dive boats and instruction, the best place to call is **Adventure Sports Limited** in Santa Cruz at ☎ **888/ 839-4286.** Point Lobos has a half dozen well-known coves and a number of boats working; reservations for diving here are highly recommended. Call the Point Lobos park office at ☎ **831/624-4909.**

Several diving-boat charter companies run out of Monterey to sites within the bay and harder-to-reach spots like the **Ocean Pinnacles** in Carmel Bay or **Chase Reef** off Point Piños.

Aquarius Dive Shop (☎ **831/ 375-1933**) has two locations in Monterey: 32 Cannery Row and 2240 Del Monte Ave. Besides running charters in the bay they offer rentals, equipment sales, certification classes, photography tours, and a wealth of local information. **Aqua Safaris** in Santa Cruz (☎ **831/479-4386**) offers a broad schedule of courses from novice through advanced, and also leads expeditions out of the Monterey area. **Twin Otters, Inc.** (☎ **408/656-9194**) is another well-run scuba charter operation running trips as far south as Granite Canyon off Big Sur and numerous sites in the bay and off Carmel.

All of the above shops will give recommendations on the best dive site for current conditions and season. If you want an invaluable description of all the shore-accessible dive sites on the Monterey Peninsula, as well as great photos and natural-history essays, pick up the *Diving and Snorkeling Guide to Northern California and the Monterey Peninsula* by Steve Rosenberg (Pisces Books, 1992).

SURFING

Santa Cruz is situated in such a way as to allow in both north and south swells while sheltering the main surf breaks from prevailing winds and chop. This miracle of geography makes it the most consistently good surf town on the entire California coast. Summertime south swells break fast and playful on the numerous rock reefs and points. Big wintertime norths roar into the bay like freighters. A big day at **Steamer Lane** can be a lesson in humility for even the best surfer. Best of all are those cold clear winter days after a big storm when you can see Monterey across the bay to the south and the redwood-covered slopes of the Santa Cruz Mountains rising behind town to your north while you drop in on headhigh waves at the Lane or **Pleasure Point.** The beaches west of town, like **4-Mile, Scott Creek,** and **Waddell Beach,** are even wilder; the closer you get to Año Nuevo the more exposed and sharky it becomes.

Año Nuevo State Reserve itself has a fantastic surf break—within a few hundred yards of the elephant-seal rookery. But be warned: A wildlife biologist once told me that elephant-seal pups from the rookery suffer a 50% mortality rate between the time they enter the water and the time they pass Año Nuevo Island about a half mile offshore. The reason? Predation by great white sharks and orcas. I've seen how I look sitting on a surfboard and it's much too close to a seal pup for my comfort.

South of town the surf poops out pretty quickly. The long sandy beaches stretching all the way to Moss Landing have periodic good surf, but just as often they're windblown and sloppy. The exception is **Moss Landing** itself. Because the submarine canyon comes right up to shore here, deep-water swells reach the sandbars around the harbor mouth relatively unimpeded and jack up. When the surf is really big in Santa Cruz, Moss Landing is unrideable. When the surf is small in Santa Cruz, it can be glassy, head high, and so hollow you'll think you're in Hawaii. Moss Landing is wide open to the wind though, so if you're going to get it, you'll have to get on it early.

Monterey is well known for diving, not surfing, and there's a reason. The surf here pretty much sucks, with two notable exceptions: **Asilomar Beach** and **Carmel Beach.** While neither offers anything like the point break perfection of Steamer Lane to the north or some of the secret Big Sur spots to the south, they are fun and playful beach-break and rock-reef waves.

Santa Cruz is the place to go for gear and lessons. During the summer, **Club Ed** at Cowell's Beach in Santa Cruz (☎ 831/459-9283) rents boogie boards, surfboards, and wet suits, and also teaches beginning surfing on Cowell's gently breaking waves. This is one of the few breaks in the area really gentle enough to make that first ride a pleasure instead of a white-knuckle drop. **Freeline Design,** at the corner of 41st and Portola near Pleasure Point (☎ 831/476-2950), rents wet suits and surfboards ranging from hybrid mini-longboards to 9-foot BZ softboards for first-timers. It also carries a good selection of boards and wet suits for sale. Santa Cruz's **Cowell's Beach n' Bikini Surf Shop** (☎ 831/427-2355), which describes itself as a "full-service surf shop," has an appropriately Endless Summer-ish ambiance. Board rentals and lessons are both available at very reasonable prices. Open daily year-round, 8am to 6pm during the summer, 9am to 5pm the rest of the year.

Richard Schmidt Surf School, also in Santa Cruz (☎ 831/423-0928), is a long-established place to learn how to ride waves. The difference between Schmidt's and other places is that they promise to have you standing, on the board, in the water, on a wave, your first day out.

WALKS & RAMBLES

Redwood Nature Trail, Big Basin State Park

0.6-mile loop. Access: A 10-ft.-tall sign across from Park Headquarters marks the trailhead.

"If I had more influence, or if I had my way, I'd zone Santa Cruz as a special conservation area where people from more crowded and polluted regions could come to see what human beings can do with their environment, nurtured with love and compassion. I envision Santa Cruz even more beautiful in a better future than it is now. . . . I would rather live with the white shark more prevalent because we protect its primary food—sea lions and sea otters—than have to surf or swim in the disease-ridden sewer outlets I learned to surf in Santa Cruz in the '50s. In my mind Santa Cruz has done more than maintain its environment. It is a progressive and controversial county—an area where the potential for a paradise continues."

—Fred Van Dyke, early California surfer, from his book *30 years of Riding the World's Biggest Waves* (Ocean Sports International Publishing Group, 1989)

This tiny loop trail is a microcosm of what you'd see in much of the rest of the Big Basin backcountry: redwoods, tan oaks, lush creek corridor full of berry vines and poison oak, maybe even a few banana slugs. Just as with any other microcosm, you are missing the richer, more diverse experience of the whole, but you'll get the big attractions. The tallest tree in the park, 329-foot tall Mother of the Forest, is here, as is the Chimney Tree, a naturally hollowed-out redwood formed when a fire burned out much of the trunk but left the living outer layers of the tree standing.

Butterfly Grove, Natural Bridges State Beach

0.5 miles. Handicapped-accessible board-walk. Access: Park at the state beach parking lot on W. Cliff and follow the signs.

Every fall and winter thousands of mon-archs come to Natural Bridges for shelter. This spot is special in that it offers two important monarch habitats: the eucalyp-tus trees they favor for congregating and the milkweed that monarch caterpillars feed on before turning into butterflies. Milkweed is highly toxic to most animals, so scientists speculate that by eating the plant monarchs gain a lifelong protection from predators.

Elkhorn Slough Interpretive Trail

1 mile. Access: Park Headquarters at 1700 Elkhorn Rd.

Several miles of trail leave from the visitor center, but before hiking any others it is useful to walk the short interpretive trail with informational signs that will help a first-timer identify some of the upland plants that surround the slough as well as plants and animals that live in the slough. The visitor center also has some great exhibits explaining the complex workings of this large wetland.

Cypress Grove Loop, Point Lobos State Reserve

0.8 miles. Access: Information station inside Point Lobos.

The short Cypress Grove Loop shows off a little of everything Point Lobos has to offer. The grove of Monterey cypress on South Point, for which this walk is named, is one of only two spots in the world where this tree grows naturally. These grizzled old-growth cypresses on their dramatic headland seem the perfect icon for the Monterey area. Beyond the grove the trail passes an overlook where sea lions are often spotted playing near the Devil's Cauldron. The trail then passes a swirling tidal surge channel and exits into the open at South Point, a favorite whale-watching site.

WHALE WATCHING & MARINE SANCTUARY TOURS

As the gray-whale population has increased in the last 15 years, it has begun to seem as if there is no longer a whale-watching season. Indeed, it's reached a point where now some whales are begin-ning to migrate south by the time others are migrating north. Now 17,000 whales make the trip every year, providing a con-stant treadmill effect. You may be able to find a whale at any time of the year, but the best season is still from December through April, when pods of whales (gen-erally two to six individuals traveling together) hug the California shoreline en route between their winter calving grounds in Mexico and their summer feeding grounds off Alaska.

Several spots on the Monterey Bay coast are well suited to whale watching. **Lighthouse Point** in Santa Cruz and all of **West Cliff Drive** up to Natural Bridges is a good area to walk while keeping an eye out for the telltale spout of passing whales. Monterey has many good look-outs on its rocky coast. The **Point Piños lighthouse grounds** is one great spot as the whales make the turn into Monterey Bay. **Point Lobos** just south of Carmel is another spot where the whales come extremely close to shore and give whale watchers a good look. The cliffs at Point

---

Feeding Time

It is with great relief that I report that the Monterey Bay Great White shark tours have been canceled. For several years in the mid-nineties, a few companies based in Santa Cruz got the brilliant idea to take a boat full of tourists out on the bay, dump a bucket of horse blood and parts overboard, and wait for the great whites to put on a show for the passengers. This worked. The downside was the sudden presence of an unusual number of very large sharks in the bay. No one's really sure whether the scheme upset the local food chain or the tourist trade worse, but in any event every government agency within earshot quickly moved to shut down the free shark lunches. *Sorry, Charlie.* If you're looking to see a great white in the water, you'll have to slip on some scuba gear and hope for the best, or go rent a movie.

Lobos are the perfect size to give you a little height to look out at the whales without placing you so far away you can barely see.

Of course, the best way to really see a lot of whales up close is to join a whale-watching tour on any of the boats that run out of Santa Cruz and Monterey. Over the years, the whales have become accustomed to being watched and often will swim right up to an idling boat.

Some companies that run whale-watching trips also offer general tours of the bays or the marine sanctuaries. There's a difference: A whale-watching boat is going to head straight out of the bay, try to locate some whales, and stay wherever they find them. These trips usually take between 1 and 1½ hours. Sanctuary tours make a circuit of the bay and its environs, taking between 1 and 3 hours to show you pelican rookeries, sea lions, and the broader ocean landscape. Sometimes you also see a whale in the process; sometimes you don't.

Olympus Sailing Charters (☎ 831/647-1957), however, offers both options at the same time. It runs trips from Fisherman's Wharf in Monterey on *Zeus,* a 67-foot sailing yacht that holds 27 passengers. Zeus was a once-famous racing yacht, setting several local speed records before retiring to a comfortable life as a bay cruiser. The boat heads out on weekends during spring and fall, and daily during the summer season, July through September. Whale-watching tours are conducted under sail; this is a quieter, slower way to approach the animals. Evening sails are timed for sunset and include champagne. $20 for day sails, $25 for evening.

Another sanctuary-specific (though motorized) day on the water is offered by **Sanctuary Explorations,** which also runs whale-watching trips out of its Monterey landing. You might see humpback as well as gray whales, seabirds, sunfish, the occasional shark, and porpoises. But the highlight is the enormously gratifying views of local sea lions experiencing the enormous glory of their hedonistic lives, lying all over each other on the breakwater at the harbor's edge. Call ☎ **831/917-1042** for schedules and reservations.

The following companies also run whale-watching tours during the winter season out of Monterey: **Chris' Fishing Trips** (☎ 831/375-5951), **Monterey Sport Fishing** (☎ 831/372-2203), **Randy's Fishing Trips** (☎ 831/372-7440), and **Sam's Fishing Fleet** (☎ 831/372-0577). In Santa Cruz, try **Chardonnay Sailing Charter** (☎ 831/423-1213), **Santa Cruz Sport Fishing** (☎ 831/426-4690), or **Shamrock Charters** (☎ 831/476-2648).

Campgrounds & Other Accommodations

CAMPING

Santa Cruz

Big Basin State Park
9 miles west of Boulder Creek on State Rte. 236. ☎ **831/338-8860.** 100 car campsites, 45 walk-in sites. Also has rustic, reasonably priced cabins for rent. Wildlife, bird watching, hiking, swimming, surfing, boardsailing. Fees range from $6–$18. Reserve through PARKNET (☎ 800/444-PARK). Store, showers, flush toilets, running water.

Big Basin is California's oldest and most popular state park, so be prepared for (1) a pain in the butt getting a site, and (2) a crowd once you're here. But it's still one of the most beautiful places within an hour's drive of the teeming millions who call the Santa Clara Valley home. Since you didn't come here looking for solitude, enjoy the whole Ranger Rick ambiance of Big Basin—the campfire programs, the interpretive signs, the kids screaming as their marshmallows catch fire. If you *did* come here looking for solitude, you better put on your hiking shoes and start walking.

Henry Cowell Redwoods State Park
On the outskirts of Felton just north of Santa Cruz. ☎ **831/335-4598.** 112 sites. Piped water, flush toilets, showers, store in Felton. Fishing, hiking, swimming, kayaking. $14–$18 per night excluding reservation fee ($7.50). Reserve through PARKNET (☎ 800/444-PARK).

Henry Cowell is often considered the ugly stepsister of Big Basin, which is really unfortunate. Though not nearly as wild as Big Basin, Henry Cowell is a great park, especially for a family with kids. The trails

around the park are manageable by all ages and clearly marked, and summer swimming holes are plentiful on the San Lorenzo River. If you need a mechanical distraction, a narrow-gauge railroad left-over from the logging days runs from here to the Santa Cruz Boardwalk and back (it's very slow; take it for the ride, not to get there quickly).

New Brighton State Beach
Right in the middle of Aptos and Capitola. Take New Brighton exit from Hwy. 1. ☎ **408/429-2850** or 408/464-6329. 105 car camping sites, 2 bike-in sites. Running water, flush toilets, disposal station, propane, grocery store, laundry, showers. Swimming. $3–$23 per night. Reserve through PARKNET (☎ 800/444-PARK).

This is one of the prettiest state beach campgrounds. The sites are spread around a wooded glade that seems as if it were in the wilderness, even though they're surrounded by homes. From the campground, trails descend to the sandy beach below.

Watsonville

Manresa Beach State Park
On Sand Dollar Dr., 8 miles south on the San Andreas Rd. exit from Hwy. 1. ☎ **408/429-2850** or 408/761-1795. 64 tent sites, some with ocean views. Running water, flush toilets, showers. Fishing, swimming, surfing. $14–$18 per night. Reserve through PARKNET (☎ 800/444-PARK).

Manresa and Sunset Beach just to the south are the two most beautiful camping beaches in the Monterey area. Surrounded by farmland and the occasional beach house, these two gems are perfect for a quiet weekend by the sea. Manresa is extremely popular with day users from the surrounding towns who come here to surf and fish. Sunset is a big hit with kids, who like to run or roll down its huge dunes. Both these parks are within easy driving distance of Elkhorn Slough, which lacks any good camping in its immediate vicinity.

Sunset Beach State Park

San Andreas Rd. exit from Hwy. 1. Follow signs to state park. ☎ **408/429-2850** or 408/763-7063. 90 tent and motor-home spaces. Flush toilets, showers. Bird and whale watching, swimming. $14–$18 per night. Reserve through PARKNET (☎ 800/444-PARK).

Wonderful dunes and well-laid-out campsites make this beach campground a welcome break. Some sites have ocean views. The others are just a short walk away from the beach. It can be very windy here, so sometimes the more sheltered sites are a better choice than the ones with great views.

Monterey

Saddle Mountain Recreation Park

5 miles from Carmel at the end of Schulte Rd. ☎ **831/624-1617.** 25 tent sites and 25 motor-home sites. Running water, flush toilets, showers, pool, playground, and store. $20–$35 per night.

Monterey and Carmel are really hurting for good camping options near town. Saddle Mountain is a nice park on the banks of the Carmel River, which is less of a draw than you might think since the river is dry most of the year. It's nothing special, but the park is only about a 15-minute drive from anywhere in Monterey—Point Lobos, Carmel, Fisherman's Wharf, and more—and is a pleasant, cheap alternative to staying in a motel.

INNS & LODGES

Pigeon Point Lighthouse AYH Youth Hostel

210 Pigeon Point Rd. ☎ **650/879-0633.** 52 beds. $15 nonmembers, $12 members, children half-price when accompanied by an adult. MC, V. Reservations mandatory. Hostel office open year-round daily 7:30–9:30am and 4:30–9:30pm.

This area has literally hundreds of nice hotels, bed-and-breakfasts, and small inns; but most of them are set right in town, a far cry from the wilderness experience. This hostel offers the wildest accommodations in the area. Consisting of several old coast guard buildings clustered at the base of 115-foot-tall Pigeon Point Lighthouse, the hostel itself is very basic, but the location is unreal: Año Nuevo is just a few miles south and the ocean is right outside the window. And how many other hostels have a hot tub?

Pleasure Point Inn

2-3665 E. Cliff Dr., Santa Cruz (right across from Pleasure Point). ☎ **831/475-4657.** 4 units. $125–$145. MC, V.

Surfers and fishermen looking for a deluxe weekend might splurge and stay at this small B&B in a neighborhood of residential homes. It offers several rooms with ocean views, fireplaces, and surfboard storage on site. The owners also charter a large motor cruiser out of the Santa Cruz harbor.

Mangels House

570 Aptos Creek Rd. ☎ **831/688-7982.** 6 units. $120–$160 double. MC, V.

This B&B sits right on the edge of the 10,000-acre Forest of Nisene Marks State Park. Though this pleasant country inn doesn't really promote itself as a wilderness retreat, it is located on its own 4 acres smack in the middle of some of the best mountain biking and hiking in the Santa Cruz Mountains and only a mile or so from New Brighton Beach.

Asilomar

800 Asilomar Blvd., Pacific Grove. ☎ **831/372-8016.** 308 units. $74–$92 double. MC, V.

Monterey and Pacific Grove have more B&Bs than you can shake a stuffed teddy bear and a dish of potpourri at, including several along Ocean Front Boulevard, but this old YMCA located right in the middle of a beautiful state park and beach is probably the best place for an action-figure type to stay. Asilomar is now a conference center owned by the state, but it still rents out some rooms to the general public. Several of the old cottages have kitchens and fireplaces. Make reservations well in advance.

4

Big Sur, the Ventana Wilderness & Pinnacles National Monument

Big Sur's residents put up with what some would consider great inconveniences—road-closing mudslides, fires, terrible television reception, wild storms, and a meager economy—in order to live a life of simplicity lost to most of the rest of California. Henry Miller, while living high above the ocean on Partington Ridge, put his finger on it in his 1957 novel *Big Sur and the Oranges of Hieronymus Bosch:* "Whoever settles here hopes he will be the last invader. The very look of the land makes one long to keep it intact—the spiritual reserve of a few bright spirits."

It's still the spiritual reserve he wrote of, but anyone hoping to be the last invader is going to be severely let down. During peak tourist season (March to October), Big Sur swarms with out-of-towners, most of them blowing through on their way from Monterey to points south and figuring they'll pull over at a few vista points and say they've seen Big Sur. Stupid mistake. Big Sur is as much a state of mind as it is a place, and the way to find that is to get out in the deep quiet of the woods or scramble down an eroding bluff to the ocean edge—anywhere away from the rush of Highway 1—and experience the wildness of this beautiful place.

When the Spanish settled Monterey Bay they didn't know what to make of the coastline to the south. This grizzly-filled, vertiginous landscape of plummeting sea cliffs and towering mountains didn't have much to recommend it by their standards, so they left it alone, calling it *El País Grande del Sur*—the big country of the south. By the time the first homesteaders moved into the area in the early 19th century to ranch cattle, Big Sur's original inhabitants, the Esselen Indians, once estimated to number about 1,000, were already extinct from European diseases. Mining and gold panning brought more settlers during the 1850s.

Big Sur, the Ventana Wilderness, & Pinnacles National Monument

In 1899, the Point Sur Lighthouse was built, lit by a kerosene lamp at the top of 395 wooden steps. Tourism to Big Sur began about the same time, centering on Pfeiffer's Resort, which opened in 1908 at the present site of the Big Sur Lodge in Pfeiffer Big Sur State Park. Florence Pfeiffer ran the place until 1934, when it became part of the state park; Big Sur's reputation as something of a bohemian enclave rests with the guests she lured— Stanford professors, writers, artists, and nature lovers.

There are still a lot of people here living the back-to-the-land, bohemian life. Though the permanent population for all of Big Sur is less than 4,000 people, the region is home to the Esalen Institute (home of the Human Potential Movement), the Tassajara Zen Buddhist Retreat Center, a Benedictine monastery, numerous inns and lodges, and more than its share of artists, recluses, and geniuses who prefer to be left to their own devices.

Farther inland, the **Salinas Valley** is one of the richest agricultural areas in the world, and towns like Soledad, Greenfield, and King City reflect that heritage; hardscrabble field workers and agribusiness money share a common bond with the land here. To the east lie the **Gabilan Mountains** and **Pinnacles National Monument.** In the Salinas Valley, lettuce is king and broccoli queen, but this is hard-core cattle country. Most of the land is tied up in private ranches; the exception is Pinnacles National Monument, which was set aside during the early part of this century because of its unique geology and important wildlife habitat.

The Lay of the Land

Where is Big Sur? Several state parks, a river, and a smattering of landmarks bear the name, not to mention stores, motels, and a post office, but it seems like no one can agree on where Big Sur begins and where it ends. The subject provides fodder for an arcane and never-ending debate among residents, to whom it is a point of pride. We'll let them work it out. For the sake of simplicity, Big Sur is everything south of **Point Lobos** near Carmel, north of **Willow Creek** and **Cape San Martin,** and west of the **Salinas Valley.** Pinnacles National Monument falls outside this boundary, but we've put it with Big Sur because of its relative proximity.

Northern California's coastal mountains peter out when they hit Monterey Bay, but rise again on the southern end, this time in the form of the **Santa Lucias,** a rocky range of dry chaparral peaks that rise out of the sea at an angle so steep you feel like you're not just standing on the edge of a continent but actually over it. To illustrate how steep the Santa Lucias really are, consider the case of Cone Peak, the summit of which rises to 5,155 feet within 3.2 miles of the ocean. That's a 30.5% gradient, steeper than even the steepest parts of the Sierra Nevada. The highest peak in the Santa Lucias is 5,750-foot Junípero Serra Peak. Numerous other peaks exceed 4,000 feet.

Though they look foreboding at first, covered as they are by brushy, thick chaparral, the Santa Lucias are also interspersed with redwood-lined valleys, pine forests, meadows, and numerous creeks. Most land here is owned by the federal government as part of the northern section of **Los Padres National Forest.** Of the nearly 200,000 acres that make up Big Sur, only about one quarter is privately owned. Big Sur, of course, is famous for its coastline, a rocky plunging stretch of often inaccessible beaches and sheer rocks. Two main rivers, the Big Sur and Little Sur, drain the Santa Lucias's west slope. Runoff from the east enters the Salinas River and eventually Monterey Bay. All creeks and waterways here can

MOUNTAIN WORDS

When writing about mountains one runs into a little problem: England, where our language developed, isn't known for its great mountain ranges. As a result, English is not a tongue rich in mountain words. Since the United States, on the other hand, has amazing mountains, we've been forced to look elsewhere for our descriptive language or make up our own. Many of the best mountain words have come from French, German, Italian, and Spanish, the Alps and Pyrenees being what they are. These are beautiful, sonorous words, subtle words, words that will teach you to see things in mountains you didn't know were there:

Arête: Sharp-crested mountain ridge

Bergschrund: Series of crevasses

Butte: A solitary, steep hill or small mountain

Caldera: Volcanic crater left by an eruption

Cirque: A steep bowl-like mountain basin

Col: Pass or saddle between mountains

Cordillera: A system of mountain chains

Couloir (*Cool*-wahr): A steep mountainside gorge or gully

Crevasse: A glacial fissure or deep crack

Defile: Narrow pass between hills or cliffs; gorge

Escarpment: Cliff formation

Esker: A gravelly or sandy mountain ridge

Glacier: Slow-moving mass of perennial ice

Hogback: Sharp-crested mountain ridge

Hoodoo: Oddly eroded rock column

Massif: A mountain range section or mass

Moraine: Glacial deposit of rocks and boulders

Moulin: A vertical shaft worn by water pouring though a crack in a glacier

Palisade: Line of cliffs

Piedmont: Area at the foot of a range

Randkluft: Chasm left by a receding glacier

Scree: Rocky debris on a mountain slope

Serac: Jagged glacial ridge or ice fall

Sierra: Chain of mountains with sawtooth peaks

Talus: Rocky debris below a cliff

Tarn: Small mountain lake with steep sides

Traverse: A place suitable for crossing a mountain face

dry up in the summer, and once away from the major creeks, water is scarce.

Across the agriculturally rich Salinas Valley to the east, the Gabilan Mountains are home to the otherworldly **Pinnacles National Monument,** a remnant volcanic plug of towering rock spires and cool tunnel caves. The two parallel ranges run in a north-south orientation for over 100 miles between Monterey and San Luis Obispo.

The **climate** here is moderate year-round. Precipitation falls mostly in the winter months and is extremely localized, falling mostly on the immediate coastal strip. Inland a few miles, less than a third as much rain falls. Snow rarely falls on the higher peaks. Summer brings coastal fog and hot inland temperatures. The beach can be drizzly and cold while 5 miles away on the ridgeline it is 90°F. Inland, it gets much hotter. The Pinnacles and the back reaches of the Ventana Wilderness often reach 100°F during the dry summer months.

Though the grizzly bears that kept early settlers guessing are gone now, plenty of **wildlife** remains. Deer, red-tailed hawks, bobcats, cougar, wild turkeys, squirrels, raccoons, and other animals are common. So are poison oak, ticks, and rattlesnakes. The area is also home to several wildlife recovery success stories. It was along the Big Sur coast in the 1920s that California Fish and Game biologists found the isolated colony of California sea otters—long thought to be extinct—from which the population recovered to now occupy the entire northern coast. In the remote backcountry of the Ventana Wilderness, wildlife biologists have reintroduced bald eagles and hope to soon have four breeding pairs. The Big Sur and Little Sur rivers, the largest wild rivers in central California, are home to winter runs of endangered steelhead trout. Gray whales, once hunted to near extinction, are now numerous in the waters off Big Sur as they migrate from their feeding grounds in Alaska to their calving grounds in Baja California.

Orientation

Highway 1, the famous coast highway, provides the main access to the Big Sur coastline and accompanying state parks. Most visitors to the Big Sur Valley come down the 29-mile stretch from Carmel and Monterey. Others drive the entire 90-mile stretch from Carmel to San Simeon. There are no roads east to west over the Santa Lucias with the exception of **Nacimiento Road** through Hunter Liggett National Guard Base. The eastern accesses into the Big Sur backcountry from **Arroyo Seco Road** and **Carmel Valley Road** are underutilized. Here, those in search of true solitude can access the most remote parts of the Ventana Wilderness by coming in the back way, away from the tourist crush.

Pinnacles National Monument has a west entrance just a few miles from Soledad, but is best reached via **State Route 25,** a beautiful winding two-lane road that threads through miles of ranch country between Hollister and King City and leads to the eastern entrance of the Pinnacles, where the most interesting features and visitor services are located.

Palo Colorado Road

This narrow two-lane road 6 miles south of Carmel on Highway 1 leads 8 miles into the hills to Bottcher's Gap, a major trailhead for the Ventana

Wilderness as well as a national-forest car camp.

Bixby Bridge

Fallacious local legend claims Bixby Bridge, 12 miles south of Carmel on Highway 1, as the longest concrete arch in the world. It's not, but the beautiful span is one of the few man-made features that actually enhances the already outrageous scenery. Before the bridge was open, travelers had to traverse miles up-canyon before continuing down the coast. Park on the north side and walk about 100 yards up the Old Coast Road for an unbeatable view of the bridge and river mouth below. It is risky but possible to scramble down the rocky slope to the pocket beach below.

Urban Big Sur

There's no such thing as an urban center in Big Sur; however, the 5-mile stretch of Highway 1 through the Big Sur Valley is the closest thing you'll find to a town. Residents do all their shopping in Carmel, 24 miles to the north. You should too, but anything you've forgotten can probably be found, outrageously overpriced, at one of the small gas stations, markets, motels, or restaurants along this stretch. The **River Inn** (☎ 408/625-5255) has a BP gas station, restaurant, grocery store, and outdoor espresso cart. Locals perform music and theater here during winter months. Adjacent is **Big Sur Garage and Towing** (☎ 408/667-2181). **Big Sur Health Center** (☎ 408/667-2580) offers emergency treatment. Just before leaving the Big Sur Valley to the south, you'll find the **Big Sur Post Office** (☎ 408/667-2305), a **Chevron** gas station, and a store.

Arroyo Seco Road

This beautiful country road loops from U.S. 101 in the Salinas Valley near Soledad, deep into the back side of the Los Padres National Forest, and exits near King City, providing trailhead access to the most remote portions of the Ventana Wilderness.

Parks & Other Hot Spots

The spots along Highway 1 are listed in north to south order, with Pinnacles National Monument at the end of the section.

Garrapata State Park

5 miles south of Carmel on Hwy. 1. ☎ 408/667-2315. Pit toilets, no water. Fishing, hiking, swimming, rock climbing, surfing, whale watching. Open dawn to dusk.

Heading south from Carmel, the first coastal access you'll come to after 4 miles of high cliffs is Garrapata, an undeveloped 2,800-acre park with a beautiful-sounding Spanish name that means, no kidding, "wood tick." Though the park extends on both sides of Highway 1 for 4 miles, most visitors come for the beaches. As one of the few places in the northern part of Big Sur where you can actually get to the water, Garrapata draws fishermen, surfers, skinny-dippers, picnickers, and beachcombers. More than 30 numbered gates lead from roadside pullouts to vistas, and beaches, on one side of Highway 1, and hiking trails, redwood forests, and chaparral-covered mountains on the other. The mountain side of the park is little used and a boon for hikers seeking solitude. A map and brochure of the park are available for sale at the entrance kiosk at Andrew Molera State Park 15 miles south.

Point Sur Lighthouse State Park

17 miles south of Carmel on Hwy. 1. ☎ 408/625-4419. Visitor center, pit toilets, no water. Whale watching. Open to guided tours only, year-round Wed 10am, Sat 10am and 2pm. $5 per person. Meet 15 min. before tour at locked gate on Hwy. 1. Reservations accepted.

Jutting 200 feet in the air like a fantasy castle at the end of a long sandpit, Point Sur, a huge solid rock monolith, provided the perfect place to situate a lighthouse along this treacherous coast. Though only open 3 days a week, and even then by docent-led tours only, it's worth setting aside a weekend morning to tour the 40-foot-tall lighthouse built of stone blocks, picnic on the grounds, and scan the ocean for passing whales. Built in 1889, the lighthouse provides great insight into what life was like on this part of the coast before Highway 1 was opened in 1937.

Andrew Molera State Park

22 miles south of Carmel on Hwy. 1. ☎ 408/667-2315, or 408/625-8664 for horseback-riding concession. Walk-in campground (reservations not accepted), picnic area. Wildlife, bird watching, hiking, swimming, horseback riding, kayaking, biking, camping, whale watching. Fee.

Just south of Point Sur, Highway 1 leaves the ocean's edge and for almost 10 miles is cut off from the sea by Pfeiffer Ridge. Most of the land here is extremely private and off-limits, but fortunately the beautiful Andrew Molera is a 4,800-acre exception. The park is almost entirely undeveloped and a hiker's paradise. At the Big Sur River mouth on the park's northern end, surfers find some of the best waves in the area and access to Big Sur's longest beach. A private concession (☎ 408/625-8664) leads horseback trail rides for a real-life ranch experience.

Pfeiffer Big Sur State Park and Big Sur Station

26 miles south of Carmel on Hwy. 1. ☎ 408/667-2315 (state park); 408/667-2423 (Big Sur Station). Public campground, showers, flush toilets. Hiking, swimming. Fees for day use and camping.

Pfeiffer's old-growth redwoods, a waterfall, cool swimming holes, and numerous trails make it Big Sur's largest public campground, the epicenter of tourist-season Big Sur. You'll also find a grocery store, restaurant, and Laundromat here, as well as Big Sur Lodge, a bleak example of what goes wrong when park concession-aires with no real investment in the physical property of a hotel defer maintenance and cut corners.

One half mile south of the state park on Highway 1 is **Big Sur Station,** a multi-agency administrative center for both national forest and state park needs; it has the best information about the backcountry, as well as wilderness and fire permits. Several major trails into the Ventana Wilderness leave from here. Parking is provided.

Pfeiffer Beach

Sycamore Canyon Rd., 25 miles south of Carmel on Hwy. 1. ☎ 408/667-2423. Pit toilets, parking. Fishing, swimming, kayaking, surfing, whale watching. Open dawn to dusk. Fee.

Though you can't look 10 feet in Big Sur without seeing the Pacific Ocean, getting to the water is notoriously difficult. Pfeiffer Beach is the closest you can get your car to the beach—about one-quarter mile, flat—so it's popular with everyone from picnickers and nude sunbathers to kayakers and surfers. At low tide, climb the two huge seaward rocks for a majestic view of the waves. Locals regularly steal the Sycamore Canyon Road sign that leads to Pfeiffer Beach in order to confuse visitors, so just keep your eyes peeled for the only paved road on the west side of Highway 1 after you pass Big Sur Station.

Ventana Wilderness/Los Padres National Forest

Access from Hwy. 1 or Arroyo Seco Rd. ☎ 408/385-5434 or 408/667-2423. Hiking, whale watching, wildlife, camping, fishing, bird watching, swimming. Fees may apply.

Within this wilderness lie 161,000 acres of varied geography ranging from redwood forests to desolate, dry ridgelines. With 400 miles of trails, lots of backcountry camps, three major rivers, hot springs, and numerous high peaks, the Ventana Wilderness offers the best winter backpacking in Northern California;

wilderness permits are required to enter (available at Big Sur Station—see above). Most hikers enter through the popular Pine Ridge Trail at Big Sur Station, but numerous trailheads lead into the wilderness from all sides. The Ventana Wilderness Recreation Map ($4.25) can point you to them. In mid- to late summer be sure to ask about trail closures due to fire danger. Los Padres National Forest also manages several beaches, campgrounds, and day-use areas in the southern reaches of Big Sur. *Hiking the Big Sur Country: The Ventana Wilderness,* by Jeffrey P. Schaffer (Wilderness Press, 1991), is an excellent, if a bit dry, guidebook to the more obscure trails of the Ventana Wilderness.

Julia Pfeiffer Burns State Park

37 miles south of Carmel on Hwy. 1. ☎ 408/667-2315. 2 walk-in campsites. Picnic area, rest rooms. Kayaking, diving, hiking, camping. Open dawn to dusk.

If you haven't figured it out already, the Pfeiffers, an early homesteading family, were the originators of tourism in Big Sur—their name is everywhere. Julia Pfeiffer Burns State Park is a small but remarkable park encompassing a lush redwood forest, two cliff-top environmental campsites, a sheltered cove, and what park literature claims is the only waterfall in California to fall directly into the Pacific Ocean. The environmental campsites here are some of the best in the state and are consequently hard to get. Kayakers willing to schlep their boats down a short but steep trail and through a 200-foot-long solid rock tunnel can launch at the remains of the old Partington Cove loading dock to explore miles of otherwise inaccessible coastline. Divers (experienced only!) are required to register with the rangers in advance to explore this designated marine sanctuary.

Pinnacles National Monument

For best results enter the park from State Rte. 25 on the east side. A secondary entrance exists just outside Soledad from U.S. 101. ☎ **408/389-4485.** Public and private campground, visitor center, picnic area, toilets. Hiking, wildlife, bird watching, rock climbing, caving. Open dawn to dusk. Fees.

Located in the rolling hills of the Gabilan Range ranch country east of the Salinas Valley, the Pinnacles are a geological anomaly, half the remains of a volcanic plug that left jutting rock spires and caves in the middle of this otherwise nondescript landscape. The other half of the volcano sits more than 300 miles south near Tehachapi—testimony to the San Andreas Fault's influence over this landscape. Popular with climbers, Pinnacles is also a great springtime destination to catch the wildflower bloom and is home to California's largest breeding population of hawks, eagles, and falcons. For more information, see "Pinnacles National Monument," below.

Limekiln Creek State Park
52 miles south of Carmel on Hwy. 1. ☎ **408/667-2315.** Water, toilets available. Hiking, beach access nearby.

This recent addition to the state park system lies 26 miles south of the Big Sur Valley. Limekiln holds a waterfall, historic lime kilns, redwoods, and a small sheltered beach. The name refers to a lime-making operation that settlers set up here in the 1870s. It's a short walk to the old kilns, with good redwood stands nearby.

Pacific Valley Area
58 miles south of Carmel on Hwy. 1. ☎ **408/385-5434** for national forest information; ☎ 408/927-8655 for store or gas station. Gas, phones, store, ranger station, campgrounds, trails, beaches. Diving, kayaking, swimming, hiking.

Between 28 miles and 38 miles south of the Big Sur Valley is a stretch of coastline containing several Los Padres National Forest beaches, campgrounds, picnic areas, and a small community (Pacific Valley). The most remote part of the Big Sur coast, this stretch doesn't bear the same tourist burden as the northern parks. There's great diving, kayaking, and hiking here. It's also noteworthy because the Nacimiento-Fergusson Road between Kings City and Kirk Creek is the only east-west road through the Santa Lucias.

Pinnacles National Monument

Once a little-known outpost of the national monument system, Pinnacles National Monument has become one of the most popular weekend climbing destinations in central California over the last 10 years. The mild winter climate and plentiful routes make this a perfect off-season training ground for climbers. It's also a popular haven for campers, hikers, and nature lovers. One of the most unique chaparral ecosystems in the world supports a large community of plant and animal life here, including California's largest breeding population of raptors.

The Pinnacles themselves, hundreds of towering crags, spires, and hoodoos, are seemingly out of place in the voluptuously rolling hills of the coast range. And they *are,* in fact, out of place, part of the eroded remains of a volcano formed 23 million years ago 195 miles south in the middle of the Mojave Desert. They were carried here by the movement of the San Andreas Fault, which runs just east of the park. The other half of the volcano remains in the Mojave. Because of this distinctive geology, Pinnacles was set aside as a national monument on January 16, 1908, though it wasn't developed for visitor use until the 1930s and 1940s.

GETTING THERE

Two entrances lead to the park. The **West Entrance** from Soledad and U.S. 101 is dry, dusty, and much less attractive than the **East Entrance.** Unless you're coming from nearby, take the longer drive on Highway 25 to enter through the east. Because the peaks of the Pinnacles face east, and the watershed drains east, most of the interesting hikes and geologic features are on this side. No road crosses the park.

WHEN TO GO

Daytime temperatures often exceed 100°F in summer, so the best times of year to visit are spring, when the wildflowers are blooming, followed by fall. Crowds are common during spring weekends.

WARNINGS & REGULATIONS

Beware of poison oak, particularly in Bear Gulch. Rattlesnakes are common throughout the park but rarely seen. Bikes and dogs are prohibited on all trails, and there is no backcountry camping allowed anywhere in the park.

THE VISITOR CENTER

The first place you should go upon entering the park from the east is the **Bear Gulch Visitors Center** (☎ 408/389-4485). This small center is rich with exhibits about the park's history, wildlife, geology, and also has a great selection of nature handbooks and climbing guides for the Pinnacles. Climbers should register here before heading out: many routes are closed during hawk- and falcon-nesting season, and rangers like to know how many climbers are in the park.

The Bear Gulch picnic ground, adjacent to the visitor center, is a great place to fuel up before setting out on a hike or, if you're not planning on leaving your car, the best place to gaze up at dramatic spires of the high peaks.

HIKING

You could spend many days here without getting bored, but it's possible to cover the most interesting features in a weekend. With a single hike you can go from

the lush oak woodland around the Bear Gulch Visitors Center to the dry and desolate crags of the high peaks, then back down through a half-mile-long cave complete with underground waterfalls (see the **High Peaks Trail** listing under "Day Hikes"). If you're coming into the park from the west entrance, there are a couple of other day-hike options. The **Juniper Canyon Trail** is a short (1.2-mile) but very steep blast to the top of the high peaks. You'll definitely earn the view. Otherwise, try the short **Balconies Trail** to the monument's other talus cave, **Balconies Cave** (bring a flashlight).

What to Do & Where to Do It

BIRD WATCHING

The list of birds you can see on the central coast is pretty much endless, given the variety of ecosystems and climatic zones that meet in this part of the state. Particularly noteworthy is the large variety of raptors common here. **Pinnacles National Monument** is the largest nesting area of raptors in California; you'll often see kestrels, black-shouldered kits, red-tailed hawks, Cooper's hawks, and the occasional peregrine falcon or golden eagle soaring over the volcanic towers, which make such fine nesting sites. Much zoological and ornithological study has been done on the Pinnacles, and the visitor center at **Bear Gulch** (☎ 408/389-4485) has extremely detailed species lists available.

Big Sur is also a raptor hot spot. Bald eagles and peregrine falcons have been reintroduced into the **Ventana Wilderness** (☎ 408/385-5434). Other woodland birds commonly seen are the chestnut-tailed chickadee, California towhee, hermit thrush, lesser goldfinch, and Lewis woodpecker. The coastal river mouths like **Andrew Molera State Park** (☎ 408/667-2315) or the **Little Sur River** are great places to look for sea and shorebirds like willets, snowy plovers, sanderlings, pelicans, grebes, and numerous migratory species. A list of birds in the area is available for 25¢ at the Andrew Molera State Park entrance.

BOARDSAILING

One thing you can say about the Big Sur coast is that the wind always blows, and it blows hard. Unfortunately, most of the 60-plus miles of coastline are inaccessible except by foot, and the trails to the beach are often precipitous. That pretty much eliminates Big Sur as a boardsailing destination except for the most hard-core. It's not that far, however, to **Cambria, San Simeon,** and **Cayucos,** beaches south of here popular with advanced, high-wind sailors.

FISHING

Inland, the fishing here is pretty limited. The **Big Sur and Little Sur rivers** both offer some beautiful fly-fishing water in the winter and spring, but are subject to closure due to runs of endangered steelhead trout that use these rivers to spawn. Higher up the Big Sur River near **Sykes Hot Spring** I've caught and released small trout on flies and lures. Always check with the Forest Service at Big Sur Station to find out the most recent regulations here before casting, as the fishery seems to be in a state of flux.

The Pacific is a different story. Cold nearshore water, rich and rocky habitat, and relatively light use make Big Sur a surf fisherman's dream come true. It's not uncommon to catch large ling cod, cabezon, and red snapper straight off **Willow Creek, Pfeiffer Beach,** or **Garrapata Beach.** Like all coastal-dependent sports in Big Sur, the hardest thing is getting to the water. That, and the often adverse wind and surf conditions.

Only at Willow Creek in the southern end of Big Sur can you launch a small inflatable or skiff.

Randy's Fishing Trips, Fisherman's Wharf, Monterey (☎ 831/372-7440), offers full-day deep-sea fishing trips down to the waters off Point Sur.

HIKES, BUSHWHACKS & BACKPACK TRIPS

More than 400 miles of hiking trails cut through the Big Sur area of Los Padres National Forest and another 30 or so miles traverse the Pinnacles. Main trails into and through the Ventana Wilderness are Pine Ridge Trail, Carmel River Trail, and the Arroyo Seco Trail.

Day Hikes
Mount Carmel Trail, Ventana Wilderness

10 miles round-trip. Strenuous. Access: Bottcher's Gap Trailhead, Ventana Wilderness. Map: Ventana Wilderness trail map (Forest Service topo maps are available, but you won't need them—the brush here is much too thick to bushwhack).

This trail leads through some of the least-used backcountry of the Ventana Wilderness to the summit of Mount Carmel. Thickly covered with scrub oak, this 4,417-foot peak would be viewless were it not for a rock outcropping that fortuitously graces the summit. From the top of the rock, the 360° views take in the Carmel Valley, Salinas Valley, Monterey Bay, and much of the Ventana backcountry. If the view from here isn't enough, a mysterious telephone pole with rungs is located on the summit and juts about 3 feet higher. Just a pole, no lines. Go figure.

Bluff–Panorama Ridge Loop, Andrew Molera State Park

9 miles. Moderate. Access: Andrew Molera State Park; trailhead at beach at the mouth of the Big Sur River (see "Beach and Headlands Trail," below,

under "Walks & Rambles"). Map: Andrew Molera State Park map.

The Bluff Trail circles most of the high points of the 4,800-acre park. It skirts the top of the ocean bluff for almost 2 miles. To the north is Point Sur and the lighthouse. South is Cooper Point. This coastal grassland blossoms with numerous wildflowers during the spring and early summer, including lupine, sage, poppies, and Indian paintbrush. Before the trail circles left, crossing the ridge and returning to the parking area, a spur trail leads down to the beach, offering the chance to hike 2 miles back to the river in lieu of the loop trail. Hikers who opt to stay on the loop will cross the ridge via a switchbacked path and return through a deeply shaded oak grove. Look for circling vultures and hawks cruising the updrafts. As the loop heads back, another cutoff, Hidden Trail, leads down to the Big Sur River. Many lush meadows carpet the river valley here. Deer are common, and summer footbridges allow you to cross over to Highway 1. Otherwise, remain on the ridge trail until you return to the river mouth and beach, then hike the short ranch road back to the parking lot.

Coast Ridge Road, Los Padres National Forest

10 miles to Terrace Creek Trail, round-trip, returning to Ventana Inn; 12 miles to Big Sur Station via Terrace Creek Trail and Pine Ridge Trail. Moderate. Access: Los Padres National Forest. Park in the clearly signed Vista Point lot at the Ventana Inn or in the pullout on Hwy. 1; please don't park in the restaurant lot or the Ventana Inn lot itself. Trailhead just below the inn. Map: Los Padres National Forest map.

The Coast Ridge Road climbs steeply to the crest of the Santa Lucias and then heads south, switchbacking over the ridge with alternating views of the ocean and wilderness. Though the road is almost 25 miles long, it's the first 4 or 5 miles you're interested in. Just below the restaurant

you'll see a locked gate swathed in ominous NO TRESPASSING signs. Take note, then head on—the Coast Ridge Road has been at the center of a public-access battle for years now. The Forest Service owns and maintains the graded dirt road; thus, taxpayers own it and have the right to walk, bike, or horseback ride on it. Several private-property owners who use the road feel differently, however, and do everything they can to keep you out. The best policy is to be extremely careful not to trespass on private land, but if anyone hassles you for being on the road, politely tell them that Coast Ridge Road is a public easement; you pay for it, and you plan on using it. Almost immediately after passing the gate, you'll enter a cool redwood grove. Several spur roads lead above and below the road. These are driveways. Stay off! In half a mile you'll come to one of the most interesting-looking waterfalls around. Marble from upstream dissolved and subsequently resolidified as it trickled down the face of a 40-foot cascade, forming a sort of stalactite hanging from the hillside.

Almost immediately after the falls, you'll exit the trees and begin traversing grassy hillsides. In spring, this area is carpeted with poppies, lupine, Indian paintbrush, and blooming yuccas. The view north is the best perspective on the Big Sur Valley I've ever found, with Point Sur and Molera Point capping the course of the winding river valley. The road heads south, leading to dramatic ridgelines and canyons where you can peer down onto Partington Ridge, an ultra-private cluster of homes where author Henry Miller lived upon his return to the United States after years in Paris. In 4.2 miles you'll come to a grove of red-barked madrones. Here you'll find the trailhead for the Terrace Creek Trail, which drops down to the Pine Ridge Trail, allowing the opportunity to loop back to Big Sur Station. But the walk back down Coast Ridge Road is shorter and just as nice.

Tan Bark Trail, Julia Pfeiffer Burns State Park

6.6 miles round-trip. Moderate. Access: Julia Pfeiffer Burns State Park; trailhead uphill from the parking pullout for Partington Cove, about a mile north of the McWay Falls parking lot. Map: Ventana Wilderness or Los Padres National Forest map.

The Tan Bark Trail is the remnant of a skid-trail system used to haul tan oaks and redwoods down to Partington Cove to be loaded onto schooners bound for San Francisco to the north. It's a fairly short trail but climbs more than 2,000 feet in 3.3 miles. The drainage of Partington Creek is home to a lush forest of tan oaks and several redwood groves. You'll switch-back through many different plant communities on the way up—including plenty of poison oak, so watch out. On a clear day, the top, near an interesting-looking tin house, offers great views and is a good place to stop for a picnic before heading down.

Vicente Flat Trail, Ventana Wilderness

6.8 miles round-trip. Moderate. Access: Trailhead at Kirk Creek Campground, Ventana Wilderness. Map: Los Padres National Forest map.

Beginning at Kirk Creek Camp on Highway 1 in the southern reaches of Big Sur, this gives some of the most consistently stunning ocean views of any trail in the region as it climbs into the Ventana Wilderness. It's a simple hike. Just find the Vicente Flat Trail (also sometimes called Kirk Creek Trail though it doesn't follow Kirk Creek) across the road from the car campground and head on up. For 3.4 miles you'll switchback through fields of wildflowers and mixed oak and bay trees. Occasionally you'll traverse gullies lined with redwoods. Overall you'll gain 2,000 feet in elevation from the starting point, which is only 164 feet above sea level. By the time you reach Espinosa Camp, the views up and down the coast

will make you dizzy. Below lie Hare Creek and Limekiln Creek canyons, home to some of Big Sur's best redwood groves. When you've had enough, return the way you came.

High Peaks Trail, Pinnacles National Monument

6 miles. Moderate. Bring a flashlight for Bear Gulch Cave. Access: Pinnacles National Monument; trailhead at visitor center. Map: Pinnacles National Monument trail map.

This wonderful day hike allows you to see almost all of Pinnacles National Monument in a single day: caves, rock spires, circling raptors, and stunning views of the Salinas Valley and San Andreas Fault. Take Condor Gulch Trail from the visitor center. As you climb quickly out of the parking area, the Pinnacles' wind-sculpted spires seem to grow taller. In less than 2 miles you are among them and Condor Gulch intersects with the High Peaks Trail. The view from the top spans miles: the Salinas Valley to your west, the Pinnacles below, and the coast ranging to the east. After traversing the high peaks (including stretches of footholds carved in steep rock faces) for about a mile, the trail drops back toward the visitor center via a valley filled with eerie hoodoos. In another 1.5 miles you'll reach the reservoir marking the top of Bear Gulch Cave. You'll need your flashlight and might get wet, but this 0.6-mile-long talus cave is a thrill. From the end of the cave you're just a short walk through the most popular climbing area of the park away from the visitor center. If the cave is closed due to rain or earthquakes, then return via Moses Spring Trail.

Overnights

There are no backpacking outfitters in Big Sur, though the **Sierra Club** (☎ **415/ 977-5630**) runs a weeklong trek through the Ventana Wilderness every spring at the peak of wildflower season; the cost is approximately $360. The **Esalen**

Institute (☎ 408/667-3005) also runs one or two wilderness backpacking courses each summer.

Pine Ridge Trail, Ventana Wilderness
18.4 miles round-trip. Strenuous. Access: Big Sur Station Trailhead, Ventana Wilderness. Map: Ventana Wilderness map.

This is the most popular trail in the Ventana Wilderness by far. The reason? Sykes Hot Spring, 9.2 miles up the Big Sur River. If hot water and backcountry crowds aren't your thing, then this isn't your trail. However, if the thought of soaking in a 104°F pool on the banks of a gurgling river after a hard day's hike appeals to you, aim for midweek or a wintertime weekend and check Sykes out. From the Big Sur Station Trailhead the path climbs directly up the mountain-side, skirting the Big Sur River Gorge. Steep and hot, this is the worst part of the entire trip. Once beyond sight of the Big Sur Valley, you'll climb up and down ridges, sometimes near the river, often high above. Midway to Sykes is the Barlow Flat Camp, a perfect place to stop and swim on your way in or a nice lay-over if you're planning a longer trip. You'll come to the river a second time 9.2 miles after leaving the road. Here the trail crosses and heads away from the river. You're there. The hot spring is about 0.25 miles downstream on the south bank. The number and size of pools vary seasonally. Campsites are strung up and down the river. Good trout fishing in both directions. Wilderness permits required.

Bottcher's Gap to Ventana Double Cone, Ventana Wilderness
30 miles round-trip. Strenuous. Access: Bottcher's Gap (Palo Colorado Rd.). Map: Ventana Wilderness map.

This 30-mile round-trip takes you through the loneliest part of the Ventana Wilderness and to the summit of 4,853-foot Ventana Double Cone, the highest peak in the wilderness reachable by trail.

Along the way you'll take in some of the most expansive country in the coast range. Unfortunately, this is one of the driest areas of the wilderness too. You'll depend on tiny creeks and the occasional spring for water, and the second half of the hike is even drier. For this reason it's often better to hike one day into Puerto Suelo Camp (11.5 miles) where there is a spring and shade, then day-hike to the summit and back (15 miles round-trip), allowing you to blast up and back with just water and food. On top of the higher southern summit you'll find the remains of an old fire lookout and occasionally a windbreak of scrap wood. From here you can see virtually all of the Ventana Wilderness. To the east-southeast you'll spot a mountain that is considerably high-er than any other. That's Junípero Serra Peak, at 5,862 feet the highest in the cen-tral coast range. Because of its dry nature it is best to do this hike in the early spring when you'll catch blooming wildflowers and running creeks. Later in the season it is hot beyond belief and the flies will eat you alive.

HORSEBACK RIDING

A private concession operating from the old barn and corral inside Andrew Molera State Park, **Molera Trail Rides** (☎ 408/625-8664) leads 2-hour trail rides through the park. Reservations required for all rides. **Ventana Wilderness Expeditions** (☎ 408/659-2153) offers 3- to 7-day packstock trips into the Ventana Wilderness.

KAYAKING

With its miles of beautiful, inaccessible coastline, Big Sur is perfectly suited to exploration by sea kayak. First, however, you have to get your boat to the water—no small feat itself—and then you have to deal with Big Sur's unpredictable wind, icy water, and waves. If you can handle that, you're in for the paddle of a lifetime. It's always prudent to head north from your put-in point. That way when the prevailing winds come up in the afternoon, they'll be at your back for the return trip.

One sunny February day, Leslie Moran (see "Outfitters," below) and I set out from Pfeiffer Beach to paddle a couple miles downcoast to Wreck Beach, an isolated beach reachable only by boat. Once we punched through the surf, it was smooth paddling offshore by huge sea cliffs and over eerie, surging, sucking rock boils. Pulling into the lee of a small point, we watched as migrating whales headed past. Several curious sea lions circled our boats. Back at Pfeiffer, the wind had come up and so had the swell. I got lucky and caught the first wave of the set and made it almost to the beach, got flipped in the shore break, and stood up in time to see Leslie scrambling over a big clean-up set. The waves kept getting bigger until eventually she just took off on one, making it halfway to the beach before the wave closed out and white water rolled her; then she swam in with her boat. We both laughed hard at our icy dunkings, but if getting wet isn't your idea of kayaking fun, then Big Sur on anything other than a totally calm day probably isn't the best place for you.

A few people do overnight kayak camp trips down the coast here. If you decide to, be aware that though the beach below the high tide line is public, most of the land along here is private. Be as subtle and discrete as possible when choosing a campsite.

Andrew Molera State Park, with its point-sheltered river mouth and long beach, would be a great launching point but for one thing—it's a mile from the parking lot to the beach here. Still, a few people do it.

The easiest launching spot in northern Big Sur is **Pfeiffer Beach**—you have to carry the boat only about a quarter mile, and it's flat. This beautiful sandy beach is located at the end of Sycamore Canyon Road. The coast in either direction is a mixture of high cliffs and secluded cove beaches. Pfeiffer is also a popular surfing spot, which tells you something about the launch. The second cove down is better; if there's a swell, you can paddle out in the lee of the rocks and scramble through the breaker zone during a lull.

A mile north of the main entrance to Julia Pfeiffer Burns State Park a small dirt road leads down a canyon, through a 200-foot tunnel blasted through stone, and out into rocky **Partington Cove.** You can still see huge eyebolts in the rock and the remains of a high lead here where schooners once tied up to take on loads of tanbark and redwood logs. The same sheltered conditions that let them come in so close let you launch the kayaks you just carried a quarter mile down that steep road. Bring a rope to help lower your kayaks into the water. Then it's just a matter of scrambling down the rocks and getting in. Downcoast is a large beach and beautiful McWay Falls. North is Fuller's Cove, a popular surfing spot and beautiful bay with a tumbling creek pouring down a side canyon.

When it's windy and bumpy up in northern Big Sur, **Willow Creek,** just past Pacific Valley, is often calm and flat. That's all relative of course, but the other plus is that you can drive your car within striking distance of the ocean here, saving you the hike with a boat on your head. Paddle upcoast from here and explore the other coves to the north. If it's really calm, head out to Plaskett Rock with a mask and snorkel.

Outfitters

The Moran sisters of **Aquatic Adventures of Big Sur,** P.O. Box 398, Big Sur, CA 93920 (☎ **408/667-2914**), take as few as 2 and as many as 12 out on open-cockpit kayaks—wet suit, boat, and paddle provided. They'll also take you diving off a kayak if that strikes your fancy. Most trips go to Willow Creek or Point Lobos, but they're flexible and specialize in small, custom adventures.

Monterey Bay Kayaks, 693 Del Monte Ave., Monterey (☎ **408/373-KELP**), concentrates mostly on the Monterey Bay but offers occasional tours of the Big Sur area.

MOUNTAIN BIKING

Big Sur would be a world-famous mountain-biking destination but for one thing: the Ventana Wilderness. Many Ventana trails would be great rides but, alas, they're off-limits to bikes, so we're out of luck.

Big Sur has no single track, but some of its fire roads make for unforgettable rides. Since the Los Padres National Forest has many inholdings (privately held land within the forest's boundaries), you'll have to be on the alert for vehicles on all the backcountry roads.

Coast Ridge Road

10–40 miles round-trip. Moderate. Graded dirt road. Access: Ventana Inn. Please do not park in restaurant or inn parking lot. Map: Los Padres National Forest map.

I just can't say enough about this ride. It's steep enough to be a workout, stable enough to be a doable, and has the best views of any ride in Big Sur. Stretching back for almost 20 miles along the edge of the Ventana Wilderness, it is also the longest ride beginning in the Big Sur Valley. Unfortunately, the Coast Ridge Road, which begins just below the famous Ventana Restaurant and scales to the crest of the Santa Lucias in a power-house 4.2 miles, is reportedly now closed to mountain bikes. The only reason I could get from the Forest Service, which maintains this dirt road as a fire access way and a trail easement into the Ventana Wilderness, is that private landowners along the route complained about bike traffic. Frankly, the Forest Service maintains this road with your tax dollars, and it is historically a public easement. You should be allowed to ride here. I'm not advocating trespassing, but I rode it anyway and no one said a word.

Old Coast Highway

14 miles one-way. Strenuous. Graded dirt road. Access: Begin at the roadside pull-out just above Andrew Molera State Park; Old Coast Hwy. to Bixby Bridge; Hwy. 1 loops back to where ride begins. Map: Los Padres National Forest map.

Before Bixby Bridge was completed at the end of 1932, travelers heading south into Big Sur from Carmel detoured 14 miles up Bixby Creek, through the Little Sur River Valley, over a few ridges, and then were deposited at the head of the Big Sur Valley at the entrance to current-day Andrew Molera State Park. Today, travelers whiz south along the coast road, cutting 9 miles and many hours off a once harrowing journey. In a rare incidence of what's good for cars is good for mountain bikers, the virtual abandonment of the Old Coast Highway other than as an access way to a few remote homes and ranches left cyclists with a splendid dirt road all to themselves.

The Old Coast Highway steeply ascends over the ridge into the Little Sur Valley. You'll wind through ranch country and drop along a few ridges before curving past a beautiful turn-of-the-century ranch compound and entering the lush river valley. Watch for wild turkeys in the open range land. Often they'll run in front of you for a mile or more, gobbling and clucking in a panic. In the river bottom, stop and absorb the scents and sounds of the Little Sur River running through an old-growth redwood forest. It's up and over another steep ridge from here, then down a long, fast hill. You'll pass a cluster of houses, including a geodesic dome. If you were a drop of water you'd be only a short distance from the bridge and ocean, but the road takes a radical detour up the seemingly vertical north side of Bixby Canyon. Just when you think the climb is going to do you in, boom, there you are, coasting down to Bixby Bridge and the Pacific Ocean. From here you can ride the 5 miles down

Highway 1 to your car with the wind at your back or get a ride with a friend. This is my favorite way to do this ride. The loop can be done in reverse, but the climbs are steeper that way, and the wind is in your face as you head north on Highway 1.

Andrew Molera State Park

Several short but sweet rides. Easy. Old ranch roads. Access: Molera Parking Area. Map: Molera trail map.

As a former ranch, 4,800-acre Molera is crisscrossed with numerous old dirt roads and trails. Some, but not all, are open to mountain bikes, and those designations keep changing. You're not going to find any long rides here, but if a short trail in beautiful surroundings is what you seek, ask at the front entrance which trails are currently open to bikes.

Nacimiento Road/Cone Peak

28 miles round-trip. Strenuous. Graded fire road and pot-holed pavement. Access: 1 mile south of the Kirk Creek Campground you'll come to Nacimiento-Fergusson Rd. Map: Los Padres National Forest map.

This is the only east-west link across the Santa Lucias. *Nacimiento* is the Spanish word for childbirth, and you'll feel like you've given birth after climbing this mother. Beginning at 48 feet above sea level, the road climbs a towering series of switchbacks to the crest of the mountains. After the first 7 miles, which are on paved (though not well-maintained) county roads, you'll be at 3,106 feet and see Cone Peak Road forking off to the left. Don't worry—it's only about another 2,049 feet of altitude and 10 to 15 miles of steep dirt road to the summit of 5,155-foot Cone Peak. Only 3 miles as the crow flies from the Pacific, Cone Peak's western escarpment is one of the steepest on the West Coast, more than a 30% incline. That's steep. It's all downhill from here. Hope you have good brakes.

ROAD BIKING

If you want to ride a road bike in Big Sur, you'll be doing a lot of riding along **Highway 1** since it's the only paved road that goes more than a few miles. Bicycle companies, like car companies, like to shoot photos of their products crossing Bixby Bridge or wheeling down the backside of Hurricane Point on Highway 1. Ooh, how romantic!, you think, fingering through the new *Trek* or *Bianchi* catalogue. I want to do that! This entire stretch of coast is a legendary bike tour, what with its incredible views, plentiful inns and campsites, and plenty of places to fill a water bottle, but those glossy images and romantic notions leave something unsaid, namely the ponderous motor homes, amphetamine-crazed sports-car drivers, and rubbernecking tourists too swept up in the views to watch out for anything as insignificant as a cyclist. With no shoulders and places where getting run off the road can mean a 400-foot fall into the drink, I've always found biking Highway 1 to be more hair-raising than worthwhile. A lot of people ride in worse places for worse reasons every day in urban California, but I'm just a country boy from Santa Barbara and the traffic here really freaks me out more than the view enchants me.

People touring through Big Sur, like all of the West Coast, generally ride from north to south to have the prevailing winds at their backs and the ocean that much closer. If you really want to bike this stretch, my advice is to do it midweek, and do the Carmel-to-Big-Sur stretch early in the day (I mean sunrise) when you can get a jump on southbound tourist traffic, or afternoon, late enough to be behind the traffic. Once south of the Big Sur Valley the traffic situation is better, though the road gets narrower and the cliffs taller.

Locally, no one is leading bicycle trips or renting equipment. Several of the larger statewide outfitters listed in chapter 1 lead road-biking trips through the area.

ROCK CLIMBING

The rotten and crumbly rock of the coast range limits the options for climbers, but this region is not without its attractions. Most climbers head to **Pinnacles National Monument,** the central coast's most famous climbing destination and home to the area's only long routes. Many routes are closed during the spring nesting season of several endangered raptors, including the peregrine falcon and golden eagle. The volcanic rock is soft and crumbly—always double-check holds before trusting your life to them. Most routes are bolted. If you're climbing a new route, be aware that protection can and will pull out of situations here where it wouldn't on better rock. The park service requests that all climbers check in at the Bear Gulch Visitors Center (☎ **408/389-4485**) on their way in. That's not a big problem, since Bear Gulch is where you'll find most of the well-marked and bolted routes. The visitor center has a free climbing supplement as well as an excellent selection of descriptive climbing guidebooks to the park.

A couple of groups and individuals lead guided climbing trips and classes to the Pinnacles: **Epic Adventures,** 993 9th St., Albany, CA 94710 (☎ **510/528-9884**), and **Pacific Edge Climbing Gym,** 104 Bronson, Santa Cruz, CA 95062 (☎ **831/454-9254**).

The **Big Sur Coast** also has a few short but exceptional climbing spots. The most well known of these are the granite outcroppings at **Garrapata Beach, Granite Creek,** and **Sea Otter Rocks** with many 5.8 to 5.10 routes. None are more than 30 feet high, and most are bolted top-rope situations. In winter, the high waves take away the sand beach below many of these routes, making for bad landings into rocky surf if you fall. Frankly, the climbing is much better elsewhere, but the fact that you're hanging out over the edge of the Pacific makes up for a lot of what the rock lacks. Several similar granite outcroppings exist down the coast at **Partington Cove** and points beyond. There are no really formal routes and the area is waiting to be explored.

SCUBA DIVING

With the world-famous diving of Monterey Bay to its north, Big Sur gets almost no visiting divers. On those rare occasions when the wind and waves cooperate, Big Sur is home to some of the wildest underwater habitat on the Central Coast. Large fish, thick kelp, and numerous marine mammals are the norm. Only dive here if you're really in shape and confident with your surf entries; the currents and surf here are extremely powerful. When conditions permit, boats from Monterey race down the coast to dive some rarely utilized spots, including several offshore rocks, and Granite Canyon in the northern edge of Big Sur.

Dive Sites

Willow Creek and Mill Creek
38 miles south of the Big Sur Valley, just past Pacific Valley.

Though often rocked by large surf, Willow Creek and Mill Creek a few miles north are the only places you can beach-launch an inflatable boat or dive board on the entire coast. Immediately north of the launch site are several rock reefs and nice cobblestone areas with thick kelp. Several more coves extend up the coast, with offshore sea-stack Plaskett Rock standing to the north. Jade is not uncommon in this area of Big Sur. In 1971, a team of three divers pulled up a 9,000-pound nephrite jade boulder near here that was valued at almost $200,000 after working for months to raise it from 30 feet. This state beach has rest rooms and picnic areas.

Partington Cove
36 miles south of Carmel on Hwy. 1, 1 mile north of the main entrance to Julia Pfeiffer Burns State Park.

By permission only (☎ 408/667-2315), divers are allowed to explore the rich environs of this sheltered cove. It's a fairly steep quarter-mile walk from Highway 1, and you'll have to enter and exit the water by clambering down a steep rock face. Still, it's one of the nicest dives in the area.

Outfitters

Sisters Laura Cuzner and Leslie Moran operate **Aquatic Adventures of Big Sur,** P.O. Box 398, Big Sur, CA 93920 (☎ 408/667-2914). They teach scuba certification classes at the River Inn in Big Sur and lead beach dives in the area. All equipment is provided. Prices vary depending on how many tanks and where you go. **Aquarius Dive Shop,** 2040 Del Monte Ave., Monterey, CA 93940 (☎ 800/833-9992 or 408/375-1933), and **Twin Otters, Inc.,** P.O. Box 8744, Monterey, CA 93943 (☎ 408/394-4235), both sometimes run trips down to Big Sur. Aquarius is also the nearest full-service dive shop to Big Sur for rentals and equipment sales.

SURFING

Big Sur's surf is fickle, but not in the usual sense of the word; here it's often too big rather than too little. Most of the really good spots are secret spots—hard to find, hard to reach, and heavily localized. **Fuller's Cove,** an insane left point-reef setup, is the hot Big Sur surf spot, and consequently the site of many ugly confrontations between extremely proprietary locals and people with less-than-perfect wave etiquette. Stay away unless you are an adept lineup diplomat. Spots that are more open to outsiders are **Willow Creek, Kirk Creek, Pfeiffer Beach,** and **Molera Point,** though localism runs strong just about everywhere here. Big Sur breaks better on a summertime south swell than during wintertime norths, when the stormy conditions often make it unsurfable.

SWIMMING

With its cold ocean temperatures, the beaches of Big Sur aren't exactly cut out for leisurely swims. The most you'll want to do is jump in to cool off on a rare hot day. Inland, however, the **Big Sur River Gorge** offers a number of great summer swimming holes. To reach them, park at Pfeiffer Big Sur State Park and walk the short Gorge Trail. From the deep pool at the bottom it's only a matter of your determination how high up the creek you go. There are numerous nice swimming holes and jumping rocks. The nicer hotels in Big Sur all have pools, but the only one open to the public is at the **River Inn** (☎ 408/667-2700) and requires a small day-use fee.

WALKS & RAMBLES

Soberanes Point Trail, Garrapata State Park

1.7-mile loop. Access: Garrapata State Park, Gate 13 on the west side of Hwy. 1, about 4 miles south of Point Lobos. Map: Los Padres National Forest map.

Once through the gate veer left at the junction onto this loop trail. In another 0.1 miles you can veer right or left depending on whether you prefer to do the loop clockwise or counterclockwise. The inland leg of the trail offers great views down the coast toward Point Sur and beautiful wildflowers in spring. A short side trail leads 0.3 miles to Whale Saddle, with short paths to the dual summits of North and South Whale Peaks. A viewing bench marks the spot. During winter months, particularly in early January, this spot and the two summits are some of the best places to spot passing gray whales, who cut close to Soberanes Point as they migrate south to calve. The seaward leg of the loop offers more intimate views of the crashing waves, tide-pool rocks, and sea stacks and arches. Hikers often spot sea otters, seals, and sea lions in the rich feeding waters just offshore. In spring, nesting seabirds colonize offshore rocks, and you can catch the whales on their way back north.

Beach and Headlands Trail, Andrew Molera State Park

2.8 miles round-trip. Access: Trailhead at parking lot near main entrance of Andrew Molera State Park. Map: Molera State Park map.

The Big Sur river mouth is one of the best birding spots on the central coast and the headlands of Molera Point are a perfect place to sit and watch a sunset and the plentiful wildlife of both the ocean and river estuary. This flat, 2.8-mile round-trip follows the Big Sur River through a beautiful riparian habitat in its last miles before the Pacific and also provides great beach access. Follow the trail on the north side of the river. In about 0.3 miles you'll pass through the walk-in camp with more than 100 sites, toilets, and running water. Continue on along the wide path past a cabin on your right. This is Cooper's cabin. Built in 1861, it's the oldest building in Big Sur.

Just past here the trail curves left, following the river through a grove of willows, blackberry, and poison oak. In about a mile, a fork to the left leads over a narrow summer-only footbridge to the beach. The right fork climbs a coastal bluff and leads out to Molera Point. Many species of shorebirds and seabirds take shelter from Pacific winds in the lee of the point and migratory steelhead trout can sometimes be spotted making their way upstream. On your way back, cross the footbridge to the long beach. During low tides it is possible to walk for miles downcoast over beautiful water-polished cobbles and past several small headlands, but you must be extremely aware of the incoming tide or it'll be a wet, cold, and potentially dangerous walk back. From the beach, return to the parking lot along an old ranch road through the beautiful riparian meadow trail south of the river.

Nature Trail, Pfeiffer Big Sur State Park

0.6 miles. Access: Just off the park road inside the entrance of Pfeiffer Big Sur State Park. Map: State Park map from front kiosk.

This trail introduces hikers to many of the plant species and habitats of the Big Sur region. Pick up the interpretive brochure at the park kiosk on your way in.

Gorge Trail, Pfeiffer Big Sur State Park

2 miles round-trip. Access: Trailhead is 0.1 miles from the Pfeiffer campground site 202, in Pfeiffer Big Sur State Park. Map: Los Padres National Forest map or State Park map.

The Gorge Trail leads you to a deep pool at the foot of the Big Sur River Gorge. Upstream from here are many more pools and falls, popular for swimming and sunbathing with locals and visitors alike in summer months, but you'll have to rock-hop and scramble to get there.

Pfeiffer Falls–Valley View Trail, Pfeiffer Big Sur State Park

1.8-mile loop. Access: Trailhead near Pfeiffer Big Sur State Park Nature Center; follow the signs. Map: State Park map.

This loop trail leads you through a beautiful redwood grove to delicate 60-foot-tall Pfeiffer Falls. In the creek bottom below the falls is a lush verdant mixture: sword fern, five-finger ferns, chain ferns, lichen, and tan oak all contribute to a rich green hue. Several footbridges cross the creek before you'll come to the tiny but beautiful ribbon of water contrasted against a dark cliff. Beyond the falls, the Valley View Trail leads onto the nearby ridge for a panoramic view of Pfeiffer Big Sur State Park.

McWay Falls, Julia Pfeiffer Burns State Park

0.5 miles. Access: Trailhead at parking lot inside Julia Pfeiffer Burns State Park. Map: Los Padres National Forest map.

It may be short, but this half-mile trail to the overlook of McWay Falls is worth stopping for. From the parking lot inside the park descend the stairs and follow a wide path through a tunnel under Highway 1. At the trail's end, watch McWay Creek splatter itself onto the beach below in one of the most ridiculously beautiful falls you'll ever see—depending on the tide it sometimes actually falls straight into the turquoise-hued Pacific. A short detour on the way back leads to the Pelton Wheel, an early water-powered generator that provided the first electricity for the Pfeiffer homestead.

Bear Gulch Trail, Pinnacles National Monument

1.5 miles. Bring a flashlight for Bear Gulch Cave. Access: Trailhead at visitor center of Pinnacles National Monument. Map: National Monument trail map.

This is one of the most unique short hikes in California. The trail leaves right from the visitor center on the east side of the park and goes through the most shaded and lush part of this otherwise harsh landscape. Numerous climbing routes exist on the overhanging walls of the canyon. Eventually you'll come to Bear Gulch Cave. If you've thought ahead to bring a flashlight, you can explore this 0.4-mile-long talus cave. Some chambers are pitch dark. Others are spacious grottos with diffuse light seeping in through high-up entrances. A creek and several falls run through the cave.

WHALE WATCHING

Nowhere on the California coast have I seen as many whales as at Big Sur. Particularly in the southern stretches of Highway 1, near Kirk Creek, it seems like every time you look at the ocean, a whale spouts. The winter months, when the gray whales are headed north to their summer feeding grounds off Alaska, are the best times to spot a spout, but whales are present here year-round. Almost any roadside pullout makes a

good whale-watching perch, but several spots are perennial favorites.

The elevated headland of **Molera Point,** at the mouth of the Big Sur River in Andrew Molera State Park, gives a good perspective on passing whales that cut nearshore on their way around Point Sur. It's a mile hike from the Molera parking lot to the point.

Another good spot is the **Point Sur Lighthouse.** This 19th-century lighthouse is only open 3 days a week by guided tour, but it's one of the most amazing spots to watch whales as they round the corner formed by the point, even if only for a few minutes. Call ☎ **408/625-4419** to reserve tour space.

Pfeiffer Beach lacks the expansive views of many other spots in Big Sur, but the two huge rocks that stick up out of the sand make up one of my favorite spots to watch the whales go by. You'll have to climb hand over hand to get up, but the intimate view more than compensates you for the struggle. Not for the faint-hearted, however.

Finally, **Soberanes Point,** a large expanse of oceanfront land in **Garrapata State Park,** is a favorite whale-watching perch, either from the cliffs or from the top of aptly named Whale Peak. (See "Soberanes Point Trail" under "Walks & Rambles," above.)

Campgrounds & Other Accommodations

CAMPING

When it comes to camping, Big Sur is more hospitable and better equipped than just about any other region in California. In contrast to many parts of the state, where pulling off the road in your

VW bus on the cliff above your favorite surf break, popping the top, and crawling into a sleeping bag for the night is probable cause for arrest and police harassment, or an invitation to every sociopath for 100 miles, here it is an ages-old and well-respected tradition; no one will hassle you at all. Heck, they might even bring you breakfast.

Obviously most campers in Big Sur still choose a more official approach to lodging, and there are plenty of choices ranging from the deluxe to bare bones. Two of my favorite coastal campsites in the state are here: one, the cliff-top environmental campsite at the top of McWay Falls in **Julia Pfeiffer Burns State Park,** is extremely hard to get; the other, the walk-in campground at **Andrew Molera,** is uncrowded even on a popular weekend. The following are my selections for the best public and private campsites in the area.

Bottcher's Gap

8 miles up Palo Colorado Rd., which leaves Hwy. 1 10 miles south of Carmel just past the Rocky Point Restaurant. Palo Colorado dead-ends into the campground. 20 sites; 9 tent-only, 11 tent or small RV. Pit toilets, running water, picnic tables, fire pits, food lockers. Dogs accepted on leash. Hiking. Open year-round. Fee charged. Call Big Sur Station (☎ 408/667-2423) for information.

Bottcher's Gap Camp is nothing special, but I'm listing it because this is the trailhead to some of the more remote hikes into the Ventana Wilderness, such as Mount Carmel or the overnight to Ventana Double Cone. It's also one of the least crowded camps on a busy weekend. The place is pleasant, but other than hiking, there's nothing much here.

Andrew Molera Walk-In Campground

21 miles south of Carmel in Andrew Molera State Park. ☎ 408/667-2315. More than 100 sites. Running water, chemical toilets, picnic tables, fire pits, and food storage boxes. Pets accepted

on leash. Bring your own wood or buy it at entrance station. Wildlife, bird and whale watching, hiking, swimming, horseback riding, kayaking, biking, surfing. Open year-round. First-come, first-served. $3 per night.

Amazing the difference a quarter-mile walk makes. Though the campsites themselves are nothing to write home about and the chemical potties will make you think twice before sucking down that second cup of coffee, Andrew Molera is one of the most spectacular settings anywhere, with its wild beach and thousands of acres of undeveloped land. This campground is often desolate when Big Sur's car camping sites are totally booked, but it's a good idea to call ahead before coming on a busy weekend. It's extremely laid back—I'm absolutely phobic about calling PARKNET to reserve campsites in advance, so I depend on Molera for those impromptu journeys up the coast.

Fernwood Park, Big Sur Campground, and Riverside Campground

On the Big Sur River between Andrew Molera and Pfeiffer Big Sur State Parks. Showers, fireplaces, rest rooms, stores, Laundromats, playgrounds, dump stations. Dogs permitted if leashed. Reservations required; Fernwood, ☎ 408/667-2422 ($24–$27); Big Sur, ☎ 408/667-2322 ($24–$42); Riverside, ☎ 408/667-2414 ($25–$28).

I wouldn't have included these except for the fact that they are the last car-camping sites in the Big Sur Valley to fill up (no doubt because they cost a small fortune) and are a good option as a last resort. I have to admit to a certain bias against most private campgrounds; they're often cramped, overpriced, and shoddy. Well, none of these three are shoddy; in fact, they're well kept and managed, but the sites are too close together and way too expensive for what you get. All three are surrounded by private (no trespassing!) land, so hiking from camp is out, and they're just too overdeveloped for my idea of a nature experience. Also, because of their location in the shadow of Pfeiffer Ridge, they don't get a lot of daylight.

Pfeiffer Big Sur State Park

29 miles south of Carmel on Hwy. 1 in the Big Sur Valley. 217 campsites for tents and RVs up to 32 ft. Also primitive bike-in camp. Piped water, flush toilets, showers, fireplaces, tables. Nearby in the park is a Laundromat, grocery, restaurant, gas, and propane. Hiking, swimming. Pets permitted on leash. Car sites $14–$23 per night. Bike sites $3. Pets $1. Reserve through PARKNET (☎ 800/444-PARK).

This is the mother of all car-camping sites in Big Sur and one of the most heavily used in the state. Normally, I'd tell you to just keep on driving, but the hikes, river, and redwoods here make the hassles worthwhile. Pfeiffer Beach is a short drive, the Ventana Wilderness begins at the park boundary, and Big Sur Station— the joint agency headquarters for federal and state information services—is a half-mile stroll. Reservations are a necessity on any summertime weekend here.

Ventana Campground

About 2 miles south of Pfeiffer Big Sur State Park, below the Ventana Inn. P.O. Box 206, Big Sur, CA 93920. ☎ 408/667-2688. 70 tent sites. Rest rooms and showers. Small store across the highway. Four-star Ventana Restaurant up the hill. Pets accepted on leash. $20 per site. Open year-round.

Okay, so it's expensive. Otherwise this is one of the most beautiful car-camping sites in the Big Sur Valley, with none of the usual negatives of a private campground. Spacious sites are interspersed throughout a towering redwood grove.

Julia Pfeiffer Burns State Park Environmental Walk-In Campsites

About 10 miles south of the Big Sur Valley on Hwy. 1. ☎ 408/667-2315. 2 walk-in sites (0.25 miles, level). Pit toilets, picnic tables, million-dollar view.

Wildlife, hiking, kayaking. Fees about $14.

I'd sleep on a bed of nails to wake up with the view these two sites have from their perch under cypress trees at the top of McWay Falls, a 60-foot-tall ribbon of water that catapults out of McWay Canyon and lands on the beach below. Crashing waves, birds, whales, and otters will be your only neighbors here at night. During the day it can be a little bit of a drag dealing with all the people who haplessly wander down "your" private trail to this choice spot. Oh well. Call the park for information on how to reserve these two special sites.

Kirk Creek, Los Padres National Forest

4 miles south of Lucia on Hwy. 1. 33 sites for tents or RVs. Also, bike-in sites. Flush toilets, running water, picnic tables, fireplaces. Hiking, biking, surfing, fishing, bird watching, wildlife, swimming. $16 per site; $5 for bike sites. Call Los Padres National Forest (☎ 805/683-6711) for reservations. Open year-round.

Located on a high bluff overlooking a cobblestone beach of gemlike agates and other exotic-looking rocks, Kirk Creek has such outrageous views you won't even notice the sites are a little too close together and the people next door are watching "The Simpsons" on their satellite TV instead of the sunset. Besides the beach, great hiking (Kirk Creek Trail) and biking (Nacimiento Road) begin just across Highway 1. Surfing and fishing are sometimes great from the beach below. Lucia, 4 miles north, is a quaint little town with most services.

Arroyo Seco, Los Padres National Forest

On the edge of the Ventana Wilderness 19 miles west of Greenfield and U.S. 101. 33 tent or motor-home sites. 1 group site. Running water, pit toilets, fireplaces, picnic tables, bathrooms, showers. Hiking, bird watching, wildlife, swimming, rock climbing, caving. Pets accepted. $15 per night. No reservations. Open year-round.

This campground in the pretty ranch lands of the Arroyo Seco area is a major trailhead into the back side of the Ventana Wilderness as well as a beautiful spot in its own right.

Pinnacles Campground, Inc.

Just outside the east entrance of Pinnacles National Monument, 2.5 miles off State Rte. 25 between Hollister and King City. 125 sites for tents and motor homes. Flush toilets, showers, running water, picnic tables, fire pits, firewood for sale, store, swimming pool, RV disposal station. Hiking, bird watching, wildlife, rock climbing, caving. Pets accepted. Group camps can be reserved by calling ☎ 408/389-4462. $4 reservation fee. Sites are $7 per person per night with a $28 maximum. Group sites $60 minimum.

I've included this campground and not the actual National Monument Campground on the west side of Pinnacles because the east side is where all the action is and the west side is dry and desolate. Rangers from the monument hold interpretive programs here on weekend nights. It's a long hike but a short drive or bike ride from here to the main park attractions around Bear Gulch. Perhaps because it's popular with climbers and hikers more than motor-homers, this is the nicest private campground I've seen: lots of room between sites, ranchlike setting, natural vegetation, minimal road system, and a nice, on-site manager. The pool can be a blessing because it gets scorching at the Pinnacles.

INNS & LODGES

Nobody (I hope!) goes to Big Sur to hang around inside a hotel, so the people here have developed their own style to bring the lodging outdoors and the outdoors inside: natural landscapes, plentiful glass to frame captivating views, fireplaces, and wood construction.

Deetjen's Big Sur Inn

5 miles south of the Big Sur Valley on Hwy. 1. ☎ 408/667-2377. 20 units. $75–$180 per night. MC, V.

With 20 highly individual rooms and several buildings, including a barn, this eclectic, funky historical inn is one of the coolest places you'll ever stay: no locks on the doors, handmade furniture, and a wildly overgrown garden as well as great food and company. The restaurant and bar are open to nonguests as well. Castro Creek runs through the grounds. Julia Pfeiffer Burns State Park is a few miles south. Very bohemian, very Big Sur. Don't make the mistake of confusing Deetjen's Big Sur Inn with the poorly operated Big Sur Lodge in Pfeiffer Big Sur State Park.

The Ventana Inn

28 miles south of Carmel on Hwy. 1. ☎ 408/624-4812. 62 rms, 3 villas. $260 and up per night. AE, DC, DISC, MC, V.

The Ventana Inn is very Big Sur in a different way. This laid-back love nest of the rich and famous is ultradiscreet and luxurious in a way only a four-star hotel on the edge of a wilderness can be. With two 25-meter pools, Japanese whirlpool baths and sauna, staff masseuse, and a clothing-optional sun deck, this is a fabulous place to lie in the sun and iron out those kinks in your psyche. The landscaping is all native plants; hammocks hang in the trees. Deer graze outside your room, and the first thing that wakes you in the morning will probably be a wild turkey gobbling outside your window. Though most people don't leave the grounds, some really great hiking surrounds the inn, and the staff will advise you or arrange for a guide.

The Ventana Restaurant (expensive) has the best dinner in Big Sur and a great view from its outside decks. Breakfast (complimentary) is a delicious mix of

California fruits, homemade granola, croissants, fresh bread, juices, and hot coffee or tea. *Tip:* Don't come here by yourself unless you feel like being the odd person out; this is very much a lovey-dovey couples sort of place, and even if you weren't lonely when you came, you'll feel like a hermit by the time you leave. I speak from experience.

Esalen Institute
10 miles north of Lucia. ☎ **408/ 667-3005.** Shared rooms begin at $80–$150 per night with 3 meals, but residence rates are usually connected to seminar or workshop fees. AE, MC, V.

Once a hippie hotbed where Joan Baez, Hunter Thompson, Carlos Castenada, and many others of that generation hung out to get back to nature, Esalen is still a counterculture haven, though now it leans more toward the crystal-clutching New Age than the good old days of gobbling acid and roaring down the coast on motorcycles. Still, Esalen is the site of many interesting seminars and workshops, ranging from shamanic healing and psychosynthesis to massage (Esalen has its own style of massage named after it) and wilderness trips. You can also come here just to chill out. Simple, shared accommodations (often in bunk beds) in a variety of buildings on the oceanfront Esalen campus include lunch and access to the famous Esalen hot springs. The hot springs here are some of the nicest in the world—terraced into a sea cliff, clothing optional. Don't come if you are uncomfortable with nudity. Call for information about programs or reservations.

5

The Wine Country & Delta

The Wine Country of Napa, Sonoma, Lake, and Mendocino counties has achieved a worldwide fame in the last 20 years for giving even the finest wine-making regions of France a run for their money. The climate and soil here are perfect for growing high-quality wine grapes, and an entire culture has been built up around the wineries. Each weekend swarms of visitors descend to trek from tasting room to tasting room, sometimes causing traffic jams on the main roads. Though it can all seem a little too precious—too much money, too many European sports cars, and too many affected accents—the rolling hills and country roads of the Wine Country are ideal for world-class bicycle touring. Several bike shops offer rentals, and almost all the big bike-touring companies, like Backroads, offer multiday trips through the area. The main roads can be a little hairy with all that traffic, but once on the rural side routes, bicycling here is a ride in heaven.

Another quirk of nature has turned the entire area into Spa Central. Numerous hot springs underlying area towns like Calistoga, Geyserville, and Middletown have been tapped to create a mecca for the sore-muscled or the stressed out—the perfect denouement to a hard weekend in the saddle or on the trail. Besides biking, the Wine Country is also blessed with great hiking in the several state parks here, and is home to Clear Lake, one of California's largest natural lakes.

If the Wine Country is southern France in California, the Sacramento River Delta, at the confluence of the San Joaquin and Sacramento rivers, is Holland. Once a huge series of tule marshes richly populated with wildlife that covered hundreds of square miles, the delta is now a diked-off maze of sloughs, below-water-level "islands," deepwater channels, and huge farms of sunflowers, rice, and soybeans. The towns in this part of the state are usually nothing more than a gas pump and a post office. Most visitors come by boat anyway, not by land, the houseboat being the best way to

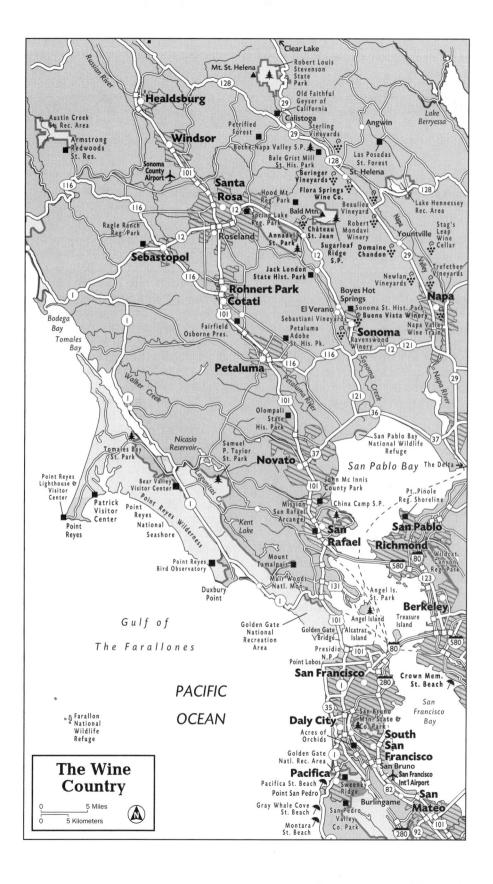

The Wine Country

0   5 Miles
0   5 Kilometers

| Napa's Average Temperatures and Precipitation | | | | | | | | | | | |
	Jan	Feb	Mar	Apr	May	June	July	Aug	Sept	Oct	Nov	Dec
High (°F)	56	61	64	69	73	79	81	81	82	76	67	58
Low (°F)	38	40	41	43	47	50	52	52	50	47	42	39
Precipitation (in.)	4.9	4.2	3.3	1.7	0.8	0.2	0.0	0.0	0.4	1.2	2.4	4.4

travel. In this Huck Finn swamp, you can hide away in a quieter time and place, whether you've officially come to fish, houseboat, bicycle the levees, camp, or bird-watch.

Since the delta is the largest break in the coast range, winds off the San Francisco Bay and Pacific Ocean funnel through the narrow straits and hit the western edge of the delta with full force. Rio Vista has become a popular speed boardsailing spot as a result. With flat water and howling winds, plus little other boat traffic, this could be the next Columbia Gorge.

The Lay of the Land

The Wine Country is actually two distinct valleys, Sonoma and Napa, separated by a low range of hills. **Napa,** the more famous, is the easternmost valley, and runs from the north end of **San Pablo Bay** to the foothills below **Mount St. Helena,** near the town of **Calistoga.** The Napa River runs down the center of the valley, with the vineyards running in a narrow strand beside it. Some of the most famous—Stag's Leap, Domaine Chandon, and Beringer— are within a few miles of each other. At the valley's north end, the grape fields give way to pines as you climb into the mountains surrounding **Clear Lake,** the state's largest natural lake.

Only a few miles west, but a world away in profile, the **Sonoma** Wine Country is less congested and slower paced. Though

it's quickly developing into a suburban corridor for San Francisco, Sonoma nevertheless retains much of the area's grassland and oak trees in broad sections of protected land. Some of the hillsides have begun to give way to vineyards here too, however, a development that may someday move the vines from the realm of postcards to that of environmental impact reports. Sonoma is a broader valley than Napa, giving the area a more spread-out, roomy feel. In the far north, the **Russian River** runs past the B&B town of **Healdsburg** and on toward the coast, while in the south, the primary waterway is the heavily channelized **Petaluma River,** which isn't good for much recreation, but offers sailors a route down to San Pablo Bay.

San Pablo Bay itself is the gateway to the Sacramento and San Joaquin river **delta,** a popular boating and fishing area where the rivers spill into the San Francisco bay system. Though also heavily managed, waters south of the Wine Country are mobbed by party boats and water-skiers every weekend. Roads dip in and out of the area where the brackish water and muddy soil allow.

Orientation

Navigation in the area boils down to three roads. Both the Sonoma and Napa valleys run generally north-to-south, with a road running down the middle. **Highway 12** runs along the floor of the Sonoma Valley, between Santa Rosa and the city of Sonoma. **Highway 29** runs down the Napa Valley, parallel to Highway 12.

Just south of the valleys, **Route 37** meanders east along the north shore of the delta, dipping into the towns along the way.

Sonoma Valley

The **Sonoma Valley Visitors Bureau,** 453 1st St. E., Sonoma, CA 95476 (☎ **707/ 996-1090**), is a great source of lodging and service information for the entire Sonoma Valley and surrounding region.

Napa Valley

The **Napa Chamber of Commerce,** 1556 1st St., Napa, CA 94559 (☎ **707/ 226-7455**), offers the best general service information for the Napa Valley.

Healdsburg

The **Healdsburg Area Chamber of Commerce,** 217 Healdsburg Ave., Healdsburg, CA 95448 (☎ **707/ 433-6935**), provides good maps and other resources about the Russian River Valley and Healdsburg proper.

Rio Vista

The **Rio Vista Chamber of Commerce,** 75 Main St., Rio Vista, CA 94571 (☎ **707/ 374-2700**), is a great source of information about the backwaters of the delta. Nearby, at Sandy Beach County Park, is some of the best boardsailing on the Sacramento River.

Parks & Other Hot Spots

Annadel State Park

Channel Dr., via Mission Blvd. and Montgomery Dr., east of Santa Rosa and south of State Rte. 12. ☎ **707/ 539-3911**. Picnic tables, museum, water,

pit toilets, ghost town. Fishing, bird watching, hiking. No dogs. Open 9am–sunset.

This 5,000-acre park, just east of Santa Rosa, is woven with an elaborate web of trails that intersect and cross so often it's easy to get lost. Luckily the park map is good. Lake Ilsanjo, a man-made 26-acre pond, is good for catching black bass and bluegill in the spring. Of particular note is the Ledson Marsh, a neat little pocket wetland that is often home to migrating waterfowl, herons, and grebes.

Sugarloaf Ridge State Park

Adobe Canyon Rd., 7 miles east of Santa Rosa, north of State Rte. 12. ☎ **707/ 833-5712**. 49 campsites. Picnic tables; hiking, horse, and mountain bike trails; pit toilets; flush rest rooms; water. Day-use and camping fee.

Midway between Santa Rosa and Sonoma, Sugarloaf Ridge State Park contains almost the entire upper drainage of Sonoma Creek—lined in places by redwoods—and mile upon mile of hiking and biking trails. The high point of the park is 2,729-foot Bald Mountain, which offers an incredible view of the surrounding Wine Country.

Jack London State Park

Glen Ellen, about 20 min. north of Sonoma. ☎ **707/938-5216**. Picnic tables; museum; hiking, horse, and mountain bike trails; pit toilets; water. Daily 10am–7pm summer, 10am–5pm winter. Fee.

Jack London may be most famous for writing about the Arctic, but he lived much of his life here, just outside the tiny town of Glen Ellen. Besides its interesting literary history and wonderful museum of London's life, filled with memorabilia from his wide-flung travels, the park is also a great outdoors spot, with plenty of hiking and nature. Horse lovers will get a kick out of the 2-hour trail rides ($45) offered by **Sonoma Cattle Company** (☎ **707/996-8566**) on the trails here.

Clear Lake State Park
Soda Bay Rd., 3.5 miles northeast of Kelseyville. ☎ **707/279-4293.** 147 campsites. Picnic tables, hiking trails, swimming area, rest rooms, showers, water, boat launch. Kayaking, bird watching, fishing, hiking, swimming. Camping and day-use fee.

Clear Lake is almost 20 miles long and has about 100 miles of shoreline. Spring-fed and fairly shallow, the lake gets into the mid-70s during the summer—perfect for swimming and boating. It's also an important bird and fish habitat. Anglers pull largemouth bass, catfish, perch, and bluegill from the lake year-round. The 600-acre park is small, but it contains some great lake frontage. In summer the water turns a brownish-green from algae blooms, but is perfectly safe; it's a result of those same 76° waters that make the lake such an inviting swim.

Delta Meadows River Park
Most accessible by boat. Limited vehicle access is via a dirt road just north of the Cross Delta Canal, 100 yd. south of Locke. ☎ **916/777-6671.** Trails, pit toilets, no drinking water, primitive boat launch. Wildlife, bird watching, hiking, kayaking. Daylight hr.

Want to see what the delta looked like before it was leveed and diked into submission? Well, this is all that's left: a small expanse of wild marshland. River otters and beavers are the most common large mammals, and the birding possibilities here are endless. You can explore the park on foot, but the best bet is to poke around the wild Railroad Slough in a kayak or canoe. Bring your own—there's nothing much here in the way of services.

Brannan Island and Franks Tract State Recreation Areas
Brannan Island is on State Rte. 160, 3 miles south of Rio Vista. Franks Tract is only accessible by boat. ☎ **916/777-6671.** 102 regular campsites, 32 boat-in sites. Boat launch and slips, picnic tables, swimming area, rest rooms, showers. Fishing, kayaking. Camping, boat launch, and day-use fees.

These two recreation areas are perfect proof that what nature giveth, nature taketh away. Bordered by the Sacramento River, Brannan Island is one of the most popular fishing and boating centers of the delta. It offers a swimming area, camping, and access to miles of delta waterways. Franks Tract was not too long ago a leveed-off area of farmland and homes. Now, since the levees holding back the water collapsed, it's a lake. This is one of the most wide-open expanses of water in the whole delta, a perfect spot for water-skiers and boaters. Franks Tract can only be reached by boat, which you'll most likely want to launch at Brannan Island.

What to Do & Where to Do It

BALLOONING
Most of the ballooning in Northern California is found in the Wine Country, and that means two things: excellent food and drink before going aloft, and views right out of a French postcard during the ride. The catch is, balloons fly best in cold air, and that means sunrise, and that means getting up *really early.* Nor does the fun come cheap: an hour flight will run you $150 per person at least, with most flights in the $185-to-$200 range. But for the price, ballooning outfits do offer an estimably tony experience, including breakfast amid the grape fields before lift-off or en route, or brunch afterwards with the traditional glass of postflight champagne.

There are a few things to look for in a ballooning outfit, not so much to ensure your safety (you're in good hands with any of these outfitters), but to guarantee a memorable flight. First, ask how many people will be along for the ride. A balloon basket with 16 or 18 people in it feels more like an open-air elevator, and the companies run them that way. Eight or nine people is optimal. Next, get a sense of who's running the show. The person piloting your balloon certainly has the skill to get you up, over, and down in one piece. But you want more than that. You want a guide, someone who knows the landscape below, can identify the vineyards and rivers by name, maybe recommend a good chardonnay. Ballooning companies are family businesses; the person who answers the phone may be the pilot. Chat him or her up. Ask where you'll be going and what you'll be seeing. Ask what's for breakfast. See if this is a person you'd like showing you around the sky. Then remember to bring a camera, sunglasses, and a sweater.

The Napa and adjacent Sonoma valleys are often considered together as "Napa," but for ballooning, the distinction between the two is important. Weather patterns differ enough for a balloon to notice, and Sonoma is slightly closer to the water. Sonoma balloon pilots say this means you'll get a better ride out their way, though that's probably just marketing bluster. What isn't bluster, however, is the superior scenery—you'll have a better chance at an ocean view, plus you'll see coastal hills and just as many vineyards and small towns as Napa. **Air Flambouyant,** in Healdsburg (☎ 800/456-4711), is a good Sonoma ballooning company, led by an amusing pilot named Captain Wim, who'll tell you all you need to know about the air and land and probably more, in the best way.

The following are more of the best balloon outfits in Wine Country: **Above the West Ballooning,** Yountville (☎ 800/627-2759); **Adventures Aloft,** Napa (☎ 800/944-4408); **Balloon Aviation,** Napa (☎ 800/367-6272); **Bonaventura Balloon Company,** Napa (☎ 800/FLY-NAPA); and **Aerostat Adventures,** Healdsburg (☎ 800/579-0183).

BIRD WATCHING

Both Clear Lake and the delta are extremely important remnants of what once was a much larger expanse of marshy waterfowl habitat. At either place you're likely to see lots of big waterbirds: great blue heron, Canada geese, tundra swans, snow geese, greater white-fronted geese, and the full spectrum of ducks. One of the best places to explore if you have a boat is **Delta Meadows River Park** (☎ 916/777-6671). Poke around the slough quietly and you might find some great surprises.

In Clear Lake, the **McVicar Sanctuary** in Anderson Marsh State Historic Park becomes an important migratory stopover during the fall and early winter. The lakeside wetlands here provide habitat for a broad variety of songbirds, as well as hawks, kites, herons, and pelicans. Recent migration reports and weather updates are available at Anderson Marsh's park headquarters (☎ 707/994-0688).

BOARDSAILING

Rio Vista is quickly becoming an important flat-water sailing destination for the high-wind crowd. Because the delta offers an opening to Pacific winds otherwise stymied by the coast range, the wind rages here. It pours through the opening like water through a funnel, and Rio Vista just happens to be at the center of the funnel. **Sandy Beach County Park** (☎ 707/374-2097) offers easy water access. Call the **Rio Vista Chamber of Commerce** (☎ 707/374-2700) for recommendations and current conditions.

FISHING

The delta is a fisherman's dream. Every migratory species headed to spawning grounds upriver must pass through here, and the rich waters support numerous year-round residents too. Striped bass run in the spring and summer. Salmon run in the summer and fall. Catfish, largemouth

TOURING THE WINERIES

California's adjacent Napa and Sonoma valleys are two of the most famous wine-growing regions in the world. The valleys that are a place of work for thousands of vintners are also a worthy trip for any wine lover. Hundreds of wineries are nestled among the vines of this beautiful countryside; most are open to visitors.

Winery tours are generally offered daily from 10am to 5pm. The tours usually chart the process of winemaking, from the grafting and harvesting of the vines to the pressing of the grapes and the blending and aging of the wines in oak casks. They vary in length, detail, and formality, depending on the winery. Most tours are free.

Conveniently, most of the large wineries are located along a single road, **State Route 29,** which starts at the mouth of the Napa River, near the north end of San Francisco Bay, and continues north to Calistoga and the top of the growing region. Every Napa Valley town and winery listed here can be reached from Route 29. The Sonoma Valley towns and wineries are over the ridge, due west of Napa Valley, roughly along State Route 12.

NAPA VALLEY

The wineries listed below are organized geographically from south to north along State Route 29, beginning in the village of Napa. You can't miss them; each winery bears a large sign to ensure that you won't. In addition to those listed here, be sure to stop at some of those you pass along the way. In the mom-and-pop wineries throughout the region, you can make discoveries, pick up bottles that are sold nowhere else but from the proprietor's front room, and talk with the colorful people who made the wine they're selling you with their own hands. The big, commercially oriented wineries offering tours are not to be missed, for sure, but don't pass up the other, more personal side of the Wine Country experience either.

Domaine Chandon. Founded in 1973, Domaine Chandon, California Drive at State Route 29, Yountville (☎ 707/944-2280), produces about 500,000 cases annually of *mèthode champenoise* sparkling wines—Chandon Brut Cuvèe, Carneros Blanc de Noirs, Chandon Rèserve, and Etoile. You can take a guided tour of this California-style champagne house. Wines are sold by the bottle or glass and are accompanied by complimentary hors d'oeuvres. There's also a gift shop and a small gallery housing artifacts from the vineyard's French parent company, Moët et Chandon, depicting the history of champagnes. The Domaine Chandon restaurant is one of the best in the valley.

Flora Springs Wine Co. While this handsome stone winery just off State Route 29 at 1978 W. Zinfandel Lane, St. Helena (☎ 707/963-5711), dates back to Napa Valley's early days, the Flora Springs label didn't appear until 1978. The label is well known for its barrel-fermented Chardonnay, a Cabernet Sauvignon, and Trilogy, a Bordeaux-style blend.

Flora Springs offers an excellent 2-hour "familiarization seminar," which can be tailored to all levels of wine enthusiast. Limited to groups of 10, the course is held Monday through Thursday and Saturday at 10am and is available by advanced reservation only. The program begins in the vineyards, where you'll taste the grapes. While the grapes are being crushed, you taste the must (the just-pressed juice) and see how it ultimately becomes a beautiful, clear wine. Then you're taught how to evaluate wines: You'll blind-taste different ones and learn how wines change with age and how to distinguish between them. You'll also learn to pair wines with different foods.

Beringer Vineyards.   This remarkable Rhine House, with its hand-dug tunnels carved out of the mountainside, is the site of the original Beringer winery. Beringer Vineyards, 2000 Main St., St. Helena (☎ 707/963-7115), was founded in 1876 by brothers Jacob and Frederick; the family owned it until 1971, when it was purchased by the Swiss firm of Nestlè, Inc. It's the oldest continuously operating winery in the Napa Valley. ("What about Prohibition?" you might ask; Beringer made "sacramental" wines during the dry years.) The modern working winery on the opposite side of the road is not open to the public. Tasting of current vintages is conducted during sales hours in the Rhine House; reserve wines are available in the Founders' Room (upstairs in the Rhine House). A modest fee is charged per taste. Tours are conducted by very knowledgeable guides.

SONOMA VALLEY

Sonoma is often thought of as the other valley, second to Napa, but it really isn't. In fact, even though there are far fewer wineries here, its wines have won more awards than Napa's. What makes a trip to Sonoma so pleasant is the intimate quality of so many of its vineyards; most of the wineries here are still family owned. California's first winery, Buena Vista, was founded in the Sonoma Valley in 1857; it's still in operation. Today, Sonoma is home to about 35 wineries and 13,000 acres of vineyards. Chardonnay is the variety for which Sonoma is most noted; it represents almost one-quarter of the valley's acreage in vines.

The wineries here tend to be a little more spread out than they are in Napa, but they're still easy to find. The visitors bureaus listed above will provide you with maps to the valley's wineries.

Buena Vista Winery.   The patriarch of California wineries is located slightly northeast of the town of Sonoma at 18000 Old Winery Rd. (☎ 707/938-1266). It was founded in 1857 by Count Agoston Haraszthy, the Hungarian émigré considered the father of the California wine industry. Haraszthy returned from Europe in 1861 with 100,000 of the continent's finest vine cuttings, which he made available to anybody who wanted them. Although Buena Vista's winemaking now takes place in an ultramodern facility outside Sonoma, the winery still maintains a tasting room inside the restored 1862 Press House.

Château St. Jean.   This winery, founded in 1973, is at the foot of Sugarloaf Ridge, at 8555 Sonoma Hwy. (☎ 707/833-4134), just north of Kenwood and east of State Route 12. A private drive takes you to what was once a 250-acre country retreat, built in 1920. Château St. Jean is notable for its exceptionally beautiful buildings, well-landscaped grounds, and elegant tasting room. A well-manicured lawn is now a picnic area, complete with a fountain and benches.

There's a self-guided tour with detailed and photographic descriptions of the winemaking process. When you're done with it, be sure to walk up to the top of the tower for a view of the valley. Back in the tasting room, Château St. Jean offers several Chardonnays, a Cabernet Sauvignon, a Fumè Blanc, a Merlot, a Riesling, and a Gerwürtztraminer. Since 1984, the winery has been part of the Suntory family of premium wineries.

The toll-free, interactive **Château St. Jean "wine line"** (☎ 800/332-WINE) offers free recorded reports on the Sonoma Wine Country, including updated information on vineyard conditions, interviews with winemakers and growers, what's happening at the winery, and descriptions of currently available wines.

bass, and sturgeon are caught year-round. To fish the delta you really should have a boat. If you don't have one, there's no shortage of guides willing to take you out for a price. **Capt. Don's Delta Charters** (☎ 707/429-2117), will take 1 to 4 anglers out for the day from Delta Bay Marina near Rio Vista. The cost is $65 to $75 per person.

HANG GLIDING

With the vineyard views below, and the combination of ocean air and hot valley air above, Sonoma is a perfect hang-gliding spot. The most popular place to glide is (not surprisingly) the area's tallest mountain, Mount St. Helena, most of which is located within Robert Louis Stevenson State Park, located north of Calistoga about 7 miles up a very windy road. The park—besides having some good hiking—offers the additional advantage of a convenient parking area where you can unload your gear. Park information is available at ☎ **707/942-4575. Mount St. Helena,** 7 miles north of Calistoga in the Wine Country, is another mountaintop launch site. Wind and weather information for various areas around the mountain can be found at a Web site, **www.sonomawings.com**.

HIKES

Warren Richardson Trail, Annadel State Park

7.5 miles. Moderate. Access: Trail begins at east end of parking lot at end of Channel Rd. east of Santa Rosa. Map: Annadel trail map.

It's actually hard to follow an exact route anywhere in this park because trails criss-cross so much and aren't always clearly marked. The basic idea is to follow the Warren Richardson Trail to Lake Ilsanjo, walk around the lake, and take Steve's Trail to Ledson Marsh. From there, follow the Quarry Trail back to your car. Along the way you're likely to see deer, plenty of interesting birds, and a wonderful landscape of rolling grasslands and oak woodland. Keep your eyes peeled for chips of obsidian. Native Americans used this site as a quarry for the valuable black-glass stone from which they fashioned many tools and weapons.

Bald Mountain Loop, Sugarloaf Ridge State Park

7 miles. Moderate to strenuous. Access: Main park day-use area on Adobe Canyon Rd. Map: Sugarloaf Ridge State Park map.

Though the chief reason for doing this hike is the splendid view from the top of Bald Mountain, the process of getting there is worthwhile in itself. Parts of the hike follow fire roads, but other times you'll find yourself walking on beautifully shaded single track through huge and healthy chaparral interspersed with even healthier oak, laurel, and madrone forests. Watch for deer—there's no shortage of them here.

Mount St. Helena

10 Miles. Moderate. Access: Robert Louis Stevenson State Park, 7 road miles north of Calistoga. Map: USGS Mt. St. Helena area map.

At just over 4300 feet, Mount St. Helena (not to be confused with it's more explosive cousin in Washington State), is the tallest thing in the Wine Country. You'll climb about half that far—more than 2,000 feet—getting from the mountain's base to the summit on this uphill trail. It's 5 miles each way, sloping gradually at the beginning through a good stand of pines, then getting steeper as you emerge into the open grasslands. In summer, the second part of the climb is in the direct sun, so bring water and sunblock and expect to get hot. From the summit, you get excellent 360° vistas of the Wine Country to the south and the lake country to the north. And the whole way home is downhill.

MOUNTAIN BIKING

Bald Mountain Loop, Sugarloaf Ridge State Park

7 miles. Moderate. Access: Main day-use area on Adobe Canyon Rd. Map: Sugarloaf Ridge State Park map.

This one almost didn't cut the mustard simply because it contains a long stretch of paved service road, but since that road is so steep, I thought I'd throw it in. The strong will be reaching for their granny gear, and the weak . . . well, the weak shouldn't try it. Once you wheeze your way up the 1,500-foot climb to the summit of Bald Mountain on the paved road, you'll want to take in the view for a few minutes. Then pull out that handy map you bought back at the visitor center to decide which trail is the Gray Pine Trail (it's the one to the right, but don't trust me). Go that way and enjoy the downhill—about 30 minutes to an hour's worth of perfect curvy trail, depending on how fast you ride. The Park Service would like you to ride 15 miles per hour tops, but that's pretty hard to do on a downhill like this. Just be careful not to run over any hikers or scare any horses. A horse had to be killed here after it broke its leg when a group of mountain bikers scared it off the trail. Other than that, though, there haven't been any major trail-use conflicts here, and it would be nice to keep it that way.

ROAD BIKING

The back roads of the Sonoma and Napa valleys are just too good to pass up on a road bike. It just seems like the roads are never too hilly and never too flat, and the temperature in spring and fall is perfect for cycling without overheating. Also, outside of the main highways, cars are actually kind of rare around here. And the scenery just keeps rolling along: vineyards, beautiful houses, wild hillsides. In short, it's great. Then to top it off, you've got a full selection of hot springs, spas, and mud baths in which to drown your sorrows after climbing a few too many of those seemingly easy hills.

The hill country around **Harbin Hot Springs** is a favorite with a lot of people for its secluded roads. (I hear there's a big nudist scene here—a clothing-optional resort complete with clothing-optional hiking trails, and so on; just thought you might want to know.) Others like the **Angwin** and **St. Helena** area.

One of the most popular ways to explore the Wine Country is with local bicycle guides. Some of these outfitters combine wine tasting with their rides. Others are more seriously aimed at covering some distance and really exploring the Wine Country roads. Ask very specific questions about exactly what the goal of each tour is; some are aimed at novices who haven't been on a bike in years; others target the strong road tourer. Whichever you are, you don't want to find yourself riding with the other. The following is a list of area outfitters offering Wine Country tours: **Getaway Bicycle Tours,** Calistoga (☎ 800/499-2453), **Good Time Bicycle Co.,** Sonoma (☎ 707/938-0453), and **Napa Valley Bike Tours,** Napa (☎ 707/255-3377). **Backroads** (☎ 800/245-3874) in Berkeley runs multiday supported tours of the Wine Country.

Easy Napa Valley Loop

12 miles. Easy. Starting point: Corner of State Rte. 29 and Pope St. in St. Helena. Map: Napa Valley road map.

Park in or near the high school and head east on Pope Street. Very shortly (less than a mile) you'll cross the Napa River on a beautiful stone bridge and hit Silverado Trail. Turn south. From here you'll enjoy a smooth, gently hilly ride through the heart of the Napa Valley. Vineyards line much of the route, and on weekends you won't be alone; you'll probably see balloons flying overhead and other bicyclists. After about 7 miles you'll reach Oakville Cross Road. Here you have two major options. You can turn right, where you'll soon hook up with the main valley thoroughfare, State Route 29, and return north, passing through a 3-mile stretch with four wineries before arriving back at your car. Or, if busy road traffic makes you as insane as it makes me, turn around and return the way you came.

Best of Napa Loop

54 miles. Moderate. Starting point: Corner of State Rte. 29 and Pope St. in St. Helena. Map: Napa Valley road map.

From the starting point you have to ask yourself, "Do I want to ride on busy State Route 29 and visit Bale Grist Mill and Bothe–Napa State Park, both interesting historic and natural landmarks between here and Calistoga, or do I want to avoid the busiest part of Route 29 and ride straight into the country in peace?" If the former, go north on State Route 29. If the latter, go east on Pope Street until you reach Silverado Trail, then head north (left). Eventually the two routes hook up again in Calistoga, and you will continue the ride on Route 29.

This ride will take you through some of the Napa Valley, but after Calistoga it immediately begins climbing. Here you'll find nice views of Sugarloaf Ridge and of the valley below. About 15 miles into the ride you will reach the high point of the climb, about 2,500 feet—the ride begins at about 250 feet. (If you're on a mountain bike or a sturdy touring bike, the unpaved road to the summit of 4,344-foot Mount St. Helena offers an interesting side-trip challenge—see "Mountain Biking," above.) From here you'll descend and reach the small country town of Middletown, where you'll turn right on Butts Canyon Road. If you're going to need food or drink on this ride, this is the place to buy it—it's a long way to anything else.

After about 10 miles on Butts Canyon the road name changes to Pope Valley, but everything else stays the same—mile after mile of beautiful rolling-hill country. Watch on your left for Hubcap Ranch, the brainchild of Litto Diamonte. He collected hubcaps throughout his life, covering every inch of the house and barn and lining the fences. He died in 1983, but the ranch has been declared a State Historic Landmark and will live on as his legacy. Soon, you'll reach tiny Pope Valley; turn right on Howell Mountain Road, climb one last steep 2-mile ascent, and then it's all downhill until St. Helena and your car.

SAILING

A cruise up the **delta** is a common weekend getaway for San Francisco–based boats, with good wind, light traffic, and no waves to speak of. For information on sailing and cruising the delta, contact **Discovery Bay Yacht Club,** 5871 Marina Rd. in the town of Discovery Bay (☎ **925/634-1210**).

Sailing up several rivers around the delta is also popular. The **Petaluma River** and much larger **Sacramento River** are common, excellent inland waterway trips. The Sacramento is large enough for barge traffic, a mixed blessing (you won't run aground, but you might run into a barge). The Petaluma is a much smaller waterway, and you might feel less nervous in a boat with a shallow draft. Whales have made it surprisingly far up each river, however. Local hero, Humphrey the Whale famously made it most of the way to Sacramento back in the early '80s, before being persuaded to turn around by marine biologists using complicated scientific methods of persuasion, like standing in the water beating on trash can lids. **Capt. Don's Delta Charters** (☎ **707/429-2117**) runs delta tours. Call for information and rates.

Campgrounds & Other Accommodations

CAMPING

Brannan Island State Recreation Area

3 miles southeast of Rio Vista on Hwy. 160. ☎ **916/777-6671** or 916/777-7701. 102 car sites, 36 boat sites. Flush toilets, showers, boat ramp, picnic tables. Boating, fishing, swimming. $12–$15 per site. Reserve through PARKNET (☎ 800/444-PARK).

For waterskiing or fishing in the delta this is the place to stay. It's nothing special as far as scenery goes, but the water access for swimming and boating is unbeatable—it's the biggest campground for year-round boating access in the heart of the delta.

Sugarloaf Ridge State Park

Midway between Santa Rosa and Sonoma at the end of Adobe Canyon Rd. off State Rte. 12. ☎ **707/833-5712** or 707/938-1519. 49 sites. Flush toilets, running water, picnic tables. Hiking, horseback riding, biking, bird watching. Dogs accepted. Fee.

Whether you come here for the hiking and mountain biking within the park, or plan to use it as a base for exploring the surrounding region, this park is a gem. It's hands-down the best camping near the Wine Country, with great scenery.

INNS, RESORTS & SPAS

Tall Timbers Chalets

1012 Darms Lane, Napa, CA 94558. From State Rte. 29 N., turn left onto Darms Lane before Yountville. ☎ **707/252-7810.** 8 cottages. Sun–Thurs $116.55 double, Fri–Sat and holidays $166.50 double. Extra person $20. AE, MC, V.

This group of eight whitewashed, roomy cottages surrounded by pines and eucalyptus is one of the best bargains in Napa Valley. All the cottages are nicely decorated and well furnished; amenities include refrigerators, toaster ovens, and coffeemakers. It's really pleasant to find, on your arrival, a basket of fresh fruit in the breakfast nook, breakfast treats in the refrigerator, and a complimentary bottle of champagne. There are no phones in the cottages, but you'll have access to one in the main office. Each unit can sleep four (there's a bedroom plus a queen sofa bed in the living room); several have decks. No smoking is allowed in the cottages.

Vintage Inn

6541 Washington St. (between Humboldt St. and Webber Ave.), Yountville, CA 94599. From State Rte. 29 N., exit at Yountville and turn left onto Washington St. ☎ **800/351-1133** or 707/944-1112. Fax 707/944-1617. 80 units. $150–$275 double; $225–$325 minisuites. Extra person $25. Rates include continental breakfast. AE, CB, DC, MC, V.

Built on an old 23-acre winery estate in the center of town, this inn is a contemporary accommodation, although the land once belonged to pioneer George C. Yount, who received it as a Spanish land grant. Famed designer Kipp Stewart, who also designed the sybaritic Ventana Inn at Big Sur, was responsible for creating this hideaway, which boasts four villas. Rooms are well equipped, with fireplaces, ceiling fans, oversize beds, coffeemakers, refrigerators, plush bathrobes, tubs with Jacuzzi jets, and a complimentary bottle of wine. A California-continental champagne breakfast (cereals, yogurt, pastries, egg salad, and fruit) is served in the Vintage Club, as is afternoon tea. Facilities

SOIL YOURSELF: TAKE A CALISTOGA MUD BATH

One thing you should do while you're in the Wine Country is head for the mud. In Calistoga, people have been doing it for the last 150 years. The natural mud baths are composed of local volcanic ash, imported peat, and naturally boiling mineral-hot-springs water, all mulled together to produce a thick mud that simmers at a temperature of about 104°F.

Once you overcome the hurdle of deciding how best to place your naked body into the mushy stone tub, the rest is pure relaxation—you soak with surprising buoyancy for about 10 to 12 minutes. A warm mineral-water shower, a mineral-water whirlpool bath, and a mineral-water steam-room visit follow. Afterward, a relaxing blanket-wrap will slowly cool down your delighted body. All of this takes about 1^{1}/$_{2}$ hours and costs about $45; with a massage, add another half-hour and $20. The outcome is a rejuvenated, revitalized, squeaky-clean you. Mud baths aren't recommended for those who are pregnant or have high blood pressure.

The spas also offer a variety of other treatments, such as hand and foot massages, herbal wraps, acupressure face-lifts, skin rubs, and herbal facials. Prices range from $35 to $125, and appointments are necessary for all services; call at least a week in advance.

You can indulge yourself at any of these Calistoga spas: **Dr. Wilkinson's Hot Springs,** 1507 Lincoln Ave. (☎ 707/942-4102), **Lincoln Avenue Spa,** 1339 Lincoln Ave. (☎ 707/942-5296), **Golden Haven Hot Springs Spa,** 1713 Lake St. (☎ 707/942-6793), or **Calistoga Spa Hot Springs,** 1006 Washington St. (☎ 707/942-6269).

include a 60-foot, year-round heated swimming pool, an outdoor heated whirlpool, and two tennis courts. Bikes are for rent, and ballooning can also be arranged.

Meadowood Resort

900 Meadowood Lane, St. Helena, CA 94574. ☎ **800/458-8080** or 707/963-3646. Fax 707/963-3532. 107 units. Apr 30–Nov 21 $395–$880 double; from $550 suite. About $20 less off-season. AE, DC, MC, V.

This exquisite resort, on 250 wooded and hilly acres, resembles a New England resort on the sea. The private, quiet accommodations are scattered around the property in four-unit clusters, close to either the golf course or the tennis and pool facilities. Some 13 rooms are located in the handsome English-style croquet lodge overlooking the perfectly manicured croquet lawn. All rooms have private porches, fine furnishings, a coffeemaker, and a toaster; most have fireplaces. Guests have use of the 9-hole golf course, seven tennis courts, croquet, bicycles, hiking

trails, pool and whirlpool, and health spa offering massages, facials, and body treatments.

Dr. Wilkinson's Hot Springs

1507 Lincoln Ave. (State Rte. 29, between Fairway and Stevenson aves.), Calistoga, CA 94515. ☎ **707/942-4102.** 42 units. Winter $89–$139 double; summer $109–$149 double. Weekly discounts and packages available. AE, MC, V.

This spa/resort was originally established by "Doc" Wilkinson, who arrived in Napa Valley just after World War II. Today, it's a typical motel, distinguished by the mud and mineral baths on the premises. Rooms range from Victorian-style units to rather basic and functional motel-like rooms, similar to Janet Leigh's room in *Psycho*. All rooms have drip coffeemakers and refrigerators; some have kitchens. Facilities include three swimming pools (two outdoor and one indoor). Facials and all kinds of body treatments are available in the salon.

Houseboats

There's no better way to satisfy that Huckleberry Finn fantasy you've had all these years than to spend a week or a weekend drifting the backwaters of the delta in a houseboat. These stable, spacious, slow-moving pontoon boats make the perfect platform for exploring the more than 70 islands and hundreds of sloughs, channels, and rivers that make up the delta. Rates vary widely with season and size of boat. **Paradise Point Marina**, 8095 Rio Blanco Rd., Stockton, CA 95219 (☎ 209/ 952-1000), rents houseboats by the week as well as fishing boats and ski boats.

Beltane Ranch
1775 Sonoma Hwy., Glen Ellen, CA 95442. ☎ **707/996-6501.** 6 units. $130–$210 double. No credit cards.

This 1892 double-porched bunkhouse is off the main road, on the slopes of the Mayacamas, surrounded by 1,600 acres. It's part of local legend, having once been owned by "Mammy" Pleasant, a former slave and abolitionist who, among other professions, was a madam and the mistress of English millionaire Thomas Bell. Mammy was suspected of his murder but was never convicted.

After the 1930s, the Heins family used the ranch to raise turkeys, but when Rosemary Wood inherited it in 1981, she turned it into a B&B. The gardens are filled with irises and roses; a terrace surrounding the house looks out over the flowers and the fields beyond. Guests can use the comfortable parlor with the brick fireplace and woodstove. Rooms are comfortably furnished in a homey style with the occasional family antique. Facilities include hiking trails and a tennis court.

6

The Sierra Nevada

To Europeans and early American settlers, the New World meant limitless expansion. They pushed west for 2 centuries, from the first explorations of Davy Crockett, Jim Bridger, and Lewis and Clark all the way through the gold rush, taking pelts, mining gold—in short, ripping through the land in search of resources to exploit. America seemed an inexhaustible resource. Kill a hundred buffalo and there were a thousand more over the next hill. Cut down a thousand trees and there were a million more across the river. When the California gold rush of 1849 brought thousands west, America's frontier mentality crashed like a wave against the shores of the Pacific. San Francisco overtook Monterey as the most important city in California, and the huge profits of the Mother Lode drove the quick development of the state. Suddenly, there was no more "west" to head to.

To early pioneers, the Sierra Nevada was simply the last of many obstacles to overcome before reaching the shining Pacific and the goldfields of the West. But as in any final line of defense, the continent threw up every last weapon at its disposal. The Sierra was raw, untamed nature, rugged and not easily bested—a lesson learned by many early settlers. The tale of the Donner party—who had to resort to cannibalism to survive a winter that came early and trapped them in the high country north of Lake Tahoe—is merely one of many.

When John Muir arrived by boat in San Francisco in the spring of 1868 he asked a passerby to point him to "any place that is wild." The answer led him across the great Central Valley and into the Sierra Nevada, where Muir found the raw nature he was looking for, and found it in danger of being eroded away by the trample of civilization. Even before reaching the range, Muir was awestruck. Looking up from Pacheco Pass in the coast range, Muir said, "It seemed to me the Sierra should be called not the Nevada, or snowy range, but the Range of Light." His experiences in the Sierra Nevada became the central focus of his writings and philosophy, which bore the seeds of the modern conservation movement.

Muir lived for years in the Yosemite Valley—which he was instrumental in having declared a national park—and traversed the whole range, often traveling with just the clothes on his back. For Muir, the Sierra embodied light not only in the literal sense, but in the metaphysical as well. "Everything in it seems equally divine—one smooth, pure, wild glow of Heaven's love." In these mountains, Muir waxed, "you bathe in these spirit beams, turning round and round as if warming in a campfire. Presently you lose consciousness of your individual nature: You blend with the landscape and become part and parcel of nature."

Obviously, Muir fell in love with these mountains, and like any good lover he fought tirelessly to protect them. In 1892, he and 27 other men formed the Sierra Club both to promote the enjoyment of the wild and, in what was a landmark declaration for the time, "to enlist the support of the people and the government in preserving the forests and other features of the Sierra Nevada Mountains."

Every year thousands come to the Sierra Nevada with perhaps less lofty but equally enticing goals, hoping to find a place where they too can seek a little quiet repose from their hurried existence in the cities below. They find one of the world's best expanses of wilderness. Three national parks cover 1.6 million acres. Eight national forests contain another 8 million acres. In all, the publicly owned portion of the Sierra is larger than most eastern states.

That is a lot of land, but the Sierra is sometimes in danger of being loved to death. **Yosemite National Park** gets more than 3 million visitors a year, most to the Yosemite Valley. **Sequoia and Kings Canyon National Parks** are visited by another 2 million. **Lake Tahoe** was once a pristine wilderness. Now home to casinos, condos, and a higher concentration of ski resorts than anywhere in the nation, it staggers under more than 12 million visitors a year. Still, for every

Yosemite and Lake Tahoe, there are a hundred backcountry lakes and isolated national-forest campgrounds with hardly any visitors.

The Lay of the Land

Nearly 450 miles from north to south and between 60 and 80 miles wide, the Sierra is carved from a huge mass of granite. If you picture the range as a single building block beginning just below **Mount Lassen** and ending just below **Mount Whitney,** the block is tilted west, and slanted so it's almost twice as tall in the south as it is in the north. The **High Sierra** is the area from just north of Yosemite to the south end of the range, characterized by high granite domes and peaks, alpine lakes, and little tree cover. Most of this stretch is relatively unsullied wilderness.

One hundred million years ago, molten granite from the earth's mantle spewed forth and was released under a seabed of sedimentary and volcanic rock. Never to reach the surface, the molten granite cooled in the gigantic dome shapes that characterize the Sierra. From about 70 million years ago until 12 million years ago the range was uplifted by geological forces. Massive erosion of the soft sedimentary deposits exposed the huge granite batholiths. It was only in the last million years that the glacial scouring of three separate ice ages put the finishing polishes on the Sierra as we know it today.

Because of its westward tilt, the west slope of the Sierra is a gentle wedge: Grassy foothills become pine-forested mountains and finally reveal themselves as the granite-spired high peaks. Large rivers drain through numerous canyons and glacial valleys. The eastern flank demonstrates no such subtlety. Viewed from the east, a huge escarpment of strikingly sheer peaks simply shoots straight out of the sagebrush desert. No rolling foothills, no messing around—it's one of the most striking mountain walls anywhere in North America.

The Sierra is still growing. As rivers and glaciers continue to gnaw away at the western slope, the range grows from the east. A 400-mile-long fault zone along the eastern base of the Sierra is the location of some of the most active geology in California. In the last 2,000 years, more than 30 major eruptions have draped a necklace of cinder cones and lava flows across the land. **Geological activity** is a daily fact here, not just something discussed in textbooks. And though there are obvious dangers to living in a land of earthquakes and volcanic eruptions, there are also benefits, like the hot water that gushes from the ground all over the eastern slope. There are more **hot springs** here than in any other part of California, some commercial but most of them free and scarcely used. Most popular is Hot Creek, near the Mammoth Lakes Airport, where boiling thermal water mixes with 40°F snowmelt for perfect bathing, but there are literally hundreds more waiting to be discovered (see "Hot Springs" in "Eastern Sierra: What to Do & Where to Do It" later in this chapter).

The precipitous nature of this eastern massif testifies to the continuing heartbeat of the Sierra Nevada. Some 700,000 years ago, say geologists, Long Valley, just south of Mammoth Lakes, was the site of an eruption so massive that one part of the flow actually crested the eastern slope and flowed down the west slope as far as the great Central Valley at speeds pushing 100 miles per hour. The loss of that much landmass caused the caldera to collapse in the wake of the great eruption, forming 20-mile by 15-mile Long Valley.

Residents of the few towns on the east side of the range have learned to take frequent **earthquakes** in stride. Generally the uplift is measured in fractions of an inch per year, but a single quake in 1872 produced a 17-foot vertical shift in mountains near the Owens Valley. The resort town of Mammoth Lakes and surrounding Long Valley are built on the still-active remains of that ancient volcanic caldera, as the steam vents on top of Mammoth Mountain and hot springs in the valley illustrate. In the wake of fears raised by the Mount St. Helens eruption, the area was ranked by the U.S. Geologic Survey as the most likely place in the continental United States to experience the next **volcanic eruption.** When the feds went so far as to release a notice saying that the town and ski mountain at Mammoth are sitting on a powder keg of potential volcanism, the powers that be nearly blew a gasket, worried that tourism and the real-estate market would suffer. Of course, the U.S. Geologic Survey was speaking in geologic terms and had never meant that an eruption was imminent, simply that the odds of one happening here in the next, say, 1,000 years were much greater than an eruption happening at Mount Hood, Oregon, or Amarillo, Texas, for that matter. The warning was downgraded to appease local land speculators and chamber-of-commerce types, but the fact remains the same: Mammoth could blow tomorrow or it could blow in 5,000 years. The mountain sleeps, but it's not dead.

Several bands of **plant species** climb the mountain flank. Though distribution of plant communities varies widely following local geography, by taking rainfall, soil type, latitude, and slope orientation into consideration, some generalizations can be made. The lower slopes from about 1,000 to 5,000 feet are covered with thick chaparral alternating with drought-resistant pine and oak species, not to mention huge patches of poison oak and blackberry vines.

Above that is what's known as the transition zone, a broad band of evergreen and deciduous forest containing the majority of timber. Douglas and white firs, incense cedar, and sugar pine are the common evergreens, while cottonwood, maple, and oak are the most common broadleaf species. Also occurring in the transition zone are the Sierra's unique groves of *Sequoiadendron giganteum,* the giant sequoia. These enormous trees are living fossils, a species that evolved 150 million years ago, before the Sierra even existed. Some of the largest living specimens are 30 feet thick and nearly 300 feet tall. The oldest is roughly 3,200 years old. Unlike the coastal redwoods, which are good for lumber, the giant sequoias splintered when felled and the remains were good only for shingles, fence posts, and other small items. As a result, they were less heavily logged and substantial groves remain in Yosemite, Kings Canyon, and Sequoia national parks and Calaveras Big Trees State Park.

Nearing timberline, one passes through the lower boreal belt: lodge-pole, Jeffrey and silver pines, red fir, Sierra juniper, and aspen. "Above timberline" is somewhat of a misnomer; there are still trees here in what is more properly called the subalpine belt. Buried under snow most of the year and subject to cruel winters, this high-altitude region is nonetheless home to hardy and isolated populations of several pine species pushing the outer limits of their survival capacity. A head-high tree here might be as old as one that soars 100 feet in the much lower altitude of the transition zone.

Though much of the Sierra has been preserved, in many ways it is not as wild as the Sierra that Muir wandered. That bear you see on the California state flag is a grizzly, once common in these mountains but now extirpated from the whole state. Wolves too were driven out. Apparently if you're a predator big enough to eat people, you aren't welcome in California.

Wildlife is still prevalent, however. Black bears are common even today, and often get into trouble when careless tourists forget to hang or lock away their food. Other predators include mountain lions, coyotes, bobcats, ringtails, foxes, raccoons, and several species of skunks. Present, but extremely rare, is the wolverine. Known for its ill disposition, territorial nature, maliciousness, and almost legendary feats of strength and cunning, the wolverine sounds almost too good to be true.

A large population of grazers summer in the range. Mule deer are common in high-country meadows and move to the foothills before the snow settles in. Sierra bighorn sheep, nearly extinct by the 1970s, have staged a comeback since the creation of special reserves and a relocation effort. They can be seen in the jagged peaks east of Tioga Pass and at other more remote sites in the High Sierra.

The endangered spotted owl, which gained national fame in the 1980s, is still here. Legal skirmishes over saving the bird and its habitat halted much of the clear-cutting that was taking place. Pygmy owls, gray owls, red-tailed hawks, and peregrine falcons are also to be found in the Sierra. Other birds, like the three-toed woodpecker and Clark's' nutcracker, make their home near timberline, and the whole Sierra is full of crested jays, finches, and warblers.

Ecologically the **eastern Sierra** is one of the great transition zones between the rugged high-country peaks and the flat sagebrush plains of the Great Basin Desert. As a result there is an incredible diversity of life here. Rivers and creeks draining this side of the range hold endangered cutthroat trout and a few of the high lakes hold golden trout, the strikingly beautiful state fish.

The plains of the desert below are filled with a whole different menagerie of wild and feral animals. Mono Lake, of course, is a whole bizarre world of bird islands, brine shrimp, and buzzing insects, but the rest of the plain is remarkable too. Perhaps because there are so few people it seems like there are more animals, or maybe it is just the lack of cover that makes them so easy to spot. Near the former Owens Lake on U.S. 395

it is common to see herds of elk grazing near the road. Pronghorn antelope, the fastest mammal in North America, are also regularly spotted racing across the plain.

You also might see one of the large groups of **wild burros,** descendants of mining-camp escapees, who forage in the lava fields between Big Pine and Bishop. The Bureau of Land Management has rounded up many of the burros in an effort to preserve important forage for the elk and other native animals, but the little jackass and its cousin the mule are such an ingrained part of the culture here that every Memorial Day weekend more than 40,000 people venture to Bishop for Mule Days, a 3-day bacchanal of mulish antics like mule look-alike contests, mule races, and much showing off of everyone's mules and burros, not to mention good music, food, and company. I've never done Mule Days myself, but a friend of mine swears by it.

Orientation

The first highway to cross the Sierra Nevada was the Lincoln Highway, promoted by early car manufacturers as the first transcontinental highway. It was mostly a rutted and dangerous collection of old wagon tracks and cow paths that would scarcely be called a road these days. The Lincoln Highway is gone now, buried under the roadbed of modern six-lane **Interstate 80,** the largest road over the Sierra, but plenty of other passes still appeal to a sense of adventure.

Several **mountain passes** cross the range. The first in the north, where the mountains are barely 5,000 feet high, is State Route 36. Farther south, Beckwourt Pass on State Route 70 and Yuba Pass on State Route 49 begin to climb higher. Near Tahoe, the Sierra begins to grow to a respectable size and Donner Summit on Interstate 80, Echo Summit on U.S. 50,

Luther Pass on State Route 89, and Carson Pass on State Route 88 are all high and dramatic roads. Then things get really interesting: The passes from State Route 88 all the way south to State Route 178 are summertime only, and in a bad year some don't open until mid-July when the last snow is cleared from the High Country. State Route 4, Ebbetts Pass, briefly leaves the timberline between Bear Valley and Markleeville, and offers astounding views of the Nevada desert. Next is Sonora Pass, State Route 108. This winding, less-than-two-lane road climbs through some of the most dramatic Sierra peaks accessible by driving. Since it's so twisted and steep, you'll find none of the commercial traffic that plagues the northern passes. (Leave the RV at home.)

Tioga Pass, State Route 120, connects the western part of Yosemite with Mono Lake and Lee Vining, traveling through high granite country and beautiful alpine meadows. In the summer of 1995, after a winter of huge snowfall, Tioga Pass did not open until nearly August. South of here, the mountains are too high and wild for year-round roads. For the 160 miles between Tioga Pass near Mono Lake and Sherman Pass (State Route 190), the Sierra is uncrossed by a single road.

The impassable wall the Sierra presents to the rest of Northern California—especially in winter—is the reason the eastern Sierra is more popular with Southern Californians than with denizens of the north. It's easy to drive up through the Mojave Desert on any given winter day. Crossing the High Sierra passes near Tahoe during a winter storm is a different story altogether.

This lack of roads in the southern Sierra, and particularly the eastern side of the southern Sierra, creates one of the greatest wilderness opportunities in the state. Running north to south, **State Route 49** on the west side and **U.S. 395** on the east parallel the Sierra about 80 to 100 miles apart. U.S. 395 runs through varied terrain, from the desert plains of

South Lake Tahoe's Average Temperatures and Precipitation											
	Jan	Feb	Mar	Apr	May	June	July	Aug	Sept	Oct	Nov	Dec
High (°F)	37	39	43	50	59	69	79	78	70	58	47	40
Low (°F)	17	18	22	26	32	37	43	42	38	31	25	20
Precipitation (in.)	6.1	5.4	3.9	2.2	1.2	0.6	0.3	0.2	0.5	1.6	3.1	5.4

the Owens Valley to the forested summit of 7,519-foot Devil's Gate before crossing into Nevada. Within easy striking distance of the road are literally hundreds of hikes and backpacking trips. In the course of its run down the eastern Sierra, U.S. 395 passes Yosemite National Park, Mono Lake, Devils Postpile National Monument, several national wilderness areas (including the John Muir and the Carson-Iceberg), two major downhill ski resorts and one major cross-country ski resort, creeks, hot springs, and lakes, and then culminates in the dramatic shadow of the Whitney Massif, the highest cluster of peaks in the Lower 48.

Several major **trails** weave through the Sierra. Most famous is the Pacific Crest Trail, which runs north-south through the entire range. The John Muir Trail from Yosemite to Sequoia National Park traverses almost 200 miles of High Sierra wilderness without crossing a single road. In winter, the Tioga Pass and the Sierra Haute Route through Sequoia and Kings Canyon are popular ski-touring crossings.

For the sake of manageability, I've divided the Sierra Nevada into three subchapters: the **northern Sierra,** which includes everything north of Yosemite; the **southern Sierra,** which includes Yosemite National Park to Sequoia and Kings Canyon National Parks; and the **eastern Sierra,** which includes everything accessible from U.S. 395 on the east side. Since even then it is a long way from, say, Pinecrest Lake on State Route 108 to Bear Valley on State Route 4, activities will be clearly marked by the pass on which they occur.

LAKE TAHOE & THE NORTHERN SIERRA

Lake Tahoe

One of the most positive signs that humankind isn't hell-bent on condo-izing every square inch of the great outdoors is the Lake Tahoe master plan, a 20-year development code. Even in the worst that Tahoe has to offer, South Lake Tahoe, the glitter gulch of the Sierra Nevada, city planners have launched an ambitious plan to return their town to a more natural state. It seems they've realized there's more money to be had from nature lovers than from Las Vegas cast-offs. Parks are being opened where motels used to stand, new buildings are designed in a more Alpine motif, and, amazingly, for every new hotel room being built, 1.31 old rooms are being torn town. At that rate South Lake should look like a mountain town in, say, 100 years. But at least they're headed in the right direction. For North Lake information, contact the **Tahoe North Visitors and Convention Bureau,** P.O. Box 5578, Tahoe City, CA 96145 (☎ 800/TAHOE-4-U). For South Lake information, contact the **Lake Tahoe Visitors Authority,** P.O. Box 16299, South Lake Tahoe, CA 96151 (☎ 800/AT-TAHOE).

Interstate 80

This six-lane monster road running just to the north of Lake Tahoe is the major commercial route over the Sierra, the last to close during winter storms and the first to reopen. Several ski areas line Donner Summit, and the headwaters of the American River fall just to the south. Just past Truckee, Interstate 80 turns north and runs downhill to Reno.

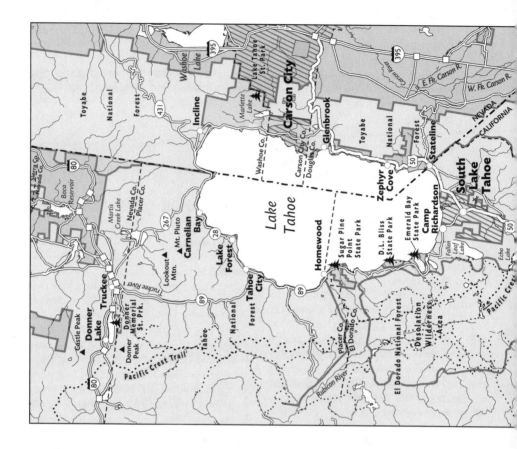

Truckee

Once a wicked little Wild West outpost of bordellos and gin mills, Truckee has mellowed somewhat but is still the most, shall we say, gritty and real town in the Tahoe Basin. It was near here that the Donner Party, trapped by early snows, was forced to resort to cannibalism to survive the winter of 1846/1847. These days the reverse is nearly true: If it hasn't snowed by Christmas the streets of Truckee are crawling with jobless ski bums looking like they just might stick a fork into you. But the snow always comes, even in the worst years, and once it does, North Shore resorts like Squaw Valley, Alpine Meadows, Northstar, and Sugar Bowl start hiring. Truckee is where you'll come to find that flashlight you forgot or to get pizza when your camp stove dies. For information, contact the **Truckee-Donner Chamber of Commerce,** P.O. Box 2757, Truckee, CA 96160 (☎ **800/548-8388** or 530/587-2757).

Fanny Bridge, Tahoe City

To see the biggest trout you're ever likely to encounter, come to Fanny Bridge over the Truckee River in Tahoe City. Bend way over and look at those lunkers lurking under the bridge (sorry, no fishing). Then back up a few steps, look at all the other people bending over to see those huge trout, and try to guess where the bridge gets its name.

U.S. 50

Much more modest than its brother, Interstate 80 to the north, U.S. 50 provides the best direct access to the south shore of Tahoe. It's a curvy and scenic two-lane road that miraculously stays open in the winter nearly as much as Interstate 80 and seems much safer because it lacks the heavy commercial traffic of the interstate. Between Tahoe and Sacramento, U.S. 50 runs past Echo Lake, with good access points into the back side of the Desolation Wilderness.

Lake Tahoe & the Northern Sierra

0—5 Miles
0—5 Kilometers

State Route 89

Running south along the west shore of Tahoe from Truckee to South Lake, State Route 89 continues south to Pickett's Junction and Sorenson's Resort, Markleeville, and finally runs into U.S. 395 along the east side of the Sierra north of Mono Lake.

State Route 88

Between the old gold-mining center of Jackson and its intersection with State Route 89 at Pickett's Junction, State Route 88 runs through high ponderosa pine forests and climbs to an elevation of 8,573 feet at Carson Pass. Beyond the summit it passes a series of small lakes and descends the Carson River Canyon to Minden, Nevada.

Sorensen's Resort, Pickett's Junction

Sorensen's Resort is the focal point of Hope Valley. It's located south of Lake Tahoe and east of the Sierra Divide, at the junction of State Route 88 and State Route 89 on the east side of Carson Pass. With cabins, good restaurants, sleigh rides, and its own cross-country center, there's plenty to do here without the hectic scene of the South Lake Tahoe glitter gulch. For information, contact Sorensen's Resort, 14255 State Rte. 88, Hope Valley, CA 96120 (☎ **800/423-9909** or 530/694-2203).

Ebbetts Pass (State Rte. 4)

Connecting Angels Camp on the west with Markleeville on the east, Ebbetts Pass is a bridge between two of the most eccentric towns you may ever find. Angels Camp is famous for its Jumping Frog Jubilee, popularized by one-time resident Mark Twain. Markleeville, population 1,200, is one of the most insulated communities in the Sierra Nevada. It doesn't have a bank, but it does have the "Death Ride: Tour of the California Alps" bike rally. In between the two extremes, State Route 4 weaves through beautiful redwoods, along the North Fork of the Stanislaus River, past the turnoff to Bear Valley Ski Resort and up to strikingly beautiful Lake Alpine. Just past here, the road narrows to less than two lanes and crosses the pass before heading down to Markleeville. For information, contact the **Calaveras Ranger District,** P.O. Box 500, Hathaway Pines, CA 95233 (☎ 209/ 795-1381).

Sonora Pass (State Rte. 108)
Built in 1901, the Sonora Pass was one of the first highways to cross the Sierra Divide. It has long since been superseded by the highways to its north and south, however, as the easiest route over the mountains. One trip over will tell you why: From Kennedy Meadows over the pass to the Walker River, State Route 108 is the most winding, steep, and gorgeous road you've ever seen. (The pass area looks so much like the Alps that it was used as a location for the filming of *For Whom the Bell Tolls*.) It isn't something you'd want to drive a truck or motor home across. Most visitors stay on the west side of the almost 9,700-foot pass. For almost guaranteed solitude, drive the extra few hours to the east slope where you'll find uncrowded hiking, fishing, and backpacking. This route is also a favorite path of cyclists over the Sierra, for exactly the same reasons cars don't like it.

SOUTHERN SIERRA: YOSEMITE TO SEQUOIA/ KINGS CANYON

State Route 168
This is the only route into the wilderness of the Sierra National Forest between Yosemite and Sequoia/Kings Canyon, and it's closed in the winter. Huntington and Shaver lakes are both located off it.

EASTERN SIERRA
Markleeville
Tiny Markleeville, located on the eastern foot of State Route 4, is the county seat of Alpine County. The population of the entire county is less than 1,200, so don't expect any big-city services. Markleeville does, however, have plenty of interesting frontier logging and mining history at the **Alpine County Historical Museum** (☎ 530/694-2317). The museum is open from early summer until fall, Wednesday through Monday, from noon to 5pm. There's no fee, but donations are accepted. Camping, fishing, hiking, biking, and hot springing are the big deal around here— this is some of the most remote and uncrowded country in the state. While Markleeville doesn't have a bank, it does have the Cutthroat Bar, a redneck delight where the standing offer is that any woman willing to give up her bra can trade it for a genuine Cutthroat T-shirt, as long as she's willing to bare-breast it in front of a crowd of slathering regulars. Gee, I wonder why there aren't more takers?

Every year the chamber of commerce sponsors the Death Ride: Tour of the California Alps—2,500 cyclists from around the country come here to test themselves on the surrounding high passes. For Death Ride registration information or more detailed information about the area, contact the **Alpine Chamber of Commerce,** P.O. Box 265, Markleeville, CA 96120 (☎ 530/694-2475).

Monitor Pass (State Route 89)
Monitor Pass connects Tahoe and summertime State Route 4 traffic with U.S. 395 down the eastern Sierra. During the fall in particular it is a great place to catch the changing colors whether on a bicycle or in your car.

Bridgeport
Bridgeport is the supply center for everything north of Mammoth Lakes. It's no

great shakes, but you can get everything from gasoline to food to fishing lures here, as well as food and lodging. More interesting are Bridgeport's weird weekend happenings: Every October brings the Big Mountain Man Rendezvous. No cars are allowed in town and participants dress in period costumes from the pioneer days while competing in shooting contests, musical performances, and craft markets. During the last weekend of June, a primitive event of a different type takes over when the annual gathering of the western states Harley Davidson motorcycle clubs roar into town. Outside town are Big Hot Warm Springs, Bridgeport Reservoir, and the Hoover Wilderness. Contact the **Bridgeport Chamber of Commerce,** P.O. Box 541, Bridgeport, CA 93517 (☎ **760/932-7500**), for info on lodging, camping, and activities. The **Bridgeport Ranger Station,** HCRI Box 1000, Bridgeport, CA 93517 (☎ **760/ 932-7070**), offers wilderness permits, maps, and camping info.

Twin Lakes Road

A major access way into the Hoover Wilderness and the popular Twin Lakes. There's great fishing for brown and rainbow trout here.

Virginia Lakes Road

Midway between Bridgeport and Lee Vining, Virginia Lakes Road cuts about 6 miles into the high mountains west of U.S. 395. It passes 10 small lakes, a campground, and the **Virginia Lakes Resort,** P.O. Box 1065, Bridgeport, CA 93517 (☎ **760/647-6484**), which has a small store, restaurant, and cabins for rent during the summer.

Lundy Lake Road

Lundy Lake, a reservoir, is a major trailhead into the Twenty Lakes Basin and is also notable on its own for good fishing and camping below the dam on the banks of Mill Creek. **Lundy Lake Resort,** P.O. Box 265, Lee Vining, CA 93541 (no phone), has cabins, camping, laundry, a store, and showers.

Lee Vining

Named for a gold miner, Leroy Vining, who was one of the first to prospect the eastern Sierra, Lee Vining is another small and peaceful supply stop at the intersection of Tioga Pass (State Route 120) and U.S. 395 near the shore of Mono Lake. Camping supplies, gas, food, lodging, and information are available—there's even an art gallery. Visit the **Mono Lake Ranger Station,** P.O. Box 10, Lee Vining, CA 93541 (☎ **760/647-6331**), west of the highway intersection on Tioga Road, for maps and information.

June Lake Loop (State Route 158)

Five miles south of Lee Vining, State Route 158 begins its westward loop through the spectacular country around the semideveloped town of June Lake and **June Mountain Ski Resort** (☎ **760/ 648-7733**). Besides skiing and snowboarding at the ski area, June Lake is great for hiking, camping, and fishing. Four lakes—Grant, Silver, Gull, and June—lie inside the loop and are popular for fishing, swimming, and boating. Camping and lodging are available at several different locations. Just to the west of the loop is the huge Ansel Adams Wilderness. Contact the **June Lake Chamber of Commerce,** P.O. Box 2, June Lake (☎ **760/648-7584**), for info.

Mammoth Lakes

Though it only officially became a town in 1984, Mammoth Lakes has been the economic center of the eastern Sierra since the ski mountain boomed in popularity during the 1970s. This is where L.A. comes to play in the snow, and Angelenos drop a lot of cash here to do it, supporting condos, nice restaurants, bars, ski shops, clothing outlets, and all the accoutrements of the glittery Southern California lifestyle. Whether this is a good thing or not is up for interpretation; a lot

The Yosemite Area

10 Miles

10 Kilometers

of old and new Mammoth locals like to complain about the weekend interlopers, but without them most people here would be out of a job. Besides the 2,500-acre ski mountain just outside town, Mammoth also boasts two cross-country–skiing centers, dogsledding, a bobsled run, mountain biking, rock climbing, hot springs, numerous lakes, fishing, hiking, Devils Postpile National Monument, and the area's only commercial airport, all within a stone's throw.

While the **Mammoth Lakes Visitors Center,** P.O. Box 48, Mammoth Lakes, CA 93546 (☎ **800/367-6572** or 760/934-2571), is ostensibly the place to call for help with lodging, trip planning, and the like, the visitor-center staff was virtually useless when I called. However, the visitor center itself on the highway into town—look for Perry's Pizza—is a good source of tourist maps and brochures. The people at **Mammoth Mountain Ski Resort,** P.O. Box 24, Mammoth Lakes, CA 93546 (☎ **800/ 367-6572** or 760/934-2571), offer info on lodging, skiing, and much more, and are *much* more helpful over the phone than the visitor center. Contact the **Mammoth National Forest Visitors Center,** P.O. Box 148, Mammoth Lakes, CA 93546 (☎ **760/ 934-2505**), for hiking maps as well as nature and camping information. **Mammoth Adventure Connection,** P.O. Box 353, Mammoth Lakes, CA 93546 (☎ **800/ 228-4947**), is the place to call if you're interested in climbing lessons, mountain-biking tours, dogsledding, and more.

Rock Creek Lake and Road

Rock Creek Road is popular for the resort area also known as Tom's Place, where the road turns off U.S. 395. The 63-acre

lake here is popular with anglers. Many trailheads leave from the lake into the John Muir Wilderness, popular in winter for cross-country skiing. Camping, fishing, hiking, resorts, boat rentals, and pack station are offered. Contact the **White Mountain Ranger Station,** 640 S. Main, P.O. Box 8, Bishop, CA 93545 (☎ **760/ 873-2500**), for more info.

Bishop

Besides being the mule capital of the world (and home of Mule Days, one of the odder annual events you'll ever see), Bishop is a pretty nice little town with lots of places to sleep and eat. It's also near a lot of places to play at the back side of Kings Canyon National Park and the southern end of the John Muir Wilderness, just west on State Route 168. Contact the **Bishop Chamber of Commerce,** 690 N. Main St., Bishop, CA 93514 (☎ **760/873-8405**), or the **White Mountains Ranger Station,** 798 N. Main St., Bishop, CA 93514 (☎ **760/873-2500**), for more info.

Big Pine/Palisade Glaciers

When you pass through the tiny town of Big Pine, look up at the Palisade Glaciers to the west. These are the southernmost "living" glaciers in North America, which means they are replenished at their top end every winter and continue to break off and melt at the bottom. This is also the most popular ice-climbing area in California (I guess to call ice climbing popular at all is a stretch, but if you're an ice climber, this is a popular place to be one).

Lone Pine and Mount Whitney

Lone Pine lies literally in the shadow of Mount Whitney. It's only 13 miles up

Bishop's Average Temperatures and Precipitation												
	Jan	Feb	Mar	Apr	May	June	July	Aug	Sept	Oct	Nov	Dec
High (°F)	52.9	58.2	63.4	70.9	80.2	90.4	97.5	95.2	88.2	77.1	63.5	55.1
Low (°F)	21.4	25.9	29.5	35.8	43.5	50.8	56.3	53.8	46.8	37.4	27.7	22.1
Precipitation (in.)	1.3	1.0	0.4	0.3	0.3	0.1	0.2	0.1	0.2	0.2	0.5	1.0

Whitney Portal Road to the trailhead where most leave for the trying but technically simple hike to the highest point in the Lower 48. Between town and the sheer wall of the range lie the Alabama Hills, popular with Hollywood directors for the desert landscape and rugged granite boulders—perfect for shooting westerns. Call the **Lone Pine Chamber of Commerce,** 126 S. Main St., Lone Pine, CA 93545 (☎ **760/876-4444**), for lodging and other tourist information. Stop by the **Eastern Sierra Interagency Visitors Center** (☎ **760/876-6222**) at the junction of U.S. 395 and State Route 136 just south of town for wilderness information, books, or the bathrooms. The **Mount Whitney Ranger Station,** 640 S. Main St., Lone Pine, CA 93545 (☎ **760/ 876-6200**), offers wilderness permits, Mount Whitney climbing permits, maps, and camping information.

Parks & Other Hot Spots

LAKE TAHOE & THE NORTHERN SIERRA

Lake Tahoe

Hiking, biking, boating, fishing, swimming, skiing, camping, boardsailing.

The statistics on Lake Tahoe, one of the world's finest alpine lakes, are impressive: It's 12 miles wide, 22 miles long, and about 72 miles around—but that doesn't begin to tell the whole story. More impressive: The lake averages 989 feet deep. That's the *average;* the deepest point is 1,645 feet. You don't lose your watch in this lake and go looking for it. Even though the lake sits high above snow line, as a result of its incredible depth it never freezes (except for a few small, shallow inlets). As winter cools the surface water, the colder water sinks and is replaced by warmer water from below.

At all times of the year, the lake is amazingly clear. Despite an increase in pollution as the population around the lake has exploded in the last 50 years, you can still see a quarter sitting on the bottom in 70 feet of water (assuming you can find a place that's only 70 feet deep to drop it in).

Of course, most of us don't come to Tahoe to drop coins in a lake. We come here to ski, camp, mountain-bike, hike, fish, and boat. A lot of visitors also come here to pour money into the Nevada-side casinos, hotels, and brothels just down the road, but that's in Nevada and this is a book about California. Sorry. On the California side you'll just have to content yourself with good clean fun.

Donner Memorial State Park

2 miles off Interstate 80 on Donner Pass Rd. ☎ **530/582-7894.** Water, toilets available. Hiking, mountain biking, boating, fishing, swimming. Closed for winter season (Oct/Nov to late May). Day-use and camping fees.

If you want to learn more about the Donner Party, go to Donner Memorial State Park. The Emigrant Trail Museum is a fascinating place to find out more about the Donners, the construction of the first railway over the Sierra, Tahoe history, and the natural history of the Sierra Nevada. Also of note is the Donner Lake campground, and fishing, canoeing, and swimming in the lake itself. Unfortunately, you can hear the noise of Interstate 80 from virtually anywhere in the park—ironic when you consider the Donners' unfortunate isolation.

Sugar Pine Point State Park

Just south of Homewood on State Rte. 89. ☎ **530/525-7982.** Water, toilets available. Swimming, hiking, mountain biking, dinghy sailing. Day-use and camping fee.

Once the summer estate of turn-of-the-century San Francisco bank tycoon Isaias W. Hellman and his family, Sugar Pine Point is now a fine park with 2 miles of waterfront for swimming, boating, and sunbathing; good hiking and biking; and year-round camping. Also worth noting is Tahoe's only lighthouse and, of course, the Hellmans' outrageous Ehrmann Mansion, which is open for tours in the summer.

D. L. Bliss and Emerald Bay State Parks

Southwest shore between Sugar Pine Point and Camp Richardson on State Rte. 89. ☎ 530/525-7982. 268 campsites. Flush toilets, showers, picnicking, beach, fishing, boating, hiking, swimming. Closed for winter season. Day-use and camping fees.

Two names, one park. Actually, the two were originally separate, but now they're managed together. This shoreline is the most spectacular publicly owned property on the lake. There's really too much here to appreciate in one visit: fantastic hikes, great shore access, and beautiful Emerald Bay marked by tiny Fannette Island, the only island in the lake. The main State Park Headquarters for the Tahoe region is also here. This is a good source of information about other places to visit.

Pope-Baldwin Recreation Area and Tallac Historic Site

Just north of Camp Richardson on State Rte. 89. ☎ 530/542-4166 (year-round); 530/541-4975 (summer only). Historical buildings, hiking, skiing, multiagency visitor center (summer only), picnic grounds, and cultural center.

The Tallac Historic Site is a publicly owned but privately managed tribute to the days when Tahoe was the place to see and be seen for California's rich and famous. Several incredible old estates have been preserved by the nonprofit **Tahoe Tallac Association** (☎ 530/541-4975) and are open for a variety of events. The Recreation Area offers lake access and several nice trails. One of the most unique trails in the entire state is

here: Rainbow Trail, which at one point descends below stream level alongside Taylor Creek. The Forest Service has constructed a Plexiglas wall allowing you to see creek life in a kind of natural aquarium.

Desolation Wilderness

Southwest of Lake Tahoe from D. L. Bliss State Park to U.S. 50. ☎ 530/573-2600. For information, contact Forest Service Lake Tahoe Basin Management Unit, P.O. Box 8465, South Lake Tahoe, CA 96158. Camping is free on Forest Service land outside state or national parks. Hiking, skiing, mountain biking.

Far from desolate, this 64,000-acre wilderness on the southwest shore of Tahoe is so popular that reservations for many backcountry destinations often fill up 90 days in advance. Fifty percent of the trail permits are held until the day of departure, though. If you are adamant about going to an exact place, try to reserve in advance. If you're more flexible, you can get away with showing up really early in the morning the day you want to leave. Hikers (or in winter, skiers) looking for tips on where to go in the wilderness or on other Forest Service lands around the lake should visit the **Forest Service Center** at 870 Emerald Bay Rd (☎ 530/573-2600).

Kirkwood and Caples Lakes

Kayaking, fishing, hiking, camping.

On the west side of the Carson Pass, 63 miles east of Jackson, large Caples Lake and its tiny neighbor Kirkwood Lake are the main center of summertime camping and boating in the area. No motorboats are allowed on Kirkwood Lake, leaving it to the canoers and kayakers to enjoy. Caples Lake is much larger, and motorized fishing boats are allowed. Rental boats are available. Fishing here is best just after the ice breaks up in spring, but good all season. Several national-forest campgrounds surround Caples and trailheads from here make a good launching point for hikes into the Mokelumne Wilderness. For information and maps, contact the **El Dorado National Forest Amador Ranger District** office in Pioneer (☎ 209/295-4251).

Silver Lake
Boating, swimming, fishing, hiking, camping.

Four hundred feet of elevation lower than Caples, Silver Lake gets warm enough in summer to make an inviting swim and is big enough for waterskiing. Several resorts rent cabins around this blue-water and granite-boulder jewel. National forest campgrounds (☎ 209/295-4251) around the lake hold plenty of campers but do fill up quickly on summer weekends.

Mokelumne Wilderness
South of State Rte. 88. ☎ 209/295-4251 (Amador Ranger District in Pioneer). Hiking, fishing, swimming, horseback riding, camping.

The Mokelumne Wilderness protects more than 100,000 acres of Sierra High Country. Countless lakes and meadows dot this enormous wilderness, and the huge Mokelumne River Canyon drains it. Miles of good hiking trails make it easy to explore this still-uncrowded retreat.

Calaveras Big Trees State Park
Off State Rte. 4 between Dorrington and Arnold. ☎ 209/795-2334. 129 camping sites. Picnic areas, visitor center, flush toilets, showers, running water. Fishing, hiking, swimming, kayaking, rafting, skiing. Day-use and camping fees.

Calaveras Big Trees was once thought to be the only place on earth where the giant sequoia grew—more than a thousand grace the park in two groves. Though this is one of the best-preserved forests of giant sequoias, it was here in 1852 that a group of promoters chopped down the Discovery Tree, a 24-foot-diameter giant, building a dance floor on its stump, a bowling alley out of its trunk, and a traveling freak show exhibit out of

the shell of its bark—all to show their appreciation for these fantastic trees. John Muir used this horrible example to rally protection for the sequoias.

Numerous trails loop through the park, and the Stanislaus River bisects the 6,300-acre forest. Swimming holes and fishing pools make it a favorite summer getaway. World-class kayaking and rafting is available a few miles downstream below Murphy. In winter, the park is open for camping and is often snow-free. If there is snow, the park is open for cross-country skiing.

Lake Alpine
Kayaking, hiking, fishing, camping, boardsailing.

Hidden under a cloak of snow all winter, Lake Alpine bursts out in an explosion of beauty every spring and summer. The several-mile-long reservoir is surrounded by four national-forest campgrounds with all the usual amenities. Other nearby camps accommodate the overflow. Boats ranging from kayaks to small motorized fishing boats (15-m.p.h. speed limit on the lake) are available to rent at the marina. Trout fishing is good. Trails surround the lake and explore the headwaters of the Stanislaus River. Ebbetts Pass is a few miles beyond, just past Mosquito Lake. Shallow and inhabited by multitudes of its namesake, the lake is an important trailhead into the Carson-Iceberg Wilderness south of here.

Pinecrest Lake
Boating, fishing, hiking, boardsailing, camping.

Winter or summer, Pinecrest is where the action is on State Route 108. Several hundred campsites are broken up into smaller camps hidden in the trees near the west side of the lake. A boat ramp and marina allow launching of private boats (20-m.p.h. limit) and rentals of canoes, sailboats, and fishing boats. The town of Pinecrest has a gas station, grocery store, sporting-goods shop, a few restaurants, condos, cabins, and post office. Best, though, is the trail around the roadless back side of Pinecrest Lake. Private cabins reached only by boat or trail are peppered among long stretches of undeveloped granite shoreline. The lake freezes in winter but don't walk or ski on the ice. Water levels change too quickly for the ice to be safe and solid. For forest information, contact the **Summit Ranger Station,** 1 Pinecrest Lake Rd, Pinecrest, CA 95364 (☎ 209/965-3434). For lodging information and reservations, contact **Pinecrest Lake Resort,** P.O. Box 1216, Pinecrest, CA 95364 (☎ 209/965-3411).

SOUTHERN SIERRA: YOSEMITE TO SEQUOIA/KINGS CANYON

Yosemite National Park

Visitor center at west end of Yosemite Village Mall in the valley. ☎ 209/372-0200. Yosemite Wilderness Office, P.O. Box 577, Yosemite, CA 95389. Information: Yosemite National Park, P.O. Box 577, Yosemite, CA 95389. ☎ 209/372-0265. Numerous activities and facilities.

Yosemite National Park tries to be everything to everybody, and often ends up shooting itself in the foot trying. Don't get me wrong. Nowhere on earth is quite like the Yosemite Valley. It's stunning—a natural cathedral of sheer rock, rushing water, and magical light. Unfortunately, it's also been overdeveloped by the very people mandated to protect it. Do over a thousand hotel rooms, fast-food joints, postcard shops, and huge traffic jams really add to the nature experience here?

Finding the wild Yosemite takes careful planning, and I've devoted some care to mapping out a strategy for taking on what's arguably the most famous of the country's national parks. See "Yosemite National Park," below.

Huntington Lake and Shaver Lake

Boating, hiking, fishing, skiing, boardsailing, camping.

The most popular weekend getaway for people from Fresno, these two lakes off State Route 168 are large enough for waterskiing, windy enough for boardsailing, and surrounded by plenty of good camping, marinas, picnic areas, lodges, and summer cabins. Huntington in particular is a good starting point for hikes into the surrounding national forest. For information, contact the **Shaver Lake Ranger Station,** P.O. Box 300, Shaver Lake, CA 93644 (☎ 209/855-5360), or the **Shaver Lake Chamber of Commerce,** P.O. Box 58, Shaver Lake, CA 93644 (☎ 209/841-3350).

Sequoia and Kings Canyon National Parks

Off State Rte. 180 from Fresno or State Rte. 198 from Visalia. Information: Sequoia and Kings Canyon National Parks, Three Rivers, CA 93271. ☎ 209/784-1500. Road and weather information: ☎ 209/565-3341. Numerous activities and facilities.

Once separate, now a single park under unified management, Sequoia/Kings Canyon is one of the most fantastic wilderness areas in the National Park System. Though it gets heavy visitation, nothing in the park compares to the traffic and crowding problems faced by Yosemite. Only the very western segment of the park, home to the sequoia groves and all the park infrastructure, is accessible by road. The rest is covered by seemingly endless expanses of jagged peaks, gorges, rivers, canyons, and alpine meadows. Since you can't just pull over and see all the sights, visiting the park takes a bit of planning, so I've devoted some time to helping you get the most out of this rugged wilderness. See "Sequoia & Kings Canyon National Parks," below.

EASTERN SIERRA

Grover Hot Springs State Park

☎ 530/694-2248. Daily 9am to 9pm during summer, more limited in winter. Showers, flush toilets, camping, swimming, hiking. $5 day use, $14 camping.

A few miles outside Markleeville on Hot Springs Road is the year-round hot-spring–soaking paradise of Grover Hot Springs State Park. Though the collection of government-issue concrete pools (bathing suits required) full of both hot and cold water is less than beautiful, a soak at Grover is a great thing after a long day of hiking in the nearby Mokelumne Wilderness. The fee is good all day, so you can exit and reenter. Showers and changing rooms are also nice for that complete makeover after several days in the wilderness.

Bodie State Historic Park
7 miles south of Bridgeport and 14 miles east of U.S. 395. ☎ **760/647-6445.** Picnic tables, museum, water in summer only, pit toilets, flush toilets in summer only, ghost town. Bird watching, hiking, skiing. Daily 8am–7pm summer; 9am–4pm winter. $2 fee.

Bodie was once the meanest, baddest mining town in the West. Now lying in a state of prolonged decay, it's the meanest, baddest ghost town in the West.

Mono Lake
Boating, bird watching, hiking, swimming, camping.

This huge inland sea offers a number of interesting things to do: birding, swimming, canoeing, and hiking are the most popular. Though its surroundings are incredibly stark, sometimes oppressively so, the natural history of Mono Lake is among the most interesting you're likely to find. So is the human history. To get a good view of the 13-mile-by-8-mile lake, hike to the top of Black Point Fissures in the **Mono Lake County Park** on Cemetery Road. **Mono Basin National Scenic Area** and **Mono Lake Tufa State Reserve** (☎ **760/647-6331**) both protect and allow access to the lakeshore. The Mark Twain Interpretive Trail is a mile-long path explaining many facts about the lake. Tufa towers—millennia-old pillars of mineral salt formed underwater and left exposed when the lake level receded owing to the Los Angeles Department of Water and Power's freshwater predations—

are an interesting sight on the south shore at either the state reserve or the county park, where boardwalks over the muddy shore make them accessible. Though you won't want to get the water in your eyes or open cuts, a soak at **Navy Beach** on the south shore is a popular local cure for aching bones and other ailments. You'll be amazed by the buoyancy of Mono's saline water.

Owens River Headwaters
Wildlife, bird watching, fishing, hiking, biking, rock climbing.

Between June Lake and Mammoth, Owens River Road cuts east, paralleling the headwaters of the river. Several private guest ranches in the area specialize in fly-fishing vacations. Other stretches are accessible to the public. Many great mountain bike rides lace the area.

Devils Postpile National Monument
A few miles outside the town of Mammoth Lakes. ☎ **760/934-2289.** Hiking, horseback riding. Closed in winter. No entry fee. $6 shuttle fee required to get into the park from Mammoth Lakes. Camping $6–$8 per night. Pets on leashes permitted.

Devils Postpile National Monument is home to one of nature's most curious geological freak shows. Formed when molten lava cracked as it cooled, the 60-foot-high blue-gray basalt columns that form the postpile look more like some sort of satanic pipe organ or a jumble of giant pencil leads than anything you'd expect to see made from stone. The three- to seven-sided columns formed underground and were exposed when glaciers scoured this valley in the last ice age some 10,000 years ago. Similar examples of columnar basalt are found in Ireland and Scotland.

Rainbow Falls on the San Joaquin River and Fish Creek Hot Springs are other popular draws, and the Pacific Crest Trail and John Muir Trail both pass through the park on their way north and south. Because of its high elevation (7,900

The Seqouia and Kings Canyon National Parks Area

0 5 Miles
0 5 Kilometers

ft.) and heavy snowfall, the monument is open only from summer until early fall. Weather in the summer is usually clear and warm, but afternoon thundershowers can soak the unprepared. Nights are still cold, so bring good tents and sleeping bags if you'll be camping. The Mammoth Lakes region is famous for its beautiful lakes—but unfortunately all that water also means lots of mosquitoes. Plan for them.

From late June until early September, cars are prohibited in the monument between 7:30am and 5:30pm to maintain the wild atmosphere of the area. Visitors must take a shuttle bus from the Mammoth Mountain Inn to and from locations in the monument. While it takes some planning, the resulting peace and quiet is well worth the trouble and makes you wonder why the park service hasn't implemented similar programs at the Yosemite Valley and other traffic hot spots.

Crowley Lake

11 miles south of Mammoth on U.S. 395. For information, contact the BLM Bishop Resource Area Office (☎ **760/ 872-4881**). Biking, boating, fishing, hiking, boardsailing.

One of the state's most productive fishing lakes, Crowley swarms with anglers on the April 1 opening of trout season. The former state record German brown trout was caught here—25 pounds, 11 ounces. A boat-launch fee is required, and fishing regulations change every year, so check them. Waterskiing season runs from July 4 to Labor Day. There is no camping here, but you will find a grocery and bait store.

Owens River Gorge

An unmarked dirt road 20.5 miles south of Mammoth on U.S. 395 connects with Gorge Parallel Rd. Turn south and follow for roughly 2 miles. Hiking, biking, rock climbing.

The Owens River Gorge is a gorge without a river most of the time, because the Los Angeles Department of Water and

Power diverts the river south, but the 700-foot walls carved when water did run here remain. Recently the gorge has become a sport-climbing destination on par with Joshua Tree and other desert locales. Routes are bolted and generally uncrowded.

Yosemite National Park

Yosemite's sky-scraping geologic formations, lush meadows, swollen rivers, and spectacular waterfalls make the park a tourist destination for travelers from around the world. It's home to three of the world's 10 tallest waterfalls and the largest single piece of exposed granite anywhere, not to mention one of the world's largest trees and most-recognized rock formations. No matter where you go, you'll see something here worth remembering.

But in spite of Yosemite's beauty, recent years have brought a disquieting sense of foreboding to this wilderness haven. One trip during peak season and you'll understand why. Traffic backs up for miles, trees and branches along the Merced River become clotheslines, and candy wrappers, cigarette butts, and discarded soft drinks litter the valley. Songbirds can barely be heard over the din of voices yelling and hooting. Preserving the wild beauty of the park despite the hordes of visitors is the biggest challenge facing Yosemite today. Big changes are expected in the next 5 years as the Park Service grapples with the best way to permit access without causing more irreparable damage to this natural wonderland. The park already provides an efficient and extensive shuttle service that runs frequently. Most importantly, you should always remember that the crowds cluster around Yosemite's most hyped attractions—once you get out into the backcountry, or even just a mile

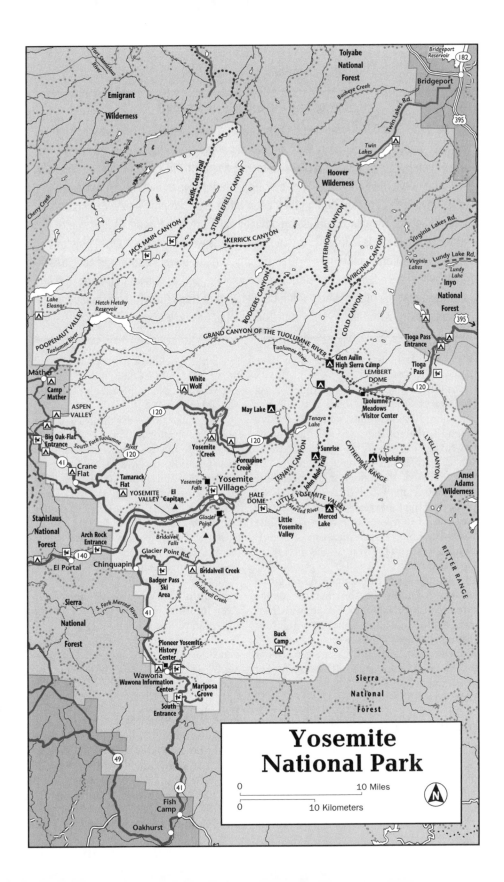

Yosemite National Park

0	10 Miles
0	10 Kilometers

Avoiding the Crowds in Yosemite

It's best to avoid holiday weekends in spring and summer if possible—during the busiest times, the park has often had to turn people away due to overcrowding. Until a more elaborate system is in place to reduce the traffic in Yosemite Valley, the park will continue to institute a policy of closing entrances when a certain number of vehicles have been admitted and, in their estimation, a maximum density of visitors has been reached. The campgrounds are usually full from June through August, and expect some crowds in late spring and early fall as well. Winter is a great time to visit Yosemite—not only is the park virtually empty, but there are a number of activities from skiing at Badger Pass to sledding, ice-skating, and snowshoeing. Keep in mind, however, that the high country along Calif. 120 and Tioga Pass Road is inaccessible to vehicles from mid-fall to early June, depending on snow levels.

---

or so down a hiking trail, you often have the place to yourself.

You'll also find that Yosemite is still living with the aftereffects of nature's rumblings. Floods and rock slides have recently altered the face of the valley, destroying campgrounds and some trails. While park workers have managed to clean most of the fallen trees, boulders, and rocks out of the heavily populated parts, half of the campsites in the valley are gone for good. The folks who live here now do so with a measure of understanding: They're living at the mercy of Mother Nature.

General park information is given below. For more on the myriad adventures you can have in Yosemite—from easy walks to scaling granite walls, from fishing and float trips to cross-country ski tours—turn to the "Southern Sierra: What to Do & Where to Do It" section. Let your fingers do the walking and have fun.

INFORMATION

If you're planning a visit to Yosemite National Park, you can get general information on accommodations, weather, and permits from the park's touch-tone phone menu at ☎ 209/372-0200 or on-line at www.nps.gov/yose/. A live operator is available weekdays from 8am to 4:30pm at ☎ 900/454-YOSE. The hearing impaired can obtain information by calling ☎ 209/372-4726.

To make a reservation to camp in Yosemite National Park, call ☎ 800/436-7275. If you are unsuccessful using this number, try the general Yosemite information line at ☎ 209/372-0200.

A superb resource is **YATI,** or the Yosemite Area Travelers Information (☎ 209/723-3153, or on-line at www.yosemite.com). This is the best Web site for Yosemite information, even surpassing the National Park Service. Also, the Yosemite Association is a nonprofit organization that publishes books and interpretive information for visitors (☎ 209/379-2646; www.yosemite.org).

Once you're in the park, buy the excellent *Map and Guide to Yosemite Valley* ($2.50); it describes many hikes and short nature walks.

GETTING THERE

Yosemite is a 3½-hour drive from San Francisco and a 6-hour drive from Los Angeles. Many roads lead to Yosemite's four entrances. From the west, the **Big Oak Flat Entrance** is 88 miles from Manteca via Calif. 120, and passes through the towns of Groveland, Buck

Meadows, and Big Oak Flat. **Arch Rock Entrance** is 75 miles northeast of Merced via Calif. 140, which passes through Mariposa and El Portal. The **South Entrance** from Wawona is 64 miles north of Fresno and passes through Oakhurst, Bass Lake, and Fish Camp. From the east, the **Tioga Pass Entrance** is the only option. It is 10 miles west of Lee Vining via Calif. 120.

FEES

It's $20 per car per week to enter the park or $10 per person per week for bike, motorcycle, or walk-in. Annual Yosemite passes are $40. Wilderness permits are free, but reserving them requires a $3 fee.

CAMPING

It costs $3 to $15 a night to camp in a Yosemite campground (☎ **800/436-7275**). Reservations are accepted in 1-month blocks beginning on the 15th of each month, and can (and should) be made up to 5 months in advance. In other words, make your reservations as near to the 15th of the month 5 months in advance of when you want to stay in the park, especially for sites in Yosemite Valley. But it's worth checking back if you're unsuccessful, because cancellations do occur.

There's a 7-day camping limit in the valley from May 1 to September 15. Some campgrounds inside and outside the valley are closed in winter. Some outside the valley are first-come, first-served. A maximum of six people and two vehicles may stay at each campsite. Check in/out is 10 a.m. at valley campgrounds and noon elsewhere in the park. Pets are allowed in a few campgrounds. Additional campground information is available by calling ☎ 209/372-0200.

SEASONS

Summer is the most popular time to visit the park, of course, and offers the best weather. But **winter** is one of the nicest times to visit Yosemite Valley. It isn't crowded, and a dusting of snow accentuates the stark contrasts of all that granite. To see the waterfalls at their best, come in **spring** when snowmelt is at its peak. **Fall** can be cool but beautiful and much less crowded.

The High Country is under about 20 feet of snow from November through May, so unless you're snow camping, summer is pretty much the only time to come. Even in summer, thundershowers are an almost daily occurrence and snow is not uncommon. Mosquitoes can be a plague during the peak of summer but get better after the first freeze.

WILDLIFE

The name *Yosemite* derives from the native *uzumati,* "grizzly bear." Grizzlies are gone from the park now, but black bears are plentiful and make their presence known through late-night depredations of ice chests and food in the campgrounds rather than by posing pretty for the cameras in broad daylight. Deer and coyote frequent Yosemite Valley, often causing vehicular mayhem as one heavy-footed looky-loo slams on the brakes to whip out the Handi-cam while another rubbernecker, equally mesmerized by Bambi, drives right into him. Metal crunches, tempers flare, and the deer daintily hop away, looking amused at the stupidity.

REGULATIONS

You'll need a **permit** to camp overnight in the backcountry. Permits are free, but it's a good idea to reserve one in advance during high season, and for that there's a fee of $3. To get one, call ☎ **209/372-0200** or stop by any ranger station or the valley Wilderness Center. Fishing licenses are required. Utilize proper food-storage methods in bear country. Don't collect firewood around campgrounds. No off-road bicycle riding is permitted. Dogs are allowed in the park but must be leashed and are forbidden on the trails. Don't feed the animals.

VISITOR CENTERS

The best and biggest visitor center is the **Valley Visitor Center** in Yosemite Village (☎ 209/372-0299). It offers exhibits on the park and its history, as well as comprehensive visitor information. The rangers here are helpful, insightful, and knowledgeable. Information boards update road conditions and campsite availability, and also serve as message boards. Maps, books, and videos can be purchased. Nearby is **Yosemite Valley Wilderness Center,** a small room with high-country maps, information on necessary equipment, and trail information. A ranger at the desk can answer all your questions, issue permits,

and offer advice. Elsewhere, the **Wawona Information Station** (☎ 209/375-9501) and **Big Oak Flat Information Center** (☎ 209/379-1899) give general park information. In the High Country, the **Tuolumne Meadows Visitor Center** (☎ 209/372-0263) is helpful.

RANGER PROGRAMS

Yosemite's wonderful rangers take time to lead a number of educational and interpretive programs, ranging from backcountry hikes to fireside talks to snow-country survival clinics. Call the main park information number with specific requests for the season and park

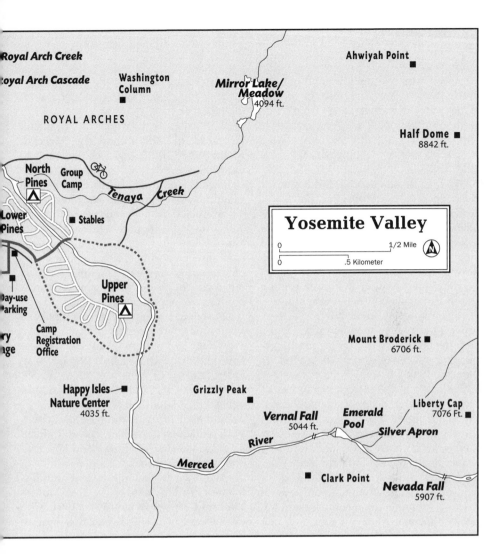

Yosemite Valley

Royal Arch Creek

Royal Arch Cascade

ROYAL ARCHES

Washington Column

Mirror Lake/Meadow 4094 ft.

Ahwiyah Point

Half Dome ■ 8842 ft.

North Pines

Group Camp

Tenaya Creek

Lower Pines

Stables

Day-use Parking

Upper Pines

Camp Registration Office

Mount Broderick ■ 6706 ft.

Happy Isles Nature Center 4035 ft.

Grizzly Peak

Vernal Fall 5044 ft.

Emerald Pool

Silver Apron

Liberty Cap 7076 Ft. ■

River

Merced

Clark Point

Nevada Fall 5907 ft.

0   1/2 Mile

0   .5 Kilometer

---

area you'll be visiting. Don't miss the free painting, drawing, and photography classes offered spring through fall and holiday weekends in winter at the Art Activity Center next to the Museum Gallery.

EXPLORING YOSEMITE VALLEY

Yosemite Valley, where 95% of tourists head, is just a small sliver of the park, but it holds the bulk of its jaw-dropping features. An estimated 4.1 million people visit the valley each year. This is the place of record-setters: the highest waterfall in North America and three of the tallest in the world (Upper Yosemite, Sentinel, and Ribbon falls); the biggest and tallest piece of exposed granite (El Capitan); and stands of the Giant Sequoia.

The 7-square-mile valley is really a huge bathtub drain for the combined runoff of hundreds of square miles of snow-covered peaks. From the 4,000-foot-high valley floor, the 8,000-foot tops of **El Capitan, Half Dome,** and **Glacier Point** look like the top of the world, but they're small in comparison to the high peaks in the park, some of which rise to nearly 14,000 feet. High country creeks flushed with snowmelt catapult over the abyss left by the glaciers and form an outrageous variety of **waterfalls,** from tiny ribbons that never reach ground to the torrents of Nevada Falls and Vernal Falls.

In concert with the shadows and lighting of the deep valley, the effect of all this falling water is mesmerizing. On a clear spring morning you'll see more rainbows than you can count and hear a bass note of roaring water echoing through the entire valley.

What most sets Yosemite Valley apart is its incredible **geology.** The Sierra Nevada was formed between 10 and 80 million years ago when a tremendous geological uplift pushed layers of granite lying under the ocean up into an incredible mountain range. Cracks and rifts in the rock gave erosion a start at carving canyons and valleys. Then, during the last ice age, at least three glaciers flowed through the valley, shearing away at the land, hauling away the rubble, and leaving vertical faces of stone. The last glacier retreated 10,000 to 15,000 years ago, but left its legacy in the incredible number of huge, high waterfalls pouring into the valley from hanging side canyons.

All that vertical stone gets put to use by hundreds who flock to the park for some of the finest **rock climbing** anywhere. Sharp-eyed visitors will spot a lot of climbers hanging off the sheer faces of Yosemite's famous walls; among these are the aforementioned El Capitan and Half Dome. The world's best climbers are here to see and be seen proving their mettle. Some spend as long as 10 days slung from the rock.

The valley is also home to beautiful meadows and the meandering **Merced River.** When the last glacier retreated, it dammed Merced River with a pile of glacial debris and formed a lake where the valley is now. Eventually sediment from the river filled the lake and created the rich and level valley floor we see today; tiny Mirror Lake, in the upper end of the valley, is all that remains of this once-huge body of water. Float trips—by raft, inner tube, or other conveyance—are a summer staple on the slow-moving Merced.

First-time visitors are often completely dumbstruck as they enter the valley from the west. The first two things you'll see are delicate and beautiful **Bridal Veil Falls** and the immense face of **El Capitan,** a beautiful and anything-but-delicate 3,593-foot-tall solid-granite rock. A short trail leads to the base of **Bridal Veil,** which at 620 feet tall is only a medium-size fall by park standards, but one of the prettiest.

Right in the middle of the valley's thickest urban cluster is the **Valley Visitors Center** (☎ 209/372-0299), with exhibits that will teach you about glacial geology, history, and the park's flora and

---

John Muir & Yosemite

The name of nature writer John Muir, one of the founders of the conservation movement, is virtually synonymous with Yosemite. Muir came here from the Midwest in the late 19th century and ended up spending the rest of his life battling for the protection of Yosemite and the greater Sierra Nevada.

Muir won the largest battle of his life when he formed the Sierra Club and convinced President Benjamin Harrison to declare Yosemite a national park in 1890. Later, though, he suffered a critical defeat when the City of San Francisco built a water diversion dam within the park, flooding Muir's beloved Hetch Hetchy Valley, the glacial splendor of which rivaled Yosemite Valley. Always the opportunist, Muir, lobbying the federal government to declare the entire Sierra Nevada a national park, once spent 3 days swapping tall tales, drinking, and sleeping under beds of pine boughs with the old rough rider himself, President Teddy Roosevelt.

Mariposa Grove

Wawona Point

UPPER GROVE

Fallen Wawona Tunnel Tree

Summer Hiking Trail to Wawona

Museum

Outer Loop Trail

LOWER GROVE

Grizzly Giant

0 — 1/2 Mile
0 — .5 Kilometer

N

Parking

Tram Boarding Area
Gift Shop
Free Shuttle Bus Stop (seasonal)

Free Shuttle Bus Stop (seasonal)

Mariposa Grove Rd.

To Wawona

41 South Entrance

fauna. Check out the **Indian Cultural Museum** next door for insight into what life in the park was once like. Excellent exhibits highlight the culture of the Miwok and Paiute people who occupied the park, and the museum also has an awesome collection of baskets and other artifacts. Behind the center is a re-creation of an Indian village. The **Museum Gallery** houses a number of fine Ansel Adams works, as well as those of other artists.

A few hundred yards from the visitor center is the **Ahwahnee Hotel.** Unlike the rest of the hotel accommodations in the park, the Ahwahnee actually lives up to its surroundings. (See "Campgrounds & Other Accommodations" for details.)

The best single view in the valley is from **Sentinel Bridge** over the Merced River. At sunset, Half Dome's face functions as a projection screen for all the sinking sun's hues—from yellow to pink to dark purple—and the river reflects it all. Ansel Adams took one of his most famous photographs from this very spot.

EXPLORING THE SOUTHWEST CORNER

You can easily slip into the park's south gate and enjoy a hike among the majestic giants of **Mariposa Grove** or along **Glacier Point Road** without having to deal with an overly stressful crowd scene. And just outside the park's southern boundary is **Goat Camp,** where you can wind through the sequoias on cross-country skis. Also in this part of the park are several meadows and the rushing south fork of the Merced River.

This corner of Yosemite is densely forested and gently sculpted in comparison to the stark granite that makes up so much of the park. Coming from the valley, State Route 41 passes through a long tunnel. Just prior to the tunnel entrance is **Tunnel View,** sight of a famous Ansel Adams photograph, and the best scenic outlook of the valley accessible by automobile. Virtually the whole valley is laid out below: Half Dome and Yosemite Falls straight ahead in the distance, Bridal Veil to the right, and El Capitan to the left.

A few miles past the tunnel, Glacier Point Road turns off to the east. Closed in winter, this winding road leads to a picnic area and visitor center at **Glacier Point,** site of another fabulous view of the valley, this time 3,000 feet below. Schedule at least an hour to drive here from the valley and another hour or two to absorb the view. This is a good place to study the glacial scouring of the valley below; the Glacier Point perspective makes it easy to picture the valley below filled with vast sheets of ice.

Thirty miles south of the valley on State Route 41 is the **Wawona Hotel** and the **Pioneer Yosemite History Center.** The Wawona, which dates from 1879, was the first lodge built in the state reserve that would later become the national park. Its Victorian architecture evokes a time when travelers spent several days in horse-drawn wagons to get to the park. What a welcome stop it must have been. (See "Campgrounds & Other Accommodations" later in this chapter for more information.) The Pioneer Center is a collection of early homesteading log buildings across the river from the Wawona.

One of the primary reasons Yosemite was first set aside as a park was the **Mariposa Grove** of sequoias. These humongous trees have personalities that match their gargantuan size. Single limbs on the biggest tree in the grove, the Grizzly Giant, are 10 feet thick. The tree itself is 209 feet tall, 32 feet in diameter, and more than 2,700 years old. Totally out of proportion with the size of the trees are

the tiny cones of the sequoia. Smaller than a baseball and tightly closed, the cones will not release their cargo of seeds until opened by fire. Many good trails lead through the grove.

EXPLORING THE HIGH COUNTRY

While it's easy to let the tremendous gravity of Yosemite Valley draw all of your attention there, remember that 95% of Yosemite is wilderness. Very few of the 4 million visitors who come to the park each year ever get more than a mile from their car. That leaves most of Yosemite's 750,000 acres open for anyone adventurous enough to hike a few miles. Even if the valley is the hands-down winner for dramatic freak-of-nature displays, the Yosemite High Country offers a more subtle kind of beauty: glacial lakes, roaring rivers, and miles of granite spires and domes.

Of the entire Sierra Nevada, the High Country of Yosemite has the most grandiose landscape. Dome after dome of beautifully crystalline granite reflects the sunlight above deep-green meadows and icy-cold rivers. Since this area of the park is under snow from November through June, the short season we call summer is really more like spring here. From snowmelt to the first snowfall, the High Country explodes with wildflowers and long-dormant wildlife trying to make the most of the short season.

Tioga Pass (on State Route 120) is the gateway to the High Country. At times it clings to the side of steep rock faces; other times it weaves through canyon bottoms. Several good campgrounds make it a pleasing overnight alternative to summertime crowds in the valley, though use is increasing here too.

Unlike the valley, a car is vital to getting around here, as the only public transportation is the once-a-day bus to Tuolumne Meadows. Leaving the valley at 8am, the bus will let you off anywhere along the way. The driver waits 2 hours at

Wawona

0   1/2 Mile

0   .5 Kilometer

Swinging Bridge

Swinging Bridge Loop

Chilnualna Falls Trail

To Mariposa Grove

Mariposa Grove Trail

Wawona Rd.

Trailhead

Parking

South Fork Merced River

Forest Drive

Wawona Meadows

Chilnualna Falls Rd.

Redwood Guest Cottages

Brook Walk

Meadow Loop Rd.

Wawona Golf Course

Pine Tree Market

Parking

Trailhead

Camp Chilnualna Cabins

Wawona Meadow Loop

Stables

Wawona Hotel

Pioneer History Center

Parking

Wawona Store

41

Alder Creek Trail

Free Shuttle Bus Stop (seasonal)

Tuolumne Meadows, which isn't much time to see anything, then heads back down to the valley, returning around 4pm. One-way fare is $12, or slightly less to intermediate destinations.

Near the top of Tioga Pass is stunning **Tuolumne Meadows,** my favorite region of the park. This enormous meadow, covering several square miles, is bordered by the Tuolumne River on one side and spectacular granite peaks on the other. The meadow is cut by many stream channels full of trout, and herds of mule deer are almost always present. Awesome day and overnight hikes lead off into the wilderness in all directions. Miles of uncrowded granite-climbing routes surround you. This is still a pristine place, unaffected by the tour-bus mentality you find in the valley. At the Tuolumne

Meadows Lodge and store, you can buy last-minute backpacking supplies and have lunch at the burgers-and-fries cafe.

Tenaya Lake is another popular High Country destination. It's great for water sports, though the water is very chilly. Many good hikes lead into the High Country from here, and the granite domes surrounding the lake are popular with climbers. Fishing here varies greatly from year to year.

SEEING YOSEMITE'S HIGHLIGHTS IN A DAY

If you're like most visitors to Yosemite, you'll stick to the valley and not stay long. It's ironic, considering the immensity and grandeur of the property, but if you have limited time, don't despair—there's a lot to see and do. The following are some

Tuolumne Meadows

0   1/4 Mile

0   .25 Kilometer

N

Pacific Crest Trail

Mt. Conness Trail

Dingley Creek

Young Lakes Trail

Tuolumne Falls

Dog Lake

Tuolumne River

Delaney Creek

Dog Lake Trail

Pothole Dome ▲

John Muir Trail

Lembert Dome ▲

Dana Meadows Trail

Tenaya Lake Trail

Fairview Dome ▲

TUOLUMNE

Dana Fork

Tuolumne River

← To Yosemite Village

Visitor Information Center

MEADOWS

Tuolumne Meadows Campground

John Muir Trail

Budd Creek

Unicorn Creek

Elizabeth Lake Trail

John Muir Trail

Cathedral Peak ▲

attractions that will give you the most Yosemite flavor in just a little time.

The **Valley Visitor Center** (shuttle bus stop nos. 6 and 9) is your logical starting point. Here, you can learn about Yosemite's unique granite landscaping, and gain an appreciation and understanding of the park. More importantly, you can orient yourself.

The base of **Lower Yosemite Fall** (shuttle bus stop no. 7) is an easy walk from the parking lot across from Yosemite Lodge. From here, you'll be able to see a portion of the magnificent water show. During peak runoff, you might get wet— the force of the fall sends spray in every direction. In winter, a huge snow cone caused by freezing water rises to heights of up to 300 feet at the base of this fall.

Happy Isles (shuttle bus stop no. 16) is another major attraction. Located at the convergence of several inlets, it's the site of the valley's new nature center. This is also the trailhead for Vernal and Nevada falls, two picturesque staircase waterfalls that can be reached on foot.

Next, I recommend a visit to **Mirror Lake** (shuttle bus stop no. 17), a small lake named for the near-perfect way it reflects the surrounding scenery. It's slowly filling up with silt and is less dramatic and mirrorlike than it used to be, but its shore still offers a beautiful view of Half Dome. This short stroll is well marked (see "Walks & Rambles," below).

If you have more time after that, don't worry. There's always plenty more to do.

Sequoia & Kings Canyon National Parks

Sequoia and Kings Canyon are two adjacent national parks managed jointly from the park headquarters near Ash Mountain on State Route 198 east of Visalia. The two are only about 200 road miles away from Yosemite but are still a world apart. Where the Park Service has taken every opportunity to modernize, accessorize, and urbanize Yosemite, leading to a frenetic tourist scene much like the cities so many of us strive to escape, at Sequoia/Kings Canyon they've treated the wilderness beauty of the park with respect and care. Only one road loops through the park, **Generals Highway,** a narrow, steep, and winding route through the forest that connects the park's two year-round entrances. No road traverses the Sierra here.

Sequoia/Kings Canyon is home to the best wilderness in the Sierra Nevada. Few roads go here because there is nowhere to build them; jagged peaks, hollowed-out canyons, and icy rivers are impediments to the smooth laying of asphalt. Hiking and backpacking are what this park is all about: 800 miles of backcountry trails connect gorges, lakes, high alpine meadows, and snowfields; 800 miles of streams and 500 lakes teem with fish. From Lodgepole, you can day hike to Twin Lakes, at 9,500 feet. At road's end on the **Kings Canyon Highway** (open from May to Nov) you can stand by the banks of the Kings River and stare up at 5,000-foot-tall granite walls rising above the river, the deepest canyon in the United States.

General park information is given below. For more on various activities in the park, see the "Southern Sierra: What to Do & Where to Do It" section.

For additional information, contact **Sequoia & Kings Canyon National Park,** 47050 Generals Hwy., Three Rivers, CA 93271-9651 (☎ **559/565-3341,** or for a live operator 559/565-3134; www.nps.gov/ seki).

GETTING THERE

There are two main entrances to the parks. Calif. 198 via Visalia and the town of Three Rivers leads to the **Ash Mountain Entrance** in Sequoia National Park. Calif. 180 via Fresno leads straight to the **Big Stump Entrance** near Grant Grove in Kings Canyon National Park. There are also three dead-end entrance roads open only in the summer: the Kings Canyon Highway (a continuation of Calif. 180) to **Cedar Grove** in Kings Canyon National Park, and two smaller roads to **Mineral King** and to **South Fork,** both in the south part of Sequoia National Park.

The parks are roughly equidistant (5 hr. by car) from both San Francisco and Los Angeles. The Ash Mountain Entrance is 36 miles from Visalia, or about an hour away. The Big Stump Entrance is 53 miles from Fresno, or about 1½ hours away.

FEES

A $10 fee per car is good for 1 week's worth of entry at any park entrance. Bikers or walkers can enter for $5. An annual pass is only $20.

THE LAY OF THE LAND

The Sierra Nevada tilts upward as it runs south. **Mount Whitney,** the highest peak in the Lower 48 at 14,495 feet, soars above the southeast corner of the park, but it is just one of the many high peaks in Sequoia/Kings Canyon. The **Pacific Crest Trail,** which runs north to south through both parks, remains at 10,000 feet most of the time and crosses through 12,000-foot-tall passes. For many miles it coincides with the **John Muir Trail,** which runs just inside the park's eastern boundary along the top of the striking east slope of the Sierra, ending just below Mount Whitney.

The Kern, Kings, and Kaweah rivers drain this huge High Country expanse, becoming incredible white-water rafting and kayaking rivers as they descend into the Gold Country. Small High Country lakes are home to some of the only remaining pure-strain golden trout. Bighorn sheep and spotted owl hide away in the craggy peaks and alpine meadows. Bear, deer, and numerous smaller animals and birds depend on the park's miles of wild habitat for summer breeding and feeding grounds.

THE TREES

Besides the snow-covered peaks, rushing white water, and plentiful wildlife, Sequoia/Kings Canyon is also home to the largest groves of giant sequoia redwoods in the Sierra Nevada. There are over 75 groves of giant sequoias in the park, but the easiest places to see the park's big trees are **Grant Grove** in Kings Canyon near the park entrance on State Route 180 from Fresno, or **Giant Forest,** a huge grove of trees containing 40 miles of footpaths, near the entrance to Sequoia National Park on State Route 198. Saving the sequoias was the reason Sequoia National Park was created in 1890 at the request of San Joaquin Valley residents, making it America's second oldest national park.

Unlike the coast redwoods, which reproduce by sprouting or by seeds, giant sequoias only reproduce by seed. The tiny cones require fire to open, so it can be decades between generations. Adult sequoias don't die of old age and are protected from fire by thick bark. Most die when they topple in high winds or heavy snows; the huge trees have surprisingly shallow roots. These groves, like the ones in Yosemite, were first thoroughly explored by conservationist and nature writer John Muir.

SEASONS & CLIMATE

Sequoia and Kings Canyon, for the most part, share a climate that varies considerably depending on the region of the park. A good rule of thumb throughout the park is to remember that the higher you go, the cooler it gets. So pack accordingly on any trip that climbs above the valley floor or ventures into the backcountry.

During the **summer,** temperatures at lower elevations can climb into the 90s and higher, and plummet into the 50s at night. Afternoon temperatures average in the 60s and 70s in **spring** and **fall,** and again, evenings are usually cool. Afternoon showers are fairly common year-round. **Winter** days average in the 40s and 50s, and seldom drop below zero, although much of the land is buried beneath several feet of snow. Remember, a particularly wet winter often leads to an incredibly stunning and powerful spring.

SPECIAL REGULATIONS & WARNINGS

The roads in the park are particularly steep and winding. Those in RVs will find it easiest to come from Calif. 180 from Fresno. Piped water is safe, but all groundwater should be boiled for 3 minutes before drinking. Rattlesnakes are common; look where you step and touch. In the foothills, check your clothes frequently for ticks. Beware also of black bears. When camping, store all food in lockers and put all garbage in bear-proof containers.

VISITOR CENTERS

There are two year-round visitor centers. **Lodgepole Visitors Center** (☎ 559/565-3782), open during the summer only, is the largest, with a full selection of park information and displays about the history, biology, and geology of this incredible place. A visit here is a great way to orient yourself in this widely dispersed park. **Grant Grove Visitor Center** (☎ 559/335-2856) is in Grant

Sequoia and Kings Canyon National Parks

Grove Village, 3 miles from the Big Stump entrance on Highway 180. **Ash Mountain Park Headquarters** also has a visitor center (☎ **559/565-3719**), on State Route 198 east of Visalia.

Also open only in summer are **Mineral King** (☎ **209/565-3768**) and **Cedar Grove** (☎ **209/565-3793**), on State Route 180 west of Hume. Park rangers lead hikes, campfire talks, and slide shows at campgrounds and visitor centers year-round (limited to weekends in winter).

EXPLORING THE PARKS

Sequoia National Park

The best-known stand of sequoias in the world can be found in **Giant Forest,** part of Sequoia National Park. Named in 1875 by explorer and environmentalist John Muir, this park consists mostly of huge meadows and a large grove of giant trees. At the northern edge of the grove, you can't miss the **General Sherman Tree,** considered the largest living thing on the planet, although it is neither the tallest nor the widest. It is believed to be between 2,300 and 2,700 years old, *and it's still growing.* Every year, it adds enough new wood to make another 60-foot-tall tree. The tree is part of the 2-mile **Congress Trail,** a foot trail that includes groups of trees with names such as The Senate and The House.

Another interesting stop in Giant Forest is **Tharp's Log,** a cabin named after the first non–Native American settler in the area, Hale Tharp, who grazed cattle among the Giant Sequoias and built a summer cabin in the 1860s from a fallen sequoia hollowed by fire. It is the oldest cabin remaining in the park.

Nearby **Crescent Meadow** is a pristine clearing dotted with wildflowers and tall grasses. A trail wraps around the meadow. This is also the trailhead for several backcountry hikes.

Also in the area is **Moro Rock,** a large granite dome that offers one of the most spectacular views in the Sierra. From atop the rock, the high-elevation, barren mountains in the Kaweah Range appear dark and ominous. Snow caps the ridgeline throughout the year. While the cliffs appear towering and steep, they are actually smaller than the summit of the Sierra, which is obscured from view. The walk to the top takes visitors up hundreds of stairs and requires about a half hour to get up. At the top is a narrow, fenced plateau with endless views. During a full moon, the mountain peaks shimmer like silver.

South of the Giant Forest is the turnoff for **Crystal Cave,** one of more than 100 caves in the park and one of just two in the area that offer guided tours (Boyden Cavern in the neighboring national forest is the other). The cave is composed of limestone that has turned to marble, and is full of stalactites and stalagmites. To reach the entrance, drive 7 miles down the narrow, winding road (RVs, trailers, and buses are prohibited), and the cave entrance is an additional 15-minute walk down a steep path. The Sequoia Natural History Association conducts 45-minute tours daily between 11am and 4pm from June to Labor Day, and less often in May and late September. Tickets are not sold

---

Avoiding the Crowds at Sequoia & Kings Canyon

Most visitors make a loop through the park by entering at Grant Grove and leaving through Ash Mountain or vice versa. To escape the crowds and see less-used areas of the park, enter on one of the dead-end roads to Mineral King, South Fork, or Cedar Grove. The lack of through traffic makes these parts of the park incredibly peaceful even at full capacity, and they are gateways to the park's best hiking.

Giant Forest

0 _____ 1 Mile

0 _____ 1 Kilometer

at the cave, but rather at the Lodgepole and Foothills visitor centers. The cost is $5 for adults, $2.50 for children and seniors with a Golden Eagle Pass, and free for children under age 6. Information is available by telephone (☎ 209/565-3759). It gets cold underground, so bring a sweater or jacket.

Lodgepole, the most developed area in both parks, lies just northeast of the Giant Forest on the Generals Highway. Here, you'll find the largest visitor center in either park. There is a large market, several places to eat, the **Walter Fry Nature Center,** a laundry, and a post office.

About 16 miles south of Giant Forest is the region of the park known as the **Foothills.** Located near the Ash Mountain Entrance, the Foothills has a visitor center,

several campgrounds, and **Hospital Rock,** a large boulder with ancient pictographs that are believed to have been painted by the Monache Indians that once lived here. Nearby are about 50 grinding spots once used to smash acorns into flour. A short trail leads down to a beautiful spot along the Kaweah River where the water gushes over rapids into deep, clear pools. Hospital Rock also has a nice picnic area.

Mineral King is a pristine, undeveloped region in the southern part of the park. This high-mountain valley was carved by glaciers and is bordered by the tall peaks of the Great Western Divide. To reach this area, patient drivers must follow the marked highway sign 3 miles outside Sequoia National Park's Ash Mountain Entrance. From the turnoff to

Mineral King, it's a 28-mile trip that makes many tight turns and takes 1.5 hours to drive. Trailers, RVs, and buses are not allowed. The road is closed in winter.

The rocky landscape in Mineral King is as colorful as a rainbow—red and orange shales mix with white marble and black metamorphic shale and granite. In winter, this area is prone to avalanches. The most prominent point in the area is **Sawtooth Peak,** which reaches 12,343 feet. Sawtooth and other peaks in this region resemble the Rocky Mountains more than the rest of the Sierra Nevada because they are made of metaphoric rocks. The trails in Mineral King begin at 7,500 feet and climb from there. Park rangers sometimes conduct hikes around here. The best way to experience Mineral King is to stay overnight in one of two nearby campgrounds.

Kings Canyon National Park

With its rugged canyon, huge river, and desolate backcountry, Kings Canyon is a hiker's dream. It consists of Grant Grove and Cedar Grove, as well as portions of the Monarch Wilderness and Jennie Lakes Wilderness. *One other point of note:* Between Grant Grove and Cedar Grove is a stretch of land not in the park, but in Sequoia National Forest instead. This region includes Hume Lake, Boyden Cavern, and several campgrounds.

Grant Grove is the most crowded region in either park. Not only is it located just a few miles from a main entrance, but the area is also a thoroughfare for travelers heading from Giant Forest to the south or Cedar Grove to the east. The grove was designated as General Grant National Park in 1890, and was incorporated when Kings Canyon National Park was formed in 1940.

Here you'll find the towering **General Grant Tree** amid a grove of spectacular Giant Sequoias. The tree was discovered by Joseph Hardin Tomas in 1862 and named 5 years later to honor Ulysses S. Grant. It measures 267.4 feet tall, 107.6

feet around, and is thought to be the world's third-largest living thing, possibly 2,000 years old. This tree has been officially declared "The Nation's Christmas Tree" and is the cornerstone of the park's annual Christmas tree ceremony.

Two and a half miles southwest of the grove is the **Big Stump Trail,** an instructive hike that can be slightly depressing as it winds among the remains of logged sequoias. Since sequoia wood decays slowly, you'll see century-old leftover piles of sawdust that remain from the logging days. Nearby, **Panoramic Point** visitors can stand atop a 7,520-foot ledge and see across a large stretch of the Sierra, and across Kings Canyon. **Grant Grove Village** also has a restaurant, market, gift shop, and visitor center.

Although in the same park, **Cedar Grove** seems a world away. That this region is around today is sheer luck. There were plans to flood Kings Canyon by damming the Kings River. Today, it's an incomprehensible move—it would have buried Cedar Grove beneath a very deep lake. Cedar Grove is covered with lush landscape, tumbling waterfalls and miles upon miles of solitude. Half the fun is driving through **Kings Canyon** as its sheer granite walls close around you and the wild South Fork of the Kings River races by. One mile east of the Cedar Grove Village turnoff is **Canyon View,** where visitors can see the glacially carved U-shape of Kings Canyon.

Easily accessible nature trails in Cedar Grove include Zumwalt Meadow, Roaring River Falls, and Knapp's Cabin. Zumwalt Meadow is dotted with ponderosa pine and has good views of two rock formations, the **Grand Sentinel** and **North Dome.** The top of Grand Sentinel is 8,504 feet above sea level while North Dome, which some say resembles Half Dome in Yosemite, towers over the area at 8,717 feet.

Roaring River Falls is a 5-minute walk from the parking area 3 miles east of the turnoff to the village. Even during

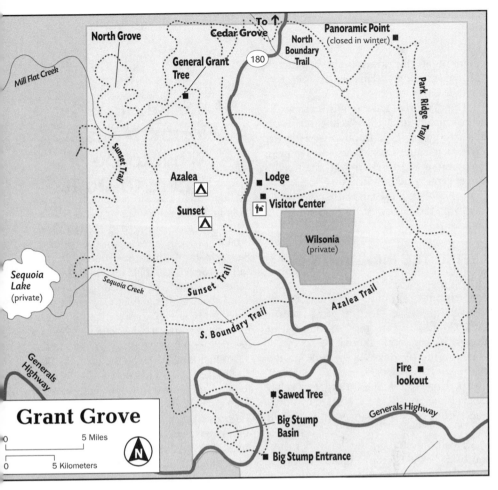

Grant Grove

0 ——— 5 Miles

0 ——— 5 Kilometers

N

summer and dry years, water crashes through a narrow granite chute into a cold, green pool below. During a wet spring, these falls are powerful enough to drench visitors who venture too close. **Knapp's Cabin** can be reached via a short walk from a turnoff 2 miles east of the road to Cedar Grove Village. Here, during the 1920s, Santa Barbara businessman George Knapp commissioned lavish fishing expeditions. This tiny cabin was used to store tons of expensive gear.

Ten miles west of Cedar Grove, in the national forest and back toward Grant Grove, is the entrance to **Boyden Cave,** the only other cave in the area to host tours. Boyden Cave hosts visitors in summertime only (☎ **209/736-2708**). Cost is $7 for adults and children age 14 and up,

and $3.50 for children ages 3 to 13. Children under age 3 are admitted free. Tickets can be purchased at the entrance. The cave is open May through October from 11am to 4pm daily.

Cedar Grove also hosts a small village with a store and gift shop, restaurant, laundry, showers, lodge, and campgrounds. This region of the park is often less crowded than others because it is at the end of the road. It is closed from mid-November to mid-April.

The **Monarch Wilderness** is a 45,000-acre region protected under the 1984 California Wilderness Act. Part of it lies on the grounds of Sequoia National Forest and it adjoins wilderness in Kings Canyon National Park. It's small, tough to reach, and so steep that hikers practically need to be roped in to climb.

You're near the wilderness area when you pass Kings Canyon Lodge and Boyden Cave.

The **Jennie Lakes Wilderness** is even smaller at 10,500 acres. Although tiny enough to hike through in a day, it exhibits a variety of wilderness features, including the 10,365-foot Mitchell Peak and several wide, lowland meadows. This region lies between the Generals Highway and Highway 180, east of Grant Grove.

SEEING THE HIGHLIGHTS IN A DAY

Day-trippers should stick to **Grant Grove** if possible—it's the most accessible. Coming from the south, **Giant Forest** is a good alternative as well, although the trip takes some time on the steep and narrow Generals Highway. Cedar Grove and Mineral King, two other destination points, are a bit farther afield and require an early start or an overnight stay.

If you only have 1 day, consider driving from Giant Forest to Grant Grove, or vice versa. It's about 2 hours through the park. Get your bearings by starting at a park visitor center—either the **Foothills Visitor Center** near the Ash Mountain Entrance or the **Grant Grove Visitor Center.** Whether traveling this route from the north or south, you'll see the varied climate within the park as you pass through dense forest to exposed meadows and then through scrubby foothills covered in oaks and underbrush. In spring and summer, much of the route is dotted by wildflowers and the southern portion runs along the Kaweah River. This route also passes near two large stands of Giant Sequoias, one at Grant Grove and the other at Giant Forest. Both have easy trails looping through the majestic stands. At Grant Grove, a footpath passes lengthwise through a fallen sequoia.

Lake Tahoe & the Northern Sierra: What to Do & Where to Do It

This is the Sierra that most people know. Often incorrectly called the High Sierra, which properly refers to the southern Sierra from Yosemite to Mount Whitney, the Tahoe-to-Yosemite region is the most accessible and developed part of the whole range. It's a relatively short drive here from the Bay Area, and a robust tourist infrastructure ensures that any creature comforts won't be overlooked.

Which doesn't mean the area has been spoiled by success: It's just too darn big for that to be true. Twenty minutes from the glitter and casinos of South Lake Tahoe you can find yourself all alone by an alpine lake. On State Route 4 and State Route 108, passes that have no connection with either Tahoe or Yosemite, you can find some of the most pristine areas in the entire range. I think the single most beautiful stretch of road I've ever driven might be State Route 108 from Kennedy Meadow to Leavitt Meadow just after the snow has melted. The combination of shimmering aspens, soaring granite peaks rushing with countless cascades, and miles of flower-filled alpine meadows made me feel like a location scout for *The Sound of Music.*

High enough and wild enough to contain incredible hiking, cross-country skiing, and mountain biking, the northern Sierra is a wilderness, but one with plenty of options for people of all different levels of ability. It doesn't require the same physical stamina and commitment as the remote, untamed parts of the southern Sierra: You need not be Sir Edmond Hillary to have a good time here. Numerous ski resorts, both alpine and Nordic, are dispersed throughout the area, and self-guided winter explorers will find no shortage of snow-covered roads, meadows, and backcountry trails to test. Another outstanding feature of this part of the range is the large number of easily accessible lakes and rivers. From the huge expanse of Lake Tahoe to the thousands of diminutive alpine ponds that dot the Sierra, you can do almost anything: fish for giant mackinaw trout, boardsail, swim, or kayak the Truckee River, stopping to fly-cast for native rainbows.

BIRD WATCHING

Birding in the Sierra Nevada is so wonderful because it isn't something you have to seek out like you would in so many other locations—the generally wild character of the mountains lends itself to surprise sightings. You might be canoeing on Donner Lake and see a family of common mergansers. Once, hiking along the top of Burst Rock near Dodge Ridge I heard a sound like an incoming artillery shell only to look up and see a peregrine falcon whoosh past me at 100 miles per hour, wings tucked in full descent mode. It circled back up and did the same thing two more times while I watched from the edge of a 500-foot precipice. Other commonly seen Sierra Nevada species are the osprey, California quail, golden eagle, bald eagle, barn owl, calliope humming-bird, and red-breasted sapsucker. In the High Country the most common birds by far are the audacious stellar jay and the friendly yet dignified Clark's nutcracker. Most Sierra Nevada state and national parks maintain bird lists and often have interpretive programs. *Discovering Sierra Birds* by Edward C. Beedy and Stephen Granholm (Yosemite Natural History Association, 1985) is a great guide to Sierra bird species and habitat.

BOARDSAILING

For Sierra boardsailing, nothing beats **Lake Tahoe.** The lake is big enough that it develops some real wind virtually every afternoon. It's also big enough that you can get in real trouble if you aren't competent. Because of the lake's incredible depth it never really warms up. Even in the warmest part of summer it doesn't rise above the 60s, with the exception of certain shallow bays. The best rigging area and access on the California side is at **Sugar Pine Point State Park,** just south of Homewood on State Route 89 (☎ **530/ 525-7982**). Wear a full suit to be comfortable. Several marinas rent gear, and private boardsailing schools operate at various locations around the lake during the summer. Contact the local visitor bureaus for up-to-date suggestions about specific instructors and schools.

Lake Alpine on State Route 4 is another popular boardsailing spot, though it lacks the daunting wind and vast surface area of Tahoe. **Bear Valley Cross Country** (☎ **209/753-2834**) rents gear and can arrange small-group or individual lessons.

Pinecrest Lake on State Route 108 is a great place for learners too, since the lake's low motorboat speed limit keeps interference to a minimum. A long sandy beach perfect for rigging and dry land practice lines the entire east shore. The water is cold.

CANOEING

So many wonderful small lakes dot the Sierra that it's almost easier to say where not to take your canoe than where to take it. It seems like every corner you turn reveals some inviting expanse of blue water. If you have your own boat, just pack a fishing rod, a picnic, and your bathing suit and go crazy. Depending on renting a canoe limits you somewhat, but not too much. Most of the bigger alpine lakes have rental fleets of canoes and small rowboats. **Tahoe Paddle and Oar** (☎ **530/581-3029**) in Tahoe City teaches canoeing and has rental boats. **Bear Valley Cross Country** on State Route 4

THE COW & THE COWBIRD

Public-lands grazing is one of the hot wildlands issues as the so-called wise-use movement butts heads with the government over grazing allotments and fees for millions of acres owned by the feds but leased to private ranchers. One side of the debate calls them welfare ranchers; the other calls them heroes of the West, upholders of a grand old tradition. The truth is probably somewhere in between. While only 3% of the nation's beef is raised on public land, more than 361 million acres are allocated to the cow, mostly marginal grazing land that is only profitable because the government leases it out for a pittance when compared to the cost of private land. The government netted nearly $25 million from grazing fees nationwide in 1981, the same year it spent $58.5 million on the program, a nearly $30 million subsidy for 3% of the country's beef. Since then things haven't gotten any better.

One thing is undeniable: There's a lot of cattle in them there hills and they ain't doing them hills a lot of good. It's a well-known fact that any large, hoofed animal is going to do a lot of damage to the ground it walks on, trampling meadows and muddying streams. It also stands to reason that if you introduce a lot of hungry grazers into an area with limited forage, something is going to lose out, most likely the deer, elk, and bighorn sheep that traditionally ate here. What is less immediately apparent is the damage done when an exotic species, in this case the cow, brings its own parade of parasites, diseases, and companion species with it. Witness the cowbird.

Prior to the 1930s brown-headed cowbirds were not seen in the Sierra. They lived in the ranch land below, where they dined happily on their favorite snack, fresh cow dung, but at that time there were very few cattle in the Sierra. When public-lands grazing took off after World War I, cows were introduced into the Sierra Nevada, and, not being the type to let all that delicious dookie go to waste, the cowbird came along.

So they eat shit, you ask? What's so bad about that? There's no accounting for taste. Well, actually it isn't their table manners that make the cowbirds bad neighbors. It's their kids. Following the herd to find its next meal makes the birds too busy to tend their own nests. Instead, the brown-headed cowbird lays its egg in the nest of a smaller native bird, where it's incubated by an unsuspecting parent. When the eggs hatch, the larger cowbird chick kills its nest mates, either directly or by outcompeting them for food. At least 22 different native bird species are threatened by the cowbird. One University of California study showed that 22.4% of warbling vireo nests contain a cowbird chick, creating an 80% loss of reproductive potential for the species overall. The vireo is nearly extinct because of the cowbird. The cowbird is here because of the cow. And the cows are here because some rancher is making a nice federal subsidy to have them here.

runs a summertime rental fleet on Lake Alpine, one of my favorite canoeing lakes.

CROSS-COUNTRY SKIING & SNOWSHOEING

If you like the sensation of busting fresh tracks through the woods after a new snowfall, head for the plentiful snow-covered logging roads and trails of the national forests that are marked for winter cross-country skiing. Try the **Castle Peak Trail** off Interstate 80 near Boreal (Sno-Park permit required), or the **Taylor Creek/Fallen Leaf Lake Trail** in the **Pope-Baldwin Recreation Area,** just north of Camp Richardson on State Route 89 (☎ 530/544-5050). **Donner Memorial State Park,** 2 miles off Interstate 80 on old State Route 40 (☎ 530/582-7894), often offers ranger-led ski or snowshoe tours, and **Sugar Pine Point State Park,** just south of Homewood on State Route 89 (☎ 530/

525-7982), has great skinny-skiing. Or stop by the **Lake Tahoe Visitors Authority** (☎ 800/AT-TAHOE) in South Lake and pick up complimentary maps of the surrounding area. The Forest Service visitor centers for each individual ranger district (see "Parks & Other Hot Spots") also keep continually updated, excellent maps of trails on their land.

Like its alpine cousin, skinny-skiing on groomed trails is big business here. The granddaddy of California Nordic resorts is **Royal Gorge** (☎ 530/426-3871) in Soda Springs, with 175 miles of groomed track, numerous warming huts, and a wilderness lodge. Purists might scoff at Royal Gorge's recently installed lifts, which allow access to the upper slopes, but telemarkers love them. At Tahoe, **Squaw Valley** (☎ 530/583-5585), with 30 kilometers (18.6 miles) of groomed trails, and **Northstar** (☎ 530/562-2475), with 65 kilometers (40.3 miles) of groomed trails, both maintain Nordic areas in addition to their considerable alpine facilities. **Kirkwood** (☎ 209/258-7248), with 80 kilometers (49.6 miles) of groomed trails, also doesn't limit itself to just pleasing downhillers. In South Lake, **Lake Tahoe Winter Sports Center,** just south of the airport (☎ 530/577-2940), has numerous groomed trails. On State Route 4 the **Bear Valley Cross-Country Center** (☎ 209/753-2834) offers an excellent network of groomed trails, warming huts, and lessons, with plentiful nearby lodging.

Castle Peak Trail

6 miles round-trip. Intermediate to advanced. Some difficult downhills and steep climbs. Access: Trailhead is at the Castle Peak/Boreal Interchange on Interstate 80 near Donner Summit. Sno-Park permit required to park. Map: USGS Norden and Soda Springs topos.

Castle Peak is extremely popular with cross-country skiers looking to get away from groomed trails and flat tracks. This route will take you up from the trailhead at 7,200 feet to more than 9,000 at Castle Pass, so be prepared to climb and descend. More experienced skiers use this route as an entry to some really wild backcountry. A great option is to make overnight reservations at the **Sierra Club's Perter Grubb Hut** just a short ski from Castle Pass. Call the **Sierra Club's Clair Tappaan Lodge** (☎ 916/426-3632) for information and reservations.

Taylor Creek

Several loops up to 4.5 miles. Beginner to intermediate. Flat trails through open meadows and aspen groves. Access: 3.5 miles north of South Lake Tahoe on State Rte. 89. Sno-Park permit required to park. Map: None needed.

The Forest Service maintains this great series of loop trails near Fallen Leaf Lake for the enjoyment of beginning and intermediate skiers. The main two loops—Fallen Leaf Dam Trail and the Sawmill Trail—both offer great views and varied terrain yet are easy enough for all but the most rank beginners. Since they're at only 6,200 feet, snow conditions can be a problem here early or late in the season.

Winnemucca Lake Loop

6 miles. Moderate. Access: Trail begins at summit of Carson Pass just west of Hope Valley and junctions of State Routes 88 and 89. Clearly marked with blue diamonds and pink flagging. Map: Eldorado National Forest map.

One of the best intermediate trails in the northern Sierra, this loop takes you through some beautiful backcountry, including several perfect telemarking bowls. En route you'll pass frozen Woods Lake and then connect with the snow-covered roadbed of old Highway 88, which you'll follow back to Carson Pass. Several steep pitches over the length of the trail make it unsuitable for skiers not confident of their turning and descending abilities.

DOWNHILL SKIING & SNOWBOARDING

The Tahoe Basin is the densest concentration of ski resorts this side of Switzerland, 17 of them at last count. An entire book could be dedicated to describing them all. Throw in Iron Mountain and Kirkwood on State Route 88 and you're pushing 20. The options range from ultramodern, ultraglitzy, and ultraexpensive Squaw Valley, known for its difficult advanced runs and home to the 1960 Winter Olympics, to the cruiser's paradise of Northstar at Tahoe, regularly ranked one of the country's best intermediate mountains, all the way down in size to tiny Soda Springs, the entirety of which can be rented by private groups for special events. Virtually all of the resorts have good ski schools, rental packages, and lodging. All Tahoe resorts except for Alpine Meadows now allow snowboarding. You can get a complete listing of Tahoe ski areas with extensive mountain descriptions and current ticket prices by contacting The **Tahoe North Visitors and Convention Bureau** (☎ 800/TAHOE-4-U) or the **Lake Tahoe Visitors Authority** (☎ 800/AT-TAHOE).

Squaw Valley

End of Squaw Valley Rd., Olympic Valley. ☎ **800/545-4350** or 530/583-6985; 530/583-6955 for snow conditions. 4,200 lift-served acres (25% beginner, 45% intermediate, 30% expert); 30 lifts including 1 cable car, 1 gondola, 4 high-speed quads, 9 triples, 10 doubles, and 3 surface; 2,850-ft. vertical drop. Full-day adult ticket $49.

Were there any justice in the world, Evel Knievel would have gotten his start here—it's the Sierra Nevada's semi-official daredevil mountain. Squaw Valley's bread-and-butter are the extremists of the ski world, who flock here for the world-famous KT-22, the mega-air to be had on Poulsen's Gully, and the seemingly vertical Chute 75, perhaps the steepest trail in Tahoe. Though primarily known as an expert area, great cruisers like Mountain Run attract intermediates, and beginners will love Bailey's Beach, a fantastic bowl. There's also a half-pipe for boarders.

Northstar-at-Tahoe

State Rte. 267 and Northstar Dr., Truckee. ☎ **530/562-1010;** 530/562-1330 for snow conditions. 57 trails (25% beginner, 50% intermediate, 25% expert); 11 lifts including 1 gondola, 3 high-speed quads, 2 triples, 3 doubles, and 2 surface; 2,280-ft. vertical drop. Full-day adult ticket $48.

While Northstar originally built its reputation on family skiing (the front side is filled with beginner and intermediate runs), the addition of a high-speed quad lift serving a dozen tree-filled expert trails on the back side is changing that image. The meticulous grooming may turn off many of the bump-lovers who frequent Tahoe, but powder days on the back side shouldn't be missed. Though Village Run gets packed in the afternoons, in the mornings it's almost perfect—a long beginner cruiser. Intermediates will have no shortage of options on the front.

Ski-Resort Hopping

For skiers, an interesting option is the interchangeable ticket program among north-shore resorts. For a fixed price you can buy a multiday ticket that allows you to ski at any of seven downhill or seven cross-country ski areas. For information about all the area resorts and lodging options, or to make reservations, contact the **Tahoe North Visitors and Convention Bureau** (☎ 800/TAHOE-4-U).

ARE THOSE MOUNTAINS THE SIERRA OR THE SIERRAS?

When talking about the large range of mountains east of the Central Valley and west of Nevada, it is common to hear people say they just spent a nice weekend in the "Sierra Nevadas," "Sierras," or "Sierra Nevada Mountains." Though common usage, the first two are technically wrong since there is only one Sierra Nevada in California, and the third makes you sound really dumb. Sierra *means* mountain range, so when you say "I went climbing in the Sierra Mountains" you're saying you climbed the mountain mountains. Duh.

When the Spaniards settling California crossed the coastal range, they encountered a huge range of snow-covered peaks to the east and offhandedly named them La Sierra Nevada: the Snowy Range. Instead of venturing into these mountains, the explorers quickly got back to the business at hand: subjugating the Indians, propagating the Catholic faith, and asking around about gold, which isn't found in the coastal range but can be found in quantity in the Sierra. But being busy people, the Spaniards didn't have the time or desire to grope around those huge peaks eating pine nuts and trout while looking under rocks, where they would have found the treasure they sought.

Later, gringos with too much time on their hands did look under rocks and find gold. Others moved here in force in the form of the gold rush of 1849. The name confused the hell out of the English-speaking prospectors. American mountains always had names like sports teams: the Rockies, the Appalachians, the Grand Tetons. Our mountains, like us, are a nation of individuals. No one thought to refer to mountain peaks in the collective but singular form. Where a Spanish speaker sees a range made from a bunch of separate mountains, we see a whole bunch of mountains standing together making a range—a subtle difference, sure, but enough to fuel the irresistible urge among Anglophones to call them the Sierras, just like the Rockies.

Just remember Sierra Nevada equals Snowy Range. As in "I spent the weekend skiing in the Sierra Nevada/Snowy Range," singular.

There, that's easy.

Soda Springs Winter Resort

Off Interstate 80, Soda Springs exit. ☎ **530/426-1010** for info and snow conditions. 16 trails (30% beginner, 50% intermediate, 20% expert); 2 lifts including 1 triple and 1 double, 2 surface tows for snow tubing; 652-foot vertical drop. Full-day adult ticket $16.

They don't have a snow-conditions line, but whoever is working the phones will be glad to look out the window and tell you what the weather's like. That should tell you what to expect at this small, friendly ski area. With the cheapest lift tickets in Tahoe, it's great for beginners. Experts might get a little bored, but if you have a very large family or just a lot of friends, you can even rent the entire area for functions.

Kirkwood Ski Resort

Kirkwood Meadows Dr., Kirkwood. ☎ **209/258-6000;** 209/258-3000 for snow conditions. 65 trails (15% beginner, 50% intermediate, 35% expert); 12 lifts including 2 doubles, 7 triples, 1 quad, 2 surface; 2,000-ft. vertical drop. Full-day adult ticket $45.

Kirkwood on State Route 88 is a short drive from South Lake, but worlds away in attitude. This is where many local skiers go on weekends, and they come for one thing: the snow, which is arguably the best in the area. With hair-raising descents like The Wall and chutes like Sisters, the terrain is also some of the Sierra's best for advanced skiers; and the Bunny Lift services a group of isolated beginner runs, so first-timers won't feel intimidated.

Bear Valley Ski Area

Hwy. 4, at Mt. Reba Rd., Bear Valley.
☎ 209/753-2301; option 2 for snow
conditions. 67 trails (30% beginner, 40%
intermediate, 30% expert); 11 lifts including 2 triples, 7 doubles, and 2 surface;
1,900-ft. vertical drop. Full-day adult ticket $35.

Bear Valley, near the summit of Ebbetts
Pass (State Route 4), is one of the best-
kept skiing secrets around. Even skiers
who've been there several times seem not
to realize that the steepest advanced runs
in California are hidden away in Grizzly
and Kodiak bowls *below* the lodge. I
came back here in the summer once and
was amazed to see waterfalls in the same
spot I'd been perfecting my steeps skiing
just a few months earlier. Another huge
slice of blue-diamond cruising runs lies on
the back side of Mount Reba. Besides traditional ski and snowboard lessons, Bear
Valley Ski Area has a nationally recognized
program for skiers with disabilities.

Dodge Ridge Ski Area

Dodge Ridge Rd., Pinecrest. ☎ 209/
965-3474; 209/965-4444 for snow conditions. 60 trails (20% beginner, 40%
intermediate, 40% expert); 12 lifts,
including 1 quad, 2 triples, 5 doubles,
and 4 surface; 1,600-ft. vertical drop.
Full-day adult ticket $39.

Dodge Ridge on State Route 108 is a
medium-size mountain trying hard to live
down a reputation as a beginners' area.
It's still no Kirkwood or Squaw, but new
runs make it a perfectly enjoyable place
for any skier to spend a day. Beginners
and intermediates love Dodge Ridge: The
slopes seem specially designed to instill
confidence, and the place is rarely crowded. A low base altitude makes Dodge a
bad bet late or early in the season unless
you're wearing your rock skis.

FISHING

There are a few different fishing options
in Tahoe and the northern Sierra. Rivers
like the Truckee, Walker, Mokelumne,
and Stanislaus all offer great fly-fishing,
and the alpine lakes are often filled with
hungry trout in the early summer after
ice-off. Unfortunately, the smaller lakes
are subject to extreme boom and bust
cycles; last year's great fishing lake might
now be dead depending on how harsh
the winter was. Lake Tahoe offers a Sierra
Nevada version of something you usually
associate with the ocean—the party
boat—only here they're trolling for lake
trout instead of mooching for salmon.
Blue Ribbon Fishing Charters (☎ 530/
541-8801) in South Lake Tahoe and **Mac
A Tac Charters** (☎ 530/546-2500) in
Tahoe City are two of the many charter
boats that will take you out trolling for
giant Mackinaw trout. Since trolling down
where the lake trout dwell takes special
gear, and finding them takes a good
degree of local knowledge, going with a
guided charter is a smart bet.

If you're anxious to do your best *A
River Runs Through It* imitation but don't
know a backcast from a backhand,
California Fly Fishing in Truckee
(☎ 800/588-7688) can help you learn
the basics and guide you to the best fishing water in the Tahoe region. **Ebbetts
Pass Sporting Goods** in Arnold near
Calaveras Big Trees State Park and the
Stanislaus River (☎ 209/795-1686) can
recommend good water and possibly
hook you up with a local guide.

HIKES, BUSHWHACKS & BACKPACK TRIPS

Day Hikes

Granite Lake, Desolation Wilderness

2.5 miles round-trip. Moderate. Short but
steep. Access: Park at Bayview
Campground off State Rte. 89 above
Emerald Bay. Map: Desolation Wilderness
map or USGS Emerald Bay topo.

This brief day sampler of the Desolation
Wilderness will show you a little of
everything the High Country can offer.

The trail climbs unrelentingly on the mountain flank above Emerald Bay. While that stinks for walking, it's great for the view. The higher you go, the thinner the lodgepole pine forest becomes, until finally you break through the trees after a little less than a mile. The granite-bouldered viewpoint here gives you a bird's-eye look at Lake Tahoe and Emerald Lake, plus a good chunk of the surrounding area. In another quarter-mile you reach Granite Lake. Lots of shoreline nooks and rocks make for fun exploring, and on a hot day a swim will cut the trail dust before you start the downhill trek to your car.

Mount Tallac, Desolation Wilderness

10 miles. Strenuous. Steep, rocky, and slippery. Allow all day. Access: Mt. Tallac Trailhead north of Lake Tahoe Visitors Information Center on State Rte. 89. Map: Desolation Wilderness map or USGS Emerald Bay topo.

In the 5 miles to the summit of Mount Tallac this hike gains almost 3,400 feet at a rather punishing pace. Along the way, though, you'll pass beautiful Floating Island Lake and Cathedral Lake, cross several creeks, and plunge through a beautiful forest before beginning the grueling climb up the ridgeline to the summit. The last 2 miles are the killer. The footpath is rocky and slippery, and no shade helps cool you down. A mile away from your goal you'll see the summit and it will look like you'll never reach it. But you will, and when you do, you'll be rewarded with an outrageous view. You're standing on a narrow ridgeline summit with a 360° view of the entire Tahoe Basin. Fallen Leaf Lake and Emerald Bay lie to your east. The Desolation Wilderness spreads out behind you. The wind on this almost 10,000-foot summit will probably push you on your way home before too long.

Rubicon Trail, Sugar Pine Point State Park

4.2 miles one-way. Easy. Access: Sugar Pine Point State Park Calawee Beach, or Emerald Bay. Map: Sugar Pine State Park map.

This is the longest waterfront trail on the California shore of Tahoe. Along the way you pass numerous tempting swimming beaches and granite cliffs where you can see the seemingly bottomless depth of the lake. You'll also meander through a scenic boat-in-only camp. The Rubicon connects Sugar Pine Point State Park with Emerald Bay State Park. Leave a car at the Emerald Bay parking lot or Calawee Beach for a shuttle or do the hike round-trip. This is a great hike to combine with a tour of the **Vikingsholm Mansion**—a Viking castle built on the shore of Emerald Bay in the 1930s, the vanity project of a local heiress apparently unaware of, or at least unimpressed by, the depression.

South Grove Trail, Calaveras Big Trees

5.25 miles. Moderate. Access: End of Memorial Pkwy. in Calaveras Big Trees State Park. Map: Purchase at visitor center or trailhead.

Most visitors to Calaveras Big Trees only visit the easily accessible North Grove, but the most rewarding nature experience with the best trees is actually on the other side of the river in the South Grove. Here, this 5.5-mile loop winds through second-growth sequoia for about a mile before getting into the really good stuff, the old-growth giants. The biggest tree in the park is here: 250-foot Agassiz Tree, named after a Swiss naturalist who was instrumental in protecting the trees. Beaver Creek provides a nice backdrop for the understory of dogwoods, poison oak, and azalea.

Paradise Valley

4 miles. Easy. Access: Located 6 miles south of Grover Hot Springs State Park.

Take the left fork off Hot Springs road, Hwy. 89 at Markleeville. Follow the private road 1.5 miles to where the pavement ends, then to the trailhead at the end of the unpaved portion. Map: USGS Markleeville area map.

While nearby Grover Hot Springs can get crowded during the summer high season, the surrounding areas in the Toiyabe National Forest remain comparatively overlooked. Paradise Valley is a lesser-known access to the High Country. The first 2 miles of this trail make for an easy day hike with good views of the Sierra ridge and an excellent variety of wildflowers in spring and early summer. From the trailhead at the end of a small dirt parking lot, it's about 0.25 miles along the meadow's edge to the pines, then a shady walk the rest of the way to the river. The river runs too fast to cross until late summer, but there's a small beach on the north bank with a cliff view behind you and the meadow opposite. It's a good spot for a picnic. Unfortunately, those flecks of gold you're finding at the water's edge are probably galena or pyrite. Then again, maybe they're not.

If you're making a weekend trip to the area and find Grover's campground full, there's also a good campsite at the river's edge. It's an easy, short walk, and a lot less crowded than the state park, so some choose to stay in Paradise Valley for the night. It's often deserted, and in the morning it's only an hour's walk out, then you can drive the few miles to Grover Hot Springs for a dip and the hike to the waterfall.

Burst Rock to Powell Lake

3.8 miles round-trip. Moderate to strenuous. Access: Off State Rte. 108 near Pinecrest. Drive to end of unpaved Crabtree Rd. and Gianelli's Cabin Trailhead. Map: USGS Pinecrest topo.

This is a good half- or whole-day wilderness sampler. Though you're less than 2 miles from your car, Powell Lake has the high alpine feel of much harder-to-reach lakes. Of course, you won't be alone. This is a very popular hike as well as the main access into a huge section of the Emigrant Wilderness. The highest point of the hike is appropriately the metaphorical high point as well. From the top of 9,150-foot Burst Rock you can see for miles into the surrounding wilderness—a vista of dramatic canyons, blue jewel lakes, and the volcanic spires of the Dardenalles.

Heiser Lake

4.5 miles round-trip. Moderate. Access: Mosquito Lake near Ebbetts Pass on State Rte. 4. Map: USGS Spicer Meadows and USGS Pacific Valley maps.

Short but sweet is the best way to describe this hike. Little Heiser Lake is a tucked-away, tree-lined lake deep enough to support a nice population of trout. Several granite islands make a good goal for a summer-day swim. The trail roller coasters up and down a few false rises before the final summit and drop into Heiser. None of them are too huge, but the combined effect of all those climbs can be pretty tiring.

Overnights

Rubicon Lake, Desolation Wilderness

16 miles round-trip. Moderate. Mostly level. Allow 2 or 3 days. Access: Park at trailhead on State Rte. 89, 0.1 miles south of Meeks Bay Resort. Map: USFS Desolation Wilderness map. Wilderness permit required.

For an 8-miler in the Sierra Nevada, the hike to Rubicon Lake is remarkably level and easy. The only really steep pitch comes in the last quarter-mile before the lake. Along the way in you pass five other lakes, including several with good campsites if you want to spend the night on the trail. Rubicon Lake is tiny, but good for swimming in the shadow of Jakes Peak. Good campsites are found in the lodgepole pine forest surrounding the lake.

Emigrant Lake, Mokelumne Wilderness

9 miles round-trip. Easy (perfect overnight). Access: Park at Caples Dam

Parking Area just off State Rte. 88. Map: USFS Mokelumne Wilderness map.

Almost half of the 4.5 miles into Emigrant Lake follow the shoreline of beautiful Caples Lake. I suppose it would be possible to cheat and hitch a ride across the lake by boat, but the walk is nice in its own right. Eventually the trail turns and follows Emigrant Creek along a gentle meadow-lined valley lushly vegetated with aspen and wildflowers. A short steep climb tells you that you're almost there. A sometimes dicey rock hop over the lake's outlet creek and you're confronted with the first glimpse of steep-sided Emigrant Lake. Carved by glaciers, steep granite talus cliffs drop straight into the water. Several coves allow fishing and swimming access, but the water is extremely cold until the end of summer, when it warms up to just plain cold.

Bull Run Lake

7.4 miles round-trip. Moderate. Allow 2 or 3 days. Access: Take Stanislaus Meadow Trailhead turnoff from State Rte. 4. Drive as far as conditions allow down the half-mile road (leave low-clearance cars on highway). Map: Carson–Iceberg Wilderness map.

Bull Run Lake was one of my first backpacking experiences as a kid. We built a raft and floated to the rock island in the center of the lake. It fell apart, so we swam back and nearly froze. That night we thought a bear was in camp, but it turned out to be my father snoring. The next day I climbed the mountain behind the lake alone to watch the sun go down and ran back to camp before darkness fell. Great times for a 10-year-old. I've been back since and it's still a magic place for me. The hike in is steep, but you can tolerate 3-plus miles of just about anything to reach a place this beautiful.

KAYAKING

The advent of the sit-on-top kayak has fostered a boom in casual lake kayakers on Tahoe. You don't need any particular ability to paddle one, and they open doors to places you'd never see otherwise. They're more or less uncapsizable and unswampable, and their low freeboard leaves them less at the mercy of Tahoe's occasionally fierce winds. **Kayak Tahoe** (☎ 530/544-2011) and **Tahoe Paddle and Oar** (☎ 530/581-3029) are both based on the west shore of the lake near some of the best paddling and both provide rental equipment, tours, and instruction.

White-water kayakers have several great Class II and III runs available to them on the **Truckee River** before it flows down into Nevada. The **River Ranch Run** is the best, roughly 11 miles of continuous Class II and III. From River Ranch to Truckee, a solid Class III paddler only has to worry about one thing: low-clearance bridges if the water is high. Call either of the shops listed above for detailed route information and recommendations. Other than the Truckee, most good white water on Sierra Nevada rivers occurs farther downriver in the Gold Country canyons. Not that these high mountain stretches don't get run occasionally—they do, and you can find excellent descriptions in Chuck Stanley and Lars Holbek's classic *A Guide to the Best Whitewater in the State of California* (Friends of the River Books, 1984), but these upper runs are volatile and dangerous Class V and VI runs. If you can handle that, you don't need me telling you where to go.

MOUNTAIN BIKING

The northern Sierra has more good mountain bike rides than you could do in a lifetime. Over a century of logging and mining did have one positive outcome: an incredible network of skid trails, mine roads, and grades into some of the most out-there outback of the Sierra. While all wilderness areas and most state parks ban mountain biking, the vast majority of national-forest land is open. The most famous ride in the area,

Tahoe's mind-bogglingly scenic and challenging **Flume Ride,** is actually in Nevada beginning in Spooner Lake State Park, but numerous less well known rides wind above the California shore as well.

A recently booming sport is summertime mountain biking at downhill ski areas. Call me a masochist, but I actually like riding up huge mountains on my own. If you prefer the easy way up, though, **Squaw Valley** (☎ 530/583-6985) will load you and your bike into the tram for a quick blast to the summit. From there it truly is all downhill. **Northstar-at-Tahoe** (☎ 530/562-2248) maintains their cross-country ski trails as a mountain-biking park in summer and rents equipment on site. In Tahoe, **City Porter's Ski and Sport** (☎ 530/583-0293) and **CyclePaths** (☎ 530/581-1171) are both great stops to get local trail maps and advice. They also offer guided half-day and full-day mountain bike tours in the surrounding area. In Truckee, **Paco's Truckee Bike and Ski** (☎ 530/587-5561) offers many similar services.

For more detailed descriptions of Tahoe area rides, including the Western States 100, Flume Trail, Paige Meadows Truckee River Loop, and many more, consult Carol Bonser's fantastically in-depth *Mountain Biking the High Sierra: Lake Tahoe–North* (Fine Edge Productions, 1993) and *Mountain Biking the High Sierra: Lake Tahoe–South* (Fine Edge Productions, 1993).

Blackwood Canyon
8–20 miles. Easy to moderate. Access: Park at Blackwood Canyon Trailhead 4 miles south of Tahoe City on State Rte. 89. Map: USGS Tahoe and Granite Chief topos.

The lower 4 miles of Blackwood Canyon Trail makes a great introductory ride for novice trail bikers. It's a single track all right, but a level and smooth one. For a loop return, head back along the gravel road when you reach Blackwood Creek. More ambitious riders will want to turn left and bike up the Blackwood Canyon gravel road to the top of Barker Pass, 7 miles and 1,500 feet of elevation gain from here.

Sugar Pine Point State Park
Distance varies. Easy. Access: Sugar Pine State Park off State Rte. 89. Map: Park map.

Though bikes aren't allowed on the foot trails in Sugar Pine State Park, numerous maintenance roads and bike paths make this a good place for kids or beginners to try out their fat wheeler. Several nice loops explore the less-developed portions of the lakeshore.

Flume Trail
24 miles round-trip. Moderate. 2,600-foot elevation gain. Allow at least 6 hr. Access: Drive east on U.S. 50 out of South Lake Tahoe and turn north on Nevada State Rte. 28. Spooner Lake State Park is 0.5 miles up on your right. Map: USGS Carson City topo.

Okay, we're not in California anymore, but it's impossible to discuss mountain biking in the Tahoe area without mentioning the Flume Ride. If you can, try to ride this on a weekday; it gets jammed on the weekends. But either way, don't miss it. Parts of this trail are grueling—steep inclines on rock-filled sand (keep your weight on your back tire)—but the flume itself is unbelievable. Four and a half miles of perfect single track looking out over Lake Tahoe far below is a worthy reward for any climb. Once you get to the top, ride the little trail down to Marlette Lake for lunch or a swim. Head back up to the trail and then it's all downhill. And yes, logs were once floated along here from man-made Marlette Lake to Lake Tahoe to be milled.

ROAD BIKING
Tour of Lake Tahoe
72 miles. Strenuous. Access: Anywhere around Lake Tahoe with a motel room or campsite for you to collapse in at the end

of your ride. Map: AAA or any other good Tahoe area road map.

For a 72-mile ride in the mountains, this one is relatively flat (total climb about 3,000 ft.). But don't jump into your biking shorts thinking it's going to be easy. First of all, you're over a mile high, so the distance alone is going to feel more like a century. The other challenge, unfortunately, is staying sane through miles of heavily trafficked roads. Sadly, this isn't the kind of road ride where you can get all delirious and wiggly without getting squished by an RV. Several stretches follow nice bike paths, but they crisscross the highway. The worst stretch is State Route 89 above Emerald Bay. The road is narrow with drop-offs, and I swear some people drive it without looking at the road once. For that reason I suggest camping at Sugar Pine Point State Park and riding the Emerald Bay to South Lake Tahoe stretch early in the morning when traffic is light and when you're fresh.

From Sugar Pine you take State Route 89 to South Lake, the bike route through town, turn northwest on U.S. 50 (scary), then turn north on Nevada State Route 28 (ahh, relief), cruise the Nevada Shore until Lake Shore Drive takes you through Kings Beach. Get back on State Route 28 until it connects back with State Route 89, and then you're nearly home. I've described the loop counterclockwise because I like it better that way, but feel free to reverse it so you can have the good views—and scary drop-offs—on your side of the road.

ROCK CLIMBING

The bad news is it isn't Yosemite. The good news is it isn't Yosemite. The atmosphere is friendlier and it's far less crowded—it's not quite the "scene" that Yosemite is. The granite this far north has a tendency to be a bit more weathered and crumbly than Yosemite's, but that's a bit like complaining that the champagne is a slightly off year of Dom Perignon.

Donner Summit and **Lovers Leap** are the two major Tahoe areas, and both have numerous routes. **Mountain Adventure Seminars** (☎ 800/362-5462 or 209/753-6556) on State Route 4 offers instruction around Ebbetts Pass.

WALKS & RAMBLES
Donner Memorial Nature Trail
0.5 miles. Access: Donner Memorial State Park. Trail begins at Emigrant Trail Museum.

Though today you can hear the roar of cars and trucks on nearby Interstate 80, this park memorializes one of the most haunting and heart-wrenching tales of California history, the terrible winter spent here by the Donner Party after a surprise October snowstorm caught them. Heroic rescue attempts failed, and by spring only 47 of the original 89 members of the party were alive. The survivors had been forced to cannibalize their dead. This short trail combines an explanation of the glacial geology that shaped this alpine lake valley with a stop at a carved granite boulder bearing the names of everyone who spent that terrible winter here. Running through the area is Donner Creek, a gentle stream perfect for kids to explore on their own.

Calaveras Big Trees North Grove Trail
1 mile. Access: Visitor center and picnic area at park entrance.

This flat, smooth loop through the Big Trees is a good way to see the grandeur of the giant sequoia for those who can't or don't want to hike into the park's more remote South Grove Trail (see above). The self-guided interpretive trail explains the interesting botany of the sequoia, and trailside signs will teach you to recognize common forest plants like the dogwood, hazel, and azalea. The strangest sight of all is the 24-foot-diameter stump of the Discovery Tree, which was used as a dance floor after the tree was felled. Unlike some other sequoia groves, this one has a rather mixed population of Douglas fir, sugar pines, and ponderosa pines, all of which seem diminutive next to the giant sequoia.

WHITE-WATER RAFTING

Most of the raftable white water in the northern Sierra begins lower down in the foothills of the Gold Country. Up high, the rivers are too extreme for most commercial rafting or for rafting period. The Truckee River, however, is a grand exception. Exciting but forgiving Class III rapids run almost nonstop for 10 miles. Contact the **Tahoe North Visitors and Convention Bureau** (☎ **800/TAHOE-4-U**) for a current list of outfitters running the Truckee.

For a bigger adrenaline surge, rafters with some experience in self-bailing paddleboats can bomb the relentless **North Fork of the Stanislaus River** right through Calaveras Big Trees. This highly technical Class IV run has a short season, usually from April until the end of June. The scenery along this run is outstanding: sequoias, waterfalls, deer, blooming azaleas and dogwoods. But you'll probably be too busy trying not to hit that huge hole after you career off that huge rock to really notice. Contact **Whitewater Adventures** (☎ **707/255-0761**) or **Beyond Limits** (☎ **800/234-RAFT**) for schedules of commercial trips down this part of the Stanislaus.

Southern Sierra: What to Do & Where to Do It

The southern Sierra from Yosemite to Sequoia/Kings Canyon is otherworldly. This, the high roadless area known as the High Sierra, is where John Muir fell madly in love with these mountains. This is his "Range of Light," which inspired so many later writings and galvanized his philosophy of protecting wilderness for wilderness' sake while others were still stuck on the idea that places should only be saved if they're scenic or contain some sort of freak of nature like an oddly shaped rock, or a bunch of geysers of interest to tourists (come to think of it, many people are still stuck on that way of thinking).

As a result of the extreme isolation of much of the southern Sierra, it's a hardcore backpacker's and peak bagger's paradise. Very few places in the Lower 48 allow you to get as far "out there" as you can in the John Muir Wilderness and the backcountry of Sequoia/Kings Canyon National Park. But there are also plenty of places that can be explored by day hike, or even from your car. The Yosemite Valley, of course, is popular with day users to the point of damage. Other great places to pack a picnic and make a mellow day of it are Tuolumne Meadows in Yosemite, or Mineral King Valley in Sequoia/Kings Canyon. Climbers will be in heaven with the huge walls of perfect Sierra Nevada granite looming all over the place, whether they're flashing a bouldering problem in the Yosemite Valley or nearing the top of a multiday climb in the high peaks near Mount Whitney. Probably the only people that will be sorely disappointed by the southern Sierra are mountain bikers, who, as a result of the National Parks Service and National Forest Service prohibitions on off-road riding into the wilderness, will find their options severely restricted.

BIRD WATCHING

Of particular interest to birders in Yosemite National Park are the **high meadows** that provide hunting grounds for raptors, such as the great gray owl, golden eagle, and osprey. These meadows are also home to many species of grosbeaks, warblers, and hummingbirds. Occasionally you'll catch a blue grouse wandering the edge of the conifer forest boundary. In the lodgepole

---

Paying for the Great Outdoors

Remember that heading into Yosemite or Kings Canyon and Sequoia National Parks for any of the activities listed below will involve shelling out just to enter the park. The paid admission to these parks is good for 1 week; if you're planning on returning even once to the park outside that week, buy an annual pass.

---

and white pine forests around **Lake Tenaya** you can find numerous pine-nut-and-needle-eating species like the white-headed and black-backed woodpeckers, Clark's nutcracker, and Steller's jay. In the majestic **giant sequoia forests** in Sequoia National Park, you might catch a glimpse of a gold-crowned kinglet or a pileated woodpecker.

BOARDSAILING

As the Sierra Nevada becomes taller toward the southern end of the range, large alpine lakes become more scarce. **Lake Tenaya** on Tioga Pass is one popular boardsailing spot—the wind here makes a gorgeous sound as it moans around the lake's granite domes and through the lodgepole pine forest. Tenaya is shallow and rocky, so beware, but the scenery is incomparable. Several good pull-outs and beaches on State Route 120 make for good rigging and launching. **Huntington** and **Shaver lakes** are also popular with boardsailors. Huntington hosts sailing regattas every summer weekend. Call the **Sierra National Forest Ranger District** (☎ 209/855-5360) or **Huntington Lake Resort** (☎ 209/893-3226) for more information about rental equipment and instruction.

CANOEING

As road access and large lakes become more scarce in the southern reaches of the Sierra, so do your opportunities to canoe. **Tenaya Lake** is a great place to paddle, but you'll have to bring your own boat. The same goes for the **Merced River** in the Yosemite Valley, and beware

of going too far downriver. Below the El Capitan Bridge the tranquil Merced becomes solid Class III and IV water, no place for a canoe. **Huntington Lake Resort** (☎ 209/893-3226) rents canoes and other small craft on that beautiful alpine lake during the summer.

CROSS-COUNTRY SKIING & SNOWSHOEING

The national parks of the southern Sierra are some of the greatest backcountry skiing regions in the world. Several trans-Sierra routes begin or end here, including the famed **Sierra Haute Route** through Kings Canyon (see "Cross-Country Skiing" under "Eastern Sierra: What to Do & Where to Do It") and **State Route 120/Tioga Pass** in Yosemite. The **Yosemite Cross-Country Ski School** (☎ 209/372-8444) leads guided 6-day trips over Tioga Pass with a cabin-based overnight at Tuolumne Meadows for approximately $435 (not counting return airfare to Lee Vining). The school's **Glacier Point overnight ski trip** is a more subdued overnight. You'll ski about 10 miles of groomed track up to Glacier Point, one of the best vistas in the entire park, where your guide cooks dinner and breakfast. No need to pack a tent; lodging is in the new log-and-stone Glacier Point Lodge. Reservations are required. Skiers not part of the overnight program are welcome to use the groomed track to Glacier Point at no charge. The 20-mile round-trip is a good all-day ski for a strong skier. The ski school is located at the **Badger Pass Ski Area** (☎ 209/372-8430) and also offers rental gear and a full slate of on-site lessons for all abilities, ranging from basic technique to trans-Sierra crossings.

If you're on your own, **Crane Flat,** located off the park road about 5 miles southeast of the Big Oak Flat entrance to Yosemite, is another good place to go. Just outside the south entrance to the park, **Goat Camp** (☎ 209/683-4665) has 18 miles of marked national-forest ski trails, some of which cross into Yosemite's amazing Mariposa Grove of giant sequoias. A snow-covered trek through these giants is something you'll never forget.

Sierra Summit (☎ 209/233-2500), near Huntington Lake, is a popular downhill resort for the Fresno-area crowd, but not many people know about the excellent cross-country skiing in this same neighborhood. Contact the **Hume Lake Ranger Station** (☎ 209/338-2252) to have them send you a trail map of the region.

Two Nordic ski areas operate in Sequoia and Kings Canyon National Parks. Just north of Giant Forest Village, the park's "downtown," **Sequoia Ski Touring,** at Wolverton near Giant Forest Village (☎ 559/565-3435), offers rentals and trail maps for 35 miles of well-marked backcountry trails through the sequoias. In Kings Canyon, **Sequoia Ski Touring** (☎ 559/335-2314) in Grant Grove near the northern entrance to the park provides the same services and an even wider selection of trails. People with their own equipment are welcome on all trails in the park at no cost. Trail maps are available at the visitor centers.

On winter weekends, park rangers at Sequoia/Kings Canyon lead introductory snowshoe hikes (snowshoes provided) at **Sequoia Ski Touring** in Grant Grove (☎ 559/335-2314).

DOWNHILL SKIING & SNOWBOARDING

Well, one thing you can say about skiing in the southern Sierra is that it's easy to decide where you want to go, since you only have two choices. There's **Badger Pass** in Yosemite, the oldest ski area in California, or **Sierra Summit** above Huntington Lake. Both mountains allow snowboarding.

Badger Pass Ski Area

Badger Pass, Yosemite National Park. ☎ 209/372-8430; 209/372-1000 for snow conditions. 9 trails (35% beginner, 50% intermediate, 15% expert); 5 lifts including 1 triple, 3 doubles, and 1 surface; 800-ft. vertical drop. Full-day adult ticket $22 weekdays, $28 weekends.

Badger is a mountain from the days when advanced skiing meant you knew how to do a stem christie and could stop without falling over or grabbing anything. Skiing's come a long way since then, but Badger just doesn't have the terrain to keep up. On the other hand, it's a great beginner and easy intermediate mountain and it's cheap. Bring on the kids and families.

Sierra Summit Ski Area

59265 State Rte. 168, Lakeshore. ☎ 209/233-2500; 209/233-3330 for snow conditions. 20 trails (10% beginner, 65% intermediate, 25% expert); 9 lifts including 2 triples, 3 doubles, and 4 surface; 1,600-ft. vertical drop. Full-day adult ticket $25 weekdays, $35 weekends.

In contrast to Badger Pass, Sierra Summit is blessed with a good amount of expert and advanced terrain, but also has enough beginner and intermediate runs to keep everyone happy.

FISHING

Numerous reservoirs in the area offer great lake fishing, particularly **Shaver Lake** on State Route 168. Depending on the season, you'll catch anything from smallmouth bass and catfish to trophy-sized brown and rainbow trout. The **Merced River** in Yosemite valley is catch-and-release only. Barbless hooks are required. You can fish for your dinner at various High Country lakes and streams, which are literally leaping with trout. A

California license is required; it's available in Yosemite at the Yosemite Village Sportshop.

Backpackers into the John Muir Wilderness and the backcountry of Sequoia and Kings Canyon will find hundreds of lakes waiting to be fished. Some are dead; others hold relentless schools of trout that will practically maul each other to get at your fly or lure. Trout fishing in the lower altitudes is fairly limited, mostly along the banks of the **Kings** and **Kaweah rivers.** High Country lakes are refuges for rare pure-strain, wild trout and are not stocked with hatchery fish. Before venturing into the High Country, inquire at a ranger station about the area you'll be visiting to find out about closures or specific regulations. A California fishing license is required for everyone over 16 years old. Tackle and licenses are available at several campgrounds and park stores.

HIKES, BUSHWHACKS & BACKPACK TRIPS

The hiking options in Yosemite and Sequoia/Kings Canyon are seemingly endless. If you've completed the hikes below and are still crying for more, consult some of the specialized guidebooks to the area. For Yosemite, *Tuolumne Meadows* by Jeffrey B. Shaffer and Thomas Winnett (Wilderness Press, 1977) and *Yosemite National Park* by Thomas Winnett and Jason Winnett (Wilderness Press, 1983) are two of the best. For Sequoia/Kings Canyon, the official park map and guide gives good basic maps for the park, but for serious hiking you'll want to check out *Sierra South: 100 Back-Country Trips in California's Sierra* by Thomas Winnett and Jason Winnett (Wilderness Press, 1993). Another good guide is *Kings Canyon Country,* a hiking handbook by Ginny and Lew Clark (Western Trails Publications, 1985). The Grant Grove and Giant Forest visitor centers both sell a complete selection of maps and guidebooks to the park.

Day Hikes
Yosemite Falls Trail
7 miles round-trip. Moderate to difficult. Steep, narrow switchbacks. Access: Yosemite Falls Trailhead at Sunnyside Campground, behind the lodge. Map: Park map.

The Yosemite Falls Trail zigzags 3.5 miles from Sunnyside Campground to the top of Upper Yosemite Falls. This trail gives you an inkling of the weird, vertically oriented world climbers enter when they head up Yosemite's sheer walls. As you climb this narrow switchbacked trail, the valley floor drops away until people below are like ants, but the top doesn't appear any closer. It's a little unnerving at first. Plan on spending all day on this 7-mile round-trip because of the incredibly steep climb.

Nevada and Vernal Falls, Yosemite Valley
7 miles round-trip. Moderate to difficult. Granite steps on the descent can be slippery. Access: Yosemite Valley. Trailhead at Happy Isles near Curry Village. Map: Park map.

This trail is the northernmost reach of the 200-mile John Muir Trail. From the valley floor you hike up the John Muir Trail to the top of Nevada Falls. For one of the most intense perspectives you'll ever get, look right over the brink of the falls. The feeling of vertigo and motion is not for the faint-hearted, but it's certainly a rush. From 2,000 feet above Happy Isles where you began, it's a dizzying view straight down the face of the fall. After taking in the view of the valley below and the strange side-angle perspective of Half Dome, return via the Mist Trail. Much of the Mist Trail consists of steps carved out of granite. Sometimes it's slippery. The trail/staircase descends alongside Nevada Falls and passes through a small flat containing Emerald Pool and the Silver Apron, a tempting-looking water slide above the pool. Just below Emerald Pool the trail descends again right along the rushing cataract of Vernal Falls. On a hot day this trail is a cool wonderland. When the water is really high, though, it can be positively scary.

Columbia Rock, Yosemite

2 miles round-trip. Moderate. Access: Trailhead next to Sunnyside Campground.

The hike mirrors the beginning ascent of the waterfall trail, but stops at Columbia Rock, 1,000 feet above the valley. There's no valley view from here, but the sights are still impressive. Because it's on the sunny side of the valley, it's also less likely to get an accumulation of snow.

Four-Mile Trail to Glacier Point, Yosemite

9.6 miles round-trip. Strenuous. Access: The trailhead is 1.25 miles from Yosemite Village, at the Four-Mile Parking Area, post V-18, or take the shuttle bus to the Yosemite Lodge stop no. 8 and walk behind the Lodge over the Swinging Bridge to Southeast Dr. The trailhead is 0.25 mile west. Map: Park map.

This trail climbs 3,200 feet and has some terrific views (OK, so does every trail climbing out of Yosemite Valley). This trail ends at Glacier Point, but if you'd like to extend, it connects with the Panorama Trail at the end. However, if you plan to hike both simultaneously, it may require an overnight stay and advanced preparation—the combined round-trip distance is 14 miles.

Panorama Trail, Yosemite

9 miles one-way. Moderate to strenuous. Access: The hike begins at Glacier Point, at the east end of the parking area. Map: Park map.

From Glacier Point, this trail drops 3,200 feet, but somehow it still feels like a climb. At one of the prettiest points, it crosses Illilouette Fall about 1.5 miles from Glacier Point. It continues along the Panorama Cliffs and eventually winds up at Nevada Fall, where it's a straight descent to Yosemite Valley via the Mist or John Muir trails.

Chilnualna Falls from Wawona, Yosemite

8 miles round-trip. Strenuous. Access: Enter Yosemite National Park on Calif. 41 and continue north. Turn right on Chilnualna Rd., just north of the Merced River's south fork. Stay on this road until it dead-ends at "The Redwoods," about 1.3 miles. This is the trailhead. Map: Park map.

One of the tallest outside Yosemite Valley, this fall cascades down two chutes. The one at the bottom is narrow and packs a real punch after a wet winter. A series of switchbacks leads to the top fall, and from here you can hike to Bridalveil Campground, or continue on to Chilnualna Lakes. If you plan to hike to the lakes, this is a great place to stay overnight, but don't forget your wilderness permit. Also remember to pack a swimsuit—there are a few swimming holes at the base of the waterfall.

Ostrander Lake, Yosemite

12.8 miles round-trip. Moderate to strenuous. Access: Take Calif. 41 to Glacier Point Rd. and turn east. Take Glacier Point Rd. to the trailhead about 1.3 miles past Bridalveil Campground, on the right-hand side of the road. Map: Park map.

The trail begins on an abandoned road. It winds through evidence of a forest fire until it reaches Bear Meadow. It begins to climb after crossing Bridalveil Creek and crosses several ridges before reaching the lake. The best camping is reportedly on the lake's west end. Ostrander Lake is popular in summer and during winter as a cross-country ski spot. The Sierra Club also manages the nearby Ostrander Hut.

Taft Point, Yosemite

2.2 miles. Easy. Access: Take Glacier Point Rd. to the Sentinel Dome Parking Lot, about 3 miles from Glacier Point. At the fork, head left. Map: Park map.

The walk to Taft Point is undemanding. It crosses a broad meadow dotted in early summer by wildflowers. Near Taft Point, note the deep chasms in the rock, known as the "fissures." Some of the cracks are 40 feet long and 20 feet wide at the top and 100 feet deep. The wall of Yosemite Valley actually overhangs the narrow ravine below and if you carefully peer over the cliff, note that your head is on the opposite side of a stream running far beneath you. A small pipe railing farther on marks the 6-by-3-foot Taft Point Overlook hanging over Yosemite Valley.

Wawona Meadow Loop, Yosemite

3.5 miles. Easy. Access: Take the paved road through the golf course on the west side of Calif. 41, and walk about 50 yd. to the trail. Map: Park map.

This relaxing stroll encircles Wawona Meadow, curving around at its east end and heading back toward the road. It crosses the highway and winds through forest until it returns at the Wawona Hotel. Some cars still use this road, so watch out.

Tuolumne Meadows to Glen Aulin High Sierra Camp, Yosemite

13 miles round-trip. Moderate. Access: From Tuolumne Meadows Visitors Center, follow dirt road sign STABLES. Park where road veers right. Trailhead on left. Map: USGS Tuolumne Meadows map.

The first part of this hike is striking enough, a flat journey through one of the best alpine meadows in Yosemite. Mule deer often graze in large herds, and you're likely to see waterfowl and large trout in the river. Stop off at Soda Springs and taste the highly effervescent water bubbling out of the ground in the small log-framed spring house. Continuing downstream, you'll leave the meadow and follow the north bank of the river for a couple of miles through a mixed conifer forest with lots of small meadows and wildflowers. Soon, the river begins to run faster. You're entering the Grand Canyon of the Tuolumne.

The next 2.5 miles down to Glen Aulin are spectacular; the river cascades through roaring cataracts and the trail crosses over the river several times on small bridges.

Finally you wind down to Glen Aulin High Sierra Camp, built at the base of roaring Glen Aulin Falls. A small store here sells snacks and drinks, but things are pricey; they came in on mule after all. Take a plunge in the river below the falls and rest before returning back upriver.

If you haven't had enough by Glen Aulin, an option is to continue on to Hetch Hetchy at the bottom of the canyon. There is a convenient trail the whole way down complete with numerous waterfalls and other natural wonders. If you plan on trekking the whole way down, though, plan on spending at least a night or two—it's about 30 miles from Tuolumne Meadows to Hetch Hetchy.

This is only one of many fantastic hikes that depart from Tuolumne Meadows; so many hikes lead from here into the backcountry it is impossible to do them justice. A good day hike is the 5-mile climb to Cathedral Lake. This steep but shady trail passes an icy cold spring and traverses several meadows.

Cathedral Lakes, Yosemite

8 miles. Moderate. Access: The trailhead is at the west end of Tuolumne Meadows, west of Budd Creek. Take the shuttle bus in summer to avoid parking problems. Map: Park map.

These lakes are set in granite bowls cut by glaciers. The peaks and domes around both Lower and Upper Cathedral lakes are worth the hike alone. Lower Cathedral Lake is next to Cathedral Peak, and is a good place to stop for a snack before heading up the hill to enjoy the upper lake.

Dog Lake, Yosemite

3 miles. Easy. Access: Take Calif. 120 to the access road for Tuolumne Lodge. Pass the Ranger Station and park at a parking lot on the left. Walk north up an embankment and recross the highway to find Dog Lake Trail. Map: Park map.

This is an easy climb through forests with great views of Mount Dana. Dog Lake is warm, shallow, and great for swimming.

Elizabeth Lake, Yosemite

6 miles. Moderate. Access: Take Calif. 120 to the group camping area of Tuolumne Meadows Campground, where the trail begins. Map: Park map.

This popular day hike attracts a slew of people, which can be a bummer, but it's magnificent nonetheless for its beauty. Elizabeth Lake glistens like ice. Don't forget your camera and some extra film—the entire route is one long Kodak moment.

Gaylor Lakes, Yosemite

6 miles. Moderate. Access: Take Calif. 120 to Tioga Pass. The trailhead is on the northwest side of the road. Map: Park map.

This trail begins with a climb, then descends to the alpine lake. It's a particularly pretty hike in early summer, when the mountainsides are dotted with wildflowers.

Glacier Canyon to Dana Lake, Yosemite

4.6 miles. Moderate to strenuous. Access: Take Calif. 120 to Tioga Lake. The trailhead is on the west side of the lake, about a mile east of the pass. Map: Park map.

This is a less-crowded alternative to the above hike to Mount Dana that doesn't top the mountain, although that alternative is available for experienced hikers. The trail begins at the Ansel Adams Wilderness and is not maintained, although it is fairly visible. This area is easily damaged so make sure to tread lightly. The route leads through the headway of Glacier Canyon to Dana Lake, which is fed by glaciers. Mount Dana looms large from the lake's shore.

May Lake, Yosemite

2.5 miles. Easy. Access: Take Calif. 120 east past White Wolf. Turn off at road marker T-21 and drive 2 miles to the May Lake Parking Area. Map: Park map.

Winding through forests and granite, this picturesque hike offers ample opportunities to fish, but swimming is not allowed.

May Lake is in the center of Yosemite National Park and is a good jumping-off point for other High Country hikes. There are numerous peaks surrounding the lake, including the 10,855-foot-high Mount Hoffman, which rises behind the lake. There is a High Sierra camp here as well, and a hikers' camp on the south side of the lake.

Mono Pass, Yosemite

8.5 miles. Moderate to strenuous. Access: The trailhead for this hike is on the south side of Calif. 120 as you enter the park from Lee Vining. Drive about 1.5 miles from the park entrance to Dana Meadows, where the trail begins on an abandoned road and alongside Parker Creek Pass. Map: Park map.

You'll pass some historic cabin sites, then hike down to Walker Lake, and return via the same route. The hike loops into the Inyo National Forest and the Ansel Adams Wilderness, and climbs to an altitude of 10,600 feet.

Mount Dana, Yosemite

5.8 miles. Strenuous. Access: The trailhead is on the southeast side of Calif. 120 at Tioga Pass. Map: Park map.

This climb is an in-your-face reminder that Mount Dana is Yosemite's second-highest peak. The mountain rises 13,053 feet and the trail gains a whopping 3,100 feet in 3 miles. The views at the top are wonderful, once you're able to stand upright after catching your breath. You can see Mono Lake from the summit. In summer, the wildflowers add to this hike's beauty.

North Dome, Yosemite

10 miles. Easy to moderate. Access: Take Calif. 120 east to the Porcupine Flat Campground, past White Wolf. About 1 mile after the campground is a sign for Porcupine Creek at a closed road. Park in the designated area. Map: Park map.

Walk south down the abandoned road toward the Porcupine Creek Campground.

A mile past the campground the trail hits a junction with the Tenaya Creek and Tuolumne Meadows Trail. Pass a junction toward Yosemite Falls and head uphill toward North Dome. The ascent is treacherous due to loose gravel, but from the top you'll catch an all-encompassing view of Yosemite Valley, second only to the view from Half Dome.

Sunrise Lakes, Yosemite

7 to 8 miles. Moderate to strenuous. Access: Take Calif. 120 to Tenaya Lake. The trail begins in the parking area on the east side of the road near the southwest end of the lake. Map: Park map.

Look for a sign that says SUNRISE. Follow the level road to Tenaya Creek. Cross the creek and follow the trail to the right. The hike parallels Tenaya Creek for about 0.25 miles, then moves away through a wooded area and climbs gently up a rocky rise. After a while the trail descends quickly to the outlet of Mildred Lake. You'll be able to see Mount Hoffman, Tuolumne Peak, and Tenaya Canyon.

At the halfway mark, the trail passes through a hemlock grove and then comes to a junction. Head left. (The trail on the right goes toward Cloud's Rest.) About 0.25 mile from the junction you'll reach Lower Sunrise Lake, tucked into the slope of Sunrise Mountain. The trail climbs past Middle Sunrise Lake and continues upward along a cascading creek coming from upper Sunrise Lake. From there it follows the lake's shore and opens in less than 0.5 mile onto a wide, bare sandy pass. It's all downhill from here. Before you is the snow-capped Clark Range. The trail then begins its descent, sharply switching back and forth in some places. There is a High Sierra camp and backpackers' camp here as well.

Redwood Mountain Loop, Sequoia/Kings Canyon

6.3 miles. Moderate. Access: Redwood Saddle Trailhead, Kings Canyon National Park Rd. off State Rte. 180. Map: USGS Giant Forest topo or Sequoia/Kings Canyon Park map.

In stark contrast to the tourist-thronged Giant Forest in this same park, the Redwood Mountain Grove of sequoias lies in a much wilder setting. You're likely not to see many other hikers on this remote trail along the ridgeline of Redwood Mountain. After passing through a stunning sequoia forest, the trail descends into the redwood creek drainage. The trees here are thick, some of the biggest in the world. Soon you'll come to a trail junction with a sign pointing you back up to the trailhead through the lush creek valley.

Mineral King, Sequoia/Kings Canyon

Various hikes. Access: Mineral King. Map: Sequoia/Kings Canyon Park map or USGS Mineral King topo.

Many of the most impressive hikes in Sequoia/Kings Canyon are in the Mineral King section in the southern end of Sequoia. Beginning at 7,800 feet, trails lead onward and upward to destinations like Sawtooth Pass and Crystal Lake. The old White Chief Trail departs from here to the now-defunct White Chief Mine. Once a silver mining boomtown in the 1870s, Mineral King was the center of a pitched battle in the late 1970s and early 1980s when developers sought to build a huge ski resort here. They were defeated, and the wilderness remains unspoiled.

Paradise Valley Trail, Sequoia/Kings Canyon

7.5 miles. Moderate. Access: The trailhead is at the end of the dead-end road to Cedar Grove, 6 miles east of Cedar Grove Village. Map: Park map or USGS The Sphinx topo.

The Paradise Valley Trail is a fairly easy day trip by park standards, leading to beautiful Mist Falls. The falls are best in the early spring and summer because snowmelt jacks up the quantity of water pouring over the edge.

BEARPAW MEADOW CAMP

It's not a hotel, nor is it a campsite. Bearpaw Meadow is a group of six wood-framed double-occupancy tents located 11 miles down the High Sierra Trail, at the precipitous edge of one of Sequoia's most astounding views. If you're one of the few hundred lucky people who manage to reserve a night there, you can day-hike in with only a water bottle and a camera, get a gourmet meal cooked for you, then sleep under a down blanket on the cots provided. It's not the Ritz-Carlton, but when you see the jealous looks from the backpackers coming through the next day, you'll feel like it is. Be kind: They'll be eating freeze-dried ramen that night, sleeping on rocks. You'll be eating grilled steaks on the mess hall porch.

It's a testament to Sequoia National Park's managers that the developed site, though located at least a day's walk into the backcountry, doesn't detract from the area's remote feel or ruin the experience for backpackers passing through. Quite to the contrary, backpackers often appreciate the fresh water available, and always seem to stop at the camp's porch for a group photo overlooking the granite chasm. The camp itself is designed like a group of European hiker's chalets. It's staffed full-time by a cook (occasionally a special visiting chef—well, la-ti-da) and provisioned by regular mule trains. A hike here is an interesting way to access the back country for people who are fit, but perhaps not interested or able to carry 40 pounds on their back for 2 days. Two of the site's tents are located literally at the edge of the cliff. The rest are located only a few yards back; each offers a million-dollar view.

A night at Bearpaw costs $125 per person per night, including breakfast and dinner. The camp usually operates from mid-June to mid-September, but be advised that the exact dates of the season depend on weather and are subject to change. Reservations are available beginning January 2, and every available spot is usually gone by the end of that first day. There is no maximum stay, but out of consideration for other interested campers, most people stay no more than 2 nights. That allows you a day to hike in, stay a second day to loll about camp or make the excellent 6-mile day hike to Hamilton Lakes (see "Hamilton Gorge" listing), and a third day to hike out.

All facilities are reserved for Bearpaw campers, with two notable exceptions. One is water—passing backpackers are invited and indeed encouraged to fill their bottles at the camp. The other is, thankfully, toilets, available to all. Backpackers aren't allowed to use the nice flush toilets, however. The line dividing the haves from the have nots forms, in this case, in front of the adjacent pit john. Try to show pity.

Copper Creek to Lower Tent Meadows, Sequoia/Kings Canyon

7 miles. Strenuous. Steep. Access: 6 miles east of Cedar Grove Village. The trailhead is off of the second parking lot on the other side of the road's end loop. Map: Park map or USGS The Sphinx topo.

Copper Creek Trail immediately rises into the high wilderness around Granite Pass at 10,673 feet. The views of snowcapped peaks and canyons are incredible, but this is one of the most strenuous day hikes in the park. The trail continues beyond Lower Tent Meadows, but unless you're prepared to spend a night or two in the wilderness, it's best to turn around.

Giant Forest, Sequoia/Kings Canyon

Various hikes. Access: Giant Forest off General's Hwy. Map: Park map or USGS Giant Forest topo.

If the altitude and steepness at the Copper Creek Trailhead are too much for you, try some of the longer hikes in the Giant Forest. The entire forest is woven with interlocking loops that allow you to hike as short or as long as you want. The 6-mile Trail of the Sequoias will take you to the grove's far eastern end where some of the finest trees are. A fascinating side trip is the 100-foot walk through the hollow trunk of the Fallen Monarch. The fallen tree has been used for shelter for more than a hundred years and is tall enough inside that you can walk through without bending over.

Azalea Trail, Sequoia/Kings Canyon
3 miles round-trip. Easy. Access: Grant Grove Visitor Center. Map: Park map.

From the visitor center, walk past the amphitheater to the Sunset Campground and cross Calif. 180. The first mile joins the South Boundary Trail as it meanders through Wilsonia and crisscrosses Sequoia Creek in a gentle climb. After 1.5 miles is the third crossing of Sequoia Creek, which may be dry in late summer, but the banks are lush with ferns and brightly colored azaleas. *Note:* Azaleas contain a toxin that can cause convulsions and paralysis if they are ingested. Return the way you came.

Hitchcock Meadow Trail, Sequoia/Kings Canyon
3.5 miles round-trip. Easy. Access: Picnic area near the entrance to Grant Grove from Kings Canyon. Map: Park map.

This trail arrives at the pretty Viola Fall. The first half mile follows the Big Stump Trail. From there, hike another quarter mile to Hitchcock Meadow, a large clearing actually surrounded by sequoia stumps. Notice the small sequoias in this area: these are the descendants of the Giant Sequoias logged in the last century. From here the trail climbs slightly to a ridge, where it re-enters Kings Canyon National Park before descending a short series of steep switchbacks to Sequoia Creek. Cross the creek and look for a sign directing you to Viola Falls, a series of short steps that join into one fall when the water level is high. It's dangerous to venture down the canyon, but above it are several flat places that make great picnic spots.

Park Ridge Trail, Sequoia/Kings Canyon
4.7 miles round-trip. Easy. Access: Panoramic Point Parking Area, a 2.5-mile drive down a steep road from Grant Grove Village. Map: Park map.

Begin this hike by walking south along the ridge, where views of the valley and peaks dominate. On a clear day, you can see Hume Lake in Sequoia National Forest, the San Joaquin Valley and occasionally, the coast range 100 miles away. Return the same way.

Sunset Trail, Sequoia/Kings Canyon
6 miles round-trip. Moderate to strenuous. Access: Across the road from the Grant Grove Visitor Center. Map: Park map.

The hike climbs 1,400 feet past two waterfalls and a lake. After crossing the highway, the trail heads left around a campground. After 1.25 miles, follow the South Boundary Trail toward Viola Falls. You'll reach a paved road where you can head to the right to see the park's original entrance. Return the way you came, or follow the road to the General Grant Tree parking area and walk to the visitor center.

Bubbs Creek Trail, Sequoia/Kings Canyon
8 miles round-trip. Moderate to strenuous. Access: East end of the parking area at Road's End. Map: Park map.

The trail begins by crossing and recrossing Copper Creek. This site was once an Indian village and shards of obsidian can still be found on the ground in this area. After the first mile you'll enter a swampy area that offers a good place to watch for wildlife. The trail here closes in on the river, where deer and bear drink. At 2 miles, you'll come to a junction. The trail to Paradise Valley heads north (left), while the hike to Bubbs Creek veers right and crosses Bailey Bridge, over the South Fork of the Kings River.

Continue hiking east over four small, wooden bridges that cross Bubbs Creek. The creek was named after John Bubbs, a prospector and rancher who arrived here in 1864. The trail will climb on the creek's north side, throwing in a few steep switchbacks to keep you alert. The switchbacks also provide nice, alternating views of the canyon of Paradise Valley and Cedar Grove. At 3 miles is a large, emerald pool with waterfalls. Far above is a rock formation known as the Sphinx. John Muir named the feature after Egypt's famous likeness. At 4 miles you enter Sphinx Creek, a nice place to spend the day or night (with a wilderness permit). There are several campsites nearby. Hike back the way you came or along the Sentinel Trail.

Sentinel Trail, Sequoia/Kings Canyon

4.6 miles round-trip. Easy. Access: Short-term parking area at Road's End, past Cedar Grove Village; follow the signs. Map: Park map.

Essentially what this hike does is encircle a small length of the South Fork of the Kings River. After hiking 2 miles on the river's north side, the trail splits and heads north to Mist Falls and Paradise Valley or east across Bailey Bridge toward Bubbs Creek. Follow the eastern trail but instead of hiking on to Bubbs Creek, follow a sign that reads ROAD'S END—2.6 miles. This will take you through dense groves of pine and cedars, with occasional views of Grand Sentinel. You'll cross Avalanche Creek before emerging into a huge meadow and returning near the riverbank. At 2 miles, you can see Muir's Pulpit, the huge boulder described above. At 2.25 miles, you'll find a footbridge that points back to the parking area.

Mist Falls, Sequoia/Kings Canyon

8 miles round-trip. Moderate to strenuous. Access: Short-term parking area at Road's End, past Cedar Grove Village; follow the signs. Map: Park map.

This is one of the more popular trails leading to the backcountry, but it's also a nice day hike. The first 2 miles are dry, until you reach Bubbs Creek Bridge. Take the fork to the left and head uphill. The first waterfall is not your destination point, although it is a pretty spot to take a break. From here, the trail meanders along the river, through forest and swamp areas before it comes out at the base of Mist Falls, a wide expanse of a fall that flows generously in spring. There are dozens of great picnic spots here, and along the way up. Return along the same route, or at Bubbs Creek Bridge, cross over and head back on the Sentinel Trail. This will add a mile to the hike. From Mist Falls, you can also continue on to Paradise Valley.

Huckleberry Trail, Sequoia/Kings Canyon

4 miles round-trip. Moderate. Access: Hazelwood Nature Trail Parking Area, 0.3 miles east of Giant Forest Village on the Generals Hwy. Map: Park map.

This is a great hike with a lot of beauty and not a lot of people. It passes through forest and meadow, near a 100-year-old cabin and an old Indian village. The first mile of this hike takes you along the Hazelwood Nature Trail. Head south at each junction until you see a big sign with blue lettering that marks the start of the Huckleberry Trail. You pass a small creek and meadow before reaching a second sign to Huckleberry Meadow. The next mile is steep, and there's a cross beneath sequoias, dogwood, and white fir. At the 1.5-mile point is a Squatter's Cabin, a log building built in the 1880s.

East of the cabin is a trail junction. Head north (left) up a short hill. At the next junction, veer left along the edges of Circle Meadow for about a quarter mile before you reach another junction. The right is a short detour to Bear's Bathtub, a pair of sequoias hollowed by fire and filled with water. Legend has it that an old mountain guide named Chester Wright once surprised a bear taking a bath here, hence its name. Continue on the trail heading northeast to the Washington Tree, almost as big as the General Sherman Tree, then on to Alta Trail. Turn west (left) to Little Deer Creek. On both sides of the creek are Indian mortar holes. Some of the largest are 3 feet in diameter and it's unknown what they were used for. At the next junction, head north (right) to return to the Generals Highway and the last leg of the Huckleberry Trail to the parking area.

Moro Rock and Soldiers Loop Trail, Sequoia/Kings Canyon

4.6 miles round-trip. Moderate. Access: 30 yd. west of the cafeteria at Giant Forest Village. Map: Park map.

This hike cuts cross-country from the village to Moro Rock. Part of the early trail is parallel to a main road, but the hike quickly departs from the traffic and heads through a forest dotted with Giant Sequoias. A carpet of ferns occasionally hides the trail. It pops out at Moro Rock, and then it's just a quick heart-thumper to the top.

Overnights

The hundreds of square miles of Yosemite wilderness make it a prime location to really get "out there." If you plan on staying in the woods for an extended amount of time, Yosemite Park wranglers can be hired to make resupply drops at any of the backcountry High Sierra camps.

Perhaps the most famous trail in Sequoia/Kings Canyon is the **Whitney Portal.** Since the trailhead is only accessible from Lone Pine on the east side of the Sierra, however, I have included it with the overnights in that section.

Half Dome Cable Route, Yosemite

17 miles round-trip. Strenuous. Access: Happy Isles Trailhead, Yosemite Valley. Map: USGS Half Dome or Yosemite Park map.

Half Dome may look insurmountable for anyone but an expert rock climber, but

thousands every year take the popular cable route up the back side; so many hikers have done this walk that the granite underfoot is grooved and polished from their footsteps. It's almost 17 miles round-trip from Happy Isle on the John Muir Trail and a 4,900-foot elevation gain. Many do it in 1 day, starting at first light and rushing home to beat nightfall. A more relaxed strategy is to camp in one of the backpacking campgrounds in Little Yosemite Valley just past Nevada Falls. The overnight campsites here fill up early, so try to make wilderness permit reservations well in advance.

Depending on your schedule, you either want to camp first and charge up Half Dome in the morning or, in the way I prefer to do things, hike to Little Yosemite, set up camp, blitz the cable route to the summit, and return at dusk to a waiting camp. From Little Yosemite to the top of Half Dome it is a little more than 3 miles, a good portion of it climbing a 46° granite slope. The Park Service has installed steel cables to help you out, and during summer, boards are installed as cross-beams, but they're still far apart. Wear shoes with lots of traction and bring your own leather gloves for the cables. Your hands will thank you.

The view from the top is an unbeatable vista of the High Country, Tenaya Canyon, Glacier Point, and the awe-inspiring abyss of the valley below. When you shuffle up to the overhanging lip for a look down the face, be extremely careful not to kick rocks or anything else onto the climbers below who are earning this view the hard way.

Cloud's Rest, Yosemite

14 miles. Moderate. Access: Take Calif. 120 to Tenaya Lake. The trailhead begins at a campground parking lot down a closed road that crosses an outlet of the lake. Map: Park map.

This hike descends through a wooded area. Head toward Sunrise Lake. Ascend out of Tenaya Canyon and at a junction, bear right (this part of the trail is usually well signed). Views begin almost at once. Your destination is clear, which is a good thing since the trail is sketchy at this point. The last scramble to the top is a little spooky, with sheer drops on each side. Yosemite River is on the right and the Little Yosemite on the left. Bravery is rewarded with spectacular views of the park's granite domes. Overnight stays are rewarded with beautiful sunrises.

Vogelsang, Yosemite

14.4 miles. Moderate to strenuous. Access: Take Calif. 120 to Tuolumne Meadows and watch for the signed trailhead for the John Muir Trail and Lyell Fork. Map: Park map.

The trail goes south through the woods to a footbridge over the Dana Fork. Cross the bridge and follow the John Muir Trail upstream. Go right at the next fork. The trail crosses the Lyell Fork by footbridge. Take the left fork 200 feet ahead. Continue onward and just before crossing the bridge at Rafferty Creek, you'll reach another junction. Veer right and prepare for switchbacks up a rocky slope. The trail climbs steeply for about a quarter mile then levels off as it darts toward and away from Rafferty Creek for the next 4 miles.

The trail then gradually ascends to Tuolumne Pass, crossing many small creeks and tributaries en route. Two small tarns mark the pass. One drains south and the other north. Just south of the tarns the trail splits. Veer left. (The right fork offers a 2-mile round-trip jaunt to Boothe Lake.) You'll climb to a meadow with great views, and here, at 10,180 feet, reach the highest of Yosemite's High Sierra camps. It's very pretty, with a great location—the base of Fletcher Peak, on the banks of Fletcher Creek and close to Fletcher Lake.

Dinkey Lakes

14 miles round-trip. Moderate. Wilderness permits available at Pineridge ranger station. Access: From State Rte. 168 near Shaver Lake, turn right on road marked Dinkey Creek and Wishon Dam.

Drive 13.6 miles to a fork in the road where you bear left toward Courtright Village and Cliff Lake Trailhead. Park at Cliff Lake Trailhead. Map: USGS Blackcap Mountain and Huntington Lake topos, Sierra National Forest map.

The Dinkey Lakes Wilderness, in a unique island of alpine High Sierra terrain, is separated from the rest of the High Sierra by a lower forested plateau. Several lakes are clustered at the 9,500-foot level, below some nearly 11,000-foot peaks. The Cliff Lake Trail climbs steadily but gently for 5 miles, the last stretch a number of switchbacks. Soon you're at Cliff Lake, named for the 400-foot cliffs that provide its backdrop. There are several good campsites here. To get beyond any possible crowd, though, I recommend going over the next pass, about 400 feet of climbing, but worth it. You'll then drop into the Dinkey Lakes Basin where stunning Rock Lake or diminutive Little Lake make good campsites. Allow an extra day to enjoy the numerous day hikes and good fishing in this area.

Hamilton Gorge, Sequoia National Park

32 miles round-trip. 3–4 days. Strenuous. Access: Crescent Meadow trailhead, near Lodgepole Visitors Center, to the High Sierra Trail, at the base of the parking lot beside the water fountain. Map: USGS Lodgepole map, available at Lodgepole Visitors Center. Backcountry permit required, available for $10 from the park's wilderness office (☎ 559/565-3708). Advance reservations recommended in summer.

Sequoia's High Sierra Trail is a narrow, spectacular route carved into the north wall of a vast gorge, tracing the side of the granite cliffs overlooking the Great Western Divide. The trail offers mountain views (with names like "Eagle's View") at virtually every turn, crosses several spectacular waterfalls, and includes a few small pools suitable for swimming and a lake surrounded by 10,000- and 12,000-foot peaks.

After climbing gradually from the parking lot for a mile, the trail evens out to a pattern of alternating flat sections and 5-minute climbs. Temperatures swing comfortably with every turn of the trail, into the shaded pines then out into the hot chaparral, then back into the pines just as you start to overheat. The first significant campsite, also a good lunch spot, is 6 miles in at a rocky overlook with a waterfall, Merhten Meadow. Metal bear boxes are available at this and most campsites and should be used, lest Yogi get too interested.

The trail continues hugging the cliff side and alternating short climbs and brief flats for another 3 miles. If you can make it, the campsite at 9 miles (called just "Nine Mile") is both larger than the 6-mile site and has a small swimming hole. It will also make your life easier the next day, when you have some serious climbing to do.

The 6 miles from Nine Mile to Hamilton Gorge include some of the park's best scenery, including lovely upper and lower Hamilton Lake, and a towering cliff face appropriately called the Angel's Wings. After 1.5 miles, you climb steeply to the overlook at the Bearpaw Meadow developed camp, where backpackers can pick up water but not food, which is reserved for the lucky camp guests (see "Bearpaw Meadow Camp," above). Another 3 miles gets you to upper Hamilton Lake. This is the most striking section of the trail, but it's also an intense, switchbacking climb. At upper Hamilton Lake, camp behind the rock face at the water's edge for a view of the High Sierra's western lip. It's 16 miles back to Crescent meadow from here, usually accomplished in 2 days. Or, if you've got the time and the stamina, you can continue up over the gorge and on another 50 miles to Mount Whitney.

Alta Peak–Alta Meadow, Sequoia/Kings Canyon

16 miles round-trip. Strenuous. Access: From Giant Village, drive about 3 miles north on the Generals Hwy. and then turn right on the Wolverton Rd. turnoff. Look for the trail at the southeast end of the parking area at Wolverton Creek. Map: Park map.

From Wolverton, hike on the Lakes Trail toward the Panther Gap Trail. Head right on the Panther Gap Trail, up through the 8,400-foot gap to Alta Trail. Turn left on Alta Trail, hike past the junction with Seven-Mile Hill Trail and the junction with Alta Peak Trail. Left takes you up Alta Peak, a 2,000-foot ascent in 2 miles that offers spectacular vistas. If climbing isn't your idea of fun, plow straight ahead to Alta Meadow, which also has a nice view and good places to camp.

Jennie Lakes Trail, Sequoia/Kings Canyon

12 miles round-trip. Moderate to strenuous. Access: From Grant Grove, drive about 7 miles south on the Generals Hwy. to the turnoff for Big Meadows Campground. The trailhead and parking are on the south side of the road next to a ranger station. Map: Park map.

This is a nice overnight hike that's not too demanding, and can be farther extended into the Jennie Lakes Wilderness Area. From the parking area, cross through the campground and across Big Meadow Creek. From here the trail climbs. At Fox Meadow, there is a wooden trail sign and register for hikers to sign. At the next junction, head right toward Jennie Lakes (left goes toward the Weaver Lake Trail) and up to Poop Out Pass. From here it's a drop down to the Boulder Creek drainage area and on to emerald-green Jennie Lakes. This hike can be combined with a second day hike to Weaver Lake. Just retrace your steps to the Weaver Lake turnoff. Weaver Lake is a relatively warm mountain lake that reportedly is surrounded by blueberry bushes that weigh heavy with fresh fruit in July.

LOOK YOGI, PICNIC BASKETS!

True story: A few years back, a group of campers in the Dinky Lakes area, worried about bears stealing their supplies, began tying two bags of camp food high in a tree. While they were doing this some hunters passed by and, claiming years of local experience, volunteered that they had never seen a bear in those woods. Happy to avoid the annoying task of hanging the food, the campers abandoned their effort, found a low boulder nearby and tied the bags only high enough to deter marmots. The bear that wasn't supposed to be living in those woods showed up a few hours later, after the campers went to bed. It quickly grabbed the group's convenient food bags, tethered together by a rope, and took off into the darkness.

Awakened by the bear's efforts, the leader of the expedition leapt from her sleeping bag and gave chase. Somehow, she caught up with the bear and got a hand on the bags of food. A tug of war ensued. The bear weighed in at a good 300 pounds, had claws, and could see pretty well at night. The human stood maybe 5'2" and 110 pounds in her hiking boots, and was more or less in the dark.

She yelled at the bear and exhorted the other campers, by this point straggling out of their tents, to throw rocks at the animal. Everyone screamed and shouted and looked for rocks. Finally the bear, performing perhaps one of the greatest acts of charity in the history of Dinky Lakes, gave up the food bag.

The campers gathered up the food and beat a hasty retreat to camp. Now working in the dark, they hung the food up high in the tree. But a few minutes later, the bear came back and managed to get at the supplies again anyway, chewing "a big slobbery hole" in the bag, though not able to dislodge it wholesale this time. "We lost the granola in the fight," lamented a witness.

Again the humans gave chase. The bear hid behind a tree, peering out at the campers. "It's eyes reflected our flashlights, and it growled a very deep growl," said the witness. "Not a 'grrrr' kind of growl. A very low, *get away* kind of growl. I think it was then that we decided we had reached an understanding, and left it alone."

The obvious point here is that bears are not necessarily going to kill you if you encounter them, but they are dangerous, and they *will* show up if you invite them. On any trip to the Sierra, bear sightings are not a remote possibility, whether you're in the backcountry or car camping.

HORSEBACK RIDING

Yosemite offers 2-hour and half-day rides from stables in Yosemite Valley and Wawona spring through fall, weather permitting. In summer, rides also depart from Tuolumne Meadows. Pack animals and private stock may also board at stables. Call **Yosemite Valley Stables** at ☎ **209/372-8348** for more information or reservations. Prices range from $35 for a few hours to $900 for a 6-day guided trip into the backcountry. Backcountry trips are available only with advanced reservations from May through September. These lead to Yosemite's High Sierra camps and trips include meals. **Yosemite Trails Pack Station** (☎ **559/683-7611**) offers riding just south of Wawona. **Minarets Pack Station** (☎ **559/868-3405**) is in the High Sierra and leads day trips to Yosemite and the Ansel Adams Wilderness.

ICE SKATING

In winter, the **Curry Village Ice Rink** in Yosemite is a lot of fun. It's outdoors and melts quickly when the weather warms up. The cost is $5 adults, $4.50 children. Skate rentals are available.

KAYAKING

There are numerous Class V and VI runs on the Kings, Kaweah, and San Joaquin rivers, most of which have been run

These encounters are usually worse for the bear than they are for you. "When bears repeatedly obtain human food and garbage, these intelligent animals learn quickly to seek more," suggests a U.S. Park Service guide on the subject. "They become destructive and dangerous, and—too often—must be killed."

Bears living in the Sierra are of the black-bear or brown-bear variety. Brown bears are larger and can be more aggressive than black ones. But they are still far less aggressive than grizzly bears—sadly, the only grizzlies left in California are the ones on the state flag.

That's a biological tragedy, but it does mean—here's the silver lining—that your only real risk of injury from bears is to stumble on a mother who feels her cubs are threatened, or somehow antagonize a lone bear, say by playing tug of war with it.

If you do see a bear, observe it only from afar. If confronted, don't run away—they'll consider you prey if you act like it, and you can't outrun a bear anyway. If possible, back away slowly, holding your arms out to make yourself look bigger. The bear will probably think you're a larger animal than you are and retreat. If it appears aggressive, use your judgment about possibly antagonizing it further, but rangers recommend you shout and wave your arms as you back away.

Most encounters with bears are actually encounters between bears and your food. Where bear boxes are available—steel boxes locked with pins, placed at many popular campsites—use them. Bear canisters, small drums made of high-impact plastic, holding six person-days of food (6 days' food for one person, or 1 day's for six) are also useful, and can be rented in Sequoia and Yosemite for a low daily fee, usually $6 per day. As a final option, hang the food from a high tree branch, at least 15 feet above ground and 10 feet out from the tree's trunk. In addition to food, make sure each night to stow toothpaste, first-aid kits, deodorant, suntan lotion, garbage, and anything else in your pack liable to give off an interesting aroma. Under no circumstances should you store food in your tent, as bears will come looking for it and don't have much skill with zippers. They might also decide you are between them and what they want; not a good position.

If a bear takes your food or makes a claim on your campsite, let it have it. Tug of war with a bear is a great story to tell, but it wouldn't sound so good from a hospital bed.

maybe two or three times total. Only recently, professional outfitters have begun taking experienced kayakers down the Class IV and V **Kaweah** and **Upper Kings rivers.** Contact park headquarters (☎ 559/565-3341) for a current listing of companies running trips. This is one of the wildest, steepest rivers in North America and only for the very adventurous.

In 1981, my friend Reg Lake with Doug Thompkins and Royal Robins hiked over Whitney Portal, a 21-mile trudge across a 13,777-foot pass, carrying boats and several days' worth of camping gear. Then they hiked back down to Junction Meadow at 8,000 feet where the Kern begins, and put in. From there it was a

mere 37 miles of gnarly Class V white water, and they'd bagged the first descent. Amazingly enough others have done the trip since they did it.

For the rest of us mere mortals the Kern, below Sequoia National Park, is the best bet. **The Forks of the Kern Run** is good Class IV and "easy" V and requires only about a 3-mile hike to the put-in. Below that, you can even drive your car to the launching points. The **Limestone Run** between Johnsondale Bridge and Fairview Dam is a good Class III and IV, and way below here, just outside Kernville, is the best beginner run in the southern Sierra, appropriately named the **Kernville Run.** The exact put-ins and take-outs for each run vary dramatically depending on your ability. Consult the blow-by-blow descriptions in Jim Cassady's *California Whitewater: A Guide to the Rivers* (North Fork Press, 1995) or Chuck Stanley and Lars Holbek's classic *A Guide to the Best Whitewater in the State of California* (Friends of the River Books, 1984) before committing to any of these runs.

Sierra South, 11300 Kernville Rd., Kernville, CA 93238 (☎ **760/376-3745**), is a kayaking school and shop with an excellent reputation for safe and quality instruction. It offers instruction on a full spectrum of white-water skills from basic paddling to advanced technique.

MOUNTAIN BIKING

If you take a look at a map of the High Sierra from the northern boundary of Yosemite to the southern edge of Sequoia/Kings Canyon, you'll recognize one thing immediately: It's one of the largest continuous wilderness areas in the continental United States, and has wisely been designated almost entirely as official wilderness area or national park. Yay, yippie, yahoo. That protection is a good thing, a great thing, no doubt about it, but it means your mountain bike isn't going to be seeing too much trail action here. You'll have to stick to the lower-elevation areas outside the parks if you really want to ride. **Kernville** is surrounded by endless miles of Forest Service roads and single track, and the **Kern River** has countless nice swimming holes to help cut the road dust. With great kayaking, camping, mountain biking, climbing, and rafting, Kernville threatens to become another Moab. Hopefully it will be spared. **Mountain and River Adven-tures,** 113 Kernville Rd. (☎ **760/376-6553**), rents bikes, leads mountain bike tours, and is a great source of local trail knowledge.

ROAD BIKING

A bicycle makes for the perfect way to see **Yosemite Valley,** which has 8 miles of bike paths in addition to the valley roads. You can rent one-speeds at the Yosemite Lodge or Curry Village for $5 per hour or $16.25 per day. If you want a fancier bike you'll have to bring it from home. All trails in the park are closed to mountain bikes.

ROCK CLIMBING

For many years, rock climbing and Yosemite were practically synonymous. The new sport-climbing focus has drawn some of the limelight away from Yosemite's amazing granite walls, but it is still an important way station on the cutting-edge–climbers' circuit. With its huge expanses of hard and perfectly textured granite, the valley is the most famous climbing spot in the world—a canvas waiting for climbers to paint their routes. Here the big walls like **El Capitan** and **Half Dome** don't simply loom over and surround you: They sink into your subconscious.

The **Salathe Wall,** a staggeringly long multiday climb up the face of El Capitan, still stands as one of the most important proving grounds for any big-wall climber. So much so that it is widely referred to as "the finest rock climb in the world." Hundreds of other multi-pitch climbs surround the valley. If you sit in a meadow near the Merced River with binoculars and scan the high walls, you sometimes see so many climbers that it looks like a family of spiders has invaded.

The valley is amazing, but for the more casual sport climber looking for single-pitch or simple multipitch climbs with easy walk-down descents, some of the best routes are in the High Country around Lake Tenaya and Tuolumne Meadows. The routes here were pioneered much later than the valley, many of them in the 1960s. Perhaps that's why you find routes with names like "The Needle and the Spoon" or the even less subtle "Drug Dome." **Lembert Dome** at the east end of Tuolumne

Meadows is a favorite spot for introducing climbers to long multipitch routes. It's clean and forgiving; an obvious escape route allows you to bug out before the final and scariest pitch if you get freaked.

The **Yosemite Mountaineering School** (☎ 209/372-1244) was one of the first in North America, and continues to set many standards for all levels of climbing instruction. A basic lesson at Yosemite Mountaineering for $100 per person per day will teach you basic body moves and rappelling and take you on a single-pitch climb. Classes run from early spring through early October in the valley, for a shorter period in Tuolumne Meadows. Call to get precise information about different clinics, lessons, and guide services. Some of the best guidebooks available are Don Reid's *Yosemite Climbs: Free* (Chockstone Press, 1994) and *Yosemite Climbs: Big Wall* (Chockstone Press, 1993).

There is no climbing school in Sequoia/Kings Canyon, but **Mountain and River Adventures** (☎ 760/232-4234) teaches rock climbing and can point experienced climbers to the local hot spot, a series of needlelike granite extrusions known appropriately enough as the **Needles.**

WALKS & RAMBLES

Yosemite Falls
0.25 miles. Access: Yosemite Valley Visitors Center.

Yosemite Falls is within a short stroll of the visitor center. You can actually see it better elsewhere in the valley, but it's really impressive to stand at the base of all that falling water. The wind, noise, and blowing spray generated when millions of gallons catapult 2,425 feet through space onto the rocks below are sometimes so strong you can barely stand on the bridge below.

Mirror Lake, Yosemite Valley
2 miles. Access: Take shuttle bus to trailhead from Curry Village.

Mirror Lake is a stunning natural reflecting pond near the base of Half Dome and the Vernal Falls, Nevada Falls Trail. The already tiny lake is shrinking every year as it fills with silt, becoming meadow, but the reflections of the valley walls and sky on its surface remain one of the valley's most tranquil sights. Twilight here is amazing. As the valley turns pink and purple, the lake reflects the changing sky. Often, it seems like you can hardly tell which one is the real sky. The walk to the lake is flat and easy. To add a little distance to it and get away from the paved trail, circle the lake on the dirt path.

Hazelwood Nature Trail, Sequoia National Park
1 mile. Access: Giant Forest Village.

This short and easy loop explains some of the interesting facts of the sequoia forest: how their cones must be heated by fire to release the seeds, how old they are, what this area was like when the often 2,000-year-old sequoias that tower here were mere sprouts. Afterwards, if you're feeling ambitious, you can try out the many miles of trail leading off into the wilder reaches of Giant Forest.

Congress Trail Loop, Sequoia National Park
2-mile loop. Access: Lodgepole Visitors Center.

The 2-mile Congress Trail Loop in the Giant Forest will take you to the base of the General Sherman Tree, the largest living thing in the world. Single branches on the General Sherman are more than 7 feet thick. Each year the tree grows enough wood to make a 60-foot-tall tree of normal dimensions. Other trees in the grove are nearly as large, and many have also been saddled with strangely militaristic and political monikers like General Lee and Lincoln. Longer trails lead to remote reaches of the grove and nearby meadows.

Moro Rock

0.5 miles round-trip. Access: Giant Forest Village.

Moro Rock is a 6,724-foot-tall granite dome formed by exfoliation of layers of the rock. A quarter-mile trail scales the dome for a spectacular view of the adjacent Kaweah Canyon. The trail gains 300 feet in 400 yards, so be ready for a climb.

WHITE-WATER RAFTING

The Kern and Kaweah are both run by commercial raft outfitters. More than 60 miles of white water are runnable on the **Kern,** most of it Class III and IV. The most demanding Kern run is the **Forks of Kern,** requiring a hike in (the rafts go on mules) and then a powerful run of IV-to-V–plus rapids, many of which must be scouted and often portaged. For a first-timer or family trip, the **Powerhouse Run** through Kernville is a perfect introduction.

The **Kaweah** is a beautiful and volatile river. The river is pure snowmelt draining Sequoia National Park, so wet suits are required. It's cold and steep; a swim here could be deadly. Since the river isn't dam-controlled, the season is short. Reserve trips early. Most outfitters require that you have previous Class V paddle raft experience.

Kaweah White Water Adventures (☎ 800/229-8658 or 559/561-1000) runs class III, IV, and V trips for beginners and intermediate paddlers. Trips usually last 5 hours; they're offered from April through August. The cost is up to $125 per person. The following outfitters also lead runs down the Kern and Kaweah: **Sierra South** (☎ 760/376-3745; Powerhouse run only), **Whitewater Voyages** (☎ 800/488-RAFT), **Kern River Tours** (☎ 760/379-4616), and **River Travel Center** (☎ 800/882-RAFT; free booking service for all California rivers).

Eastern Sierra: What to Do & Where to Do It

The eastern Sierra puts on display the startling contrasts between the Great Basin high desert and the abrupt, soaring peaks of the Sierra. From Lone Pine it is only 13 miles to the base of Mount Whitney—the highest peak in the Lower 48—but 10,000 feet practically straight up to the 14,495-foot summit. Whitney is not alone; five other peaks over 14,000 feet surround it. Another five 14,000-foot peaks are located just outside Big Pine, 50 miles north, and another, White Mountain, is just to the east. In all, 13 of the state's 14 peaks taller than 14,000 feet are here within a geological stone's throw of the Owens Valley (Mt. Shasta in the Cascades being the 14th).

It's a bit of geographic irony that the lowest point in North America is only 60 miles from here—Badwater in Death Valley. Besides being the tallest, the peaks of this end of the Sierra are some of the most dramatic in the country—soaring spires, high granite cirques, the southernmost living glacier in the United States, hanging valleys, waterfalls, dramatic ridgelines—kin in form and spirit to Wyoming's Grand Tetons.

Because of the dramatic vertical contrast, one can cover a lot of different types of geography in a single trip. It is actually possible to start a backpacking trip in scrub desert, climb the summit of Mount Whitney, descend into lush sequoia redwoods on the west slope, and soak your weary bones in a riverside hot spring, all in a few days. In winter, when State Route 120 closes, the ski crossing from Crane Flat in Yosemite to Lee Vining following the roadbed is the favorite haute route across the range.

BALLOONING

Weather permitting, **Mammoth Balloon Adventures,** P.O. Box 8561, Mammoth Lakes, CA 93546 (☎ **760/934-7188**), flies year-round from the meadows outside town. Their sunrise flight is the most popular and also least likely to be scrubbed by the high winds that pick up in the late morning and afternoon. Reservations are recommended.

BIRD WATCHING

Two hundred ninety-five separate bird species have been spotted at **Mono Lake,** east of Yosemite. More than 50,000 California gulls come each spring to breed on the lake's two major islands. Other seabirds use Mono as a staging area for winter migrations. As many as 800,000 eared grebes have been known to gather here in the fall before heading south. Other migratory species include waterfowl, like green wing and cinnamon teal, Canada geese, loons, common mergansers, and bufflehead. Besides the county park and state park, many quiet side roads lead to remote wetlands. Go past Mono Lake County Park on Cemetery Road to the **DeChambeau Ponds,** where you can see many local species in the ponds and scope the breeding island from a clear vantage point.

To the north of Mono Lake, the ghost town of **Bodie** is a great raptor-viewing spot. Vultures no longer circle over town waiting for the scraps of the next gunfight, but plenty of golden eagles, horned and burrowing owls, and red-tailed hawks hunt the surrounding scrub desert, while sage grouse strut through the empty streets.

BOARDSAILING

This side of the Sierra has plenty of wind but not nearly enough large bodies of water to make boardsailing a popular option. If, by some fluke of transport, you happen to be here and have your gear with you, I'd recommend **Crowley Lake.** It's open enough to get some real wind and big enough that you won't be tacking every 15 feet. You will, however, have to contend with trout fishermen, lots of them, and water-skiers. **June Lake** is also a good sailing lake without so much boat traffic. Any number of other smaller lakes *could* be sailed, but none really stand out.

BOBSLEDDING

Bobsledding. Are you out of your mind?
Well, no.

Bobsledz International (☎ **760/934-7533**), a commercial bobsledding operation, has mellowed out the course, tuned down the sleds, and brought bobsledding to the masses. For a fee, you and your friends can take the T-bar up and slide down a specially designed bobsled run to your heart's content. To find the place, head out of Mammoth Lakes toward Mammoth Mountain on State Route 203. It's 1.5 miles south of town on the right.

CANOEING

With hundreds of lakes small and large accessible by car, the **Mammoth** area is a canoeing heaven. If you don't have your own boat, rent one at Lake Mary's **Pokonobe Lodge** (☎ **760/934-2437**), or at Silver Lake's **Silver Lake Rentals** (☎ **760/389-0057**).

For a totally different canoeing experience, sign up for one of the **Mono Lake Committee** (☎ **760/647-6595**) canoe tours. Led by local environmentalists and ecologists, these tours are given each weekend in the summer, leaving early to beat the blasting winds that pick up in the afternoon. Only 12 spots are open for each trip. You'll see seabird-nesting islands, tufa towers, brine shrimp, and a whole lot of other things you've probably never even imagined. Call ahead to reserve a spot and get directions to the put-in place. If you

BELATED GOLD RUSH: SETTLING THE EASTERN SIERRA

The Owens Valley/eastern Sierra area was one of the last regions settled in California. Spanish settlers never crossed the Sierra from the west, leaving the native Paiutes in peace to hunt the herds of pronghorn antelope and deer. After Mexico seceded from Spain in 1821, however, the Mexican government began to lose its grip on California, leaving a power vacuum that the United States would seize as an opportunity to expand its territory. Between 1825 and 1845, explorers like Peter Ogden, Jedediah Smith, Joseph Walker, and Captain John Fremont led expeditions that mapped the Great Basin and crossed the Sierra Nevada but established no settlements on the eastern side. Even the gold rush left the southeastern Sierra unsettled. Then, as now, the best mountain pass for wagon trains and heavy traffic was Donner Pass, north of Lake Tahoe, and settlers streamed that way, leaving the land to the south unexplored until later. Until the boomtown growth of Los Angeles in the second half of the 20th century made Mammoth the closest major mountain resort to millions of people, this side of the Sierra was a peaceful backwater.

Leroy Vining, from whom the present-day town of Lee Vining gets its name, was the first to cross back over the range and begin serious gold exploration on this side. He found gold, though not in the quantities being extracted from the placer fields and hard-rock mines of the west slope, but enough to make other miners take notice and begin their own explorations.

By the 1880s, the initial gold rush was petering out on the west slope and thousands crossed back over the Sierra in search of new gold deposits. **Mammoth City,** a town of 2,000 on the site of modern-day Mammoth Lakes, boomed and busted between 1878 and 1881 at an incredible cost in human suffering when a fire destroyed most of the town during a harsh winter and miners were left to fend for themselves without substantial shelter.

Near Mono Lake, the gold and silver mining community of **Bodie** fared better. At one point more than 30 mines employed 10,000 miners and created a booming economy of vice based on hookers, whiskey, and guns. Sixty-five bars and brothels competed with only two churches for the townspeople's attention. Murders were so common they scarcely rated mention in the paper. The town's own people bragged that it was the most lawless place on earth, and for a few years it probably was. More than $30 million worth of gold and silver was scraped out of the hills above town, but by 1890 most of the mines were closed. The turn of the century left Bodie a ghost town, much of which remains preserved in Bodie State Historic Park.

have your own boat and decide to do it yourself, put in at **Navy Beach** off State Route 120 on the south shore. Keep a large (1-mile) buffer zone between yourself and the nesting birds to prevent them from panicking and crushing eggs.

CROSS-COUNTRY SKIING

The eastern Sierra boasts some amazing cross-country skiing. The snow here is dryer and lighter than on the west slope, so you'll stand less chance of becoming mired in the legendary Sierra cement. Terrain ranges from groomed flat tracks to the ultimate Sierra haute route through

Kings Canyon National Park, with lots in between.

Backcountry

The mining and logging history of the eastern Sierra has laced the range with countless dirt roads that go unplowed in the winter, perfect for self-guided backcountry skiing. Possibilities range from an easy ski to a beautiful hot spring to hair-raising plunges down the couloirs of the Sherwins.

Avalanche danger is high in this part of the Sierra; heavy snows, steep pitches, and changing weather make for perfect avalanche conditions. Before heading into the backcountry, make yourself aware of local conditions by calling the nearest ranger station. I once was snowed in at Tamarack Lodge for 4 days when an avalanche buried the snowplow (a huge Caterpillar tractor) up to its roof and closed Lake Mary Road. The driver was okay, but then again, he was inside the cab of a huge tractor. A lone skier wouldn't have fared so well.

Strong intermediate and advanced skiers may want to tackle something a little more intense than the standard single-day backcountry trips and try a multiday trek. But unless you're an expert on winter camping, emergency first aid, avalanche dangers, and alpine weather conditions, setting out alone and unprepared can be extremely dangerous. Contact **John Fisher, Mountain Guide,** P.O. Box 694, Bishop, CA 93515 (☎ **760/873-5037**), who will provide guidance. **Alpine Skills International,** P.O. Box 8, Norden, CA 95724 (☎ **530/426-9108**), teaches multiday advanced ski mountaineering courses each spring in the Palisade Glacier area to prepare strong skiers for the challenges of High Country crossings. *Backcountry Skiing in the High Sierra* by John Moynier (Chockstone Press, 1992) is a great guidebook to the more advanced backcountry skiing in the Sierra, including the High Route and other trans-Sierra crossings.

Bodie State Park

Distance depends on how far from the park the road is closed by snow. Strong beginner/intermediate. Varied trails. Access: 7 miles south of Bridgeport, turn east on State Rte. 270. Park is in 13 miles; road will probably be closed a short distance before.

It's a simple thing to ski into Bodie down the summertime road, and you're likely to have it all to yourself. Nothing could be more ghostly than this ghost town blanketed with snow during a winter storm. The weather here sucks in winter—you'll understand why the people left.

Obsidian Dome Trails, June Lake Area

Approximately 10km (16 miles) of trails but varies widely with snow conditions. Strong beginner/intermediate. Varied trails. Access: 11 miles north of Mammoth Lakes on U.S. 395. Forest Road 2S10. Park just off highway.

All trails begin with a 0.3 kilometers (half a mile) ski west from the trailhead until you reach a large meadow. From here, trails branch off into three loops, two beginners and an intermediate. The beginner trails circle through trees and small meadows. The intermediate loop climbs gently to a great view of Obsidian Dome, a large volcanic dome. The loop circles counterclockwise and returns to the parking area.

Shady Rest Loop, Mammoth Lakes

7.4km of trails. Beginner. Access: Trail begins at the USFS Visitors Center on State Rte. 203 as you enter Mammoth Lakes. Park in the Forest Service lot.

One of the most popular beginning ski areas in Mammoth Lakes, the flat Shady Rest Loop begins practically at the **USFS Visitors Center** (☎ **760/934-2505**) door. Stop by the center first and pick up the brochure describing the several loops that wind through a grove of Jeffrey pines.

Pay to Park

Certain parking areas for cross-country skiing trails now fall under the category of California Sno-Park. You need to purchase a permit to park here or you'll get a hefty fine. Daily or annual Sno-Park permits can be bought in most sporting-goods and ski shops.

CALIFORNIA'S GREAT SALT LAKE

Mono Lake, just east of Yosemite National Park, is a remarkable inland sea and one of the most troubled ecosystems in the state. The first pioneers to see this great saline lake in the 1800s described it as lifeless and hideous, the Dead Sea of California, but the Kutsadika Paiute tribe of Native Americans who lived here knew different. Brine fly grubs, a fantastic source of protein, were their chief staple, and they traded them with neighboring tribes for acorns.

Though the lake's water is so saline that only brine shrimp can live in it, and the surrounding salt plains so brutal as to only support brine flies, this seeming lack of diversity creates an interesting and delicate ecosystem. Those swarming brine flies that you'll find so annoying on your visit are food for the 85% of California's seagull population that comes here to nest each spring, as well as another 300 bird species that nest here in lesser numbers. Because the brine shrimp's traditional predators—fish—can't survive here to cull their numbers, the tiny shrimp multiply with such fecundity that by the middle of summer the lake is teeming with an estimated 4 trillion of them. At the same time the fledgling gulls reach maturity and turn to this rich and plentiful food source while they begin to fly and forage for themselves, generally the most dangerous time for young birds. Soon they are strong enough to fend for themselves and migrate back to their more traditional habitat, the ocean and bays of the West Coast.

Crowded on weekends, this is a great place for a midweek ski.

Hot Creek, Mammoth Lakes
16km round-trip. Beginner/intermediate. Access: Take Rte. 203 from Mammoth Lakes for 3 miles, then turn left on Fish Hatchery Rd. Continue another mile to sign for Hot Creek. Park where road ends, depending on snow levels, and continue on the snow-covered road on skis.

Four miles out of town near the Mammoth Airport, Hot Creek is one of the most popular winter attractions for skiers, snowshoers, and, unfortunately, snowmobilers. From the end of the road, you'll have no trouble following other tracks on the slightly pitched trail. Clouds of steam should be visible to your left in all but the worst conditions. Eventually you'll pass a gate (if the snow isn't too deep) and slope downhill. About 1 kilometer (1.6 miles) later you'll see Hot Creek with the bubbling thermal springs feeding it. The USFS discourages people from bathing in the creek as certain areas reach 210°F, but hundreds of people ignore the warning every year and have a great time. If you choose to take a dip, be extremely careful; people have died here. To return to your car, follow the same route in reverse.

Inyo Craters, Mammoth Lakes
8km round-trip. Intermediate. Access: From State Rte. 203 turn right on Mammoth Lakes Scenic Loop. Parking area in 3.5 miles on north side of road.

Begin by skiing a short distance down the snow-covered road. You'll see a blue diamond marker on the right saying Inyo Craters. Follow blue diamonds through a few zigzags and then the trail becomes more obvious. In about 3 kilometers (5 miles) is the final ascent to the summit of the craters. While the trail is mostly easy, some very steep cornices and drop-offs are nearby. Be careful. The view is worth the climb. Return the way you came.

Red Cones Trail, Mammoth Lakes
17.5km round-trip. Advanced intermediate/advanced. Large elevation changes. Access: Tamarack Lodge at the end of Lake Mary Road.

Though you'll ski right through the Tamarack area on your route, resist the temptation of those groomed tracks and follow the free public access corridor up the snow-covered roadbed of Lake Mary

Road until you reach Horseshoe Lake 5 kilometers later. It's a gentle but steady climb with beautiful views back toward town and of the surrounding peaks. Once you reach Horseshoe Lake, begin looking for the blue diamond trail that leaves from the north end of a large flat expanse (no, not the frozen lake) that is a summer parking lot. Follow the blue diamonds another 4 kilometers up through a rolling forest. Red Cones summits are hidden until you are nearly upon them. You'll break out of the trees and climb a few hundred yards to the summit where on a clear day you can see incredible distances in every direction.

Rock Creek (Tom's Place to Rock Creek Road)

6 to 8km round-trip. Beginner/intermediate. 400-ft. elevation gain. Access: 17 miles south of Mammoth Lakes on 395, turn off at Tom's Place on Rock Creek Rd. In a little more than 5 miles you'll see the Sno-Park Area (fee required) and East Fork Campground.

From the parking area, ski the 3 kilometers uphill to Rock Creek Lodge. You're in a steep canyon, so be aware of avalanche danger. When you reach the lodge you can either turn around and head home, or ski another kilometer (intermediate) or so to the Twelve Peaks View, a striking spot with a view of some of the biggest peaks in the Sierra Nevada and all the valleys below. Return to your car the way you came.

Overnights

Sierra Haute Route (Independence to Kings Canyon)

51 miles total over 7–9 days. Advanced. Guides strongly recommended. Access: Trailhead begins at Symmes Creek and ends at Wolverton Cross-Country Ski Area inside Sequoia/Kings Canyon National Parks.

There are more famous multiday routes in North America, but the High Route, with 40 miles of backcountry skiing over 10,000 feet, is widely held to be the best high-altitude crossing in the Lower 48. Above tree line for all but a few miles of its course, the High Route has a little of everything the advanced skier could ask for: high traverses, several 12,000-foot–plus passes, open bowls, unbelievable scenery, and great snow. It can be heaven or it can be hell, depending on the weather you encounter, but there's no place in the state like this: views for literally hundreds of miles, untracked powder, 4,000-foot downhills, and probably not another person within miles. Following the boundary between Sequoia and Kings Canyon National Parks along the divide between the Kings and Kaweah rivers, the route climbs from the Symmes Creek Trailhead at 6,300 feet outside Independence to the route's high point at 13,000-foot Milestone Pass. After days above tree line the trail ends as you ski down into the giant sequoia groves of the national park's Giant Forest. For a good primer on routes and resources, read *Backcountry Skiing in the High Sierra* by John Moynier (Chockstone Press, 1992).

Nordic Skiing Centers

Two well-managed Nordic skiing operations are within close distance of Mammoth Lakes. **Tamarack Lodge and Cross-Country Ski Area (☎ 760/934-2442)** has 30 miles of groomed trails in the stunning Mammoth Lakes Basin at the very end of Lake Mary Road. With rentals, nice lodgings, lessons, and a four-star restaurant on the edge of a stunning winter wilderness, Tamarack is a great all-in-one resort. The groomed runs are arranged in a series of interlocking loops with dual tracks spaced wide enough apart that you can skate in the middle. Most of the larger loops are relatively flat and marked BEGINNING. To spice things up you can take the steep connector trails, marked blue or black, between loops. Beyond that, miles of backcountry skiing in the Lakes Basin begin where the groomed trails end. Adult ski passes are $15 per day, and afternoon passes are $10.

DOGSLEDDING

Dogsled Adventures (☎ 760/934-6270) runs daily half-hour and hour-long sled tours (weather and snow conditions permitting) from the Mammoth Mountain Inn next door to the Main Lodge of Mammoth Mountain. For between $40 and $70, depending on the length of the trip, you'll be trundled in a sled driven by a professional musher and pulled by 10 specially bred dogs on a tour of the Minaret Vista Loop. An interesting side trip is to visit the Dogsled Adventures Kennel, the only professional breeding kennel for sled dogs in California. Most of the puppies are spoken for well ahead of time, so you'll be safe from impulse buying.

DOWNHILL SKIING & SNOWBOARDING

For better or worse, downhill skiing is the economic engine that drives the part of the eastern Sierra around Mammoth Mountain. If it weren't for skiing, the town of **Mammoth Lakes** would have no reason to exist. The ski area employs almost 2,000 people directly, and tourist traffic supports many more. Though it's 350 miles away, this is where Los Angeles comes to play in the mountains. It's interesting to spend an entire week here: Monday through Friday it's a nice mountain town filled with nice mountain people. Friday night the glitter and clamor of Los Angeles comes roaring up U.S. 395 in a thousand ski-racked luxury wagons, the condos light up, the mountain is a sea of speeding neon, and the Ralph Lauren Polo outlet does brisk business. Come Monday the hordes go home and it's a mellow mountain town again.

A different kind of boomtown was born in the 1930s when Dave McCoy, a hydrologist for the Los Angeles Department of Water and Power, was sent into these mountains to measure winter snowfall. He discovered that Mammoth Mountain gets more snow than any other similarly sized peak in the Sierra, more than 25 feet per year, and some of the best.

Starting with a Model A engine-powered rope tow, McCoy eventually turned **Mammoth Mountain** and its smaller sister **June Mountain** into one of the biggest skiing operations in the country, with the longest season. In 1995, a record snow year, the mountain opened in November and was still open into August. The ski area regularly stays open until late May or June. And since both June and Mammoth are owned by the McCoy family, they are run on a completely interchangeable lift-ticket system—two mountains for the price of one. Make sure to ask about package deals when you call.

Mammoth Mountain

1 Minaret Rd., Mammoth Lakes, CA 93546. ☎ **760/934-2571** for tickets; 760/934-6166 for snow conditions. 150 named trails (30% beginner, 40% intermediate, 30% expert); 30 lifts including 7 high-speed quads, 3 quads, 7 triples, 10 doubles, 2 gondolas, and 1 poma; 3,100-ft. vertical drop. Full-day adult ticket $49.

Though named after a fossilized woolly mammoth skeleton found years ago near what is now the base lodge, Mammoth is mammoth in the other meaning of the word too: 11,053-foot summit elevation, 3,500 skiable acres, 30 modern lifts, 150 trails, and some of the woolliest terrain of any California ski area. Any talk of the mountain being a certain percentage beginner, a certain percentage intermediate, and a certain percentage advanced is pretty much beside the point; there's too much of all of it for any one person to ski in a weekend.

Maybe it's the Southern California surfer influence, maybe just economic prudence, but Mammoth was a snowboard-friendly mountain back when everyone else was telling boarders to beat it. It has several full-time snowboarders on the ski-patrol staff as well as a nationally recommended snowboard school and a full supply of quality gear for sale and rent in the base lodges. There's also a half-pipe and trick area just for snowboarders.

June Mountain

85 Boulder Rd., June Lake, CA 93529. ☎ **760/648-7733** for tickets; 760/934-2224 for snow conditions. 35 trails (35% beginner, 45% intermediate, 20% advanced); 8 lifts including 2 high-speed quads, 5 doubles, and 1 rope tow; 2,590-ft. vertical drop. Full-day adult ticket $40.

Forty-five minutes to the north of Mammoth, June Mountain is the place to get away from the glitz and glam, not to mention the crowd, of Mammoth. At 10,135 feet, June Mountain is no small potato, but it somehow feels much more intimate than the mammoth Mammoth. It also has better weather. When the wind closes most of Mammoth, come here and you'll likely find more manageable conditions.

The first thing you'll see driving into the base area is a daunting wall of advanced runs. Don't worry—the top half of the mountain is where all the intermediate and beginning runs are located. A tram will take you up and down. For snowboarders, June has one of the best half-pipes in the country and all sorts of trick riding props. This was the first California mountain to open all its terrain to snowboarders and remains a leader on the snowboard scene.

FISHING

Despite the wholesale looting of most of the water on this side of the Sierra by the Los Angeles Department of Water and Power, the eastern Sierra and Owens Valley remains an incredible trout fishery. Fly fishermen flock to Bishop to cast the few remaining stretches of the **Owens River,** and each spring hundreds of boats troll for trophy trout on **Lake Crowley.**

The landscape has changed, but it's still beautiful and rich.

Virtually every species of trout can be caught here, including the rare golden trout and cutthroat trout. Trophy German brown and rainbow trout have come out of too many lakes to even bother mentioning. Just go look at the photos in Tamarack Lodge or the marina at Crowley Lake and you'll get the picture. For detailed recommendations of where to satisfy your particular fishing itch, call one of the following shops: **Mammoth Sporting Goods** (☎ 760/934-8474), **The Trout Fly** (☎ 760/934-2517), or **Village Sports Center** (☎ 760/934-8220).

Two resorts cater to fly fishermen on private stretches of catch-and-release creeks. **Hot Creek Ranch** (☎ 760/935-4214) has 2.5 miles of private frontage on Spring Creek as well as easy access to the public areas of Hot Creek. With cabins, a fly shop, and beautiful views, you could drive in once and never want or need to leave.

Alpers Ranch (☎ 760/648-7334) is farther north of Mammoth Lakes, near the headwaters of the Owens River. Several miles of the Owens are available for ranch guests to catch-and-release. Ranch owner Tim Alpers allows catch-and-keep fishing on a pond where he raises trout to plant in local lakes and rivers. Accommodations are in simple cabins and there's a small store on site.

HIKES, BUSHWHACKS & BACKPACK TRIPS

Two of the most famous West Coast trails, the **John Muir Trail** and the **Pacific Crest Trail,** run through this area and lure hikers from all over, but you can find just as much solitude and beauty on hundreds of other hikes and overnights. The ranger stations for each particular section of the eastern Sierra are good places to ask for hikes geared toward a special interest or ability level. There aren't really any great general-interest hiking guidebooks to this area other than R. J. Secor's *The High Sierra* (The Mountaineers, 1992), which concentrates largely on peak bagging.

Day Hikes

San Joaquin Ridge, Devils Postpile

4 miles round-trip. Moderate. Steady uphill and then back down. Allow 3 hr. Access: Minaret Vista parking lot on State Rte. 203 past Mammoth Mountain. Map: Devils Postpile map.

To get that High Country feeling without too much actual climbing, San Joaquin Ridge is a great hike. Shortly after beginning the hike in a lodgepole pine forest, you'll break through tree line and remain here most of the hike. Above tree line doesn't mean barren, though, and during the summer you'll find an incredible garden of tiny wildflowers and rock-clinging lichen. After about 2 miles of steady uphill along this rocky ridge, you'll reach an unnamed 10,255-foot summit. Soak up the view and return the way you came.

Convict Lake Round-Trip

3 miles. Easy. Access: Take Convict Lake Rd. to lake. Park near boat ramp. Trail circles lake.

This is a great choice for a leisurely afternoon that combines a hike with a picnic, some fishing, or a nice swim. You can hike either direction around the lake. A boardwalk will help you cross the boggy meadow where the creek enters the lake. For swimming, fishing, and the like, shoreline access is better along the northwest side of the lake. This hike is good for kids, though there are a few spots with steep drop-offs. Allow several hours and you'll have time to play.

Little Lakes Valley

4–8 miles depending on turnaround. Moderate. Access: From U.S. 395 drive to dead-end of Rock Creek Rd. at Mosquito Flat. Map: Inyo National Forest map.

Little Lakes Valley is one of those magical remnants of the glacial age. Surrounded by peaks and ridges that tower several thousand feet above the valley floor, this glacial valley is sprinkled with 40 lakes, streams, and beautiful meadows. From the trailhead, it's about 2 miles to Long Lake. From here, it's about another 2 miles to the crystalline Gem Lakes. There's plenty in between. Pack a picnic and just explore the area. You won't be let down.

Lundy Lake to Crystal Lake and May Lundy Mine

6 miles round-trip. Moderate. Allow 4 hr. Access: North of Lee Vining on U.S. 395, turn west on Lundy Lake Rd. Drive 3 miles until the road forks. Take the left fork and park near the gate below the dam. Map: Inyo National Forest map.

This hike grants a glimpse of the hardscrabble life of a hard-rock miner. As you climb the 2,000 feet to the May Lundy Mine, you'll feel for the poor suckers who spent years scouring gold from these hills. When the climb passes the cascading falls, look for evidence of the old waterwheel and pipes in the creek. At Crystal Lake you'll find the remains of a small town: boarding houses, cabins, old stores, and the old stamp mill that brought crushed ore down from the May Lundy. The lower tunnel of the May Lundy is located at 11,000 feet, on the slope of Lake Canyon; other shafts are much higher. Oneida Lake is behind the old settlement. Return the way you came.

Rainbow Falls, Devils Postpile

4 miles round-trip. Moderate. Allow 2.5 hr. Access: Via Devils Postpile shuttle bus. Map: Devils Postpile National Monument map.

From the separate Rainbow Falls Trailhead (stay on the shuttle past Agnew Meadows), this short hike will take you to the edge of spectacular Rainbow Falls, where the entire middle fork of the San Joaquin River catapults 101 feet off a lava cliff. The falls is more notable for the sheer volume of water pouring over it than anything else, though it's also one of

THE OWENS VALLEY WATER WARS

A little history is crucial to any understanding of contemporary water politics on the eastern slope of the Sierra Nevada. At the turn of the century, Los Angeles was a sleepy little city with lots of orange trees, nice beaches, and virtually no water. Not such a bad place really, but a group of "visionary" city businessmen and politicians had a different idea about the future of L.A. Led by city water-czar William Mulholland and with the complicity of the *Los Angeles Times,* the city began to pursue a two-pronged strategy of scaring people in Los Angeles into believing that there was a drought and they'd soon be drinking sand if something wasn't done, and of using underhanded techniques like lawsuits and physical threats to condemn land and purchase water rights from ranchers in the Owens Valley.

By November 1913, the first water flowed into the Owens Valley Aqueduct, destined for the so-called City of Angels. Though local opponents went as far as bombing the aqueduct 17 times in protest, the plug had been pulled on the Owens Valley and there was no going back. The ranching economy withered, and the formerly lush valley was transformed into a desolate, dusty place dominated by an alkali flat where Owens Lake once was.

Owens Lake was only the first place to fall to quench L.A.'s thirst. By 1930, Mulholland's aqueduct had created blossoming growth in L.A. and the city numbered over 1 million citizens. Still convinced that they needed more water for more growth, city residents voted in 1930 to expand the Owens Valley Aqueduct all the way to Mono Lake. By 1941, every major tributary to the inland sea had been diverted south.

As a result, the level of the lake began dropping and the ecology of the lake suffered. One of the two largest bird-breeding islands became a peninsula as the water level dropped, and coyotes ravaged the nesting bird population. Increasing salinity also affected lake species. By the 1970s, a band of loosely knit environmentalists, local residents, and ranchers began to take on the Los Angeles Department of Water and Power, first with guerrilla theater actions and protests, later with lawsuits. One of these lawsuits, which reached the state Supreme Court in 1983, would impact all California environmental battles.

The justices ruled that all the natural resources in the state—lakes, rivers, beaches, open space, the air—are owned by the people and must be managed by the state for the good of the people. Called the Public Trust Doctrine, this legal precedent established the right of citizens' groups to sue for compensation or injunction whenever and wherever the public trust is infringed. It soon became one of the most powerful tools for environmental protection.

The Owens Valley is still an artificial desert, while Los Angeles is an artificial oasis. Because of court rulings, the level of Mono Lake has stopped dropping and the ecological damage has been stabilized, but no real agreement has been reached between the warring factions about what the final level will be and how much water can be diverted.

---

the highest falls outside the Yosemite Valley. A small trail leads to swimming and fishing holes below the base of the falls.

Thousand Island Lake Loop, Devils Postpile
18 miles. Strenuous. Allow all day and pack a flashlight just in case. Access: Agnew Meadows Trailhead (take Devils Postpile Shuttle from Mammoth Mountain Inn). Map: Devils Postpile and John Muir Wilderness maps.

Eighteen miles is one hell of a long day, especially at high altitude, but this is one of the finest loop hikes in the world. Taking its name from a strange lake at the headwaters of the San Joaquin River speckled with hundreds of small granite islands, the loop begins following the San

Joaquin River Gorge for 7 steady uphill miles, puts you at Thousand Island Lake in time for lunch and a swim, and then sends you home via the High Trail (trail junction 1 mile below the lake on the river trail). The High Trail takes you far above the river gorge on a ridge overlooking the surrounding peaks. Since the last bus leaves the Agnew Meadows lot around 5:30pm, either hoof it out in time or plan to drive into Agnew before the 7:30am cut-off time for private traffic into Devils Postpile.

Overnights

Lake Sabrina to Hungry Packer Lake
12.6 miles round-trip. Moderate. 3 or 4 days. Access: From Bishop follow State Rte. 168 west where a sign says NORTH LAKE AND SOUTH LAKE. At 9 miles you'll pass a ranger station where wilderness permits are available. Follow the signs until you reach the Sabrina Basin hikers' parking lot. Map: Inyo National Forest map and Mt. Goddard topo.

Lake Sabrina Basin is the more popular name for the Middle Fork Bishop Creek Drainage, the largest drainage in this part of the Sierra. This incredible glacier-carved bowl has more than 40 lakes between the altitude of 9,000 and 12,400 feet. The north and south forks of Bishop Creek have almost 60 more. During peak season, from July 1 to September 15, the Forest Service limits the number of hikers allowed into Sabrina Basin to enhance the wilderness experience and protect habitat. With some planning, though, you should have no trouble getting a permit for this hike.

Because no trails lead from Sabrina Basin to Kings Canyon National Park, the middle fork doesn't see quite the heavy use that the other Bishop Creek drainages do. From the parking area walk south 0.5 miles to the signed trailhead. As the trail skirts the east shore of Lake Sabrina, you'll have a good view of what's to come through stunted pines and junipers. In a mile or so you'll be joined by the George

Lake Trail. Steer right and head up a switchbacked trail to Blue Lake. Beautiful and close to the trailhead, Blue Lake is a popular layover and destination in its own right, but keep going. You'll cross Blue Lake's outlet creek and continue along the west shore.

The trail then gets faint and heads in several directions. You want to bear west toward Emerald Lakes and then Dingleberry Lake—13,435-foot Mount Haeckel is a good landmark because it is just behind your destination. Just above Dingleberry you'll have to cross the middle fork (be careful in early season). The trail heads over a ridge where you can see most of the middle fork below. Soon you'll cross the outlet creek of Hungry Packer and climb to the lake's basin. Campsites are plentiful and the fishing is good. Many good day hikes round out a long weekend here.

Mount Whitney
22 miles round-trip. Difficult. 10,000-ft. elevation gain/loss. The longest overnight of your life. Access: Take Whitney Portal Rd. from Lone Pine until it dead-ends. Map: USGS Mt. Whitney topo.

You wouldn't think that the highest point in the Lower 48 could be reached by walking up a clearly marked trail with no technical climbing required, but that's exactly what Mount Whitney is, a walk up. From Whitney Portal Road you'll follow the Whitney Trail, a virtual superhighway, through an astounding number of switchbacks until it intersects with the John Muir Trail. You'll probably want to camp as high up the Whitney Trail as you can at Trail Camp, beyond which the only water is snow. In the morning, it is 2 miles of switchbacks to the John Muir Trail and another 2 miles to Whitney Summit. At 14,494 feet, this is the highest you can get in the continental United States. A hut and outhouse mark the summit. Even though the walk up is relatively easy, be aware of any symptoms of acute mountain sickness such as nausea, confusion, loss of coordination, and headache. If any in your party are experiencing these symptoms, turn around and head down. They'll improve quickly as you lose altitude.

The hardest thing about the Whitney Trail is securing a permit to do it. The Forest Service only accepts applications for summit permits by mail and strictly enforces the system. Conceivably you could do the whole hike in 1 day and circumvent the permit process, but you better be in really good shape before attempting it. Almost half the people who attempt Whitney, including those who camp partway up, don't reach the summit. Weather, altitude, and fatigue can all conspire to stop even the most prepared party. Send your application to the rangers' office in Lone Pine in the spring to guarantee a permit for the summer. The address is **Mount Whitney Rangers Station,** 640 S. Main St., Lone Pine, CA 93545 (☎ **760/876-6200**). Make sure to include the date you want and the number in your party. You can also receive a permit by writing to the rangers' office at **Sequoia National Park,** Ash Mountain, P.O. Box 10, Three Rivers, CA 93271 (☎ **209/565-3341**). When parking is a problem at the trailhead, the chamber of commerce in Lone Pine runs a shuttle.

HORSEBACK RIDING

Horses are big business on this side of the Sierra, and there are lots of people just itching to take you on a packstock trip of the High Sierra or a short day ride. These are the biggest operators, but many other smaller ones are available seasonally or part-time:

- **Agnew Meadows Pack Station,** Minaret Vista Road (☎ **760/934-6633**), offers 2-hour, half-day, and extended overnights into the wilderness around Devils Postpile.

- **Mammoth Lakes Pack Outfit,** Lake Mary Road past Tamarack Lodge (☎ **760/934-2434**), leads 3- to 6-day

backcountry trips all over the eastern Sierra. Trips are tailored to individual groups. It also runs horseback riding and wilderness photography workshops.

- **McGee Creek Pack Station,** McGee Creek Road, Crowley Lake (☎ **760/935-4324**), specializes in long backcountry trips into the John Muir Wilderness through McGee Canyon.

- **Mike Morgan's Bishop Pack Outfitters** in Bishop (☎ **760/873-4785**) leads 2-hour, half-day, and all-day rides into the Sabrina and Humphrey basins, as well as a dinner ride by special request for large groups.

- **Red's Meadow Resort and Pack Station** (☎ **760/934-2345**) offers overnights, multiday trips, and dinner wagon rides near Rainbow Falls, Red's Meadow, and Red's Meadow Hot Springs.

- **Sierra Meadows Ranch,** practically in the town of Mammoth Lakes (☎ **760/934-6161**), is a complete equestrian center oriented toward daily events rather than overnight pack trips. Sleigh rides are given in winter.

- **Wolf Creek Pack Station** in Markleeville (☎ **702/345-6104**) specializes in backcountry fishing, hunting, and camping trips in the Mokelumne Wilderness.

HOT SPRINGS

The violent volcanism that is still forming the Sierra Nevada has one very soothing and gentle side effect: hot springs. The eastern slope is positively dripping with them. Besides well-known ones like **Hot Creek** near the Mammoth Airport, and **Grover Hot Springs State Park** outside Markleeville, hundreds of others dot the landscape. *Great Hot Springs of the West* (Capra Press, 1993) is a good guide to developed springs in the whole West, but for the really out-there and hidden springs, you'll need to seek out local advice. For obvious reasons, locals are sometimes loath to reveal their secret skinny-dipping spot to the first yahoo to stagger up to them on a street corner bellowing, "Where are all the cool hot springs?" Take a more subtle approach and you might be rewarded with some great surprises.

MOUNTAIN BIKING

No other place in the state is as well suited to the serious mountain biker, and no other place is as unforgiving. Rides out here usually begin somewhere around 9,000 feet and head up. For someone coming from any of California's sea-level population centers, the effect is like having one of your lungs removed, and I don't care how bad-ass you think you are. Also, except for right around Mammoth, rides in the eastern Sierra tend to take you a long way from nowhere and then a little farther. Know how to fix anything that can break on a ride or you'll find yourself 25 miles from help and walking. Of course, the bright side is that you can do a 50-mile bike ride and never see another cyclist. And where else can you bike to the top of a 14,000-foot peak or out into a desert filled with hidden hot springs?

Far and away the best local guidebook for any sport on the eastern Sierra is Don and Reanne Douglass's *Mountain Biking the High Sierra: Mammoth Lakes and Mono County* (Fine Edge Productions, 1992). If you are really serious about biking the eastern Sierra, buy this book.

Several shops in the area rent mountain bikes. In Mammoth Lakes, call **Kittredge Sports** (☎ 760/934-7566), or **Village Sports Center** (☎ 760/934-8220). In Bishop, call **Bikes of Bishop** (☎ 760/872-3829).

Mammoth Mountain Bike Park
Various trails for all levels of ability. Access: Mammoth Mountain Ski Area (1 Minaret Rd., Mammoth). Map: Mammoth Mountain map.

When the snow finally melts off Mammoth Mountain, generally in July, the ski company turns Mammoth into a mountain biking park. For a price, you and your bike can ride the lifts to the top of Mammoth Mountain and spend the 3,000 and something feet of vertical you just cheated headed down any number of trails. Each year at the beginning of July, the mountain is host to the Grundig World Cup/Reebok Eliminator National Mountain Biking Championships, where you can watch clinically insane pros hurtle down the kamikaze hill, pushing 70 and 80 miles per hour. The mountain also rents bikes and will sell you any bike parts you break trying to mimic those pros.

Inyo Craters Loop
8 miles. Moderate. Access: From Mammoth Scenic Loop park at Forest Rd. 3S22 or 3S30.

A whole mess of fire and jeep roads cut through this area, and it's likely you'll get lost. So what. Just remember that the Scenic Loop is to the southeast and have a good time. Ideally you'll be able to follow the signs marking the trail to the top of Inyo Craters. You'll have to walk your bike to the edge of the craters themselves. These mini-volcanoes are the youngest major geologic feature in the Sierra Nevada, probably only about 1,500 years old. Several hundred feet deep, the craters blew more than 5 million tons of debris in a violent explosion of volcanic gas. Think about that on your ride back to town.

Deadman Creek to June Lake
About 20 miles. Difficult. Access: Upper Deadman Campground. Map: Inyo National Forest map.

This all-day ride is the high road for advanced cyclists between Mammoth and June lakes. It requires good route-finding skills, as well as the stamina to tackle a grueling rocky climb. There are many ways to hook up with the trail in the before-mentioned mess of jeep trails near Inyo Craters. Either way, what you're looking for is Upper Deadman Campground. (Use your Forest Service map.) From there the narrow dirt road continues up for about 5.5 miles until reaching a ridge and veering into the headwaters of Deadman Creek. In another mile, the road shoots uphill again and gets really rocky. At 7 miles (after a hellacious climb) you crest out in the very headwaters of the Owens River, where the water pouring out of all those taps in Los Angeles gets its start. The road peters out in the debris of an old avalanche. A hiking trail leads from the nearby knoll down into June Lake for several miles of tough and bushy single track.

Upper Owens River Gorge Loops

Distances vary. Easy. Mostly flat roads and trails. Access: North and east of Tom's Place, take Rd. 4S02 off U.S. 395. Park immediately.

A number of relatively flat and easy loops take advantage of the numerous roads and trails out to the Owens River Gorge, a dramatic rift carved by the river into soft volcanic stone. This is also a famous climbing area. It may appear barren at first glance, but the sagebrush plain is home to hawks, deer, burros, and the occasional pronghorn. From U.S. 395 the gorge is north and slightly west toward Crowley Lake. Head off across the sagebrush plains and hills until the earth opens in front of you. Head up- or downstream on the rim or take the hand-carved trail to the canyon bottom and follow the creek upstream to Crowley. A paved road will take you to the canyon rim. Return to U.S. 395 when you've had enough. I know these directions are really nondirections, but the beauty of this spot is that you are able to explore so many options on a whim and the road will always be to

your south. Go ahead, get lost. Then figure out which way south is and take a fire road that way. Wow, look, a highway and your car.

Shady Rest to Lookout Mountain

16 miles round-trip. Moderate. Access: Shady Rest Campground off State Rte. 203 in Mammoth Lakes. Map: Inyo National Forest or Mammoth Lakes tourist map.

This is a good first ride to get acclimated to the elevation before heading for the bigger stuff. In 16 miles you only gain about 1,000 feet, yet the view of the surrounding area is fantastic. The route is entirely paved or well-graded dirt. As you climb Lookout Mountain, the last 2 miles to the summit are steep but not unreasonable and the road-bed is good. When you reach the top, the Sierra Nevada is to your west and the White Mountains to the east. You should be able to see for miles on a clear day.

ROAD BIKING

There really aren't many paved roads on this side of the Sierra, so the ones that are here tend to be popular with cars too. Unless you're training for some gnarly road race and want to ride skinny wheels at altitude (many great road racers do train here for the hills, altitude, and good weather), I recommend using a mountain bike or at least a good cross bike, even for road rides, simply because there are so many tempting dirt roads and side paths you won't want to miss. See "Mountain Biking," above, for rental shops.

Long Valley Crowley Lake Road Ride

16 miles round-trip. Easy. Moderately hilly. Access: Crowley Lake Dr. junction with U.S. 395. Crowley Lake Rd. parallels U.S. 395 south to Tom's Place and Rock Creek Rd.

Moderate hills and light traffic make this a perfect ride to get acclimated to the thin air here. You're between the freeway and the mountains, with amazing views in every direction and a perfect spot to call the sag wagon (from Tom's Place) if the altitude is slaying you. Return to your car the way you came.

Rock Creek Road

16–24 miles round-trip. Very difficult. Access: Park at Tom's Place 17 miles south of Mammoth Lakes on U.S. 395.

Okay, so yesterday you rode Crowley Lake Road and it didn't even make you sweat. Drive or ride back out to Tom's Place and ride up Rock Creek Road and back. The 3,000-foot elevation gain within 12 miles will put the fear into you, especially considering you started at about 9,000 feet. When you're not dying from exertion, take a look around; this is one of the prettiest glacial valleys in the Sierra, filled with meadows of flowers and lakes jumping with trout. Rock Creek Lake has a store where you can buy some food or a drink before flying back down to Tom's Place or continuing another 4 miles to the end of the road at Mosquito Flat. Then head for home. Hope you have good brakes.

Death Ride Tour of the California Alps

48–130 miles. Difficulty: Read the name. Access: Town of Markleeville.

Every summer 2,500 registered riders pay good money to come to Markleeville and ride till they practically drop.

This beautiful and little-used part of the Sierra has endless opportunities for self-torture. Luckily, it's a tour, not a race, and you have several different options. Contact the **Alpine County Chamber of Commerce,** P.O. Box 265, Markleeville 96120 (☎ **530/ 694-2475**), for information and registration.

ROCK CLIMBING & MOUNTAINEERING

Long a destination for hard-core adventurers who came to ice-climb and mountaineer on the huge peaks of the Palisades and the Whitney Massif, the eastern Sierra has also suddenly boomed as a sport-climbing area. Though relatively new to the scene, the Owens River Gorge is beginning to eclipse Joshua Tree as Southern California's favorite sport-climbing outpost. Plentiful granite domes and spires around Mammoth Lakes provide more rock-climbing options.

There are several local guidebooks with route maps to areas like Rock Creek, Buttermilk, and the Owens Gorge. Check out *Rock Climbs of the Sierra East Side* by Erret Allen and Alan Bartlett (Chockstone Press, 1988), *Owens Gorge Climbs* and *Mammoth Area Rock Climbs* by Marty Lewis, or *Climber's Guide to the High Sierra* by Steve Roper (Sierra Club Books, 1976). For more advanced backcountry mountaineering and a wonderful index of peaks and their history, read *The High*

Swim at Your Own Risk

Sign at Hot Creek, the most popular hot spring in the Mammoth Lakes area:

Twelve people have lost their lives in Hot Creek since 1968 and many more have been seriously injured. Some of the hazards are scalding water, broken glass, arsenic in the water, sporadic high pollution, sudden temperature changes, unpredictable eruptions, unstable ground. It is recommended that you remain on paved and wood paths and that you do not enter the water. Some of the more dangerous areas are fenced. However, new hazards are a constant threat. Please use extreme caution.

Sierra by R. J. Secor (The Mountaineers, 1992).

SNOWSHOEING

Snowshoeing came back in fashion with the invention of smaller, lighter shoes that enable you to more or less run with snowshoes on. I, frankly, don't see why in the hell you'd want to run with snowshoes on, but then I never really got into jogging with ankle weights either. **The Great Outdoors** in Mammoth Lakes (☎ 760/924-2070) rents snowshoes, and the Tamarack Resort hosts the Great Snowshoe Race, a 10-kilometer race around the lakes basin, every January.

WALKS & RAMBLES

Hot Creek

1 mile. Well-traveled paths. Access: From U.S. 395 turn on Hot Creek Hatchery Rd. and drive to the Hot Creek Overlook (about 3 miles).

People flock here year-round to soak in the hot spring creek, but Hot Creek itself is a lot more than just a bubbling bathtub. This officially designated Wild Trout Stream is home to a great population of native trout, and fishing is catch-and-release only. Bald eagles are commonly sighted in the winter. During spring and summer, the dramatic cliffs are home to nesting swallows and other small birds. Cougars are rarely seen, but leave their sign in the form of paw prints and scat. Park at the Hot Creek Overlook and follow the trail down the hill. Dirt and wooden paths lead through the beautiful and striking thermal site with geysers and bubbling pools. You can hike either direction up and down the creek to get away from the crowd that is probably here for the spring.

Mono Lake Mark Twain Interpretive Trail

1 mile. Boardwalk trail. Access: From State Rte. 120 turn off at road to South Tufa Area–Navy Beach. Trail starts in parking area.

Interpretive signs quoting Mark Twain on this 1-mile boardwalk trail explain Mono Lake, while the trail winds through some of the best tufa towers and past a hot spring. The trail ends at Navy Beach, a popular area for taking a Mono Lake swim. Don't get the water in your eyes.

Devils Postpile

Various trails. Access: Devils Postpile National Monument Visitors Center.

There's more to Devils Postpile than a bunch of rocks, no matter how impressive they might be. Located on the banks of the San Joaquin River in the heart of a landscape of granite peaks and crystalline mountain lakes, the 800-acre park is a gateway to a hiker's paradise. Short paths lead from here to the top of the Postpile, and to Soda Springs, a spring gushing cold carbonated water.

Campgrounds & Other Accommodations

CAMPING

Ninety-nine percent of the places covered in this chapter are public land, controlled by either the National Forest Service, the National Parks Service, or the State Parks Department. While phone numbers and addresses vary for individual parks and jurisdictions, bookings for campground reservations are centralized. For all state parks call ☎ 800/444-PARK (many Forest Service campgrounds are nonreservable). To reserve campsites in Yosemite, Sequoia/Kings Canyon, and Devil's Postpile national parks call ☎ 800/365-CAMP.

Lake Tahoe & the Northern Sierra

Donner Memorial State Park

2 miles west of Truckee on Donner Pass Rd. ☎ 530/582-7892. 150 sites. Flush toilets, showers, running water, picnic tables. Hiking, mountain biking, boating, fishing, swimming. Dogs on leash permitted. $16 per night. Reserve through PARKNET (☎ 800/444-PARK).

This campground is set along Donner Lake in exactly the same location where the ill-fated Donner Party met its tragic fate You'd find it hard to believe that this beautiful spot was the site of such a horrible tragedy. There's good fishing, canoeing, and cross-country skiing here; the only drawback is the drone of nearby Interstate 80.

Sugar Pine Point State Park

18 miles north of South Lake on State Rte. 89. ☎ 530/525-7982. 175 campsites. Flush toilets, showers (summer only), store and laundry (in town), fire pits, picnic tables. Swimming, hiking, mountain biking, dinghy sailing. Dogs on leash permitted. Open year-round. $12–$16 per night. Reservations recommended in summer only (☎ 800/444-PARK).

This huge state park positively crawls with tourists in the summer. Reserve well in advance. It has nice beaches and great lakefront hiking. If you're bringing a boat, ask about the boat-in campground, far removed from the hustle and bustle of the main camping area.

East Silver Lake

State Rte. 88 near Carson Pass. ☎ 209/295-4251 (Eldorado National Forest). 62 sites. Pit toilets, running water, boat ramp, store, marina. Boating, fishing, hiking, swimming. Pets on leashes permitted. $10 per night. Reserve through PARKNET (☎ 800/280-CAMP).

Silver Lake gives the feeling of being in the backcountry even though it's easily reached by road. There's great fishing, swimming, and hiking into the Mokelumne Wilderness. The campground is wooded; some sites front the lake.

Lake Alpine

29 miles east of Arnold on State Rte. 4. ☎ 209/795-1381 (Stanislaus National Forest). 4 campgrounds with a total of nearly 100 sites. Flush toilets, showers, picnic tables, fire pits, boat launch, grocery store, rental boats, laundry. Boating, fishing, hiking, boardsailing. Pets on leashes permitted. Summer only. $14 per night. No reservations.

Lake Alpine, on the Stanislaus River, is one of the prettiest man-made lakes I've ever seen. Numerous fingers of granite reach into the lake, making perfect casting points. Several great hikes go into the Emigrant Wilderness from here or around the lake.

Pinecrest Lake

Pinecrest Lake Rd. off State Rte. 108 at 5,600 ft. ☎ 209/965-3434 (Stanislaus National Forest Summit Station). 200 sites. Running water, flush toilets, grocery store, boat ramp, marina. Sailing, fishing, hiking, boardsailing. Pets on leashes permitted. $15 per night. Reservations recommended (☎ 800/280-CAMP).

Pinecrest is another beautiful Sierra lake that could fool you into believing it's not a reservoir, except when the water level drops. It's popular with small-boat sailors because of the 20-mile-per-hour speed limit. A great trail circles the lake. Fishing for rainbow trout is good. Downstream from the dam, the Stanislaus River offers great fly-fishing.

Yosemite National Park

All car campsites in Yosemite can be reserved up to 8 weeks before date of arrival through the **PARKNET** ticket service (☎ 800/365-CAMP). During the busy season all valley campsites sell out within hours of becoming available on the service. The campgrounds below all have access to Yosemite's many activities.

Yosemite Valley Car Campgrounds

In the village. ☎ **209/372-0299.** 404 sites. Drinking water, flush toilets, pay phones, fire pits, and a heavy ranger presence. Showers are available for a fee at Curry Village. Only Upper Pines allows pets on leashes. $15 per night.

If you are expecting a real nature experience, skip camping in the valley, unless you like experiencing nature with 4,000 of your closest friends. The five car campgrounds here are always full except in the dead of winter. All are located along the Merced River. North Pines, Upper Pines, Lower Pines, and Lower River allow small RVs (less than 35 ft.). Upper River is for tents only.

Sunnyside Campground, Yosemite Valley

In the village on the west side. ☎ **209/ 372-0299.** 35 sites. Drinking water, flush toilets, pay phones, fire pits. Showers are available for a cost at Curry Village. No pets. $3 per night.

Sunnyside is the only walk-in campground in the valley, and fills up with climbers, since it costs only $3 per night. Hard-core climbers used to live here for months straight, but the Park Service has cracked down on that. It's still a much more bohemian atmosphere than the other campgrounds.

Wawona and Bridal Veil Creek

Near the south entrance to the park. ☎ **209/372-0302.** 210 sites. Drinking water, flush toilets, pay phones, fire pits. $10 per night. Reservations accepted in summer.

Outside the valley, things start looking up for campers. Two campgrounds near the south entrance of the park, Wawona and Bridal Veil Creek, offer a total of 210 sites with all the amenities. Wawona is open year-round. Because it sits well above snow line at more than 7,000 feet, Bridal Veil is open summer only.

Crane Flat

20 miles southeast of Big Oak Flat entrance on Big Oak Flat Rd. ☎ **209/ 372-0302.** 141 sites. Water, flush toilets, fire pits. $15 per night. Open May–Oct. Reservations.

Crane Flat, Hodgdon Meadow, and Tamarack Flat are all in the western corner of the park near the Big Oak Flat entrance. Crane Flat, set at 6,200 feet, is the nearest to the valley, about a half-hour drive.

Hodgdon

Adjacent to the Big Oak Flat entrance. ☎ **209/372-0302.** 105 sites. Water, flush toilets, fire pits. Pets on leashes permitted. $15 per night. Reservations.

Hodgdon Meadow is directly adjacent to the Big Oak Flat entrance at 4,800 feet. It's one of the least-crowded low-elevation car campgrounds, but there's not a lot to do here.

Tamarack Flat

Off Tioga Pass Rd. near the Big Oak Flat entrance. ☎ **209/372-0302.** 52 sites. No water, pit toilets, fire pits. No pets. $6 per night. No reservations. Open June–Oct.

This is one of the least-known car campgrounds in the park. Open June through October, Tamarack Flat is a bargain at $6 per night.

Tuolumne Meadows

Tuolumne Meadows. ☎ **209/372-0302.** 314 tent and RV sites, 25 walk-in sites. Water, flush toilets, pay phones, fire pits. Showers available nearby. Pets permitted. $15 per night; $2 per night for walk-in sites. Summer only.

Tuolumne Meadows is the largest campground in the park at more than 300 spaces, but it absorbs the crowd well and has all the amenities, including campfire programs and slide shows in the outdoor amphitheater. Half the sites are reserved in advance; the rest are set aside for first-come, first-served.

White Wolf

West of Tuolumne Meadows. ☎ **209/ 372-0302.** 87 sites. Water, flush toilets, hot showers, pay phone, fire pits. Pets on leashes permitted. $10 per night. Summer only.

White Wolf is the other full-service campground in the High Country. It has a drier climate than the meadow and doesn't fill up as quickly.

Porcupine Flat and Yosemite Creek

Near Tuolumne Meadows. ☎ **209/ 372-0302.** No water, pit toilets, fire pits. No pets. $6 per night. No reservations. Summer only.

The High Country's two primitive car camps, Porcupine Flat and Yosemite Creek, are the last to fill up in the park.

Shaver Lake Area

Campgrounds in this area have access to boating, fishing, hiking, skiing, and boardsailing.

Rancheria Camp, Huntington Lake

20 miles north of Shaver Lake on State Rte. 168. ☎ **209/855-5360** (Sierra National Forest). 150 sites. Flush toilets, running water, store, picnic tables, fire pits. Pets on leashes permitted. $14 per night. Reserve by calling ☎ 800/280-CAMP.

This is one of the best of the half-dozen camps surrounding beautiful Huntington Lake. Nearby is Rancheria Falls, a good day hike. Fishing and boating on the lake are great.

Camp Edison

On Shaver Lake, State Rte. 168. ☎ **209/ 841-3444.** 252 sites. Flush toilets, showers, motor-home hookups, boat ramp, rentals, bait shop. Pets permitted. $15–$22 per night. Call for reservations.

It's a zoo, but so is Shaver Lake. Still, this is a great place to come for fishing and boating. Other campgrounds are available around the lake, but they're all pretty comparable. Open year-round but the best season is May through November.

Sequoia & Kings Canyon National Parks

There are 13 campgrounds in the park, by far the most convenient and economical accommodations here. Only Lodgepole on the Kaweah River in Sequoia accepts reservations. Others are first-come, first-served, and often fill up on weekends. Three campgrounds, Azalea, Lodgepole, and Potwisha, are year-round. The rest are open from snowmelt through September. Even in summer, campers should prepare for rain and possible snow. Bring a good tent and warm sleeping bags. Campgrounds here all have access to the many activities in the Sequoia/Kings Canyon area.

Lodgepole

5 miles northeast of Giant Forest on the Marble Fork of Kaweah River. ☎ **209/ 565-3341.** 260 sites. Running water, flush toilets, showers, public phones, fire pits. Pets on leashes permitted. $16 per night. Reserve through PARKNET (☎ 800/365-CAMP).

This is one of the main campgrounds in the park, and with more than 200 sites, tends to be one of the noisiest. It's within a short stroll of restaurants, gas stations, and the main visitor center. If you're seeking solitude, lace up your hiking boots.

Dorst

14 miles northwest of Giant Forest on Dorst Creek. ☎ **209/565-3341.** 219 sites. Running water, flush toilets, public phones, fire pits. Pets on leashes permitted. $16 per night.

This is the park's other main campground, though it only stays open from June through September. It's set on Dorst Creek at 6,700 feet, near a backcountry trailhead.

Foothills/Mineral King Area Campgrounds

Near Giant Forest Village. ☎ **209/565-3341.** 143 sites total. Facilities vary. Pets on leashes permitted.

Smaller and more peaceful are South Fork, Potwisha, Buckeye Flat, Atwell Mill, and Cold Springs. South Fork, Atwell Mill, and Cold Springs, with no water and pit toilets, are $8 per night. The others, with flush toilets, running water, and public phones, charge $14.

Cedar Grove Area Campgrounds

Near Cedar Grove Village. ☎ **209/565-3341.** 351 sites total, plus 4 group sites. Running water, flush toilets, fire pits. Pets on leashes permitted. $12 per night.

Campers in the remote Cedar Grove area near the Kings Canyon River Gorge can choose from Moraine, Sentinel, Sheep Creek, Canyon View, and Canyon View Group Camp. All five sit at 4,600 feet and are convenient to some of the park's best hiking. The small Cedar Grove Village offers a restaurant, store, showers, and gas.

Grant Grove Area Campgrounds

Near Grant Grove. ☎ **209/565-3341.** 360 sites total. Running water, flush toilets, fire pits. Pets on leashes permitted. $12 per night.

Three campgrounds in the Grant Grove area will put you near the sequoias without the noise and crowds of Giant Forest Village. Sunset, Azalea, and Crystal Springs are all set at 6,600 feet. Showers are available at Grant Grove.

Eastern Sierra

Car camping in the eastern Sierra still remains a fairly pristine experience (other than the car), with few of the hassles associated with other parts of the state. There are so many national-forest campgrounds here (24 in Mammoth/June Lakes alone) that you can always find a site—some of the lesser-known areas have the best camping. The national-forest ranger stations for the area you want to visit are the best sources of information about specific camps and activities. The Inyo National Forest map that covers this entire area shows all campgrounds and is worth the $2 investment.

Lundy Creek

Just east of U.S. 395, 5 miles north of Lee Vining. 51 sites. Pit toilets, no water. Kayaking, bird watching, hiking, swimming. Pets permitted. $5 per night. No reservations.

This campground, set on the shore of Lundy Lake, is the closest decent campground to Mono Lake. It's a moonscape, but you wouldn't be visiting Mono Lake if you didn't like moonscapes. You wouldn't come here except for the fact that you want to check out Mono Lake, but it does the trick. Purchase any supplies you may need in Lee Vining.

June Lake Oh! Ridge Camp

Right on the shore of June Lake. 148 sites. Flush toilets, running water, Laundromat. Skiing, swimming, fishing, boating, hiking, biking, boardsailing. Dogs accepted on leash. $10 per night plus $7.50 reservation fee (☎ **800/280-CAMP**).

It's huge but it's nice. This is the summertime equivalent of downtown in Camping USA. If you don't mind company, the fishing is great, the swimming is great, and the boating is great. Even if you do mind the company, there are plenty of good hikes into the surrounding hills where you will lose the crowd.

Twin Lakes

4 miles outside the town of Mammoth Lakes on the shore of beautiful Twin Lakes. 95 sites. Flush toilets, running water. Boating, fishing, hiking, swimming. Dogs permitted. $11 per night. No reservations.

There are actually several campgrounds around Twin Lakes, all near a grocery store, laundry, great fishing, and hiking. Trophy fish come out of these two lakes every year. Boating, especially canoeing, is popular. *Note:* You can't swim in lower Twin Lake; it's the town water supply.

Rock Creek Lake
7 miles from Tom's Place on Rock Creek Rd. 28 sites. Flush toilets, running water. Boating, fishing, hiking, skiing. Dogs permitted. $8 per night. No reservations.

It gets cold up here at 9,600 feet, but the scenery is worth it. Countless great hikes head into the hills, and the fishing is good.

Big Trees
In the Bishop Creek Drainage, 11 miles from U.S. 395 on State Rte. 168. 9 sites. Flush toilets, running water. Hiking, biking. Dogs permitted. $8 per night. No reservations.

This campground is in the middle of one of the most popular backpacking and hiking destinations in the area. Lake Sabrina and hundreds of other lakes are up the road. Mountain bikers can explore several dirt roads.

INNS & LODGES

Lake Tahoe & the Northern Sierra
Sierra Club Clair Tappaan Lodge
2.4 miles east of Interstate 80 on Donner Pass Rd.; take Soda Springs/Norden exit. P.O. Box 36, Norden, CA 95274. ☎ 530/426-3632. 16 small single, 10 family-size rooms, 2 large dorms. $35 for Sierra Club Members, $39 for nonmembers, including 3 meals. MC, V.

This rambling, wood-shake lodge hearkens back to the days when the Sierra Club was the world's greatest hiking club. The dorm-style bunk rooms, private rooms, and family suites are all rustic and beautiful. The lodge has its own hot tub, library, kitchen, and dining room. Three family-style meals per day are included in the rates, which begin at $35 per night for

dorm accommodations. Winter cross-country ski rental available.

Rainbow Lodge (Royal Gorge Nordic Center)
6 miles west of Soda Springs on State Rte. 40. P.O. Box 1100, Soda Springs, CA 95728. ☎ 530/426-3661. 32 units, some with shared bathrooms. $89–$139. MC, V.

The dramatic timber and granite construction of this lodge, which was built in 1925 with lots of cheap labor, makes you feel like it could have been built by giants. A fine restaurant and bar are here, so you'll have plenty to do after a hard day's ski.

Yosemite National Park
Ahwahnee Hotel
Yosemite Valley. ☎ 209/252-4848. Reservations required. 123 units. $265–$739 double. AE, DC, DISC, MC, V.

The Ahwahnee Hotel is one of the most romantic and beautiful hotels in California, if not the world. The lodge was built in 1927 out of native granite and timber, and reflects an era when grand hotels were, well, grand. Fireplaces bigger than most Manhattan studio apartments warm the immense common rooms. Parlors and halls are filled with Native American rugs and antiques. With its ballroom, pool, tennis, gourmet dining, outstanding views, and high-digit price tag, the Ahwahnee is a special-occasion sort of affair. Rooms are booked a year in advance. Try to reserve one of the cottages, which cost the same as the rooms in the main hotel but are more spacious. And don't worry about what you're wearing, unless you're going to dinner—this is Yosemite after all.

Wawona Hotel
Hwy. 41, Wawona. ☎ 209/252-4848. 104 rms. $70.75–$97.50 double. CB, DC, DISC, JCB, MC, V. From Yosemite Valley, take Hwy. 41 south 27 miles toward Fresno.

The next best thing to the Ahwahnee (and much more affordable) is the

Wawona Hotel. Now a National Historical Landmark, the Wawona is a romantic throwback to another century. That has its ups and downs. Private bathrooms were not a big hit yet in the 19th century, and rooms were small to hold in heat. Still, the Wawona is a great place to play make-believe. It offers a restaurant, pool, stables, and a lounge.

Yosemite Lodge

Yosemite Valley. ☎ 209/252-4848. 249 rms. Reservations suggested. $70.50–$107.25 double. Lower rates Nov–Mar. CB, DC, DISC, JCB, MC, V.

Yosemite Lodge is the next step down in Yosemite Valley accommodations. It's actually a huge complex, not a lodge, with accommodations ranging from luxurious suites with outdoor balconies and striking views of Yosemite Falls to one-room cabins with shared baths in a separate building. There's also a pool. Two restaurants and a cafeteria serve mediocre meals.

Curry Village

Yosemite Valley. ☎ 209/252-4848. Reservations recommended. Moderate to inexpensive.

Curry Village is the valley's low-rent district. This compound of almost 200 cabins and almost 400 tent cabins varies widely in quality. Some have private baths. Others share campground-style bathrooms. Ironically, the oldest cabins are the nicest; shoddy construction gives the others a slapped-together appearance, not to mention making them cold and drafty in winter. The tent cabins have wood floors and canvas walls; they lack any sort of privacy, but they're fun in that summer-camp way. You'll have to sustain yourself with fast food from the Curry Village shopping center, because no cooking is allowed in the rooms.

High Sierra Camps

Reservations through High Sierra Reservations, Yosemite Park and Curry Co., 5410 E. Home Ave., Fresno, CA 93727. ☎ 209/454-2002.

Yosemite's five backcountry High Sierra Camps are an intriguing option bridging the gap between backpacking and staying in a hotel. These wilderness lodges are simple tent cabins and cafeteria tents located in some of the most beautiful, remote parts of the park. The five camps—Glen Aulin, May Lake, Sunrise, Merced Lake, and Vogelsang—make for good individual destinations. Or you can link several together, since they're arranged in a loose loop about a 10-mile hike from each other—a nice wilderness circuit. Overnight rates include a tent cabin, breakfast, dinner, bathrooms, and showers. High Sierra Camp reservations are accepted beginning in December for the following summer and usually book solid by January.

Shaver Lake Area

Mono Hot Springs Resort

End of State Rte. 168 at the edge of the John Muir Wilderness, P.O. Box 215, Lake Shore, CA 93634. ☎ 559/325-1710. Cabins $65 per night and up. Groceries and restaurant nearby.

This private hot-spring resort on the edge of the Ansel Adams Wilderness might just be the ultimate tonic for city-induced stress syndrome. With hot mineral baths, massage, rustic cabins (reasonably priced), and good food, you'll decompress in no time. And nobody can beat Mono Hot Springs for location. Hiking into the John Muir Wilderness from here is extraordinary. Call well in advance for reservations; the season is short and weekends are filled early.

Sequoia & Kings Canyon National Parks

Lodging in the park ranges from rustic one-room cabins with no bath or heat to a luxury motel. None of the complexes are very big. All lodging in the park is operated by the park concessionaire, **Sequoia Guest Services,** P.O. Box 789, Three Rivers, CA 93271 (☎ 209/561-3135). Call or write for information and reservations.

The heaviest concentration of accommodations is in **Giant Forest,** where you'll find something in every price and taste range. **Grant Grove** offers a variety of cabins with private or shared baths. **Cedar Grove** is the site of an 18-room motel. Each room has its own bath and two queen-size beds.

Eastern Sierra

Tamarack Lodge and Cabins

Twin Lakes Rd. ☎ **800/237-6879** in Calif., 760/934-2442 elsewhere. 25 cabins, 11 rooms. $75–$360 per night. AE, MC, V. No pets.

Located on the shore of Twin Lakes, this beautiful old lodge is a cross-country–ski resort in winter and a lakeside hotel in summer. The restaurant has been written up by *Bon Appetit,* and its prices reflect its four-star quality. Rooms in the timbered lodge are quaint, but the walls are a little thin. The upstairs suite in the lodge is a veritable palace, perfect for a family or two. The restaurant and a large common room centered around a beautiful fireplace occupy the entire bottom floor. About a dozen cabins with kitchens and baths are scattered around the grounds. In winter, they're secluded and can be a little hard to get in and out of during big storms, but they're very romantic.

Red's Meadow Resort

P.O. Box 395, Mammoth Lakes, CA 93546. ☎ **760/934-2345** or 760/873-3928. 6 cabins. $59–$89. MC, V.

This resort offers cabins right in the gateway to the Ansel Adams Wilderness and Devils Postpile. Trout fishing on the San Joaquin is a popular pastime, as are hikes into the backcountry. There is a store on the premises and a cafe.

7

The Gold Country

Few periods in time have captured the American imagination like the gold rush of 1849. The promise of gold to be had just for a little sweat and digging was exactly the kind of Horatio Alger dream needed to fuel the usurpation of California from the Mexicans and Native Americans to whom it previously belonged. As long as it was a desolate wilderness, they could have the durn place, but once it became known that thar's gold in them there hills, thousands of Yankees descended on the place and California was well on its way to becoming the Golden State. These days a few hardy miners still chase their dreams of hitting the mother lode, but most people here are riding a different kind of boom, the real-estate boom of the early 1990s that turned former mining camps like Sonora and Angels Camp into fashionable enclaves of Bay Area and Los Angeles equity refugees. Along with espresso, art galleries, and BMWs, the new wave of Gold Country pioneers have a lot of free time on their hands and an appetite for recreation. As a result, camping, fishing, river rafting, hiking, and mountain biking enjoy a popularity like never before in this area. It's not that any of those things are new here, just that suddenly there are a lot more people living here and doing them regularly.

The Lay of the Land

Gold was first discovered in California at Sutter's Mill on the American River in the foothills above Sacramento. In keeping with history, the Gold Country is commonly defined as the region from 1,000 to 3,000 feet in altitude along the west slope of the Sierra Nevada, even though gold was found in many other regions of the state in later years. From **Quincy** in the north to **Oakhurst** in the south, this is a region of dry range land and oak hillsides interspersed with large canyons cut by such major California rivers as the Feather, American, Tuolumne, and Merced.

Black bear and mule deer use this snow-free strip as a wintering area to escape the cold winters of the High Sierra. Rattlesnakes abound, and the plant community is pretty rough-and-tumble: a thorny, prickly mix dominated by a hardy chaparral cover on the hillsides, black-berry- and poison-oak–covered riverbanks, and the occasional cluster of pines and firs. Spring, however, brings out the Gold Country's flashier side; the grassy hillsides explode in a display of golden California poppies beginning in early May. By the time the June heat arrives they are gone.

Orientation

Highway 49
Though every major road over the Sierra passes through the Gold Country, it is Highway 49 that embodies the spirit of the forty-niners (no, not the football team, the miners) who settled this tough coun-try. Winding almost 300 miles from Portola to Oakhurst, Highway 49 is a road-tripper's delight, going through great old mining towns like Jackson and Angels Camp and over long stretches of isolated cattle country. Often the road switchbacks down steep river canyons before crossing on some high bridge and winding back up the other side. This is not a road for people prone to car sickness, but it is a great way to unwind from the urban superhighway mentality.

Auburn
Auburn is pretty much the northern end of what is traditionally considered the Gold Country. The American River runs practi-cally through Auburn, with great white water, and Folsom Dam is just a few miles downstream. My favorite feature of the Auburn area, though, is the half-mile-long, 800-foot-high **Foresthill Bridge,** built to connect the tiny community of Foresthill with Auburn when Auburn Dam was to be

constructed. The dam was put permanent-ly on hold when a huge earthquake fault was discovered nearby, but the bridge stands as a monument to man's impudent desire to control unruly nature. In June, downtown is the finish line of the Western States 100, a sadistic footrace from Squaw Valley through the Granite Chief Wilderness. For Auburn information con-tact the **Auburn Chamber of Com-merce,** 601 Lincoln Way, Auburn, CA 95603 (☎ 916/885-5616). The **Foresthill Ranger District Office** can be reached at 22830 Foresthill Rd., Foresthill, CA 95631 (☎ 916/367-2224).

Coloma
Coloma is a summertime white-water mecca, and becomes almost unbearably crowded—still, it's a great gold-rush–era town. It was near Coloma that John Marshall triggered the gold rush of 1849 by announcing to his workers, "Boys. By god, I believe I have found a gold mine." Earlier that morning he had spotted some shining flecks in the tailrace of a sawmill he was building for John Sutter on the South Fork of the American River. The **Marshall Gold Discovery State Historic Park** (☎ 530/622-3470) nearby still offers gold panning. The **Coloma Outdoor Discovery School** (☎ 530/ 621-2298) is a special environmental learning center for children that offers 3-day programs October through May.

Placerville
Once a rough-and-tumble mining town known alternately as Hangtown, Placer-ville today is more or less a glorified west-ern theme-park truck stop, an off-ramp from the U.S. 50 Corridor to the slow lane of Highway 49. For Placerville information, contact the **El Dorado County Chamber of Commerce,** 524 Main St., Placerville, CA 95667 (☎ 530/621-5885).

Jackson
Far from a ghost town, Jackson was and still is one of the most stable mother-lode cities. The Mokelumne River runs nearby, and the

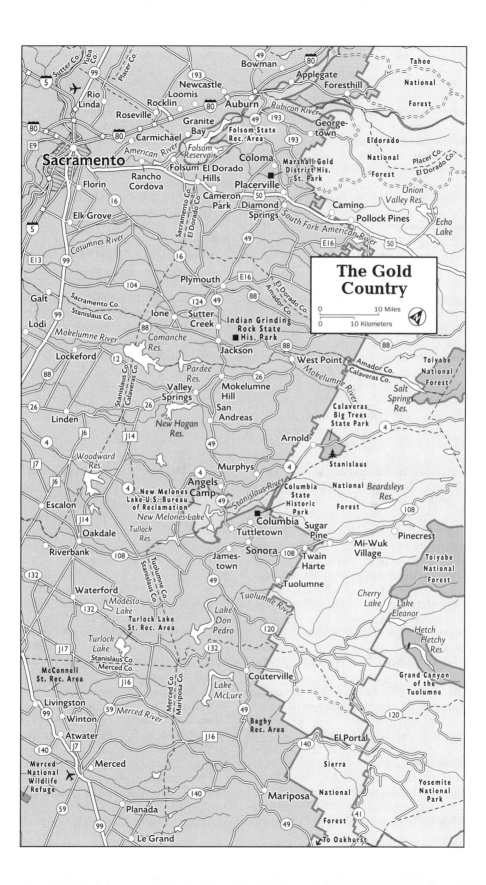

The Gold Country

0   10 Miles
0   10 Kilometers

Camanche and Pardee reservoirs offer nearby fishing and camping. Also worth a visit is the interesting **Indian Grinding Rocks State Historic Park** (☎ 209/ 296-7488). For Jackson information contact the **Amador County Chamber of Commerce** on Highway 49, P.O. Box 596, Jackson, CA 95642. (☎ 209/ 223-0350).

Angels Camp

Immortalized by Mark Twain's story "The Celebrated Jumping Frogs of Calaveras County," Angels Camp is another weird example of life following art. Twain *made up* the story of the jumping frog jubilee, a fantastic tall tale about bored miners and the stupid things they'll do for fun. Angels Camp, of course, couldn't leave well enough alone and actually started holding the frog-jumping contest in 1928. Now it's a famous tourist draw every May. For information contact the **Calaveras County Lodging and Visitors Association,** 1301 S. Main St., P.O. Box 637, Angels Camp, CA 95222 (☎ 800/ CAL-FROG).

Columbia and Sonora

Columbia is a fantastic state park encompassing an entire 19th-century mining village. The town is still "alive," in a sense: tours, exhibits, and shops relive the gold rush. Sonora is a booming foothill town on State Route 108 and Highway 49. It's gone a little hog-wild since Bay Area refugees discovered it in the late eighties. Now you can't throw a rock without hitting a bed-and-breakfast or a fancy cafe, but the change has actually been nice. For information contact the **Tuolumne County Visitors Bureau,** 55 W. Stockton St., P.O. Box 4020, Sonora, CA 95370 (☎ 209/ 533-4420). The **Stanislaus National Forest Headquarters** can be reached at 19777 Greenley Rd., Sonora, CA 95370 (☎ 209/532-3671).

Mariposa

Mariposa is the gateway to the Yosemite Valley to most people who whiz through here at top speed, but it merits its own visit. Great cycling surrounds the town, and the

town's mining-history exhibit at the county fairgrounds is really interesting too. For information visit the **Mariposa County Chamber of Commerce** at the corner of Highway 49 and State Route 140, P.O. Box 425, Mariposa, CA 95338 (☎ 209/ 966-2456). The **Mariposa Ranger District,** P.O. Box 747, Mariposa, CA 95388 (☎ 209/966-3638), is at the same corner.

Oakhurst

What little there is to say about Oakhurst is probably best said by the talking grizzly statue downtown at the corner of State Route 41 and Route 426. This is the end of the mother lode and the Gold Country. Like Mariposa, Oakhurst is largely a way station on the journey into the south entrance of Yosemite. For information visit the **Eastern Madera County Chamber of Commerce,** 49015 Rd. 426, Oakhurst, CA 93644 (☎ 209/683-7766).

Parks & Other Hot Spots

While Yosemite National Park to the southwest (see chapter 6, "The Sierra Nevada") garners most outdoor attention in this neck of the woods, the Gold Country still has a fair amount of outdoor offerings, particularly if white water is your thing. The **American River** runs practically through the town of Auburn. In summer, the small city of Coloma is transformed into the Grand Central Station of river rafting. Traffic jams back up the streets and the South Fork of the American River. The **Marshall Gold Discovery State Historic Park** (☎ 530/ 622-3470), also in town, has great swimming in the American River, and nice hiking trails past the old historic buildings.

The **Mokelumne River** runs near Jackson, and **Camanche and Pardee reservoirs** are two popular fishing and camping lakes surrounded by more than

15,000 acres of public land. A really interesting state park here is the **Indian Grinding Rocks** (☎ 209/296-7488), a meadow containing a limestone mesa that is marked by more than 1,100 ancient mortar-and-pestle grinding holes. The grinding rock (*Chaw'se* in the Miwok language) is the largest in the United States. A museum and Native American roundhouse are also here.

Beyond the jumping-frog contest, other good reasons to visit Angels Camp are the fantastic white water of the **Stanislaus River,** nearby **Moaning Cave** and **Mercer Caverns** (The county gets its name—*Calaveras,* which means "skulls" in Spanish—from these caves, once a sacred Miwok burial site), and miles of great bicycling. South of Sonora on Highway 49 is some of the state's best white water, the famous **Tuolumne River,** as well as two huge reservoirs: **Lake Don Pedro** and **Lake McClure.**

While Mariposa is primarily a stopping point on the way to Yosemite, there is some great cycling in the surrounding area. Northeast of Oakhurst before you come to Yosemite National Park, a large swath of **Sierra National Forest** cut by dirt roads and seldom-used trails offers a good alternative to the crowds of Yosemite. **Bass Lake,** a beautiful, tree-circled reservoir owned by Pacific Gas and Electric, is a popular fishing, swimming, and waterskiing lake just outside Oakhurst. Contact the **Bass Lake Ranger District** (☎ 209/683-4665) for information about the lake and national forest.

What to Do & Where to Do It

BIRD WATCHING

The oak woodlands and chaparral communities of the Gold Country foothills are an important habitat for numerous species, including woodpeckers, raptors, and owls. Not surprisingly, the acorn woodpecker is one of the most common species you'll see here, almost as common as the California quail that seem to scamper out from under every bush. You might also spot the hairy woodpecker, Nuthall's woodpecker, and downy woodpecker in the oak forests, and spot large raptors like the red-tailed hawk, northern goshawk, and golden eagle. A special treat is the occasional twilight sighting of great horned, western screech, and northern pygmy owls. Wild turkey have become common in the foothills in the last few decades, and sometimes you'll spot them right in the middle of Highway 49.

Public land is less common here in the rolling ranch country than high up in the Sierra, but several places offer good access: **Hangtown Gold Bug Park** (☎ 530/642-5232) in Placerville (62 acres of woodland), **Indian Grinding Rock State Historic Park** (☎ 209/296-7488) near Jackson, and the numerous public parks around **Bass Lake.**

Bobelaine Sanctuary, located 35 miles north of Sacramento, is a 430-acre preserve on the west bank of the Feather River. It is primarily a songbird habitat, with sparrows, warblers, finches, orioles, and flycatchers predominant. Spring migration runs from mid-April to mid-June. Fall migration is best in early September, but continues through late October and into the first half of November. Drive north from Sacramento on Highway 99, for 35 miles to the Feather River. Continue 2 miles after the bridge to Laurel Avenue, where you head east. The road ends at the sanctuary parking lot.

At the other end of the Gold Country, between Los Banos and Highway 99, lies **Grasslands International Reserve,** both a natural and a political miracle. This nearly 20,000-acre reserve encompasses about one-third of the state's remaining noncoastal wetlands. As many as 200,000 shorebirds, half of all the migrating birds in the area, pass through the reserve in spring (dropping to merely 60,000 in winter and 14,000 in fall). Western sandpipers, longbilled dowitchers, least sandpipers, sunlins, and black-necked stilts are among the local visitors. The reserve is administered by a remarkable coalition of federal and state agencies and private landowners, mostly duck-hunting clubs. The U.S. Fish and Wildlife Service considers the area to be the most important wintering area for waterfowl in the country. Public access is available year-round at the **San Luis National Wildlife Refuge,** 8 miles north of Los Banos on route 165. For recent migrations, weather, and other questions, call the refuge at ☎ **209/ 826-3508.**

CANOEING

The **American River,** half an hour north of Sacramento, has dozens of possible put-ins and many options for great canoe trips lasting from an hour to several days. Near the city, the water is quite placid. Farther up, you get into rafting territory and white water. For information and rentals, contact **California Canoe and Kayak,** 8631 Folsom Blvd., Sacramento, CA 95826 (☎ **800/366-9804**).

FISHING

Whether you're a fly-fisherman looking for a perfect patch of river or a bass buster searching for bucket-mouthed hogs, the Gold Country probably has what you're looking for. As they tumble through the foothills, the **American, Mokelumne, Stanislaus, Merced,** and **Tuolumne rivers** all offer great trout fishing. Local seasons and closures change from river to river and from mile to mile on certain rivers like the Tuolumne, where sections are closed or are catch-and-release only.

Lake fishermen have a hard time deciding where to go in this neck of the

woods. Depending on the season (and the water level) the large foothill reservoirs like **Folsom Reservoir, Lake Don Pedro, Lake McClure,** and **Bass Lake** are hot spots for trout, Kokanee salmon, largemouth and smallmouth bass, crappie, and catfish.

GOLD PROSPECTING

It's hard to visit the Gold Country and not get a little itch of the greed that drove the rush. Panning is harder than you might think; standing around waist deep in gold water can sap your enthusiasm right off if you don't know what you're looking for. Luckily, a number of outfitters are just itching to take you out and show you how to do it right (for a price—this is a gold rush after all). Try **Columbia State Park Hidden Treasure Gold Mine** (☎ 209/532-9693), **Gold Country Prospecting** in Placerville (☎ 530/622-2484), **Gold Prospecting Expeditions** in Jamestown (☎ 209/984-4653), or **Jensen's Pick and Shovel Ranch** in Angels Camp (☎ 209/736-0287).

HIKING

Hiking is hard in this area for the simple reason that much of the land is private, and that which isn't private is so darn steep and desolate that you'd be really hard-pressed to walk up or down it without falling off. The river canyons are the only real choice, and they are often impassable. There are good hikes that reach back into some of the remote canyons, however.

Western States Pioneer Express Trail, Auburn State Recreation Area
3 miles round-trip, but 20-some miles possible. Moderate. Access: End of Driver's Flat Rd. at Ruck-A-Chucky Campground. Map: Auburn State Recreation Area map.

Beginning at the Ruck-A-Chucky Campground, this trail heads upstream about 200 feet above the Middle Fork of the

HOW TO PAN FOR GOLD

Find a gold pan—ideally a 12- to 15-inch steel pan. Place the pan over a burner, or better yet, in a campfire. This will darken the pan, making it easier to see any flakes of placer gold. On a stream, find some gravel, sand, or dirt that looks promising or feels lucky. Fill the pan nearly full and then place it under water and keep it there while you break up the clumps of mud and clay and toss out any stones. Then grasp the pan with both hands. Holding it level, rotate it in swirling motions. This will cause the heavier gold to loosen and settle to the bottom of the pan. Drain off the dirty water and loose stuff. Keep doing this until gold and heavier minerals called black sand are left in the pan. Carefully inspect the black sand for nuggets or speck traces of gold. When you find gold, rush immediately to San Francisco and scream "Gold! Gold! Gold!" at the top of your lungs. This will inevitably start the next gold rush.

You can dredge from June 1 to October 15. A dredging permit is required. Apply at Regional 2 Headquarters, **California Department of Fish and Game,** 1710 Nimbus Rd., Rancho Cordova, CA 95670 (☎ **916/358-2900**). You can also sign up for one of the many tours offered in Gold Country towns. See "Gold Prospecting" above.

American River. Down below you can see dark deep pools broken up by the occasional riffle. Look for heron and other waterbirds waiting to catch trout in the shallows. In about 0.75 miles you'll see roaring Ruck-A-Chucky Falls, one of the most feared rapids on the Middle Fork. A small side trail leads down to the falls for a close-up look at the action. Careful, though—the water-worn rocks around the falls get really slippery. Continuing up the main trail you'll pass over Ruck-A-Chucky and descend again. This time you come out near a nice sandy beach and an inviting swimming hole. Give in to the temptation, but don't forget what's downstream. Sometimes blackberry vines along the river offer up a perfect feast. Return the way you came.

KAYAKING

For a really strong kayaker this is heaven; the **Class IV and V** south fork of the Tuolumne, Cherry Creek, north fork of the American, and north fork of the Stanislaus are some of the finest white water in the West. More moderate **Class II and III** runs are the **Chili Bar Run** on the south fork of the American, the **Electra Run** on the Mokelumne near Jackson, and sections of the Merced

between Yosemite and Lake McClure. Don't hop into your boat on any of these rivers because you *think* it is safe to go downstream; numerous easy Class III sections lead into harrowing Class V sections, and knowing where to take out is imperative. *California Whitewater: A Guide to the Rivers* by Jim Cassady (North Fork Press, 1995) is the definitive mile-by-mile guidebook to all these rivers and is well worth the purchase.

California Canoe and Kayak, 8631 Folsom Blvd., Sacramento, CA 95826 (☎ **800/366-9804**), runs 2-day introductory kayak classes on the lower American, a beginning class on the South Fork, as well as intermediate and advanced classes. The school operates out of several locations in the Bay Area and Sacramento.

The River Store, 1032 Lotus Rd., Lotus, CA 95651 (☎ **530/626-3435**), is the center of the white-water kayaking scene on the South Fork of the American. No lessons, but great information and plenty of gear for sale.

For a copy of the *Boating Trail Guide to the North and Middle Forks of the American River,* a publication showing put-in and take-out sites, rapids and their difficulty rating, and emergency information, phone the **Whitewater Management Office** (☎ **530/885-5648**). For river conditions contact the **California River Flow Hotline** (☎ 800/952-5530).

MOUNTAIN BIKING

Though growing in popularity, mountain biking in the Gold Country is still relatively untapped. Unfortunately, much of the area is private property or too steep to ride, but there are some great exceptions, including the Merced River ride, one of my favorite rides in the world. Shorter rides like the Western State Pioneer Express Trail through Auburn State Recreation Area along the American River, or the single-track Darrington Trail circling Folsom Lake, are great for getting the feel of the area.

For other mountain-biking adventures, contact the local ranger district in the area you'll be visiting. They know the ins and outs of public access, and can point you to great mining roads and trails into little-known spots. Particularly attractive is the **Stanislaus National Forest** above Sonora and near Groveland.

Merced River Ride

28 miles round-trip. Moderate. Gravel road. Access: Where State Rte. 140 joins the Merced River 20 miles west of Yosemite, take the 1-lane bridge across the river. Follow the dirt road downstream until you find a suitable parking place. Map: Mariposa County road map.

For the first 14 miles the dirt road sticks with the river. You'll have perfect views of one of the best Class III and IV whitewater runs on the river, great swimming holes, stunning side canyons, even a few national-forest campgrounds if you should decide to do it overnight. I like to ride it down and back, but it's possible to hook up with Highway 49 by Bear Valley and arrange a car shuttle (Why you'd do this I don't know, as the drive is much worse than the ride). The only drawback to this ride is that the road is open to cars, so you must be alert and try not to run them over—trust me, you'll be going faster than they are.

Western State Pioneer Express Trail

14 miles. Moderate. Access: Trail begins at Hwy. 49 bridge over American River. Map: Auburn State Recreation Area map.

The Western State Trail is a long-distance trail connecting Sacramento with Carson City, Nevada, a remnant of the days when trails, not highways, were how most people crossed the Sierra Nevada. These days the trail is open to hikers and horses, with only certain sections open to cycling. This section along the banks of the American River is one of the finer ones. Deep swimming holes will entice you off your bike and the foothill scenery is really nice. For entertainment keep your eye peeled for rafts careening down Murderer's Gorge Rapid.

Darrington Trail

7.8 miles. Moderate to difficult. Steep and rocky single track; intermittent creek crossings. Access: Trail begins at Skunk Hollow Trailhead on Pilot Hill–Salmon Falls Rd. Map: Folsom Lake State Recreation Area map.

The Darrington Trail flanks the shore of Folsom Lake. It's steep here, so sections of the trail are not for the faint-hearted. Much of the ride is on open grasslands, and in the summer the heat can be intense. Bring plenty of water for this one.

ROAD BIKING

With Highway 49 weaving its way up and down throughout the area, the Gold Country is a great place to hit the blacktop.

Highway 49

Anywhere from 20–200 miles. Moderate to difficult. Steep sections, busy traffic throughout. Access: Anywhere along Hwy. 49. Map: AAA road map or equivalent.

Sinuous Highway 49 makes a great bike tour from end to end, and the towns along the route are spaced just the right distance apart so that you can make an unsupported ride sleeping in a hotel or

B&B every night. If you decide to do it, plan to ride between March and the middle of June. After June you can pretty much forget about riding here until the end of September, when the 100°F days finally abate.

American River Bikeway
32 miles one-way. Moderate. Access: Begin at Beal's Point Campground in Folsom Lake State Recreation Area (☎ 916/988-0205). Map: Sacramento County road map.

One of the most well used and beautiful bike routes in California is the American River Bikeway, which travels from Beal's Point Campground in Folsom Lake State Recreation Area all the way to Sacramento, 32 miles west. Following the north bank of the American, you get beautiful views of the river and down into the Central Valley. Parts of the Sacramento end of the trail are unsafe at night, so plan to have plenty of time and a shuttle or ride waiting.

WALKS & RAMBLES

Marshall Gold Discover State Historic Park Walking Tour
Distance varies. Access: Coloma historic quarter.

This is a ramble in the best sense of the word: The historic quarter of Coloma doesn't lend itself to directed, goal-oriented trekking. Instead, take an hour or two and wander around. You'll find a mining museum, with exhibits of ore carts and stamp mills—as common in their day as computer monitors and fax machines are in ours—plus plaques explaining the various methods used to extract gold. Standing close by is the old Wah Hop Store, a leftover from the days when Chinese laborers built the stone walls and embankments you see all over the mother lode. Across Highway 49 on the banks of the South Fork of the American you can explore a replica of John Sutter's sawmill, where James Marshall discovered gold on January 24, 1848, and set off the

rush that would leave California a vastly different place. Near the south end of town take little Cold Springs Road to the cemetery, where the oldest grave marker dates back to 1850; many others followed soon after, grim testimony to the hard lives of the prospectors.

Indian Grinding Rock State Historic Park Tour
0.75 miles. Access: Visitors center on Volcano Rd., 1.5 miles south of State Rte. 88 near Jackson.

By combining the nature-walk self-guided trail (get brochures at the visitor center) with a stop at the huge grinding rock and the reconstructed Miwok village, a visitor can quickly get a picture of the way the Native Americans lived in harmony with their ecosystem here. The numerous oaks that still shade the trail were the main staple of the Miwok, and nearby forests provided game and construction materials for their cedar bark houses.

WHITE-WATER RAFTING
Not too long ago river rafting in the Gold Country was pretty limited because the rivers here were simply too tough to take commercial passengers down. Well, that's changed. Improvements in raft design and a more gonzo attitude among outfitters has opened all but the most insane Gold Country white water to commercial rafts. Almost every commercial rafting company in the state runs at least one of the Gold Country canyons, and for many this area is their bread and butter. There are literally more river rafting companies in California than there are runnable rivers—at last count about 40 full-time outfitters. Overall the quality of service is really good; with that kind of competition the bad ones are weeded out fast. For a list of outfitters operating on a particular river, or just for general information, contact the **River Travel Center,** Box 6, Point Arena, CA 95468 (☎ **800/ 882-7238**). This is a booking service for all outfitters on all rivers in California (at

no charge to you) and is extremely knowledgeable about the sport. Be advised that the American River in particular is notorious for having white-water "guides" with only marginally more experience than most of the clients.

Several outfitters are known for a certain specialty: **Beyond Limits Adventures,** P.O. Box 215, Riverbank, CA 95367 (☎ 800/234-RAFT), is best known for its Team Extreme trips for thrill-seeking rafters who want to tackle Class V white water, but it also offers beginning and intermediate-level trips. **ARTA** (the American River Touring Association), Star Rte. 73, Groveland, CA 95321 (☎ 800/323-ARTA), is one of California's oldest outfitters. It's been around since 1963 and offers runs on virtually every California river and many out of state as well.

Easy Runs

- **South Fork American River (Chili Bar and Gorge sections)** This moderate Class II and III run through the Gold Country around Coloma is the best introductory white water in the state and is popular to the point of overcrowding. More than 50 rapids—great gravel bar, wave train whompers—keep things exciting but never become technical or unforgiving. Most runs are done with guide-directed paddle rafts.

- **Mokelumne River (Electra Run)** This 5-mile run near Jackson is a great one for kids. The water is all Class II–plus, meaning you can send junior out for a spin in one of the inflatable kayaks that outfitters bring along on these trips and not worry about him or her missing a take-out and going over Death Trap Falls. It's short enough to run twice in a day.

Difficult Runs

- **Middle and North Forks of the American (Oxbow to Mammoth Bar, Chamberlain Falls, and Giant Gap)**

Mostly heavy Class IV pool and drop rapids with the exception of the sketchy Giant Gap Run (Class V). These three runs are all popular with rafters looking for a step up in the excitement level. Giant Gap is several steps up: You hike 2 miles down a trail and then bomb almost 14 miles of constantly technical white water. Outfitters require that you have previous experience on at least Class IV water before they'll take you on this one.

- **North Fork Stanislaus River (Sourgrass to Calavaras Big Trees)** Some of the world's most beautiful Class III boating now lies buried under New Melones Reservoir, but these 5 miles of Class-III-and-IV–plus rapids are far upstream of the dam's reach. The season is short for the Stanislaus because of sporadic upstream releases, but the ride is worth it—5 miles of constant white water through beautiful rock canyons and sequoia forests, and past striking waterfalls.

- **Middle Fork Stanislaus River (Dorrington to Camp 9)** Like the Giant Gap run on the American, this run also requires a 2-mile hike 3,000 vertical feet down to the river to access 10 miles of almost constant Class-IV-to-V–plus action. This is a relatively new commercial run. You should have some experience with heavy water before signing on for one of these trips.

- **Tuolumne River (Lumsden Launch to Ward's Ferry Bridge)** The long-time classic of heavy-water California rafting. From put-in to take-out, the Tuolumne dishes out nearly constant Class IV white water, including Clavey Falls, one of the biggest drops in western white water, but what's most stunning is the scenery. This stretch of the Tuolumne has been declared a Wild and Scenic River, and certainly deserves it. Don't be surprised to see mule deer, bear, or even a golden eagle. You can do this run in a day, but many outfitters offer it as a 2- or 3-day overnight run to get in some exploring up Cherry Creek, do a little fishing, and enjoy the beauty of this gorge.

- **Merced River (El Portal to Bagby)** Just outside the Yosemite National Park Arch Rock entrance on State Route 140, the Merced River enters about 30 miles of really amazing Class-III-to-IV–plus white water. For the first half the road runs alongside the Merced, perfect for motorists to watch the action, but a little distracting as a wilderness experience for the boaters. Downstream of Briceberg, the road and river go separate ways and the canyon is one of the most beautiful you've ever seen. The Merced is also part of the National Wild and Scenic River System.

Campgrounds & Other Accommodations

CAMPING

Camping is a great way to go here, year-round. Though winter nights can get cold, even snowy, the days are often clear and beautiful; it's always a gamble, but the lack of crowds could be your jackpot. Spring is beautiful almost without fail—wildflowers, clear skies, the whole package. Summer and early fall are a little too hot for my taste, unless I happen to be camped right near a river or lake. Luckily, most campgrounds in the area *are* located right on rivers or lakes.

Auburn State Recreation Area
1 mile south of Auburn on Hwy. 49. ☎ **530/885-4527.** 53 tent sites; 22 boat-in sites, dispersed throughout park. Pit toilets, no piped water. Fishing, hiking, swimming, horseback riding, kayaking, biking. Dogs accepted. Reservations only for boat-in sites, call PARKNET (☎ 800/444-PARK); other sites are first-come, first-served; $7–$9 per night.

Just outside the reach of Sacramento's urban sprawl, Auburn State Recreation Area is a great place to get a little taste of wilderness. The park offers 42,000 riverfront acres along the American River, which runs through the park, with some of the river's most difficult rapids easily visible to hikers. Good fishing, biking, and swimming, too.

Indian Grinding Rock State Historic Park
11 miles northeast of Jackson on State Rte. 88, then 1.5 miles south on Pine Grove–Volcano Rd. to the park. ☎ **209/296-7488.** 23 sites. Flush toilets, running water. Bird watching, hiking. Pets accepted. $10–$12 per night.

This park reminds you that before the gold rush there was another civilization living here in a way very different from ours. The Miwok museum and the enormous

---

Camping Pitfalls

Mosquitoes and ticks can be a problem, but they're nothing compared to the poison oak. It grows everywhere in the river bottoms, usually mixed in with blackberry vines just to tempt you. Rattlesnakes are common, but not really a problem as long as you give them the space they deserve. If you see them, please don't smash, chop, shoot, or otherwise maim them just because they scare you. You scare them too. Let them slither away and you can both live happily ever after.

grinding-stone area is fascinating. You can stay in one of some 20 campsites, but for a change stay in one of the park's five bark houses, built in the traditional Miwok way out of cedar poles and bark. They sleep about six. Call ahead for an application. Other park offerings include petroglyphs, a nature trail, reconstructed Miwok houses, and a sweat lodge.

Glory Hole
Midway between Angels Camp and Sonora on Hwy. 49 on the shore of New Melones Reservoir. ☎ 209/536-9094. 140 sites. Flush toilets, piped water, showers, boat ramp. Boating. Pets accepted. No reservations; $14 per night.

New Melones Reservoir kind of gives me the creeps. I just can't help thinking about all the great white water that used to run through here before the Stanislaus River was dammed to create this rather tepid reservoir; and in the fall the lake drops, exposing a huge bathtub ring of mud. This is the best place to camp in the Angels-Camp-to-Sonora corridor, though. If you're a boater, you'll love it here. Nearby is a cabin where Mark Twain supposedly lived for a winter.

River Ranch Campground
5 miles northeast of the tiny town of Tuolumne on Buchanan Rd. ☎ 209/928-3708. 55 sites. Flush toilets, piped water, showers, store, laundry. Fishing, swimming. Pets accepted. Call ahead for reservations; $14 per night.

In contrast to most of the other campgrounds in the area, this privately operated camp seems a bit overdeveloped, but it's pretty nice. The best feature is the Tuolumne River, which runs past here, with good fishing and swimming.

INNS & LODGES
Virtually every small town on Highway 49 has at least one and probably two or three funky old B&Bs, some of them dating all the way back to the gold rush. The following are two that I think are really neat.

Coloma Country Inn
345 High St., Coloma, CA 95613. ☎ 530/622-6919. 5 rms (3 with private bath), 2 suites. $90–$130 double; $130–$185 suite. No credit cards.

Located in the middle of a state park (albeit a state historical park), this restored 1852 country farmhouse on 5 acres is a great place to spend a night away from your tent. And it's quite romantic. The two suites are in a separate cottage; one has a full kitchen. There's a pond complete with ducks, and bicycles are available for guest use. Best of all, innkeeper Alan Ehrgott is a balloon pilot. You can sign up for an hour-long flight with this 12-year veteran.

The Murphys Hotel and Lodge
457 Main St., Murphys, CA 95247. ☎ 209/728-3444. 29 units. $70–$80 and up. AE, MC, V.

During the gold-rush years, this was the grandest hotel in California outside of San Francisco. As a result, numerous famous and infamous characters of that period stayed here and played here. Mark Twain, Horatio Alger, Ulysses S. Grant, Daniel Webster, J. P. Morgan, and even stagecoach bandit Black Bart were all guests. In keeping with the Wild West history of the place, the bar downstairs has been known to party well into the night. Murphys is about 10 miles east of Angels Camp on State Route 4.

8

The Northern Mountains

It's often overlooked that not all of California's best mountain wilderness is in the Sierra Nevada. I guess that's easy to understand when you take into consideration the grandeur of the Sierra, the distribution of much of the state's population near the Sierra, and the relative impenetrability of the Klamaths and Cascades to the automobile.

Still, it is a mystery how so many people can drive along Interstate 5 on a clear day, see the Trinity Alps to their west and the obvious, in fact, startling, Mount Shasta just a few miles east of the highway, and never bother to explore the possibilities here.

Of course, the people who do come to the state's northern mountains aren't going to cry any tears over the lack of crowds, nor are the people who live here. They know about the awesome kayaking, trout fishing, backpacking, backcountry skiing, climbing, camping, and a million other things to do here, and they probably aren't anxious for many more people to hear about it.

Maybe it's because most of the land is simply national forest and national wilderness, not glamorous, big-name national parks. Maybe it's because people were scared off by Bigfoot rumors in the 1970s and tales of renegade pot growers in the 1980s. Who knows? But anyone who drives 5 hours from the Bay Area to trudge along behind an ant trail of other hikers on an overcrowded Yosemite pathway when they could have driven 5½ hours to the Trinity Alps and been all alone is missing out.

Since the white man came to these parts, the area's history has been a sad litany of abuse and exploitation. Though first explored by Peter Ogden in 1828 and 2 years later by Jedediah Smith, the northern mountains were mostly ignored until the 1850s gold rush, which brought destructive hydraulic mining that ripped up riverbeds and banks with enormous spouts of water to free trapped gold. Hard-rock mines yanked millions of dollars from the hills. Towns like Happy Camp, Scott Bar, Orleans, and Somes Bar were the final outposts of miners seeking their fortune from these remote canyons and hillsides.

Later, logging became the next big boom. It's hard to believe, but virtually every tree in the Klamaths was cut down between the early part of this century and the 1980s, when the last old growth was chopped. The trees you see growing now are second and third growth. Though today almost 2 million acres are included in the Klamath, Siskiyou, and Six Rivers national forests, and management practices are improving slowly, rampant clear-cutting and destructive mining practices continue. The people who live here walk a thin line between their ties to and love of the land and the necessity of balancing economic needs with ecological concerns.

The Lay of the Land

Using **Interstate 5** as a dividing line, you can bisect the northern mountains into two manageable pieces. On the east side of I-5, between Redding and the Oregon border, lies a high plateau dotted with the southernmost peaks of the **Cascade Range,** most importantly **Mount Shasta** and **Mount Lassen,** both dormant (but not dead) volcanoes. Shasta rises nearly 10,000 feet from the surrounding countryside to a summit height of more than 14,000 feet, dwarfing everything for miles around. Though they seem like small fry next to Shasta, the surrounding mountains are impressive: deep forests, open range, fantastic fly-fishing, hiking, and white water. Farther north and east the Modoc Plateau becomes flatter until you hit Tule Lake and the Walker Mountains.

On the west side of I-5, you have the **Klamath Mountains,** a series of ranges with very blurry boundaries and distinctions between them. The Klamaths reach from southern Oregon about 130 miles into northwestern California. The range includes the Siskiyous, Salmons, Marbles, Scott Bars, and Trinity Alps. The glaciated

Trinity Alps, covering hundreds of square miles of forest, meadows, and above-tree-line rocky peaks are the highest and most dramatic part of the Klamaths, reaching heights of 8,000 feet. **Trinity County,** in which the Trinities lie, has the distinction of being the only county in California without a single traffic light or parking meter, though it does have more than 400 miles of hiking trails and several of the best white-water rivers in the state.

The Klamaths were formed, together with the Sierra Nevada, about 225 million years ago as the floor of the Pacific Ocean began to slide under the North American continent. The wreckage of the ocean bottom crumpled up like bent sheet metal and formed the beginnings of the range. It took millions of years for these pipsqueak mountains to achieve a respectable size, and then around 140 million years ago the Sierra split into two.

The northern third drifted 60 miles northwest to become the Klamaths. The other two-thirds, of course, became the Sierra Nevada. At the time the entire Central Valley would have been under water, and the Klamaths were probably an island chain for a few million years. While the Sierra shot skyward again in a dramatic surge of uplift that began about 3 million years ago, which has yet to subside, and was then scoured by glaciers to form the great mountain valleys, the Klamaths remained relatively stable; hence their more eroded and confused topography. Still, the Klamaths bear many similarities to their southern brethren: Geologists like to describe the rock layers in the two ranges as matching up like the type in a newspaper page torn in two. During the gold rush some of the richest deposits in California were actually found here, not in the Sierra Nevada, and individual rock specimens from both ranges are virtually identical.

Flora and fauna in the northern mountains include many of the same species to be found in the evergreen forests of the Sierra, only here they have much more room to move around. Because the Klamaths are relatively low and their terrain more varied, there exists an abundance of richly productive evergreen forest, thickly wooded river valleys, and fertile meadow grasslands. Black bear, deer, cougar, eagles, hawks, and other large animals are common sights. Salmon and steelhead, though endangered due to dam building and siltation caused by clear-cutting the hillsides, still return to the Klamath, Smith, Trinity, and Salmon rivers each year to spawn.

Orientation

Transit in the northern mountains is not too efficient, and generally follows the same pattern: take massive **I-5** to a place roughly parallel on the map from where you want to be, then wind into either the Trinities or the Klamaths by painfully slow mountain roads. **Highway 299,** which heads east-to-west out of Redding, is a good bet for the Shasta-Trinity area, while **Highway 89** is the road to take into Lassen. Both are reached via exits off I-5. Expect delays—and road closures on Highway 299—in winter, and slow going most times. Fortunately, you won't find anything but scenic routes up here, so enjoy the ride.

Weaverville
The county seat of Trinity County, Weaverville, population 3,500, is the big city in these parts—a beautiful town of gold-rush–era Victorians, brick storefronts, and the oldest continually used Chinese temple in California. If you're going into the Trinity Wilderness, rafting the Trinity River, or visiting Trinity Lake (creative naming, huh?), you'll probably pass through Weaverville coming or going. For information contact the **Trinity County Chamber of Commerce,** 317 Main St., Weaverville, CA 96093 (☎ **800/421-7259** or 916/623-6101).

Yreka
The only town with a population over 5,000 in the entire central northern area, Yreka was founded by proud ranching and mining pioneer stock and seems almost unchanged since the gold-rush days. The county seat of Siskiyou County, it is home to the **Siskiyou County Museum,** 910 S. Main (☎ 530/842-3836), the **Klamath National Forest Interpretive Museum and Headquarters,** 1312 Fairlane Rd. (☎ 530/842-6131), and a stunning display of gold nuggets at the **Siskiyou County Courthouse,** 311 4th St. (call the museum for info). For information, contact the **Yreka Chamber of Commerce,** 117 W. Miner St. (☎ **800/ON-YREKA** or 530/842-1649).

Mount Shasta City
This tiny town of about 1,000 citizens is one of those wonderful mountain towns seemingly crafted for the traveling wilderness bohemian. There's a health-food store here with good hippie staples like soy milk and granola; several good restaurants; climbing, bicycling, and ski shops (try **The 5th Season,** 300 N. Mount Shasta Blvd., Mount Shasta, CA 96067; ☎ **530/926-3606,** for all of the above); art galleries; and a used-book store. For information contact the **Mount Shasta Visitors Bureau,** 300 Pine St. (☎ **800/ 926-4865** or 916/926-4865).

Traveler's Tip: The World-Famous Yreka Bakery

Spelled backwards, the name of a Yreka bakery, the Yreka Bakery, is Yreka Bakery. Please do not point this out to the woman working there. She already knows.

Mount Shasta City's Average Temperatures and Precipitation												
	Jan	Feb	Mar	Apr	May	June	July	Aug	Sept	Oct	Nov	Dec
High (°F)	42.1	47.3	50.9	57.9	67.0	75.4	85.1	83.3	77.5	65.4	50.9	43.9
Low (°F)	25.5	28.6	29.6	33.2	39.6	46.2	50.7	49.0	44.3	37.4	30.8	26.7
Precipitation (in.)	7.2	5.7	4.2	2.8	1.6	0.8	0.3	0.5	0.9	2.0	5.2	6.0

McCloud

This tiny lumber town on State Route 89, about 6 miles off Interstate 5, is going through a rejuvenation. The mills and lumber jobs that were lost in the 1980s are slowly but surely being replaced by a tourist economy. Excellent fishing and white-water boating on the McCloud River draw plenty of visitors, some of whom seem to be staying and refurbishing the beautiful old homes sold for next to nothing when the economy faded. The lesser-known summer estate of William Randolph Hearst is near here on the McCloud River. In addition, the Nature Conservancy manages a nature preserve along 7 miles of McCloud River frontage.

Parks & Other Hot Spots

Trinity Alps Wilderness

West of I-5. Access: From State Rte. 299, State Rte. 3, and any number of smaller roads in between. ☎ 530/623-6106 (Big Bar Ranger Station). Skiing, fishing, hiking, swimming. The wilderness has no facilities; the surrounding towns and national-forest campgrounds have everything under the sun.

The Trinity Alps Wilderness is the second largest in California—more than 500,000 acres. The wildest and least-charted country in the state is here. Though 400 miles of trail explore the wilderness, huge

blocks can only be reached by blazing your own path.

Trinity Lake

Fishing, boating, swimming, rafting, camping.

With 150 or so miles of wooded shoreline, Trinity Lake is a popular fishing, camping, and waterskiing lake. The lake is actually named Clair Engle Lake after the U.S. Senator Clair Engle, who ramrodded the water project through as budget-fattening pork. The dam drowned several small towns, and the antipathy left behind is such that nobody, and I mean nobody, who lives near here calls the lake Clair Engle. For information contact the **Weaverville Ranger District Office,** State Route 299 in Weaverville (☎ **530/ 623-2121**).

Salmon and Klamath River Drainage

Fishing, hiking, kayaking, rafting, camping.

The Klamath is the largest and longest river in Northern California, reaching from the Oregon border near I-5 all the way to Klamath in Redwood National Park. Roads follow the Klamath most of the way and most of the surrounding land is national forest. There are countless places to fish, camp, hike, and run white water. The Salmon, a tributary of the Klamath, is a designated Wild and Scenic River and holds some of the most striking white water in the state. For information contact the **Six Rivers National Forest** (☎ **707/442-1721**) or the **Klamath National Forest Headquarters,** 1312 Fairlane Rd., Yreka, CA 96097 (☎ **530/ 842-6131**).

Marble Mountain Wilderness

West of I-5 via State Rte. 96 or State Rte. 3. ☎ **530/842-6131** (Klamath National Forest Headquarters). Hiking, kayaking, fishing.

Another of the Klamath Ranges, the Marbles aren't nearly as high as the Trinities, but are extremely well forested and lush. The wilderness, with 250,000 acres and little visitor use, spans the Marble and Salmon mountains, but you won't know the difference. Marble Valley, Sky High Valley, and Spirit Lake are some of the more popular backcountry camps, but with this much land and this few visitors, crowding is never a problem.

Mount Shasta

Take I-5 to Central Mount Shasta exit, then go east onto Lake St. Continue about 10 miles to the Mt. Shasta area. Hiking, biking, skiing.

The Native Americans believed Shasta was the home of the Great Spirit. Today, things haven't changed at all. A number of New Age religions center around the mountain, and it is considered one of the energy spots of the universe. Some of us just come here to climb, ski, and hike, but even that is somewhat of a holy experience. A ski area once existed on the flanks of the mountain but repeated avalanches took care of that. Now the Mount Shasta Ski Park is located on a much tamer adjoining mountain. The 14,162-foot summit of the real thing can be reached in a single day hike with no really technical climbing involved. You do, however, need an ice axe, crampons, and a hell of a lot of willpower. There is talk of building a trail around the base of the mountain, but it is currently incomplete.

Castle Crags State Park

Castle Crags Exit from I-5. ☎ **530/ 235-2684.** Camping, picnicking, showers, rest rooms, store. Skiing, hiking, rock climbing. Fees.

There's 6,000 acres of hiking, camping, and fabulous rock climbing here just

south of Shasta City. The Pacific Crest Trail passes through the park and the Sacramento River runs nearby.

Ahjumawi Lava Springs State Park

3.5 miles north of McArthur; accessible only by boat. Put in at PG&E Rat Farm launching area 4 miles north of McArthur on Main St. ☎ **530/335-2777.** Environmental camping, boating.

This unique park contains the outlet of an underground river that drains Tule Lake, 50 miles away. The 6,000 acres are open for exploration by canoeists and boaters.

Lava Beds National Monument

Loop road through park begins and ends on State Rte. 139, south of Tulelake. P.O. Box 867, Tulelake, CA 96134. ☎ **530/ 667-2283.** Campsites, interpretive center, ranger-led hikes, rest rooms. Wildlife, bird watching, hiking, caving. Day-use and camping fees.

From above, this park looks like a wind-blasted, rugged lava bed with a few scrubby hills and trees. Well, it is. But it's what you don't see on first glance that makes this park remarkable—hundreds of lava tube caves, many open for your exploration. Lava tube caves are fairly simple to navigate, unlike limestone caverns, and so even the novice spelunker can have a great time here. The history of the park is interesting too. It was here that the last band of Modoc Indians led by Captain Jack stood off the U.S. Army for 6 months in 1873 before being starved out, tricked, and executed. See "Lava Beds National Monument," below.

Burney Falls, Hat Creek, Fall River Mills

State Rte. 299 northeast of Shasta City. Fishing, camping.

Just north of Lassen on State Route 299, these three rivers arguably offer the best trout fishing in the entire state. The town of Burney is well equipped with fly-fishing shops and several fishing guides. Hat Creek is one of the best fly-fishing streams in the nation. For information, contact the **Burney Chamber of Commerce,** P.O. Box 36, Burney, CA 96013 (☎ **530/335-2111**).

McArthur–Burney Falls Memorial State Park

6 miles north of State Rte. 299 on State Rte. 89. ☎ **530/335-2777.** Hiking, camping. $5 day use; $14 camping.

15 miles northeast of Burney is McArthur–Burney Falls Memorial State Park, where a huge spring-fed waterfall pours over a richly mossy 129-foot cliff into a deep pool below. More impressive than the height of the falls is the fact that 100 million gallons of water pour over them each day.

Shasta Lake

Boating, skiing, fishing, swimming.

When it's full, which in recent decades has been a rare thing, Shasta Lake on the Sacramento River is huge: 30,000 acres and 370 miles of shoreline. Hundreds of houseboats cruise the lake, as well as hordes of skiers and fishermen. There are several marinas in different arms of the lake. The **Shasta–Cascade Wonderland Association** (☎ **800/326-6944** or 530/365-7500) is an excellent source for boat-rental, lodging, camping, and activity information about the lake.

Lassen Volcanic National Park

State Rte. 89. P.O. Box 100, Mineral, CA 96063. ☎ **530/595-4444.** Camping, rest rooms, showers, cross-country ski rental, natural-history museum, backcountry camps, wilderness lodge. Skiing, biking, boating, wildlife, bird watching, hiking. Entrance fee.

Though it is a lot like Yellowstone with its geothermal wonders, Lassen is one of the least-visited national parks. Those who do visit tend to stick to the loop road and rarely venture into the backcountry. Big mistake. The park contains boiling lakes, great hiking (150 miles of trail), a backcountry lodge, fishing, and in the winter,

great cross-country skiing. See "Lassen Volcanic National Park," below.

Lava Beds National Monument

Lava Beds is one of those places that takes a while to grow on you. It's a desolate, windy place: high plateaus, spiky buttes, and rolling hills covered with lava cinders, coyote bush, and tortured-looking junipers. Miles of land just like it cover most of this corner of California. So why, asks the first-time visitor, is this a national monument? The answer lies underground.

The ground here is like Swiss cheese, so porous in places that it actually makes a hollow sound. When lava pours from a volcano it doesn't cool all at once; the outer edges cool first and the core keeps flowing, forming underground tunnels like a giant pipeline system. More than 200 **lava tube caves** lace the earth at Lava Beds; many of them are open to the public to explore on their own or with park rangers (see "Spelunking" under "What to Do & Where to Do It"). Whereas most caves lend themselves to a fear of getting lost, with their huge chambers, multiple entrances, and bizarre topography, these are simple, relatively easy-to-follow tunnels with little room to go wrong. The feeling once inside is that this would be a great place for a game of hide-and-seek.

For more information, contact **Lava Beds National Monument,** P.O. Box 867, Tulelake, CA 96134 (☎ **530/667-2283;** www.nps.gov/labe).

ESSENTIALS

The loop road through Lava Beds National Monument begins and ends on State Route 139, south of Tulelake. **Indian Well Visitor Center** is located at the southern end of the monument. The entry fee is $4 per vehicle or $2 per motorcycle, bicycle or walk-in.

WHEN TO GO

Park elevations range from 4,000 to 5,700 feet, and this part of California can get cold, even snowy, any time of year. **Summer** is the best time to visit, with average temperatures in the 70s; **winter** temperatures plunge down to about 40°F during the day and as low as 20°F by night. Summer is also the best time to participate in ranger-led hikes, cave trips, and campfire programs. Check the visitor center bulletin board for schedules.

THE PARK'S HISTORY

In the winter of 1872, a band of 53 Modoc Indians held off a siege by more than 1,000 well-armed U.S. cavalrymen for nearly 6 months using the lava tube tunnels as hideouts in a deadly game of cat and mouse. The Modocs, who had left a reservation where they were forced to live with a rival tribe, returned here to their traditional homeland and demanded their own reservation. General E. R. S. Canby was charged with returning them. By May 1873, weakened by starvation and exhausted, almost all the Modocs had been captured or killed. On June 1, 1873, their leader, "Captain Jack," surrendered with the last of his tribe. On October 3, 1873, he and three other Modoc leaders were hanged. The surviving members of his band were banished to an Oklahoma reservation. There's very little of historical note remaining to see aboveground here besides a white cross marking the spot where General Canby was killed during surrender meetings with the Modocs, an act that led to the final blood bath.

EXPLORING THE PARK

A hike to **Schonchin Butte** (0.75 miles, one-way) will give you a good perspective on the wild, stark beauty of the monument and nearby Tulelake Valley. Wildlife lovers should keep their eyes peeled for terrestrial animals, such as mule deer, coyote, marmots, and squirrels. Birders can attempt to spy bald eagles, 24 species of hawks, and enormous flocks of ducks and geese headed to the Klamath Basin, one of the largest waterfowl wintering grounds in the Lower 48. Sometimes the sky goes dark with ducks and geese during peak migrations.

Lassen Volcanic National Park

Stashed away in the far northeastern corner of California, Lassen Volcanic National Park is a remarkable reminder that North America is still forming, that the ground below is alive with forces of creation and, sometimes, destruction. Mount Lassen is the southernmost peak in a chain of volcanoes, including Mount Saint Helens, that stretches all the way from British Columbia; though dormant, the chain is still very much alive.

Mount Lassen last awoke in May 1914, the beginning of a cycle of eruptions that spit lava, steam, and ash until 1921. The cycle climaxed in 1915 when Lassen blew its top, sending up a 7-mile-high mushroom cloud of ash that was seen for hundreds of miles. The peak itself has been dormant for 65 years now, but the area still boils with a ferocious intensity; hot springs, fumaroles, mud pots, and geysers are all indicators that Lassen hasn't had its last word. Monitoring of geothermal features in the park shows that they are getting hotter, not cooler, and some scientists take this as a sign that the next big eruption in the Cascades is likely to happen here.

Until then, the park gives visitors an interesting chance to watch a landscape recover from the massive destruction brought on by the last eruption. To the north of Lassen Peak is the aptly named **Devastated Area,** a huge swath of volcanic destruction steadily repopulating

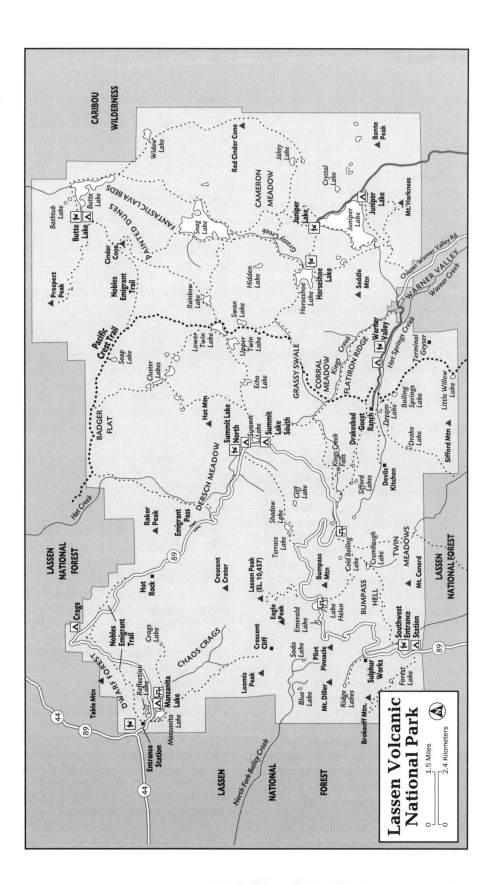

Lassen Volcanic
National Park

CARIBOU
WILDERNESS

Bonte
Peak

Widow
Lake

Jakey
Lake

Red Cinder Cone

Crystal
Lake

Mt. Harkness

Bathtub
Lake

Butte
Lake

CAMERON
MEADOW

Butte
Lake

Juniper
Lake

Juniper
Lake

Juniper
Lake

Cinder
Cone

Snag
Lake

FANTASTIC LAVA BEDS

Grassy Creek

Chester Warner Valley Rd.

Prospect
Peak

PAINTED DUNES

Nobles
Emigrant
Trail

Hidden
Lake

Horseshoe
Lake

Horseshoe
Lake

Saddle
Mtn

WARNER VALLEY

Warner Creek

Rainbow
Lake

Swan
Lake

Pacific
Crest Trail

Lower
Twin
Lake

Upper
Twin
Lake

GRASSY SWALE

CORRAL
MEADOW

Kings
Creek

FLATIRON RIDGE

Warner
Valley

Hot Springs Creek

Terminal
Geyser

BADGER
FLAT

Soap
Lake

Cluster
Lakes

Echo
Lake

Boiling
Springs
Lake

Little Willow
Lake

Hat Creek

Hat Mtn

Summit Lake
North

Summit
Lake

Summit
Lake
South

Kings Creek
Falls

Sifford
Lakes

Drakesbad
Guest Ranch

Dream
Lake

Drake
Lake

Sifford Mtn

DERSCH MEADOW

Cliff
Lake

Devils
Kitchen

Raker
Peak

Emigrant
Pass

Shadow
Lake

LASSEN
NATIONAL
FOREST

Crescent
Crater

Lassen Peak
(EL. 10,457)

Terrace
Lake

Bumpass
Mtn

Cold Boiling
Lake

Crumbaugh
Lake

TWIN
MEADOWS

Mt. Canard

LASSEN
NATIONAL FOREST

89

Hot
Rock

Crags

Crags
Lake

Nobles
Emigrant
Trail

Eagle
Peak

Emerald
Lake

Lake
Helen

BUMPASS
HELL

Southwest
Entrance
Station

89

DWARF   FOREST

CHAOS CRAGS

Crescent
Cliff

Soda
Lake

Pilot
Pinnacle

Sulphur
Works

Forest
Lake

Table Mtn

Reflection
Lake

Manzanita
Lake

Loomis
Peak

Blue
Lake

Mt. Diller

Ridge
Lakes

Brokeoff Mtn.

44

89

Manzanita
Lake

Entrance
Station

North Fork Bailey Creek

LASSEN

NATIONAL

FOREST

1.5 Miles
2.4 Kilometers
0

N

with conifer forests. Forest botanists have revised their earlier theories that forests must be preceded by herbaceous growth after watching the Devastated Area immediately revegetate with a diverse mix of eight different conifer species, four more than were present before the blast.

In addition to the volcano and all its geothermal antics, Lassen Park includes miles of hiking trails, huge alpine lakes, large meadows, cinder cones, lush forests, a cross-country ski area, and great camping. Only one major road, State Route 89, the Park Road, crosses the park in a 39-mile half circle with entrances and visitor centers at either end. Three-quarters of the park is designated wilderness.

For more park information, contact **Lassen Volcanic National Park,** P.O. Box 100, Mineral, CA 96063-0100 (☎ **530/ 595-4444;** www.nps.gov/lavo).

GETTING THERE

The best route is to take Calif. 44 east from Redding (via I-5), which leads directly to the park's **Northwest Entrance.** A shortcut if you're coming from the south along I-5 is Calif. 36 in Red Bluff, which leads to the park's **Southwest Entrance.** If you're arriving from the east via I-80, take the U.S. 395 turnoff at Reno and head to Susanville. Depending on which end of the park you're shooting for, take either Calif. 44 (to the Northwest Entrance) or Calif. 36 (to the Southwest Entrance) from Susanville.

Only one major road, **Calif. 89** (also called the Park Road), crosses the park in a 29-mile half-circle with entrances and visitor centers at either end. Most visitors enter the park at the Southwest Entrance Station, drive through the park, and leave through the Northwest Entrance, or vice versa. Two other entrances lead to remote portions of the park. **Warner Valley** and **Juniper Lake** are reached from the south on the road from Chester. **Butte Lake entrance** is reached by a cutoff road from Calif. 44 between Calif. 89 and Susanville.

FEES

Entry into the park for up to a week costs $10 per vehicle or $5 per person on foot or bike. Camping fees range from $8 to $14.

WHEN TO GO

Modoc County (Lassen National Park does not lie in Lassen County) is one of the coldest places in California. Winter lasts from late October and doesn't release its grip until June. Even in the summer, plan for possible rain and snow. Temperatures at night can drop below freezing at any time. Winter, however, shows a different and beautiful side of Lassen that more people are starting to take advantage of. Since most of the park is over a mile high, and the highest point is 10,457 feet high, snow accumulates in incredible quantities. Don't be surprised to find snowbanks lining the Park Road into July.

In winter, the park becomes a cross-country skier's fantasy. Snow closes the park roads, leaving skiers and snowshoers with their run of the place. See "Cross-Country Skiing & Snowshoeing" under "What to Do & Where to Do It" for more information.

THE PARK'S HISTORY

The Lassen area was inhabited by four groups of **Native Americans** before the arrival of whites. The Atsugewi, Maidu, Yana, and Yahi all used portions of the park as their summer hunting grounds. The white man's diseases and encroachment into their territory quickly decimated their population. By the turn of the century, they were thought to be gone from the wilds of the Lassen area. In 1911, however, a nearly naked Native American man was discovered by butchers at a slaughterhouse in Oroville. When they couldn't communicate with him, the sheriff locked the man in a cell. News of the "Wild Man" found a receptive audience among anthropologists at the University of California in Berkeley, who quickly rescued him. Ishi, as he came to be known, turned out to be the last of the Yahi tribe and lived at the UC Museum of Anthropology for 5 years before succumbing to tuberculosis. Through sharing his knowledge with anthropologist Alfred Kroeber and others, Ishi is responsible for much of what is known about California Indian culture.

WILDLIFE

The 106,000-acre park is a place of great beauty. The flora and fauna here are an interesting mix of species from the Cascade Range, which stretches north from Lassen, and species from the Sierra Nevada, which stretches south. The resulting blend accounts for an enormous diversity of plants: 715 distinct species have been identified in the park. Lassen is an important summer feeding ground for transient herds of mule deer and numerous black bears.

VISITOR CENTERS

The largest visitor center is just inside the **North Entrance** at the Loomis Museum; there is also the **Southwest Information Station,** just inside the Southwest Entrance. Both are open daily from late May to late September, and provide the full spectrum of interpretive displays, ranger-led walks, and informational leaflets.

The **park headquarters** in Mineral, located on Calif. 36, southwest of the park, offers information and publications Monday to Friday (except holidays) year-round. There are additional ranger stations at Summit Lake, and also in the more isolated reaches of the park in the Warner Valley and at Butte Lake.

When visitor centers are closed you'll need to get information by phone or mail, or at park headquarters.

REGULATIONS

Because of the dangers posed by the park's thermal features, rangers ask that you remain on trails at all times. Fires are allowed in campgrounds and the backcountry, but please make sure they are dead before leaving them. Mountain bikes are prohibited on all trails.

EXPLORING THE PARK

The highlight of Lassen is, of course, the **volcano** and all of its offshoots: hot springs, fumaroles, and mud pots, among others. It's possible to see many of the most interesting sites in a day. *The Road Guide to Lassen Park* (available at the visitor centers) is a great traveling companion that will explain a lot of the features you'll see.

Bumpass Hell, a 1.5-mile walk off the Park Road in the southern part of the park, is the largest single geothermal site in the park: acres of bubbling mud pots cloaked in a stench of rotten-egg-smelling sulfur. The name comes from an early Lassen traveler, Bumpass, who lost a leg after he shortcut through the area while hunting and plunged into a boiling pool. Don't make the same error in judgment.

Sulphur Works, 2 miles from the southwest park exit, is another stinky, steamy example of Lassen's residual heat. The ground roars with seething gases escaping from the ground.

Boiling Springs Lake and **Devils Kitchen** are two of the more remote geothermal sites located in the **Warner Valley** section of the park, which can be reached by hiking from the main road or entering the park through Warner Valley Road from the small town of Chester.

Most Lassen visitors drive through in a day or two, see the geothermal hot spots, and move on. That leaves 150 miles of trails and expanses of backcountry to the few who take the time to get off-road. The Lassen Trails booklet, available at the visitor centers, gives good descriptions of some of the most popular hikes and backpacking destinations. Anyone spending the night in the backcountry must have a wilderness permit issued at the ranger stations. For more information, see "Hikes, Bushwhacks & Backpack Trips" under "What to Do & Where to Do It."

Canoes, rowboats, and kayaks can be paddled on any of the park lakes except Reflection, Emerald, Helen, and Boiling Springs. Motors, including electric motors, are strictly prohibited on all park waters. Park lakes are full of trout and fishing is popular. You must have a current California fishing license.

What to Do & Where to Do It

BIRD WATCHING

There's good birding all over the northern mountains: everything from the endangered and controversial spotted owl to the brown sparrow calls this area home. But the big news in these parts is the incredible numbers and diversity of waterfowl you can see at **Tule Lake** and **lower Klamath Lake wildlife refuges,** almost 100,000 acres of wetlands and agricultural fields. They are an incredible breeding ground for the geese and ducks that congregate in stunning numbers during the spring and fall migrations. By official estimate, 45,000 ducks and 2,600 geese are hatched and reared here every year. The number of adult waterfowl stopping through reaches the millions. During the winter, when birding for waterfowl is slow, Tule Lake and lower Klamath are the site of a winter congregation of between 500 and 800 bald eagles, and a lesser number of golden eagles. For a complete list of birds and information about self-guided tours of the refuges by canoe or on foot, contact Refuge Manager, Klamath Basin National Wildlife Refuges, Route 1, Box 74, Tulelake, CA 96134 (☎ **530/667-2231**).

CANOEING

One of California's most unique state parks, **Ahjumawi Lava Springs State Park** (☎ **530/335-2777**), is inaccessible by foot or car and perfectly suited to exploration by canoe. The Pit River Indians, who were the original residents of this huge spring-fed freshwater lake, creek, and wetland system, named it *Ahjumawi:* "where the waters come together." The waters originate from huge lava springs in enormous upwelling of cold, clear water that seems to turn every shade of blue and green while reflecting striking views of Mount Shasta, Mount Lassen, and the surrounding area. Boaters can camp overnight at any of nine backcountry sites. Put in at the PG&E Rat Farm launching area 4 miles north of the town of McArthur on Main Street.

CROSS-COUNTRY SKIING & SNOWSHOEING

Expert backcountry skiers have their work cut out for them on the flanks of **Mount Shasta,** where you can climb as high as your skills and legs will take you. For beginners, the area between Bunny Flat and the Sierra Club hut is a safe and relatively easy place to practice your first backcountry skills. If the hills are too daunting, continue up the unplowed Everitt Memorial Highway beyond Bunny Flat. Since an avalanche peeled the old ski lifts off the mountain at the former downhill ski area, Caltrans no longer plows the last 3 miles of road. The **House of Ski,** 1208 Everitt Memorial Hwy. (☎ **530/926-2359**), is on your way up to the mountain and rents a full line of cross-country gear.

Lassen Volcanic National Park (☎ **530/595-4444**) is an amazing place to check out on skis or snowshoes. Snow closes the park road in November and most years it doesn't open until June, so cross-country skiers have their run of the park. Snowmobiles were once allowed but are now forbidden. Marked trails of all skill levels leave from Manzanita Lake at the north end of the park and Lassen Chalet at the south. Most visitors come to the southwest entrance, where the ski chalet offers lessons, rental gear, and a warm place to stay.

Popular trips in the park include the beginners' trails to Lake Helen or Summit Lake. More advanced skiers can make the trek into Bumpass Hell, a steaming valley of sulfuric mud pots and fumeroles. A popular overnight is to ski the 30-mile course of the park road from the north entrance through the park to the chalet, but doing this involves a long car shuttle. Because of the remoteness and dangerous geological features of the park, rangers require that all skiers register at the trailheads whether they're heading out for an overnight or just the day. Park staff also lead snowshoe hikes into the park emphasizing ecology and winter survival.

The following resorts offer groomed trails, rental equipment, and lessons: **Mount Shasta Nordic Center,** 5 miles east of Shasta City on State Route 89 (☎ 530/926-8610), and **Lassen Ski Touring,** State Route 36 at southwest entrance to Lassen Volcanic National Park.

DOWNHILL SKIING & SNOWBOARDING
Mount Shasta Ski Park
104 Siskiyou Ave., Mount Shasta City. ☎ 530/926-8610; 530/926-8686 for snow conditions. 21 trails (20% beginner, 60% intermediate, 20% expert); 3 lifts including 2 triples and 1 surface. Full-day adult ticket $31 weekends and holidays, $26 weekdays, $18 on Tues.

The Native Americans believed Mount Shasta was the home of the Great Spirit, and so they left it to higher powers, never climbing above timberline. When the white man built a ski area on the flanks of Shasta in 1958, the Indians remained confident that it wouldn't last. It didn't, but the Great Spirit took a while to take his revenge. Avalanches and bad weather kept the mountain closed much of the

time and the resort always trod a thin line between profit and insolvency, but it always held on. Then, in 1978, a huge avalanche swept most of the chairlifts from the mountain. That did the trick, and the ski bowl closed for good.

In 1985, a new resort opened on Mount Shasta, this time below timberline and hopefully out of the range of the Great Spirit's wrath. Snowmaking and night skiing are recent additions, and the resort is looking to expand even more. There's a little bit of everything here, and yes, snowboarding is allowed.

FISHING
The fly-fishing in this part of the state is simply among the best anywhere in the world. The most famous trout-fishing rivers here are **Hat Creek, Fall River, McCloud River, Pit River,** and **Burney Creek.** The Trinity, Salmon, and Klamath once supported huge runs of steelhead and salmon, but dams and siltation caused by clear-cutting of the forest have drastically reduced their number. **Canyon Fly Fishing** (☎ 530/623-330), in Weaverville, is one of the area's best outfitters. Others include **Andrew's Guide Service** (☎ 530/632-3465) in Gridley, and **Trinity Fly Shop** (☎ 530/623-6757), in Lewiston, which has bait and tackle and also runs a guide service.

Lake fishermen will go crazy with pleasure on **Lake Shasta** just trying to figure out what to chase. The enormous reservoir on the Sacramento River has a surface area of 30,000 acres and more than 370 miles of shoreline. Spring and summer are the best fishing seasons when the lake warms and fish go into feeding mode. Deep-water trollers pull out trophy-worthy rainbow trout, while fishermen working the shallows often score big with largemouth and smallmouth bass. To keep the kids happy, Lake Shasta has a huge population of crappie that will practically jump into your boat during the spring. Call the **Shasta–Cascade Wonderland Association**

(☎ 800/326-6944 or 530/365-7500) for information about boat rentals or tackle shops.

HANG GLIDING

The place to hang-glide in the northern mountains is **Hat Creek Rim,** located in Lassen National Forest. It's popular with gliders and paragliders from all over the northern part of the state. The rim is about 1,000 feet above the valley and is known for excellent ridge running conditions from June through September (occasionally into Oct). Hat Creek Rim is located about 75 miles east of Redding. Take 299 east out of Redding to Burney; head south on 89; and then drive into Lassen and stop at Fireside Village for fuel, food, and flight information. A bulletin board for pilots is posted at the village store.

A second launch is located nearby in Burney, north on Highway 89 on the slopes of **Burney Mountain.** This site is less popular than Hat Creek Rim, and slightly harder to find. At Burney, ask directions to Burney Lookout. Gliders launch nearby. Winds here and at Hat Creek Rim reportedly get very high early in the day and calm in the midafternoon.

HIKES, BUSHWHACKS, & BACKPACK TRIPS

Day Hikes

Mount Eddy Summit and Deadfall Lakes

9.5 miles round-trip. Moderate to strenuous. Access: Trailhead at dead end of Forest Rd. #17, 14 miles west of Edgewood/Gazelle exit off I-5 north near Weed. Map: USGS Mount Eddy topo.

The best place to appreciate the splendor of Mount Shasta isn't on Shasta itself, but rather from the summit of 9,025-foot Mount Eddy. Rising above a mixed forest of red and white fir, Jeffrey and ponderosa pine, and numerous smaller deciduous species, Mount Eddy was the site of a now-abandoned national forest lookout, because of its astounding views of the

Trinity Mountains to the west and Shasta to the east. This trail is a segment of the Pacific Crest Trail. After the first 2 miles of hiking through forest, you'll hit a basin containing three small lakes: upper, middle, and lower Deadfall lakes. Middle has great sunbathing rocks and deep spots perfect for a cool-off swim. After the lakes the Mount Eddy Trail begins steadily climbing; the total elevation gain on this hike is almost 3,000 feet. Several steep switchback sections might require some work, but the view will keep you going. After enjoying the summit, return the way you came.

McCloud River Preserve

5-plus miles round-trip. Moderate. Access: In McCloud, turn south on Squaw Valley Rd. Follow for 12 miles and pass McCloud Reservoir until you come to a dirt road signed AH-DI-NA. Follow signs to AH-DI-NA Campground and go past campground to end of road. Map: Shasta–Trinity National Forest map; Nature Conservancy brochure.

Access to the McCloud River is really difficult in most places; private land lines much of the area. Thanks to the Nature Conservancy's reserve in the McCloud River Canyon, however, hikers and fishermen can enjoy this spring-fed stream. Wandering downriver from the reserve entrance, you'll pass through a nice forest of oak and maple mixed with the occasional large Douglas fir. Keep your eyes peeled for wildlife: the Nature Conservancy has documented the presence of wolverines, mountain lions, and black bears here. More likely you'll see a bald eagle or a small herd of deer grazing by the river. Continue downstream until you reach the signed boundary of the conservancy's wildlife study area, which is off-limits to visitors. Return the way you came.

Whitney Butte Trail, Lava Beds National Monument

6.8 miles round-trip. Moderate. Access: 2 miles north of the visitor center, take the turnoff for Merrill Cave. The trailhead is at the end of the road. Map: Free brochure available at visitor center.

Whitney Butte Trail leads from Merrill Cave along the shoulder of 5,000-foot Whitney Butte to the edge of the Callahan Lava Flow along the park boundary. Though stark, the views from this trail are some of the most spectacular in the park: over a foreground of jagged lava and hardscrabble juniper bushes, you can look out onto the huge expanse of Tule Lake National Wildlife Refuge and the Warner Mountains to the east.

Lyons Trail, Lava Beds National Monument

8.2 miles. Strenuous. Access: Trailhead begins at visitor center. Map: Park map.

The 8.2-mile (one-way) Lyons Trail spans the wildest part of the monument, where you're likely to see plenty of wildlife. Besides numerous birds of prey, like red-tailed hawks, kites, and the occasional bald eagle, you might see the large herds of mule deer grazing on the greenery that grows among the brutal-looking lava flows and pumice fields.

Lassen Peak Trail, Lassen Volcanic National Park

4.8 miles round-trip. Moderate. Access: Trailhead is on Park Rd., 7.5 miles past the south park entrance. Map: Lassen Trails booklet available at visitor center.

Probably the most popular hike in Lassen is the 2.5-mile climb from the Park Road to the top of Lassen Peak. The trail may sound short, but it's steep and generally covered with snow until late summer. At 10,457 feet in elevation, though, the view of the surrounding wilderness you'll get from the summit is worth every step of the way. On clear days it's possible to see south all the way to Mount Diablo near Oakland and north into the Cascades.

Cinder Cone Trail, Lassen Volcanic National Park

4 miles round-trip. Moderate. Access: Trail begins at the Butte Lake campground at the far northeast corner of the park. Map: Lassen Trails booklet available at visitor center.

Cinder Cone, in the northeast corner of the park, is best reached from the Butte Lake campground at the far northeast corner of the park. If 4 miles seems too short, you can extend the hike (and shorten the drive) by walking in about 8 miles from Summit Lake on the Park Road. Now dormant, Cinder Cone is generally accepted as the source of mysterious flashing lights that were seen by early settlers to the area in the 1850s. This black and charred-looking cone is bare of any sort of life and surrounded by dunes of multihued volcanic ash.

Pacific Crest Trail Day Hike, Lassen Volcanic National Park

10 miles round-trip. Moderate. Access: Trail begins at Drakesbad on the Warner Valley Rd. in the southeast corner of the park. Map: Lassen Trails booklet available at visitor center.

A 17-mile segment of the Pacific Crest Trail cuts through the park and can be accessed via the Warner Valley Road or by a long hike from Hat Lake. The most interesting section of the trail for non–through-hikers is the 5-mile segment south of Drakesbad that leads toward the park's southern boundary via Boiling Springs Lake and Terminal Geyser. This little-visited part of the park is actually one of the most spectacular geothermal displays this side of Yellowstone, and you're likely to have it to yourself.

Nobles Emigrant Trail, Lassen Volcanic National Park

10 miles round-trip. Easy. Access: Northwest Entrance. Map: Lassen Trails booklet available at visitor center.

One of the park's easiest longer hikes is this scenic trail that passes though an old-growth forest, past Choas Crags (pink-hued rocks from an old weathered volcano), and into Lassen's Dwarf Forest, a bizarre region of stunted trees.

Paradise Meadow, Lassen Volcanic National Park

3.5 miles round-trip. Moderate. Access: Hat Lake parking area, off Calif. 89 between Emigrant Pass and the Summit Lake Campgrounds. Map: Lassen Trails booklet available at visitor center.

This hike rises at a steady grade along a creek, eventually coming to a series of small waterfalls and a postcard-perfect meadow with outstanding wildflower displays during midsummer.

Summit Lake, Lassen Volcanic National Park

8 miles round-trip. Moderate. Access: Start from either Summit Lake Campground.

This popular day hike is a longer version of the Summer Lake Trail loop. It passes a myriad of lakes and wildflower-filled meadows on the way to lower Twin Lake. After you pass the first moderately steep crest, the rest of the hike is less strenuous.

Overnights

Trinity Alps Overnight, Alpine Lake

18 miles round-trip. Allow 3 or 4 days. Strenuous. Steep and rocky. Access: Trail begins at Bridge Camp, 2 miles up Stuart Fork Rd. from Trinity Alps Resort. Map: USGS Rush Creek Lakes and Siligo Peak topos.

This is a good backpack for a long weekend. The forest service campground at Bridge Camp is a nice layover before beginning your hike early in the morning. You quickly leave the beautiful Stuart Fork of the Trinity and begin a relentless climb. The first 5.5 miles aren't so steep, but after you pass the trail junction at Oak Flat and follow the Alpine Lake Trail, you'll gain almost 3,000 feet in just over 3 miles. The payoff? Well, you get to camp beside a beautiful alpine lake in a glacial valley. Great day hikes surround the area. If you feel like breaking up the hike in or out, make a halfway stop at the really nice campsite on the Stuart Fork, just about a quarter-mile west of the Stuart Fork/Alpine Lake Trail junction.

HORSEBACK RIDING

Coffee Creek Ranch, HC 2, P.O. Box 4940, Trinity Center, CA 96091 (☎ 530/266-3343), is located right on Coffee Creek and has every possible dude-ranch activity you could think of (and a few you probably wouldn't think of). It has a heated pool, fishing pond, square dancing, and, of course, a huge stable of beautiful horses waiting to be ridden into the surrounding mountains.

For a more rugged adventure, the **Hank Pritchard Cattle Drive,** in Manton (☎ 530/474-3355), does the *City Slickers* thing, bringing soft city folk along on a genuine multiday cattle drive and making them do real work for a change. There are two trips each year; one begins June 1, the other October 15.

KAYAKING

If what you dream of is miles and miles of Class III and IV water, with relatively easy portages around the hard stuff, this is your neck of the woods. For an intermediate kayaker, the runs are almost limitless: the lower Klamath, the Trinity, the McCloud River, the upper Sacramento between Lake Shasta and Lake Siskiyou, the Salmon. Mixed in with all the *easy* water are some gnarly stretches of Class IV–plus and Class V: the Gorge Run of the Salmon, Burnt Ranch Gorge on the Trinity, and the upper Klamath, any of which will keep all but the most jaded boater happy.

The best resource for mile-by-mile descriptions of any of these rivers is either *California Whitewater* by Jim Cassady and Fryar Calhoun (Cassady and Calhoun, 1985) or *A Guide to the Best Whitewater in the State of California* by Lars Holbec and Chuck Stanley (Friends of the River, 1988). Kayakers seeking instruction would do well to contact **Otter Bar Lodge,** which is widely considered to be one of the best and certainly the most luxurious kayaking school in the world (see box). **Cutting Edge Adventures** in Mount Shasta, P.O. Box 1334, Mount Shasta, CA 96067 (☎ 530/926-4647), runs two 5-day kayak clinics each summer on the Klamath. Evenings are spent camping on the river, and all gear is carried by rafts.

MOUNTAIN BIKING

The mountain bike is king here—not surprising in an area where you can count the number of stoplights on both hands and where there's at least as many dirt roads as paved ones. In the **Klamath National Forest** you could literally ride a new logging road every day for a year and never cover the same ground twice. That's not even taking into account all the single track. The option is there for extended multiday touring through all the northern mountain areas. National-forest campgrounds are plentiful, and small towns are fairly evenly spaced to restock on food every day or two.

For a really cushy stay at a beautiful wilderness lodge with awesome guided mountain-bike rides every day, look into **Otter Bar Lodge** (☎ 530/462-4772) on the Salmon River. This famous kayaking school has branched out in recent years to include a mountain-biking program. You'll bike to secluded swimming holes, up to fire lookouts, and descend as many miles of single track as you could ever stand. It's expensive, close to $1,590 per person per week double occupancy, but Otter Bar provides all meals and equipment, and the staff is great. (See "Otter Bar Lodge" feature and look under "Campgrounds & Other Accommodations" for more information.)

Siskiyou Lake Loop
11 miles. Easy. Flat. Access: Begins where North Shore Rd. turns to dirt 3 miles west of Mt. Shasta City. Map: Shasta–Trinity National Forest recreation map.

Though this ride is almost entirely on gravel and dirt roads, and never gains more than 80 feet of elevation, there is one tricky spot: the ford through the headwaters of the Sacramento River. From the parking area follow North Shore Road around the lake. At the intersection of North Shore Road and Dead End Road, you'll want to go straight on North Shore. After crossing a bridge over Deer Creek and then riding through another small stream, you should see a dirt road to the left that has been blocked off to car traffic. It will take you to the Sacramento River. Carry your bike across. (In high water you may not be able to ford the river. Be careful!) Continue back along paved Barr Road, which will follow the south shore back around and over the dam to your starting point. At the dam take a look down into Box Canyon, the dramatic gorge below.

The Ride Around Mount Shasta
63-plus miles. Extremely difficult. Access: Park your car in downtown Mt. Shasta City and ride south on Mt. Shasta Blvd. Map: Shasta–Trinity National Forest recreation map.

Even though this route is relatively flat with only one serious climb, don't go into it ill-prepared. The elevation gain is moderate, but the ride is long and rough, on dirt and gravel roads, plus 2 hellish miles along a railroad grade. Since you'll be riding on dirt forest service roads that may or may not be currently open to logging trucks and woodcutters, stay alert for traffic. Take a lot of water, full tool kit, extra tubes, and plenty of food—the only town on the route is Mount Shasta City. Note that the climate around Mount Shasta is so weird and varied that you could leave Mount Shasta City in warm sunshine and get snowed on when you reach the other side of the mountains.

Along the route you'll pass everything from evergreen forest to volcanic moonscape, and then go through a long stretch of high desert in the rain shadow of hulking Mount Shasta. Along the eastern side of the mountain, many small streams drain the mountain. With a water pump filter, these could save you a lot of weight in carrying extra bottles of water. For the most current information on the conditions of fire roads on this route, contact the staff at **The 5th Season,** 300 N.

OTTER BAR LODGE

One of the most pleasant weeks of my entire life was spent at Otter Bar Lodge on the Salmon River (often called the Cal Salmon to differentiate from the Salmon River in Idaho). Peter and Kristy Sturgis started Otter Bar as just a wilderness lodge. Peter was—and still is—a hotshot white-water kayaker, so his boating buddies kept coming here for the fantastic white water on the Salmon and the nearby Klamath. One thing led to another, and now 15 years later, Otter Bar Lodge is widely considered to be among the top three kayaking schools in the nation and unequivocally the most luxurious. The lodge is a beautiful, hand-built work of art, the fruit of years of Sturgis's labor. It has four double rooms, two cabins, multiple decks, a wood-burning hot tub, and my favorite, an outdoor shower where I once watched a golden eagle circle while I washed my hair. The food is delicious, so good in fact that *Bon Appetit* has written about Otter Bar. You will not suffer a lack of creature comforts here.

Teaching at Otter Bar is done in small groups of three or less, and the emphasis is placed on practical hands-on river learning rather than repetitive drills in the pond. Sturgis employs a rotating corps of some of the best kayakers in the world as his instructors. Groups rotate days with instructors to benefit from a variety of different teaching styles. During my session we rotated between three instructors.

Creek Hanauer is a mid-40s local resident who lives up the river from Otter Bar. He has a gift for the gab and an easy way of laughing at his own and everyone else's follies. Creek was great at letting you make a mistake, but then would explain perfectly what you'd done wrong and how to avoid it in the future. His wealth of local natural and human history made him a great river companion.

Reg Lake, at 51, is somewhat of a legend in kayaking circles. He's done numerous first descents around the globe and spends half the year sea kayaking around South America. The Zen master of the instructors, Reg on a river is a living example of excellence through economy of motion. Rivers have taught him a lot over the years, and he was very into letting the river do the teaching, sometimes to the point that I wanted to strangle him. "What am I doing wrong, Reg?" I'd ask after a sound thrashing. "Why don't you try it again and let the river show you?" Well, Reg, because I figured I'd let you save me the trouble. Inevitably he'd relent and share some brilliant nugget of kayak technique, but not before you threatened to shove a paddle up his nose.

Brennan Guth was the youngest instructor at 25, but somehow has found enough time to fit in stints as a mountaineering instructor and professional river guide. He's also worked with Native American tribes in Idaho and finished a degree in philosophy at the University of Montana. All this in between running some of the hardest white water in the world. By far the most gonzo boater I've ever seen, Brennan is a genius of technical, cutting-edge kayaking and his teaching style reflects it: precise, insightful, and calm in the face of what seemed to the rest

Mount Shasta Blvd. (☎ **530/926-3606**), or the **Mount Shasta Ranger District,** 300 Pine St. (☎ **530/926-4511**).

ROAD BIKING

Lassen Volcanic National Park Metric Century

62 miles round-trip (100km). Strenuous. Access: Lassen Chalet, just inside south-west entrance of park. Map: Lassen Volcanic National Park map.

This road is only open 6 months of the year, but during those 6 months it is simply one of the greatest metric century rides in the world. Starting at the chalet, you'll tour through beautiful wooded countryside with occasional views of Mount Shasta and Lassen Peak. In the first of us to be overwhelming hardship. He's also got a killer wit and is a great conversationalist about almost any subject.

Each day they'd take us down increasingly harder stretches of river. By virtue of being the third best boater in our nine-person session, when the groups were divided up I wound up being the worst kayaker in the hardest group. Michael and Kristin, my fellow students, were a young married couple who'd recently escaped the Bay Area to live in Mount Shasta. Michael was pretty much unstoppable. Throw a rapid in front of him, any rapid, and he'd run it. Flip him over, he'd pop back up smiling. Kristin and I, on the other hand, took turns reassuring each other that we probably wouldn't die and really were doing this for fun. When one of us would take a beating, screw up our Eskimo roll, and swim, we'd laugh together and exchange knowing looks. Meanwhile, Michael was looking for bigger, faster thrills and seemed a little dissatisfied with the pace of things.

The high point for all of us came on the last day when Brennan led the three of us down a section of the Klamath that a week earlier would have spelled certain destruction. At the top of a scary-looking rapid named Aikens Creek, the run called for us to ferry out to a midriver boulder, catch the eddy behind the boulder, then peel out downriver around some rocks and slam through a long and frightening wave train that emptied into a big pool. Brennan probably ran it backward just for kicks, but for the rest of us it was pretty intense. Even Michael looked a little put off by it.

I caught the eddy easily enough, looked over my shoulder at Brennan and Kristin, who'd already made it through, and then, mysteriously, flipped over. Hanging there, about to run the biggest rapid of my life backward and upside down, I had a moment of incredible calm and clarity. I took inventory of my situation. . . .

"Andrew," I told myself underwater, "if you screw up now it's curtains for you."

That out of the way, I did what they'd been coaching us to do all week: I set up my roll, went through my mental checklist to make sure I was doing it right, then snapped my paddle and body around in an amazing display of grace and coordination I didn't know I had in me. Next thing I knew I was upright, paddling like a son of a bitch to keep from slipping backward over the lip of the rapid. After hiding out in the safety of an eddy for a minute, I caught my breath and ran it, this time flawlessly.

That rapid was a huge mental victory for me. The worst possible thing that could happen to me did, and I handled it fine. The fear that had been holding me back all week left me, and that day my kayaking improved fivefold. On the last rapid of the day I got slammed over a 4-foot drop, punched through a huge wave still upright, and actually caught air. When I landed, I wiped out and rolled up laughing so hard I nearly choked. That, to me, is what it's all about.

Otter Bar Lodge, Forks of Salmon, CA 96031 (☎ **530/462-4772;** www.outterbar. com), offers 1-week sessions at $1,590 per person, including all meals, equipment, and instruction.

10 miles you'll climb almost 2,000 feet to crest the 8,512-foot Park Road summit. (If you're feeling really ambitious it's a short hike from here to the top of Mount Lassen.) Early in the season watch for ice on the road near here. Now you'll descend through more striking alpine scenery and pass the occasional bubbling mud pot or sulfur vent, eventually reaching Manzanita Lake at Lassen Park's northwest corner. Manzanita Lake is a stunning spot to rest; Lassen Peak makes a spectacular backdrop to this large, tree-encircled gem. Don't linger too long, because from here you have to climb almost 3,000 feet back up to the Park Road summit before you can coast back to the chalet and your car.

CLIMBING MOUNT SHASTA

Mount Whitney and its surrounding peaks may be higher, but as far as the experience of climb-ing a *mountain* goes, nothing in the state rivals 14,162-foot-tall Shasta. Unlike the other moun-tains over 14,000 feet in the state, Shasta stands all by itself, a perfect cone rising 10,000 feet above the surrounding countryside.

Though just about anyone in good physical condition can climb Shasta by the popular **Avalanche Gulch Route,** it's not something to be taken lightly. You won't need a rope, but most of the climb is on ice and snow, meaning that crampons and ice axes are indispensable.

In a normal snow year, the prime climbing season on the mountain is from early June through late July or early August. Too early, and you'll be slogging through waist-deep soft snow on your way to the summit. Too late, and after a few miles of slipping and sliding on scary pumice and scree slopes, you'll be making pacts with the devil just to get off the mountain. What you want is to find the whole route covered in nicely hardened, sun-and-wind-packed snow, making for a smooth walk all the way to the top.

The winter of 1994/1995 was an incredible snow year on Shasta, and the mountain was still covered in late August when my friend Kristin Williams and I set out for the summit at 3am under a full moon. As we hiked through the pines above the Bunny Flat parking area, the moon-glow gently lit Avalanche Gulch and Casaval Ridge, and we were able to sleepwalk our way up the mountain without flashlights.

Two miles later, the **Sierra Club cabin** at Horse Valley popped out of the darkness. We filled our water bottles at the spring-fed tap (about 2 gal. each—there's no water above here unless you melt it) and stumbled on up the **Olberman's Causeway,** an amazing elevated path built of huge flat rocks by one of the original caretakers of the Sierra Club hut.

From the hut to the summit it's only 4.1 miles, but more than 6,000 vertical feet. The stone pathway soon gave way to well-packed snow. By sunrise we were at 10,400 feet on the frozen "shores" of **Lake Helen,** a semiglacial tarn that's only a lake in years of extremely light snow. Though we'd been walking on snow and ice for almost 2 miles now, Lake Helen is where the climb really begins.

After a breakfast of Power Bars and oranges, we strapped on our crampons and pulled out the ice axes. Ahead we could see several other parties strung out along the 2,500-foot snow-field leading to the top of Avalanche Gulch and the red pumice cliffs of Red Banks. In the 15 minutes it took us to eat and gear up, it looked like they moved about half an inch.

About an hour later I was where those people had been, on a 40° slope of sun-cupped icy snow, and it was me who was barely moving. They, on the other hand, were nowhere to be seen. No doubt they were on top snapping summit pictures and jeering the slowpokes behind them. To the casual observer it must have looked like Kristin and I had fallen asleep standing upright, but if they looked closely, they might have been able to discern the rhythm of our forward progress: Pick up ice axe . . . drive ice axe into snow . . . shuffle left foot up 4 inches to new ice axe placement . . . follow with right foot . . . lean on ice axe . . . gasp like a carp . . . pick up ice axe . . . every 20 steps stop to drink water or eat. God, I've never seen anything go on as long as that snowfield. Luckily, the views below us were beautiful and kept us entertained.

Avalanche Gulch is narrow and steep at the top. Soon we were working our way over a slight headwall and into a narrow chimney through the **Red Banks.** Kristin, who'd been feeling bad for the last hour or two, suddenly got her second wind and bolted ahead out of sight. Me? I lost my wind and got scared. One slip here might not have meant death, but wouldn't have been a cake-walk either.

Looking from the bottom you think that once you crest the Red Banks it's just a hop, a skip, and a jump to the summit. Ha! After the Red Banks you still have more than 1,000 feet of altitude to climb, most of it in a single rock-covered nightmare called **Misery Hill.** We'd been hiking in beautiful sunshine the whole way when we hit Misery Hill and suddenly, boom, we were socked in by a thick cloud bank. Great, I thought, you mean I climbed all this way to look at the inside of a cloud? That's right brother, said the mountain, as it started throwing 60-mile-per-hour gusts at us just to stir up the mix.

After conferring for a second, we decided to bolt for the summit. After hauling my ass up Avalanche Gulch, I thought Misery Hill looked like something you'd see at a putt-putt golf course. At least I couldn't fall off it, or if I could, the clouds prevented me from peering morbidly into the abyss. Inexplicably, I was feeling strong and fast. Kristin, on the other hand, started to feel really sick. As we stumbled across the last ridge to the summit, it was so windy that we had to hunker down and brace with our ice axes when the 60- to 70-mile-per-hour gusts hit and stagger onward whenever they let up; but I noticed Kristin was bracing in the calm periods and trying to walk during the wind blasts. Occasionally she'd wander in a small circle and look confused.

By the time we reached the base of the summit col, a 50-foot-tall pile of rocks that is the actual highest point on Shasta, it was obvious that my climbing buddy was in a bad way. She had all the classic symptoms of altitude sickness. Slurring her words, Kristin told me she was about to vomit and collapse and that I should go on. Then she staggered up to some guy coming up behind us, took off his sunglasses, and stared into his eyes with a crazed look. There was no time for a picnic or a nice session of yodeling. We snapped a hasty almost-summit shot and before you could say "Acute Mountain Sickness" we'd shed our crampons and were lurching arm in arm back down the rocks of Misery Hill.

From the base of Misery Hill you can glissade—the nice-sounding French word for sliding on your butt—all the way to wherever you run out of snow. Kristin mysteriously pulled a Hefty garbage sack out of her pack, stuck her legs through it, sat down, and was gone. I followed right behind, but I was too gripped with fear to keep up. I used my ice axe as a brake the whole way down and even then I thought I was a goner once or twice. I don't know what she did to maintain control but I swear that from above Kristin looked like an Olympic luger, just a cloud of snow quickly pulling away from me, the occasional arm or leg sticking out. By the time we hit Lake Mary, the thicker air and the adrenaline blast had made her as good as new. What took us 13 hours to hike up took exactly an hour-and-a-half to slide down. We were lucky that there was snow almost to the Sierra Club hut. A month later and we'd have been walking down. We got back to car at sunset.

PRACTICALITIES

Rent crampons, ice axes, mountaineering boots, and any other climbing gear you'll need at **The 5th Season,** 300 N. Mount Shasta Blvd. (☎ **530/926-3606**). The staff there is a good source of general mountain wisdom and lore.

The Mt. Shasta Book by Andy Selters and Michael Zanger (Wilderness Press, 1990) gives accurate and easy-to-understand descriptions of all the major climbing routes up Shasta and ski mountaineering areas on the volcano. It comes with a redrawn Mount Shasta topographical map covering the whole mountain, rather than splitting it into two separate quadrants like the USGS maps.

Note: We did the hike in 1 day, leaving our car at 3am and returning at about 7pm. It can be done, but it hurts. Next time I'm going to bivouac at least as high as the Sierra Club hut and possibly as high as Lake Helen to make the summit hike less of a grueling ordeal.

ROCK CLIMBING & MOUNTAINEERING

The jagged granite spires of the **Castle Crags** are the easternmost vestiges of the Klamath Range, which was once joined with the Sierra Nevada before dramatic geological forces drove the two ranges apart. The climbing here is very similar to the Sierra too: good clean routes on granite domes and spires with single faces as tall as 1,500 feet. Numerous shorter routes are popular with sport climbers. There is so much variety here it would be hard to get tired of the place. Perhaps the greatest treat of climbing the crags is the exquisite view of Mount Shasta and the surroundings you get from the top. For specific routes and climbing advice, contact **The 5th Season** (☎ **530/926-3606**) in Shasta City.

SPELUNKING

The caves at **Lava Beds National Monument** (☎ **530/667-2282**) are open to the public with little restriction or hassle (see box). All you need to see most of them is a good flashlight or headlamp, sturdy walking shoes, and a sense of adventure. Many of the tunnels are entered by ladders or stairs, others by holes in the side of a hill. Once inside, walk far enough to round a corner, then shut off your light. Imagine the Modocs, knowing they're surrounded, sitting here waiting for the cavalry. Then imagine the cavalry knowing that anywhere they go the ground could open to a bunch of armed and desperate men. A chilling impasse, to say the least.

The one-way **Cave Loop Road** just to the southwest of the visitor center is home to many of the best cave hikes. About 15 lava tubes have been marked and made accessible. Two of the caves are ice caves, where the air temperature remains below freezing all year and ice crystals form on the walls. If exploring on your own gives you the creeps, check out **Mushpot Cave.** Almost adjacent to the visitor center, this cave has been outfitted with lights and a smooth walkway; you'll have plenty of company. Hardened spelunkers will find enough remote and relatively unexplored caves in the monument, many requiring specialized climbing gear, to keep themselves busy.

WALKS & RAMBLES

Bumpass Hell, Lassen Volcanic National Park

1.5 miles. Access: Trailhead clearly marked on Lassen Park Road. Map: Lassen National Park map.

The beginning of this walk leads you through a quiet and peaceful meadow of wildflowers and chirping birds before depositing you right in the middle of Bumpass Hell, a churning, roaring, stinking display of volcanic power. The bubbling mud pots and hot springs here cover acres. Stay on the path: Bumpass Hell is named for a hunter who fell in a mud pot and lost his leg.

Clear Creek, Mud Creek Trail

1.5 miles. Access: Trailhead is located at the end of Clear Creek Rd., about 17 miles northeast of McCloud. Contact Shasta Ranger Station for the latest road status—detours are common on local roads. Map: Shasta–Trinity National Forest map.

The remote Clear Creek and Mud Creek drainages on the south side of Shasta are good places to get a look at the different ecosystems of the mountain in one compact area. From here you'll explore the pine forests of the mountain flanks, pass mountain hemlock and running meadows, and see where a mud flow in 1960 nearly slid into the little logging town of McCloud. Several waterfalls grace the area. On the mountain above, you can see the Konwakiton and Wintun glaciers, permanent ice fields cut with numerous crevasses and ice falls.

WHITE-WATER RAFTING

This area gives the rivers of the Sierra Nevada a good run for their money. The

Klamath and Trinity rivers in particular are popular with commercial outfitters. The Klamath is the best late-summer white water in the state; its steady flow is controlled by a dam in Oregon. The Trinity, too, is kept at a steady pace by releases from Lewiston Dam. Depending on your ability and desire for thrills, you might choose a single-day Class III trip down the **lower Klamath** or **upper Sacramento.** Looking for something a little more hairy? Try the **Salmon** in early spring (a wild river with a very short season), the **Burnt Ranch Gorge of the Trinity** (Class V, scary water), or the **upper Klamath** (Class IV–plus).

Numerous rafting companies run all these rivers. Contact the local chamber of commerce or the **River Travel Center,** Box 226, Point Arena, CA 95468 (☎ **800/ 882-7238**), for complete listings, prices, and recommendations.

Campgrounds & Other Accommodations

CAMPING

Bridge Camp, Shasta–Trinity National Forest

2.5 miles up the Stewarts Fork Trinity River from Trinity Reservoir on Trinity Alps Rd. off State Rte. 3. ☎ 530/623-2121. 10 sites. Pit toilets, running water. Skiing, hiking, swimming, horseback riding, biking. Pets accepted, horse corrals available. $4 per night; no reservations.

Bridge Camp is a world apart from the hustle and bustle that characterizes most campgrounds near Trinity Lake. The Stewarts Fork tumbles by the camp, providing numerous swimming holes. This is also the trailhead for the Stewarts Fork Trail into the Trinity Alps Wilderness.

Castle Crags State Park

6 miles south of I-5, Dunsmuir exit. ☎ 530/235-2684 or 530/225-2065. 64 sites. Flush toilets, showers. Skiing, hiking, rock climbing. Pets accepted. $12–$14 per night. Call MISTIX (☎ 800/ 444-PARK) for reservation; fee charged.

With the granite spires of the Castle Crags looming above, Mount Shasta in the distance, and the Sacramento River nearby, this is a hard spot to beat. The only drawback is that I-5 runs nearby and can sometimes be heard. There are plenty of nearby places to explore.

Lake Siskiyou Camp

On Barr Rd. across I-5 from Mt. Shasta City. ☎ 530/926-2610. 300 sites. Flush toilets, running water, showers, store, boat rentals, laundry. Kayaking, fishing, hiking, swimming, biking. Pets accepted. $16.50–$22.50 per night. Reservations accepted.

Lake Siskiyou is a great place to camp with kids. The sandy beach and warm water make for an inviting swim. Fishing on the lake is also good, and motorized boats are prohibited. Since the lake was built for the sole purpose of recreation, it stays full all summer long. Great hikes and mountain biking into the nearby hills, as well.

Indian Well, Lava Beds National Monument

0.75 miles from the park headquarters. ☎ 530/667-2282. 40 sites. Picnic table, fire ring, cooking grill, pit toilets, no water. During summer, water and flush toilets are available. Wildlife, bird watching, hiking, caving. $10 per night in summer; $6 per night in winter. No reservations.

If you really want to stay inside Lava Beds, there isn't much in the way of selection. Fortunately, Indian Well, the park's only campground, is great. In the winter particularly, it lacks in facilities, but with 20 lava tube caves nearby just waiting to be explored, who's complaining about having to use a pit toilet?

Lassen Volcanic National Park Campgrounds

P.O. Box 100, Mineral, CA 96063. ☎ 530/595-4444. 7 car campgrounds with 375 sites total. Various facilities. Skiing, biking, boating, wildlife, bird watching, hiking. Fees vary from $8–$14. Reservations only for Lost Creek Group Campground (fees charged).

Car campers have their choice of seven park campgrounds in Lassen, more than enough to handle the trickle of visitors. In fact, so few people camp in Lassen that there is no reservation system except for the Lost Creek Group Campground, and stays have a generous 14-day limit. Sites do fill up on weekends, however, so your best bet is to get to the park early on Friday to secure a place to stay. If the park is packed, there are 43 campgrounds in surrounding Lassen National Forest, so you'll find a site somewhere.

By far the most "civilized" campground in the park is at **Manzanita Lake,** which has hot showers, electrical hookups, and the like. When Manzanita fills up, rangers open the **Crags Campground** overflow camp about 5 miles away. It's much more basic. On the southern end of the park you'll find **Southwest Campground,** a walk-in camp directly adjacent to the parking lot for Lassen Chalet.

The two remote entrances to Lassen, Warner Valley and Butte Lake, have their own campgrounds. **Butte Lake** has flush toilets, no showers, and charges a fee. **Warner Valley,** along with the **Juniper Lake** campground, is primitive, with pit toilets and no water, but the price is right—free. Backcountry camping is allowed almost anywhere. Ask about closed areas when you get your wilderness permit.

INNS & LODGES

Trinity Alps Resort

Just off State Rte. 3, 1750 Trinity Alps Rd., Trinity Center, CA 96091. ☎ 530/286-2205. 43 cabins. Cabin rentals average $495–$955 per week in summer. No credit cards.

The Trinity Alps Resort reminds me of something out of the 1920s: a family resort where everyone gets together for group hikes and campfire sing-alongs, big kids flirt on the beach, and younger kids are fascinated with trying to catch the savvy trout that live downstream. The resort was in fact built in the 1920s but recently underwent a major renovation. The cabins here are rustic but beautiful. There's also a store, horseback rides, rec room, and video games.

Otter Bar Lodge

14026 Salmon River Rd., Forks of Salmon, CA 96031. ☎ 530/462-4772. Exclusive wilderness lodge/kayaking school. Maximum occupancy 14 guests. 1-week stays, roughly $1,590 per person depending on activities. Reserve well in advance. MC, V.

Otter Bar is well known in the kayaking world for its excellent instruction, awesome location, and, last but certainly not least, cushy accommodations and great food. When you're here, you know you're in the middle of nowhere. Located right on the Salmon River, Otter Bar has great swimming and mountain biking in addition to its white-water kayaking program. See "Otter Bar Lodge" feature and "Mountain Biking" under "What to Do & Where to Do It" for more information.

Drakesbad Guest Ranch, Lassen Volcanic National Park

Inside Lassen Volcanic National Park at the end of a dead-end road. Contact California Guest Services, 2150 N. Main St. #5, Red Bluff, CA 96080. ☎ 530/529-1512. 19 units. Doubles begin at $185, meals included. Reserve well in advance. MC, V. Open mid-June to mid-Oct.

This incredible wilderness lodge was built around the turn of the century in one of the most remote parts of the Lassen backcountry. Today little has changed.

Drakesbad is deluxe in the way that only a place with no electricity or phones can be. At night, guests read by kerosene lamps and huddle under hand-stitched quilts in the rough-hewn pine rooms. Full meal service is available and very good. Daily horseback rides are scheduled to a variety of scenic park locations every day, but it's hard to beat where you are; Drakesbad is surrounded by meadows, lakes, streams, and mature forests. Hundreds of miles of hiking trail leave from your doorstep. When your day is over, you can slip into the 116° hot-spring pool to soak away any sore muscles. Unbeatable.

9

The North Coast

North of the Bay Area's sphere of influence lies a weird and wild coast. Between Jenner, at the mouth of the Russian River, and the Oregon border, the California coast is a land of deep dark forests, slimy banana slugs, tiny timber and fishing towns, Bigfoot, pot-growing hippies, redneck loggers, crashing surf, and salmon as big as rottweilers. That's the stereotype at least. Some of it is even true. The north coast of California is a bizarre conglomeration of everything good about the state, everything weird under the sun, and a healthy (or is it unhealthy?) dose of human and ecological tragedy.

Maybe it's the weather that sets the North Coast apart. California, after all, is the Golden State: sunshine, Malibu Barbie, the Beach Boys. But from San Francisco to the Oregon border, California is the land of gum boots and Gore-Tex, not bikinis and Coppertone. Your skin is more likely to erode away in the rain than to get burned in the sun. Whatever it is, the North Coast is the outlandish cousin of the California that people who grew up on *Gidget* and *The Brady Bunch* imagine.

Much of the year the thick **coastal fog** lies over the land like a soggy wool blanket, dripping slowly but constantly onto the land below. From this constant moisture, the world's original drip irrigation system, springs a verdant world of thick forests, huge rivers, and dramatically eroded coast-line. Of course, half the time you can't see any of it through the fog, which cloaks the area in an omnipresent fuzziness that softens everything and washes the color out of a landscape filled with bright reds and greens and blues. There is a certain serene beauty about the fog, though, that makes you focus on the things in front of you without distraction. Given that the area receives an average of 80 to 135 inches of rain a year, most of it in the form of a slow drizzle, a sunny day on the North Coast is nothing less than spectacular, inducing a dropped-jaw feeling of "You mean that's what's out there in the fog?" as you marvel at a stand of redwoods or the striking violence of waves crashing into a rocky headland.

Once predominant, now endangered, the defining feature of the North Coast is still the **redwood forest.** When the coast redwood was first noted as a species in 1794, an estimated 2 million acres of the trees covered much of the coast between Santa Cruz and the Oregon line. By 1965 that number was down to 300,000 acres, so the state and federal governments set aside almost 110,000 acres in Redwood National Park. Cutting on private land continued, though. Today a heated battle over cutting down the last 5,000 acres of privately owned old-growth redwoods has reached a feverish pitch, with the trees perhaps saved, but the forest's fate still greatly in doubt.

The economy here was once based on a seemingly stable tripod of three natural resources: timber, salmon, and marijuana. All over the North Coast, loggers, lumber-mill workers, fishermen, and pot growers existed happily side by side (they were often, in fact, the same person), and the money they earned was the foundation for most area business: the car dealers, restaurants, gas stations, and supermarkets.

Then the system collapsed. Silt and dirt eroded into the rivers from logging clear-cuts year after year, covering up the gravel needed by the king and silver salmon for their spawning beds. With very few new salmon being born, the fishery plummeted and has yet to recover. Then in the mid-1980s, the big timber companies discovered that they could save money by shipping raw logs to Japan to be processed in high-tech automated lumber mills and then shipping the finished lumber back here to sell, rather than paying the local mill workers union wages. With the loss of those mill jobs, the timber economy seized up and has never recovered.

Which left the North Coast standing on one leg, and a dubious one at that. Pot growing didn't go over very well with law enforcement during the Reagan-Bush–era "War on Drugs," and after a few seasons of massive raids, helicopters buzzing overhead, and midnight arrests of prominent local citizens, the big growers left, running off to wherever it is that dope growers go when the heat gets too bad. And that's where it stands now. The North Coast exists largely on an economy of tourism and retirement money from people fleeing the urban life of L.A. and San Francisco. Meanwhile, there are a lot of unemployed fishermen and timber-industry workers sitting on their hands waiting for things to take a turn for the better, and a lot of pot growers sitting in jail. Not the way the American Dream was supposed to turn out.

The Lay of the Land

All problems aside, the North Coast is still some of the most beautiful country around, and the opportunities for outdoor sports here are almost limitless. Most of the coast is still wild. From Eureka to Rockport, for example, there are only three roads that reach the beach in a 75-mile stretch of coast, and 4,000-foot-tall mountains rise straight out of the sea. Within that area is the longest undeveloped stretch of wilderness coast in California, the **Lost Coast:** 24 miles of plunging cliffs, secret waterfalls, cobblestone beaches, redwood trees, an abandoned lighthouse, and huge crashing surf. It's a backpacker's paradise. The numerous fire roads and trails of the **King Range Conservation Area** are perfect for extended mountain-biking forays. All along the North Coast, state and national parks allow great access to the ocean and the mountains of Sonoma, Mendocino, Humboldt, and Del Norte counties.

The general topography of the North Coast is one of extremely steep mountains rising straight out of the sea. Only in

The Northern Coast

PACIFIC OCEAN

a few spots do you find a large coastal plain, usually near the mouths of rivers such as the Smith or the Klamath, or where large dune fields have formed around bays and lakes. The largest coastal plain surrounds Humboldt Bay and Arcata Bay near the mouth of the Eel River. **Eureka,** the largest town on the North Coast, fills the central portion, and farms line much of the rest. Most places on the coast, though, are pretty much straight up and down. **Highway 1** south of Leggett along the Mendocino and Sonoma coast is an exercise in patience and steady nerves as you wind up and down huge sections of sinuous road with scarcely a foot or two of asphalt between you and a thousand-foot fall. It's worth the effort, though. Isolation has left much of the North Coast a window into the past: small towns of Victorian houses, seaside ranches, redwood trees looming high on the ridges, and the constant crashing of ocean waves against a rugged, rocky shoreline.

Orientation

Travel in the North Coast is by necessity north/south, with the rugged coast range making most east/west roads windy and slow. **Highway 101,** a massive freeway in San Francisco, is a fairly mellow two-lane road up here, a scenic but still fast route between Mendocino County and the Oregon border. North of Garberville, 101 heads toward the coast and runs along the shore the rest of the way to the northern state line.

On the west side of the coastal mountains, **Highway 1** is the only way to reach the towns and parks along the north coast. It's among the most beautiful drives in the country, but it's not a fast way to get anywhere and services are few and far between.

A lattice of **mountain roads** cross from Highway 101 to Highway 1 from

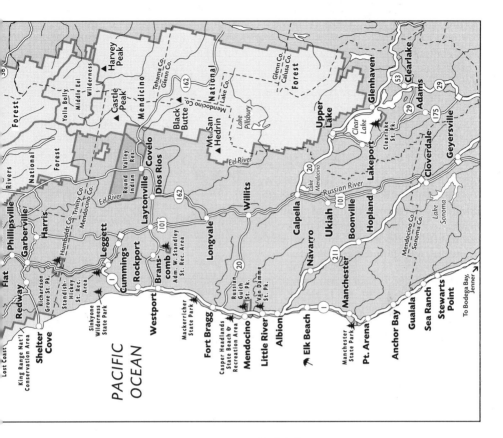

Mendocino north. Getting lost on these roads is a fantastic adventure, but some of them go nowhere, and many are unmapped logging roads. Make sure the tank is full, and try not to leave anyone waiting for you on the other end.

Bodega Bay

This small town and snug harbor is a busy fishing port and home to a 128-campsite **county park** on the beach (☎ 707/875-3540); a beautiful high headland perfectly situated for whale watching; and the **Bodega Marine Laboratory** (☎ 707/875-2211), a University of California marine research station offering public tours from 2 to 4pm every Friday.

Jenner

Situated at the mouth of the Russian River, this tiny town has long been a successful summer resort. The 110-mile-long Russian River drains into the sea here through an impressive estuary and sandbar system.

Point Arena

Port Arena is the site of the only boat launch between Bodega Bay and Fort Bragg. It's also home to the 115-foot-tall **Point Arena Lighthouse** (☎ 707/882-2777), built in 1870. Tours are offered from 11am to 2:30pm daily. **Arena Cove** is a popular and highly localized surf spot.

Mendocino and Fort Bragg

These two towns constitute the "urban" centers of coastal Mendocino County. Both support numerous B&Bs, fine restaurants, art galleries, and other tourist services. Mendocino is quaint and precious. Fort Bragg is sort of Mendocino's redneck cousin, and in my opinion a lot more fun. For information, contact the **Fort Bragg–Mendocino Chamber of Commerce,** 332 N. Main, P.O. Box 1141, Fort Bragg, CA 95437 (☎ 800/726-2780 or 707/961-6300).

Leggett

Small and kitschy Leggett, which boasts a drive-thru tree and isn't far from the "house inside a redwood," is located at the important intersection where Highway 1 disappears into Highway 101 and runs inland. There's a small cafe here boasting burgers and fries. If you're heading south, Leggett is the last food before the Sinkyone wilderness, 10 miles east as the crow flies. Mountain bikers heading to the coast can stop here for water before tackling the steep 6-mile hill and narrow, winding canyon out to the ocean, and the numerous fire trails branching out from either side.

Garberville

A small stopover just off Highway 101, Garberville is the last reliable place to get supplies and gas before heading into the Avenue of the Giants or west into the King Range. The road to Shelter Cove, one of the few to cross the mountains to the Lost Coast, begins here. Cozier than Eureka 60 miles north, Garberville is a nice round 200 miles from San Francisco, making it an ideal first-night motel stop before trips into the nearby redwood forests.

Ferndale

Located amid the ranches and farms 5 miles west of Highway 101, Ferndale was once the first town stagecoaches stopped at after the rough trail through the Lost Coast. Now it's a minor tourist destination playing off the Victorian architecture in its one-street downtown. It's also the jumping-off point for a steep, beautiful, not-for-the-weak mountain bike route over the northern end of the King Range.

Eureka and Arcata

The largest town on the North Coast by a long shot, Eureka is a heavily industrialized port city. Until fairly recently a nuclear power plant and several pulp mills were the town's biggest employers. The port of Humboldt Bay is an important harbor—one of the largest between San Francisco and the Columbia River. Since the economy has been in a slump the last 10 years, property crime has become a problem here. Arcata, a small community on the north end of the bay, is Eureka's alter ego. Home to Humboldt State University, one of the most countercultural schools in California, Arcata is a bohemian artist and student community.

Trinidad

A small coastal town with a state beach (Trinidad State Beach) and a state park (Patrick's Point), Trinidad manages to feel secluded despite being half a mile from Highway 101. Many private campgrounds are also available here, as are several of the area's classier restaurants and a handful of B&Bs.

Crescent City

A hardscrabble logging and port town of 3,500, Crescent City has had a tough history. In 1964, a tsunami caused by an earthquake in Alaska sent 12-foot waves roaring inland a quarter-mile through the business district of Crescent City. Nearly the entire waterfront was leveled and numerous people were killed. In 1972, a freak typhoon destroyed much of the town again. Crescent City is now rebuilt, but has the look of a town that expects to get leveled every decade. Besides the port, the biggest business in Crescent City is Pelican Bay Maximum Security Prison, where the baddest of the bad in the California prison system are sent.

Parks & Other Hot Spots

Sonoma Coast State Beaches

Between Jenner and Bodega Bay on Hwy. 1. Russian River Ranger District Station. ☎ **707/875-3483.** Swimming (though the water is very cold), whale watching, kayaking, diving, camping, hiking, fishing. No lifeguards. Bodega Head and Russian Gulch State Beach have toilets and water.

A series of more than 20 separate beaches, access ways, coves, and coastal trails. Most units of the park are free, with the exception of the Bodega Head Campground and Russian Gulch State Beach.

Salt Point State Park
20 miles north of Jenner on Hwy. 1. ☎ 707/847-3221. Boat launch, campground, rest rooms, beaches. Wildlife, hiking, swimming, diving, biking. Camping fee.

Salt Point is one of the best-known dive sites on the Sonoma coast—the spear fishing and abalone diving are excellent, but be aware of the underwater reserve boundaries. Less well known is the fact that the 4,300-acre park contains substantial upland areas laced with great hiking and riding trails. Not immediately adjacent to the park but nearby is the **Kruse Rhododendron State Reserve**, a stunning 300-acre rhododendron forest that blooms from April to June. Call Salt Point for information.

Elk Beach
At Elk, 20 miles south of Mendocino on Hwy. 1. Beach access, picnic areas.

The beach below this cliff-side B&B town is perfect for a picnic, with a small grocery store (fresh fruit in season) across the street and bench tables at both ends of the steep, quarter-mile trail to the ocean. There's no swimming at Elk Beach; the attraction here is the dramatic rocks just offshore, and the bizarre piles of driftwood scattered over the sand, entire trees worn into bonelike shapes by the surf and tossed onto the shore. Park in the dirt

lot opposite the general store and follow the signs left to the beach.

Manchester State Park
0.5 miles north of Manchester on Hwy. 1. ☎ 707/937-5804. Diving, surfing, hiking. Day-use and camping fees.

This 1,400-acre beach park has a large number of sand dunes and a long sandy beach. There's good diving and surfing.

Van Damme State Park
3 miles south of Mendocino on Hwy. 1. ☎ 707/937-5804. Diving, surfing, hiking. Day-use and camping fees (no fee for beach use).

This very popular campground is located across Highway 1 from a small sandy beach and the mouth of the Little River. There's good diving in the offshore underwater preserve and nice hiking in the upland portion of the park.

Russian Gulch State Park
2 miles north of Mendocino on Hwy. 1. ☎ 707/937-5804. Toilets and water available. Diving, hiking. Day-use and camping fees (no fee for beach use).

Once a rough-and-tumble port for timber schooners, Russian Gulch is now one of the most beautiful parks on the California coast. The spectacular campground here is tucked into a forested canyon. Hiking trails lead around the headlands and pass a huge, 200-foot-wide ocean blowhole.

MacKerricher State Park
3 miles north of Fort Bragg on Hwy. 1. ☎ 707/937-5804. 15-acre freshwater lake. Diving, swimming, boating, fishing, wildlife viewing (mostly sea lions).

Eureka's Average Temperatures and Precipitation											
	Jan	Feb	Mar	Apr	May	June	July	Aug	Sept	Oct	Nov	Dec
High (°F)	54	55	55	56	58	60	61	62	62	61	58	55
Low (°F)	41	43	43	45	48	51	52	53	51	49	45	42
Precipitation (in.)	6.2	5.0	5.2	2.8	1.8	0.6	0.2	0.3	0.8	2.9	5.8	6.3

Day-use and camping fees (no fee for beach use).

MacKerricher has one of the longest sandy beaches in Mendocino County, though the beach is somewhat severed from the rest of the park by an elevated logging haul road. Lake Cleone is good for freshwater fishing and canoeing. The campground here, like those of most state parks in the area, is extremely nice.

Sinkyone Wilderness State Park
For maps and information contact Eel River State Parks District Office, P.O. Box 100, Weott, CA 95571. Camping, swimming, hiking.

This spectacular 7,312-acre park of undeveloped coastline begins where Highway 1 turns inland to Leggett. A one-lane dirt road through the park is passable during good weather, and several good campsites are located on the beach. A 17-mile coastal backpacking trail runs the length of the park.

Richardson Grove State Park
8 miles south of Garberville on Hwy. 101. ☎ 707/247-3319. Toilets and water available. Hiking, camping, swimming, fishing.

The "grove" of the park's name is an impressive stand of redwoods along the Eel River. The Eel is warm and calm enough to swim in during the summer and early fall, and is rumored to have good trout fishing (no eels, though). Ten miles of hiking trails offer an alternative to the sun and the water, and the temperature difference in the cool redwood microclimate is a welcome change after some time on the river. There's also a hiker/biker campsite here (see "The Hiker-Biker Program" in chapter 1).

The "Lost Coast" and King Range National Conservation Area
For information contact Eureka Resource Area, U.S. Bureau of Land Management, 1695 Heindon Rd., Arcata, CA 95521. ☎ 707/825-2300. Camping, hiking, beaches, biking.

This incredible area is probably the wildest piece of coastline in the Lower 48. Other than the tiny town of Shelter Cove, there is no population center in the entire 63,000-acre area, a steep and densely forested range of 4,000- to 5,000-foot peaks rising right out of the sea. It's possible to hike the entire length of the Lost Coast from the Mattole River to Shelter Cove as a 3- to 5-day backpack trip. Other good backpacking trails are located back in the King Range.

Humboldt Redwood State Park
45 miles south of Eureka on Highway 101. ☎ 707/946-2409. Rest rooms, showers, visitors center. Camping, hiking, biking, swimming, kayaking, fishing. Fees for some park areas.

The largest redwood park in the state park system, Humboldt Redwood State Park is a stunning 51,000-acre forest containing more than 40% of the remaining old-growth coastal redwoods. Some groves are easy to reach; others require long hikes and offer the rare chance to visit these huge trees in solitude. The Eel River runs through the park for 30 miles; it's a popular summertime fishing, canoeing, and swimming spot. The park also contains a total of 250 campsites, which fill up quickly.

Grizzly Creek Redwoods State Park
On state highway 36, 17 miles east of Hwy. 101 at Fortuna. Camping, bird watching, kayaking, fishing, swimming.

Grizzly Creek Redwoods is a small park set in an unlikely area: amid the logging grounds east of the mill town of Fortuna, at one end of the wide Van Duzen Valley. Still, the range of wildlife here is impressive: bald eagles, pileated woodpeckers, black bears, river otters, and perhaps the coastal redwood's most famous resident, the spotted owl. A trip to the park takes you first past the marks of the nearby logging industry, clear-cuts, and dramatically eroded hills that have lost their vegetation. Not too uplifting if you were hoping for a day in the trees. But within another few miles you're plunged into the protected areas, and the contrast makes an impression. In winter, the Van Duzen River swells with Humboldt County's constant rain, and becomes a challenging canoe or kayak opportunity.

Patrick's Point State Park
25 miles north of Eureka, 5 miles north of Trinidad on Hwy. 101. ☎ 707/677-3570. Camping, hiking.

This family-oriented park has one of the best beaches on the north coast, Agate Beach. It's best visited in late summer, when the incessant coastal fog lightens up slightly. The views from several areas in the park, all accessed via a mile-long coastal trail, are postcard-perfect, the best on the coast. Bring the camera, and if it's foggy, a jacket as well. A re-created Yurok Indian Village illuminates some of the history of the area. Inexplicably, there's also a canvas "yurt" cabin for rent, which looks less like a yurt than a small space capsule and seems unrelated to anything else in the park.

Redwood National Park
South of Crescent City on Highway 101. Information: 1111 2nd St., Crescent City, CA 95531. ☎ 707/464-6101. Encompasses 3 state parks: Del Norte Coast Redwoods, Jedediah Smith Redwoods, and Prairie Creek Redwoods. Many activities and facilities. Day use and camping fees for some portions of the park.

The establishment of Redwood National Park in 1968 consolidated several state parks, federal reserves, and privately owned forests into this huge tribute to what much of the North Coast looked like before intensive logging cropped the old-growth forests. Most people whiz through here on Highway 101, stop to take a few pictures, and carry on. That's a shame. Take some time and explore the more remote portions of the park—it's worth it. See "Redwood National Park," below.

Humboldt Lagoons State Park and Harry A. Merlo State Recreation Area
31 miles north of Eureka on Highway 101. ☎ 707/488-2041. Camping, boating, hiking, swimming, biking. Open year-round; visitor center open only in summer.

Three lagoons lie inside these two parks. During heavy storms, two of the lagoons overflow into the ocean, carving huge channels in the beach, and dropping the lagoon water levels by up to 6 feet an hour. The surf and tides repair the beach.

Smith River National Recreation Area
For maps and other information contact the Gasquet Ranger District Office, 10600 Hwy. 199 N., P.O. Box 228, Gasquet, CA 95543. ☎ 707/457-3131. Fishing, hiking, swimming, rafting, kayaking, camping.

Long eyed by dam developers, the Smith River was recently declared a Wild and Scenic River and protected by the 305,000-acre Smith River Recreation Area. Almost a third of the area is old-growth Douglas-fir forest. There's great fishing, hiking, camping, and white-water rafting and kayaking.

Redwood National Park

When he was governor of California, Ronald Reagan once said that if you've seen one redwood, you've seen them all. Redwood National Park is living proof that he couldn't have been more wrong. While he was right that a 367-foot-tall coast redwood (the world's tallest, located in the Tall Trees Grove) does in fact look pretty much like the next one, Reagan was guilty of not seeing the forest for the trees.

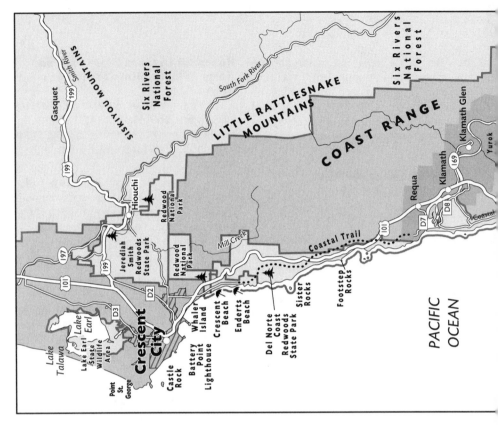

It's impossible to explain the feeling you get in the old-growth forests of Redwood National Park and its attached Redwood state parks without resorting to Alice-in-Wonderland comparisons. Like a tropical rain forest, the redwood forest is a multistoried affair, the tall trees being only the top layer. Everything is incredibly big, misty, and primeval. Flowering bushes cover the ground; 10-foot-tall ferns line the creeks; and the smells are rich and musty. It's so "Land of the Lost" that you half expect to turn the corner and see a dinosaur.

When Archibald Menzies first noted the existence of the coast redwood in 1794, more than 2 million acres of redwood forest carpeted the North Coast. By 1965, heavy logging had reduced that to 300,000 acres and it was obvious something had to be done if any redwoods were to survive. The state created several parks around individual groves, and in 1968 the federal government created Redwood National Park.

The 110,000-acre park offers a lesson in bioregionalism. When the park was first created to protect the biggest coast redwoods, the federal government allowed loggers to clear much of the surrounding area. Redwoods in the park began to suffer as the quality of the Redwood Creek drainage declined, because of upstream logging. In 1978 the government purchased the entire watershed, having learned that you can't preserve individual trees without preserving the ecosystem they depend on.

No one has ever lacked for things to do at Redwood National Park. Everything from river kayaking to bird watching is available here (for more information, see "What to Do & Where to Do It," below). In addition to the redwoods, the park includes miles of coastline, several miles of rivers and streams, a herd of elk, three California state parks, and several small towns.

For more information, contact **Redwood National and State Parks,**

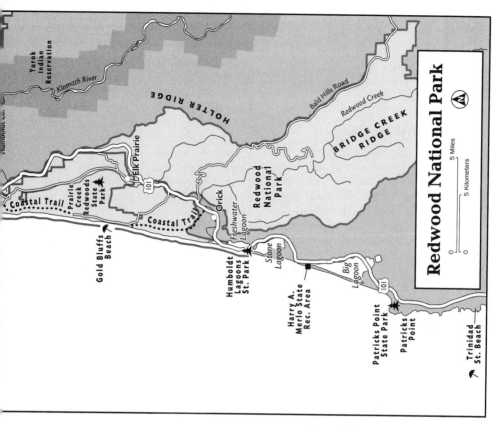

Redwood National Park

1111 Second St., Crescent City, CA 95531 (☎ 707/464-6101; www.nps.gov/redw).

GETTING THERE & GATEWAYS

Redwood National Park and the three Redwoods state parks are located on a narrow strip near the coast in Northern California, about 375 miles north of San Francisco. There are three major routes to the Redwood Coast. **Highway 101** travels up from San Francisco and down from Brookings, Oregon, to traverse much of the length of the parks. **U.S. 199** leads from the north of the park to Grants Pass, Oregon, to the northeast. The main route to the east is **Calif. 299,** which goes from Redding, California, to meet up with Highway 101 south of the park.

If you're heading from the south, you'll want to stop in **Orick.** If you're heading from the north (Oregon), you'll want to stop in **Crescent City.** Why? Because both towns have excellent information centers crammed with useful (and important) information about the

Redwood National and State Parks, including free maps.

FEES

Admission to the national park is free, but to enter any of the three state parks (which contain the best redwood groves), you'll have to pay a $5 day-use fee. It's good at all three.

SEASONS & WEATHER

Frankly, all those huge trees and ferns wouldn't have survived for 1,000 years if it didn't rain one heck of a lot. Just count on rain or at least a heavy drizzle, then go ecstatic when the sun comes out. It can happen anytime. **Spring,** of course, is the best season for wildflowers. **Summer** is foggy (watch out for the "June gloom," which often lasts until July). **Fall** is the warmest, sunniest (relatively!) time of all, and **winter** isn't bad, though it's cold and some park facilities are closed. A storm can provide the most introspective time to see the park, since you'll probably be alone. And after a storm passes through, sunny days often follow.

RANGER PROGRAMS

The parks run interpretive programs at the Hiouchi and Redwood information centers and in the Crescent Beach area during summer months, as well as year-round at the park headquarters in **Crescent City** (☎ 707/464-6101, ext. 5064). Park rangers lead campfire programs and numerous other activities throughout the year as well. Call the **Parks Information Service** (☎ 707/464-6101, ext. 5265) for current schedules.

WILDLIFE

One of the most striking aspects of the park is its herd of **Roosevelt elk,** usually found in the appropriately named Elk Prairie at the southern end of the park. These gigantic deer can weigh 1,000 pounds. The bulls carry huge antlers from spring to fall. Elk are also sometimes found at Gold Bluffs Beach—it's an incredible rush to suddenly come upon them out of the fog or after a turn in the trail. Several hundred **black bears** also call the park home but are seldom seen. Be sure to observe food-storage etiquette while camping and by disposing of garbage properly.

VISITOR CENTERS

The southern gateway to the Redwood National and State Parks is the town of Orick, on Highway 101. You can't miss it: Just look for the dozens of burl stands alongside the road. Here you'll find the sleek **Redwood Information Center,** P.O. Box 7, Orick, CA 95555 (☎ 707/464-6101, ext. 5265), where you can get a free map and see a variety of exhibits. It's open daily from 9am to 5pm year-round. If you missed the Redwood Information Center, don't worry: About 7 miles farther north on Highway 101 is the

Prairie Creek Visitor Center (☎ 707/464-6101, ext. 5300), which carries some maps and information. It's open daily from 9am to 5pm in the summer, daily 10am to 2pm in winter.

The northern gateway to the Redwood National and State Parks is Crescent City. This "city" is a real eyesore (at least along Highway 101), but it's your best bet for a cheap motel, gas, fast food, and outdoor supplies. Before touring the park, pick up a free guide at the **Redwood National and State Parks Headquarters and Information Center,** 1111 2nd St. (at K Street), Crescent City, CA 95531 (☎ 707/464-6101, ext. 5064). It's open daily from 8am to 5pm.

If you happen to be arriving via U.S. 199 from Oregon, the rangers at the **Hiouchi Information Station** (☎ 707/464-6101, ext. 5067) and **Jedediah Smith Visitor Center** (☎ 707/464-6101, ext. 5113) can also supply you with the necessary maps and advice. Both are open daily in the summer months from 9am to 5pm and when staffing is available in spring and fall.

EXPLORING THE PARK

A number of scenic drives cut through the park. Steep, windy **Bald Hills Road** will take you back into the Redwood Creek watershed and up to the shoulder of 3,097-foot Schoolhouse Peak. The partially paved 8-mile **Coastal Drive** wanders among redwood groves and along the banks of the Klamath River. Watch for the old World War II radar tracking station disguised as a barn and farmhouse to fool the Japanese.

The most amazing car-friendly trail in all of the Redwood National and State Parks, however, is the hidden, well-maintained gravel road called **Howland Hill Road** that winds for about 12 miles through Jedediah Smith Redwoods State Park. It's an unforgettable journey through a spectacular old-growth redwood forest—considered by many one of the most beautiful areas in the world. To get there from Highway 101, keep an eye out for the BP gas station at the south end of Crescent City; just before the station, turn right on Elk Valley Road, and follow it to Howland Hill Road, which will be on your right. After driving through the park, you'll end up at U.S. 199 near the town of Hiouchi, and from there it's a short jaunt west to get back to Highway 101. Plan at least 2 to 3 hours for the 45-mile round-trip, or all day if you want to do some hiking or mountain biking in the park.

The park's beaches vary from long white sand strands to cobblestone pocket coves. The water temperature is in the high 40s to low 50s year-round and it's often rough out there, so swimmers and surfers should be prepared for adverse conditions. **Crescent Beach** is a long sandy beach just 2 miles south of Crescent City that's popular with beachcombers, surf fishermen, and surfers. Just south of Crescent Beach is **Endert's Beach,** a protected spot with a hike-in campground and tide pools at its southern end.

High coastal overlooks (like **Klamath Overlook** and **Crescent Beach Overlook**) make great whale-watching outposts during the December and January migration. The northern sea cliffs also provide valuable nesting sites for marine birds like auklets, puffins, murres, and cormorants. Birders will also thrill at the park's freshwater lagoons. They are some of the most pristine shorebird and waterfowl habitat left and are chock-full of hundreds of different species.

The area streams are some of the best steelhead trout and salmon breeding habitats in California. Park beaches are good for surf casting but be prepared for heavy wave action. A California fishing license is required, and you should check with rangers about any special closures before wetting a line.

What to Do & Where to Do It

BIRD WATCHING

The combination of remnant old-growth forests, large coastal wetlands, and the presence of a rich marine environment make the North Coast one of the most diverse birding spots in the state, overshadowed only by Point Reyes. **Lake Earl,** just south of Crescent City, is a good spot to scope shorebirds and migrating waterfowl. Look for Aleutian goose, canvasbacks, wood duck, and green-winged teal, plus sandpipers, phalaropes, and other beach dwellers.

Redwood National Park is home to several endangered species that dwell in the old-growth forest. The marbled murrelet is a seagoing bird that only comes ashore to nest in the crowns of redwood trees. Also residing in the park is the endangered spotted owl. The listing of the owl as endangered caused an uproar among logging towns in California and Oregon, where SAVE A LOGGER, EAT A SPOTTED OWL bumper stickers became the hot accessory for a while.

Trinidad Beach, a few miles north of Arcata, is the southernmost spot where you can regularly spy the tufted puffin. Large offshore rocks are frequented by nesting puffins and storm petrels.

CANOEING

The **Eel River** in Humboldt Redwood State Park is one of the few long stretches of river in coastal California gentle enough to paddle in an open canoe. Water levels can drop dramatically in late summer, so spring and early summer are the best. Few pleasures can match paddling through dense redwood groves on a sunny day. Also, the **Russian River,** just north of Bodega Bay, is calm most of the way from inland Sonoma county, though it's narrower and slightly faster east of the bed-and-breakfast town of Healdsburg. Some inner-tubing, swimming, and rope swinging on the lower Russian, near the river's mouth, may present drunk obstacles during the summer. Contact **Adventure's Edge** in Arcata (☎ 707/ 822-4673) or **Burke's Canoe Trips** in Forestville (☎ 707/887-1222) for rentals and current advice on the best stretches of river.

FISHING

Once upon a time, salmon and steelhead were so plentiful in North Coast rivers that it was almost hard not to catch them. Habitat loss from dams and destruction of spawning grounds by logging-induced erosion, however, have sent the number of salmon and steelhead plummeting. In some rivers the annual run has fallen from the hundreds of thousands into the hundreds. Many longtime local residents I know have stopped fishing for salmon altogether, figuring that the fish have enough problems already. If you feel you must catch a steelhead or a salmon you certainly won't be alone—hundreds of fishermen line local riverbanks every winter—but you will do better if you hire a guide.

The **Smith River,** the northernmost river in California, is the best place to catch salmon and steelhead, since it hasn't been dammed and logging damage to its watershed has been light compared to other areas. **Smith River Salmon and Steelhead Trips,** 2095 U.S. 199, Hiouchi, CA 95531 (☎ 800/248-4704 or 707/ 458-4704), offers excursions with all tackle provided, as well as expert guides, and will arrange multiday packages with meals and lodging.

The **Van Duzen River** runs best in late fall and early winter, with fishing for rainbow trout, steelhead, and king salmon. Some bait and tackle is available in nearby Carlotta, a town that looks suspiciously like a single general store, 2.5 miles west down Highway 36.

Offshore, **Bodega Bay** includes crabbing opportunities in addition to ocean fishing. **Will's Fishing Adventures** (☎ 707/875-2323) has four boats working out of the bay year-round.

HANG GLIDING

Located north of the Russian River's mouth, the town of **Jenner** is a spectacular seaside area for hang gliding off the cliffs above Highway 1. One mile north of town, **Goat Rock State Beach** is the usual gathering spot for hang gliders heading to the top of the coastal bluffs. Other takeoff areas can be found a few miles farther north on Highway 1.

HIKES, BUSHWHACKS & BACKPACK TRIPS

For an excellent source of thousands of miles' worth of well-written trail listings and maps of the North Coast, check out the *Hiker's Hip Pocket Guides to Mendocino, Humboldt, and Del Norte Counties,* which you can order from Bored Feet Publications, P.O. Box 1832, Mendocino, CA 95460 (☎ 707/964-6629). Written by Bob Lorentzen, a former timber cruiser for the logging companies turned guidebook author, the Hip Pocket Guides are a stunning example of local knowledge and familiarity with this beautiful area.

Day Hikes
Pygmy Forest Loop, Salt Point State Park
5-mile loop. Moderate. Access: Salt Point State Park. Trail begins in Woodside Camp on east side of Hwy. 1. Map: Salt Point State Park map.

Though most of this hike follows fire roads and utility corridors—not normally my favorite hiking paths—it's worth noting because it passes through one of the most unique botanical displays you'll see. By following the North Trail uphill, within 1.5 miles you'll enter the pygmy forest from which this trail gets its name. Here you'll find a profusion of 15-foot pine trees and 5-foot cypress trees. Well, so what? There are 15-foot-tall trees in every Christmas-tree lot. Ah, but these are hundred-year-old old-growth trees, which, due to highly acidic, nutrient-poor soil, never grew taller than your average 5-year-old tree in richer forests.

If that doesn't do it for you, don't worry—there are other things to see on the hike. After exiting the pygmy forest, you'll enter a beautiful grass prairie that's spectacular in springtime. Watch for deer here. Leaving the prairie you'll descend through second-growth redwoods until the trail turns and follows Highway 1 back to Woodside Camp.

Russian Gulch Trail, Russian Gulch State Park

6 miles round-trip. Moderate. Access: Park near campground on east side of Highway 1, 2 miles north of Mendocino. Trail departs from the campground. Map: Russian Gulch State Park map.

Russian Gulch is one of the most beautiful coastal canyons on the entire California oceanfront. This trail begins just above Russian Gulch Cove and follows a park access road and the loop trail 3 miles back into a lush redwood forest. At the far end of the trail you'll find a beautiful waterfall, which the loop trail circles. Return the way you came, and take some time to poke around the stunning ocean headlands and cliffs on the beach side of the park.

10-Mile Beach Trail, MacKerricher State Park

You guessed right, 10 miles. Moderate. Access: Laguna Point parking area at MacKerricher State Park. Map: MacKerricher State Park map.

It's hikers' good fortune that a wild 1982 storm washed out several sections of the beachfront haul road at MacKerricher Beach. Once upon a time, logging trucks roared back and forth along the beach road, taking logs to the nearby mill, but now, due to two washed-out sections, the elevated road is closed to motorized traffic and makes a perfect walking route. My advice is to walk the first half of this route on the sand of MacKerricher Beach, taking plenty of time to poke around tide pools and watch the seals that often haul out here.

When you reach the mouth of the 10-Mile River, you can return via the road. While you were walking on the beach you probably didn't notice the fantastic sand dunes that lie on the inland side of the haul road. Well, now is your chance. Check out Sand Hill Lake and Inglenook Fen. Both are beautiful marsh and wetland areas where you'll often spot waterfowl. Whenever you tire of walking through the soft dune sand, the haul road offers an easy walking surface back to your car.

Tall Trees Trail, Redwood National Park

1.3 miles one-way. Moderate. Access: End of Tall Trees Access Rd., off Bald Hills Rd. Permit required. Map: Park map.

To see the world's tallest trees—some 360 feet tall and more than 600 years old—you'll first have to go to the Redwood Information Center near Orick to obtain a free map and permit to drive to the Tall Trees Grove Trailhead. (*Note:* Only 50 permits are issued per day on a first-come, first-served basis.) After driving to the trailhead, you have to walk a steep 1.3 miles down into the grove, but what a small price to see the tallest trees in the world, some reaching 360 feet high. By the way, the average time spent gawking at the world's largest trees is 1 minute 40 seconds, even though the whole expedition takes about 4 hours.

Friendship Ridge, Coastal Trail Loop, Redwood National Park

7.5 miles. Moderate. Some steep climbs, seasonal creek crossings. Access: Park at Fern Canyon Trailhead, end of Davison Rd. off Highway 101 in Prairie Creek Redwoods State Park. Map:

Redwood National Park or Prairie Creek Redwoods map.

This is possibly the most varied and beautiful hike in Redwood National Park. Beginning at the Fern Canyon Trailhead, you'll follow the Coastal Trail north from the trailhead. Soon you'll come to a fork where you'll veer right and follow the Friendship Ridge Trail. For the next 3 miles you'll walk through a magical fern and redwood forest, interspersed with lush meadows and grasslands. Occasional ridge-top sections grant you views in all directions. After about 3 miles of this you'll join the West Ridge Trail, which will soon descend the Butler Creek watershed through old-growth forest and arrive at Butler Creek Camp.

From here, it's a simple thing to follow the Coast Trail back south. This time, instead of weaving high through the trees, you skirt the fringe of high ocean cliffs and beach. If you have the time and energy left for a short detour, several short spur trails to the left lead to beautiful waterfalls. While walking this stretch, keep your eyes peeled for elk. Give them wide berth if they are blocking the trail—they've been known to stand their ground. The Coast Trail will take you back to the junction where you veered onto Friendship Ridge 7 miles ago. Continue back to the Fern Canyon Trailhead.

Boy Scout Tree Trail, Redwood National Park

6 miles round-trip. Easy. Access: Ask for directions and a map at the Jedediah Smith Information Center. Map: park map.

After taking this trail through Jedediah Smith Redwoods State Park, you'll understand why an activist like Woody Harrelson would chain himself to the Golden Gate Bridge to protest logging old-growth forests. This is nature primeval, a lush, cool, damp forest brimming with giant ferns and majestic redwoods.

Overnights
The Lost Coast

25 miles one-way. Strenuous. Allow 3–4 days. Access: From Highway 101 in Fortuna take Ferndale exit and follow signs to Petrolia. In Petrolia take Lighthouse Rd. to its dead-end at the Mattole River mouth. Map: Trails of the Lost Coast, California Coastal Foundation.

The Lost Coast is one of the most famous and most daunting hikes in California. This is the longest completely wild stretch of coastline in the Lower 48. From the Mattole River to Shelter Cove 25 miles south, you'll cross some 15 creeks, climb over huge boulders, scramble up eroded cliffs, camp near crashing surf on black-sand beaches, and be amazed by the utter wildness of this place. You can do this hike in either direction, but most choose to do it north to south, with the prevailing wind at their back.

Since you're walking along the beach much of the way, it's important to be aware of the tides—several places along the route are impassable at high tide. Also, be constantly aware that large rogue waves are common in the North Pacific, and can easily reach high above the normal waterline. If you look out to sea and see a really big wave looming, walk up the beach a little and give it some space—it certainly beats swimming with your pack on. Other hazards to be alert for are poison oak, which is everywhere, and the numerous timber rattlesnakes that live in driftwood piles on the beach and surrounding meadows. The local timber rattlers are small almost to the point of being cute, but they're very venomous.

Three or 4 days of hiking through paradise will eventually lead you out of the wilderness to Shelter Cove, a tiny fishing and vacation-home village. This is where you want to leave your second car for the shuttle, or have your ride waiting.

Since you're following the beach the entire way, a more useful resource than the map is the *Hiker's Hip Pocket Guide to the Humboldt Coast* by Bob Lorentzen (Bored Feet, 1992), which contains a lengthy mile-by-mile description of the route and hazards that existed at the time of publication. For more information contact the **Bureau of Land Management** in Arcata (☎ **707/825-2300**).

Redwood Creek Overnight, Redwood National Park

16 miles round-trip. Moderate to difficult. Access: Turn right off Highway 101 onto Bald Hills Rd. In approximately 0.5 miles, turn right on turnoff to trailhead parking in another 0.5 miles. Map: Redwood National Park map.

This hike is a beauty. What you're in for is a wilderness trek to the tallest grove of sequoias in the world, the aptly named Tall Trees Grove. En route you'll pass through a primeval forest of giant ferns, dogwood, alders, and willows (and poison oak—watch out). Occasional openings near Redwood Creek, or in the periodic meadows along the route, will really give you the perspective to appreciate these stunning trees from a distance.

Though most of this area is old growth, you'll pass through a few sections that were logged before the government created the park—the contrast is striking, even though the second growth is quite beautiful. Just before you reach the Tall Trees Grove, after about 8 miles of hiking, you'll crest a small hill to the high point of the hike, 290 feet above sea level. From here you get an incredible perspective on the grove. The bottoms of the trees are down there, way down, almost 300 feet down, but when you look straight out you notice that the tops of many are higher than you are. This is probably the closest thing you'll ever feel to being in the top of one of the trees. From here a small bridge will carry you into the grove, but from below, these giants look pretty much like every other redwood tree—tall.

Camp downstream at least 0.5 miles away from the bridge on one of the many fine sandbars of Redwood Creek. There are bears in the area, so hang your food. The bridges on Redwood Creek are only installed from May 15 to September 15. For about a month before and a month after that you can probably ford the creek when the bridges are gone, but from the end of October to the beginning of April you don't want anything to do with this hike. The rain is horrendous, and the creek crossings are extremely dangerous.

HORSEBACK RIDING

Chanslor Riding Stables, in Bodega Bay at 2660 Hwy. 1, has trails on the beach for novice through advanced riders, and offers guided rides on request. Call ☎ **707/875-3333** for more information.

KAYAKING

White-Water Kayaking

White-water kayakers will enjoy runs like the Class II and III **Russian River** in Sonoma County, which is the closest real white water to the Bay Area, the 32-mile Wilderness Run on the **Middle Fork Eel,** the Pigeon Point Run of the **Trinity,** and all three forks of the **Smith River. Adventure's Edge** (☎ **707/822-4673**) in Arcata is a great store specializing in white-water kayaks and canoes.

Aurora River Adventures (☎ **800/ 562-8475** or 530/629-3843) offer a guided kayak tour through Redwood Creek or the Smith River during spring. The 2-day, Class 3 trip costs approximately $200 per person (for a minimum of four people) and includes all the requisite kayak gear and food. This trip is extremely weather-dependent.

In **Redwood National Park** (☎ **707/ 464-6101**), kayakers can join park rangers for a 4-hour float down the **Smith River** twice a day Thursday through Monday during June and July, when water levels are prime. A $6 donation is requested. Reserve a space at the Hiouchi Visitors Center at the north end of the park no more than 2 days in advance.

Experienced boaters are free to enjoy the Smith and a number of other creeks on their own.

In spring, the **Van Duzen** river, which runs through Grizzly Creek Redwoods, swells enough to provide some good white water in stretches. At other times of the year, the river is too low for any kayaking, much less the white-water variety. Call **Grizzly Creek Redwoods** at ☎ **707/777-3683** for flow information.

Sea Kayaking

If you're venturing out on the open sea here you better know what you're doing. The entire North Coast is exposed to whatever storm conditions the Gulf of Alaska is dishing out, and the surf can go from nonexistent to booming in a matter of an hour. Don't go paddling up here if you're not comfortable with that possibility. Still, the payoff of going out is well worth the effort—you'll see a rare perspective on this rocky and wild coast. Bird-watchers will like the numerous offshore nesting rocks, and you might see whales, sea otters, and other wildlife.

Force Ten, P.O. Box 167, Elk, CA 95432 (☎ **707/877-3505**), located in Elk, offers several different options for beginning through advanced kayakers. Beginners can take advantage of owner Steve Sinclair's expertise by signing up for one of his K-2 tours—a tandem kayak thrill tour of the rocky Mendocino sea caves, wave channels, and seabird and seal rookeries. He'll take the back seat and handle the tricky stuff; you stay in front and paddle or just hold on for the ride. Force Ten also offers even wilder and woollier "Storm Surf" tours for intermediate and advanced sea kayakers.

MOUNTAIN BIKING

Mountain biking the North Coast can be incredibly rewarding or excruciatingly frustrating, often both on the same ride. The same rain that makes this country so beautiful can quickly turn roads and trails into a quagmire. That wonderful single track you follow down through a redwood forest can become a poison-oak–choked hell ride when you reach the bottom. Still, this is some of the least explored and most potentially rewarding riding in the whole state. Come prepared for rain and mud and bring lots of spare parts—you'll probably destroy a few things with all the goo caked to your bike.

Arcata Community Forest

2 to 10 miles. Moderate. Access: Park at end of California St. near Humboldt State University in Arcata. Follow dirt road until trails begin branching off. Map: Arcata Community Forest map.

The Arcata Community Forest is the favorite playground of Humboldt State students. All trails, single track and fire road, are open to bicycling, but be aware that they're also heavily used by walkers and hikers. This is a perfect place for a day of exploring the watersheds of Janes Creek and Jolly Giant Creek through second-growth redwood forests.

Whiskey Flat Out and Back, Humboldt Redwoods State Park

10 miles. Moderate. Access: Trailhead is near Albee Creek Campground on Mattle Rd., Humboldt Redwoods State Park. Map: Humboldt Redwoods State Park map.

The bad news about this ride is there's something blocking the potentially dramatic views on almost the entire ride. The good news is *what* is blocking your view—huge groves of old-growth redwoods. After the trailhead you'll ascend the Grasshopper Road for about a mile, then turn right on Squaw Creek Ridge Road. You'll follow this through a fairly constant and gentle climb until you reach Whiskey Flat Trail Camp, which is named after a prohibition-era bootleggers' camp that once graced the spot. Return the way you came.

ROAD BIKING

Avenue of the Giants, Humboldt Redwoods State Park

32 miles. Easy to moderate. Access: From the south, take the Phillipsville exit off Hwy. 101, north of Garberville. Follow the signs right to the Avenue. From the north, take the Jordan Creek exit off 101 and follow the signs under the freeway.

This flat, two-lane road through the redwoods is a popular scenic auto route, but the best way to see the massive trees is from a bicycle. When the state built wide Highway 101, the lovely stagecoach road along the Eel River became a route through the redwoods. From the north, begin at the turnoff from 101 5.9 miles south of Scotia, a mill town. At the sign for Avenue of the Giants, pass under the freeway and immediately enter the forest on the Avenue. There's no shoulder on the road, but traffic is slow and infrequent most of the year, with peak times in July and August. Still, wear bright colors and a helmet year-round, particularly under the thick redwood canopy, where the light is dusky even in the middle of the day.

The Avenue is easily ridden in short stages, as it's heavily shaded and sheltered from the wind and has turnoffs at 3 to 5 miles intervals for stops in the massive groves. The Rockefeller Grove, Chandler Grove, and Bolling Grove are particularly stunning. Day-use areas are clustered along the Avenue's midpoint, at the Garden Club Grove, Williams Grove, and park headquarters near the town of Weott, about 12 miles from the south entrance. Food is available in the small towns of Pepperwood, Redcrest, Myers' Flat, and Miranda (listed north to south). Remember to bring food and a spare inner tube, anyway—you may not see another soul here for hours at a time, and the lone store in each town will be closed if the owner happens to be away.

If you aren't riding the Avenue's full length, any of these spots makes for a convenient turnaround back to your car.

Overnight camping is available at the Garden Club Grove campsite, 15 miles from the Avenue's north entrance. Hidden Springs Campground is another 10 miles. Both have hiker/biker sites.

At the end of the route, the trees thin as the road nears the river, until finally the Avenue ends and meets busy Highway 101 in the town of Pepperwood. Have someone pick you up at the sign for the Avenue's south entrance a mile south of Phillipsville, or turn around and ride back the way you came.

SCUBA DIVING

I use the term *scuba diving* loosely here, since most diving on the North Coast is done without tanks. Why, you ask, would anyone want to dive up here without tanks? Well, it's really quite simple: a good 90% of diving in Sonoma and Mendocino County is done in pursuit of the red abalone, and California Fish and Game regulations strictly prohibit taking abalone while diving with tanks. So free-diving is the name of the game. That doesn't mean you can't dive with tanks; in fact, the scuba diving is quite good, but most people don't. Either way, the big problem here is getting to the ocean front, and once you're there, getting in through the surf zone.

The water in the far northern coast is rumored to be clearer than it is in Sonoma. That's perhaps because it's a good deal colder. **Mackerricher State Park,** north of Fort Bragg, has an underwater park for divers, including a kelp forest. The following are other popular dive spots.

Stillwater Cove, 14 miles north of Jenner, is the most popular beginning diving spot on the entire North Coast. The reason is immediately apparent: The cove is protected from high swells from almost any direction and is generally calm and safe to enter. Underwater, the terrain is a little less spectacular than some other sites in the area, but that's the price you pay for easy access. The rocky outcroppings on the north and south sides of the cove have the best fish and invertebrate life.

Salt Point State Park, 20 miles north of Jenner, is famous throughout California for its fantastic abalone diving. The two most popular dive sites here are Gerstle Cove and South Gerstle Cove. Both are fairly well protected from all but a heavy northwest swell. Gerstle Cove is a game preserve, so you can look but you can't touch. Check out the incredible beds of strawberry anemones here. South Gerstle is open to abalone diving and spearfishing and is good for both.

The farther north you go, the harder the diving gets. **Russian Gulch,** 2 miles north of Mendocino, is one of the last really desirable dive spots on the Mendocino coast. The beach inside the state-park cove makes for easy water entry. The cove is long and well protected, though as you explore the outer areas you'll find it prone to fairly heavy surge. Good abalone diving and spearfishing.

Underwater Adventures, located inland in Cotati (☎ **707/795-6510**), offers instruction and information. Several dive shops in the San Francisco Bay Area also teach diving off the Sonoma Coast: **Marin Skin Diving** in San Raphael (☎ **415/ 479-4332**) and **Cal School of Diving** in Berkeley (☎ **510/524-3248**) are among the area's best-known dive schools.

WALKS & RAMBLES

Kruse Rhododendron Loop

2.25 miles. Access: Follow signs off Hwy. 1 onto Kruse Ranch Rd. Trailhead at dead-end. Map: Kruse Rhododendron State Reserve map.

The rhododendron is usually just one of many plants growing in the understory of a dark forest dominated by Douglas fir and redwoods, but here logging and several large fires have opened the forest to more sunlight and consequently more rhododendrons. The best time for this

walk is in spring, when the flowers are in full bloom. Other trails lead from here into surrounding Salt Point State Park.

Gold Bluffs–Fern Canyon Loop, Redwood National Park

0.75 miles. Access: Trail begins at end of Davison Rd. in Prairie Creek Redwoods State Park. Map: Redwood National Park or Prairie Creek Redwoods State Park map.

This spot is one of the most otherworldly locations you'll ever see. Walking through Fern Canyon, an unbelievably lush grotto of sword, five-finger, and maidenhair ferns cut by a babbling brook, it's easy to imagine a dinosaur or some other prehistoric beast lumbering ahead. The trail wanders back and forth through this always-dripping landscape, ripe with the thick, earthy aroma of decomposing wood and prospering ferns. Gold Beach, at the end of the walk, was the site of a minor gold rush when miners found some gold in the beach sand. The boom soon became a bust when it turned out there wasn't enough gold here to be worth mining.

Lady Bird Johnson Grove Loop, Redwood National Park

1 mile. Access: Lady Bird Johnson Grove. Take the Bald Hills Rd. exit off Highway 101, 0.5 mile north of Orick.

This self-guided tour loops around a glorious lush grove of mature redwoods. It's the site at which the national park was dedicated by Lady Bird Johnson in 1968. The following year the trail was named for her.

Yurok Loop Nature Trail, Redwood National Park

1 mile. Access: 6.5 miles north of the Klamath River Bridge on Highway 101 at Lagoon Creek.

This self-guided trail gradually climbs to the top of rugged sea bluff (with wonderful panoramic views of the Pacific) before looping back to the parking lot. If someone's willing to act as shuttle driver, have him or her meet you at the Requa Trailhead and take the 4-mile coastal trail to the mouth of the Klamath.

Memorial Trail and Harriet Hunt Bard Loop, Grizzly Creek State Park

1 mile. Access: Trail begins opposite the bridge over the Van Duzen River. Cross the bridge behind the amphitheater and go up the hill toward the Rathert Grove. Maps available at the visitor center, located at the park entrance.

This is a great walk that takes in a lot of old-growth redwoods in a short distance. The trail is the access for the adjacent Rathert, Philip Bard, and Harriet Hunt Bard groves of redwoods, all of which feature trees over 200 feet tall and several centuries old. To see all three groves, follow the trail up the hill and go right at the fork. Walk through the Rathert Grove for a quarter mile, then walk another quarter mile to the cutoff to the Loop Trail. The Harriet Hunt Bard Grove will be on your right at the trail's beginning. After you rejoin the Memorial Trail, the Phillip Bard Grove will be between you and the river most of the way back to the trailhead. Keep your eyes peeled for bald eagles in winter, as well as pygmy owls, pileated woodpeckers (enormous animals—that jackhammerlike sound you hear is not a jackhammer), and the elusive spotted owl.

Agate Beach trail, Patrick's Point State Park

0.3 miles to the beach and back. Access: From the park entrance, follow the road straight 1 mile toward the water, then head right at the fork and follow the signs to Agate Beach. The trail begins at the overlook beside the parking lot.

This short, steep trail passes a small waterfall and offers panoramic views of the beach and ocean all the way down.

Once on the beach, it's another mile to the end, where it narrows to a narrow spit and separates the ocean from a broad lagoon. True to its name, Agate Beach is the place to go to look for agates, glasslike stones that wash up with the area's intense surf. The beach is made almost entirely of pebbles, many of which are striking in their own right. You'll have to hunt for a while to find good agates amid all the colors. The park allows you to take home what you find to put on your shelf, but it's illegal to sell the mysterious stones to your local New Age bookstore back home.

WHALE WATCHING

The wild seas cut down drastically on the number of whale-watching charters on the North Coast, but there is one. **King Salmon Charters,** 1875 Buhne Dr. #67, Eureka, CA 95503 (☎ 707/442-3474), often runs trips off the Humboldt coast.

Land-based whale watching is particularly fine in the **Sonoma** and **Mendocino** stretch of shoreline. Here, high cliffs make it easy to find an elevated perch from which to sight the passing whales. Each March, Mendocino has its annual whale festival, a wine-tasting, chowder-chomping good time, including plenty of staring out to sea from the Mendocino bluffs looking for those telltale puffs of spray.

Campgrounds & Other Accommodations

CAMPING

Salt Point State Park

20 miles north of Jenner on the Sonoma coast. 140 sites. Flush toilets, running water. Wildlife, hiking, swimming, diving, biking. Pets accepted. $16 per night. Reservations through MISTIX (☎ **800/ 444-PARK**).

Salt Point is the most popular state park with divers, since you can camp and dive all at the same spot. Don't overlook the great hiking on the other side of Highway 1, where the park extends way back into the hills.

MacKerricher State Park
On the beach about 5 miles north of Fort Bragg. 153 sites. Flush toilets, running water, showers. Diving, swimming, boating, fishing, wildlife viewing (mostly sea lions). Pets accepted. $16 per night. Reservations through MISTIX (☎ 800/ 444-PARK).

MacKerricher is unique to the Mendocino coast as one of the few places where a long beach fronts the ocean without large cliffs. The campsites are located back in a pleasant forest a short walk from the beach and 20-acre Lake Cleone, which offers good freshwater fishing for trout. North of the park lies an enormous field of sand dunes.

Stone Lagoon Boat-In, Humboldt Lagoons State Park
Boat-in only. Launch boats at the parking area 3 miles south of the Redwood Information Center on Highway 101. The campground is 0.75 miles away, across the lagoon. ☎ 707/488-2041. No water, pit toilets, picnic tables, fire rings. Boating, hiking, swimming. No pets. $7 per night. No reservations.

This boat-in campground is an interesting option. Reachable only by canoe, kayak, or rowboat, it's on the bank of the lagoon, just a short walk to the ocean beach.

Patrick's Point State Park
30 miles north of Eureka. 64 tent sites. $16 per night. Hot showers, flush toilets, fire rings. Hiking. Pets accepted. ☎ 707/ 677-3570 for reservation info.

Patrick's Point is a family-oriented park with one of the best beaches on the North Coast, Agate Beach. The sites here fill up quickly in summer.

Redwood National Park Camping
South of Crescent City on Highway 101. Information: 1111 2nd St., Crescent City, CA 95531. ☎ 707/464-6101. Encompasses 3 state parks: Del Norte Coast Redwoods, Jedediah Smith Redwoods, and Prairie Creek Redwoods. Various facilities and activities. Day-use and camping fees for some portions of the park.

Five small campgrounds are located in the national park proper. Four are walk-in camps and are free, but you must get a permit from the visitor center in advance. The fifth, a car-camping strip along the freeway at Freshwater Lagoon, requests an $8 donation.

Most car campsites are in the **Prairie Creek and Jedediah Smith state parks,** which lie entirely inside the national park. Sites there are $12 to $16 per night and can be reserved by calling the state's infuriating MISTIX reservation system (☎ 800/ 444-7275), which requires an additional $6.75 reservation fee. Be prepared to deal with a truly annoying computer when you call and know exactly what campground and, if possible, which site you would like. (The state park service has promised improvements in this system, but we'll see.)

Farther from the park attractions but also farther from the crowds are four **National Forest Campgrounds** in the mountains above the park. Sites are $8 per night and can be reserved by calling ☎ 800/280-2267—where an actual person can help you make decisions.

INNS & LODGES
Benbow Inn
445 Lake Benbow Dr., Garberville, CA 95542. ☎ 800/355-3301 or 707/ 923-2124. Fax 707/923-2897. 55 units, 1 cottage. $115–$325. AE, DISC, MC, V.

This national historic landmark, overlooking the Eel River, off Highway 101, was designed by Albert Farr in 1925; pretty Benbow Lake State Park is right out the front door. It's built in a mock Tudor style, and guests enter to a grand hall with cherry-wood wainscoting. Rooms in the main building have fireplaces, TVs, private entrances, patios, and some have VCRs, too. A comfortable annex, with elegant woodwork, was added in the 1980s. Bicycles are available.

Rachel's Inn

N. Hwy. 1 (P.O. Box 134), Mendocino, CA 95460. ☎ **707/937-0088.** 9 units. July–Oct and weekends and holidays year-round $120–$220; Mon–Thurs Nov–June $96–$190. Rates include breakfast. MC, V.

This B&B is set 2 miles south of Mendocino, on an acre of land that abuts 82 acres of **Van Damme State Park** (☎ 707/937-5804). The ocean is very close and a beach is a short walk away. Two things make this inn so special. One is Rachel herself, a solicitous host who loves the Mendocino coast and who was responsible for organizing against the threat of offshore oil drilling in the 1980s. The second is that, unlike most inns in town, this one is *not* decorated in Laura Ashley style. Instead, it has a refreshing contemporary style, with modern art and an emphasis on comfort.

From the house, guests can walk down to the cove, and there's also a trail from the house across the headlands. Rachel cooks a superb breakfast of huevos rancheros or something similar, plus fruit, baked goods, and cereals. The main house, built in the 1860s, contains four rooms, including the parlor suite, which has its own sitting room with piano and ocean view. The South Room is a state-of-the-art unit for the guests with disabilities, with an extra large shower (with seat) into which you can wheel a wheelchair.

Redwood AYH Hostel, Redwood National Park

14480 Highway 101, near Klamath. ☎ **707/482-8265.** Dorm-style accommodation. 30 beds. $14. MC, V.

This turn-of-the-century inn is the only lodging actually within Redwood National Park. It has kitchen facilities, three showers, and 30 beds in shared rooms. The staff leads nature walks and is well versed in local history.

Trinidad Bed & Breakfast

560 Edmonds St. (P.O. Box 849), Trinidad, CA 95570. ☎ **707/677-0840.** 4 units. $105–$125 double; $145–$155 suite. Rates include breakfast. MC, V. Closed Dec–Jan.

Set 175 feet above the ocean, the site was selected because of its sweeping views; on a clear day, you can see up to 65 miles of the rugged coastline. Your hosts are Paul and Carol Kirk, innkeepers who have created what might be the most charming inn around. Rooms contain antique dressers, modern beds, and ocean views. The larger of the two suites has a wood-burning fireplace. Decor throughout is an eclectic mix of New England–style antiques and more recent reproductions.

Index